BARALAM AND YEWASEF

This text, the first English translation of the Ethiopic version of a Christianized Buddhist legend, will certainly be of interest to any reader with a penchant for the unusual or an appetite for the abstruse. The book also contains descriptions of numerous other versions of the story, including Syriac, Hebrew and Western European. Budge's clear, literal translation is a delight to read and is supplemented by numerous illustrations.

BARALAM AND YEWASEF

The Ethiopic Version of a Christianized Recension
of the Buddhist Legend of the Buddha and the
Bodhisattva

E. A. Wallis Budge

Routledge
Taylor & Francis Group

LONDON AND NEW YORK

First published in 2004 by
Kegan Paul International

This edition first published in 2011 by
Routledge
2 Park Square, Milton Park, Abingdon, Oxfordshire OX14 4RN

Simultaneously published in the USA and Canada
by Routledge
711 Third Avenue, New York, NY 10017

First issued in paperback 2016

Routledge is an imprint of the Taylor & Francis Group, an informa business

British Library Cataloguing in Publication Data
A catalogue record for this book is available from the British Library

ISBN 13: 978-1-138-98768-5 (pbk)
ISBN 13: 978-0-7103-0994-5 (hbk)

Publisher's Note
The publisher has gone to great lengths to ensure the quality of this reprint
but points out that some imperfections in the original copies may be
apparent. The publisher has made every effort to contact original copyright
holders and would welcome correspondence from those they have been
unable to trace.

PREFACE

THE object of this work is to put into the hands of those who are interested in the "spiritual romance" of Barlaam and Iôasaph, as it is commonly called, the complete Ethiopic text of the Christianized version of this remarkable work, together with an English translation of the same. Until now this version has only been known to the student of the literary history of the romance through the text of a few of the Parables or "Apologues" which Zotenberg edited in his valuable work from a manuscript in the Bibliothèque Nationale. The Ethiopic text given in the first volume* of the present work is edited from two good, though late, manuscripts preserved in the British Museum, which probably represent with considerable accuracy the received text in the sixteenth, seventeenth and eighteenth centuries. I have reproduced from the manuscript that I have called B (Oriental 753) all the variants that seem to me to be of importance, but only in very few cases do they make it necessary to alter the text in A (Oriental 699). The late Professor William Wright considered Baralâm and Yĕwâsĕf to be a work of importance for illustrating the flexibility of the Ethiopic language, though he regarded it as possessing little value as a historical document.

I have made the translation as literal as possible, but for the convenience of the English reader I have broken it up and added a series of short headings, which may help him to find his way easily through the work. These are enclosed in square brackets and are printed in italics. The Ethiopian scribes

* *Not re-produced in this volume.*

were never tired of illustrating the Old and the New Testaments, and the Lives of Saints and Martyrs, and the Miracles of the Virgin Mary, with brightly coloured pictures, which are often of considerable interest, and sometimes possess artistic value. But unfortunately works like Baralâm and Yĕwâsĕf, the Kebra Nagast, etc. are entirely without illustrations, and the sea of Ethiopic text has nothing to break its monotony. Whatever the feeling about the need of pictures in such works may have been in Abyssinia when the Book of Baralâm became common cannot be said, but in some parts of Europe, in the fifteenth century and earlier, illustrated editions of Western versions of this work were published. Thus the German Version that was printed at Augsburg in 1477 is illustrated by sixty-four woodcuts drawn in outline, which add to the interest of the text, and are very fine examples of the craft of book-illustration in the fifteenth century. About the same time great activity prevailed in Abyssinia in making copies of native works and translations of Indian, Arabic and Coptic books, both sacred and profane. I have there-fore reproduced all the illustrations in the Augsburg edition of the German Version of the Book of Bar-laam, and inserted them in the English translation here given, not only for the sake of the text that they illustrate, but also for their originality and quaint excellence. It seems to me that they deserve to be better known, even though in attempting to bring about this result I lay myself open to the charge of inconsistency.

Much has been written about the literary history of the Barlaam Romance by Kuhn, Zotenberg and

Jacobs, who have thrown great light upon the subject, but the book, in which its elements, Indian, Persian, Arabic, Egyptian, Greek and Christian, are clearly distinguished, has yet to be written. Thirty years ago when I copied the Ethiopic text Prof. Rhys Davids told me that he intended to write such a book, but alas, it was never written. In the Introduction to the present work I have collected what seem to me to be the essential facts about the transmission of the Romance in various versions and languages from Asia to Africa and Europe, and in it the reader will find references, I believe, to the works of all the principal authorities on the subject. No satisfactory account of the Arabic Versions can be given until the Arabic texts are published from the manuscripts in the Bibliothèque Nationale, and it is much to be hoped that, in the interests of the Romance, some scholar will soon undertake this work.

The reader will notice in the translation (see p. 4) a definite statement to the effect that St Thomas, one of the Twelve Apostles, preached the Gospel of Christ in India and converted the Indians to Christianity. This statement is also found in the Greek and Syriac texts which have been edited, translated and described by Bonnet, Wright and Lipsius, and in the Arabic translations which were made from Syriac or Coptic. Throughout the section of the Ethiopic Literature which deals with the Lives and Acts of the Apostles, the Preaching of Thomas in India is regarded as a historical fact. In the GADLA HAWÂRYÂT, or "Contendings of the Apostles," two long sections are devoted to the Preaching and Miracles of St Thomas in India, and as they are found in manuscripts written in the fifteenth century, it is quite clear that they were regarded as ancient and authoritative accounts of the life and works of the Apostle in Abyssinia. In 1899 I published the Ethiopic texts of these, with English translations, in my edition of the GADLA HAWÂRYÂT, but as this work is out of print I have added as an Appendix to this volume revised English translations of the Preaching and Miracles of St Thomas.

My thanks are due to the Trustees of the British Museum for permission to reproduce the Ethiopic texts, and also the sixty-four line illustrations in the Augsburg edition of the German Version of the Book of Barlaam from the rare copy in the Grenville Collection (No. 11766); to the Royal Asiatic Society for permission to reproduce the first and the last palm leaves of the Codex of the *Lalita Vistara*; to the authorities of the Library of the India Office for permission to copy the photographs printed on Plates III—V; to Mr F. W. Thomas, Librarian of the India Office, for his courteous assistance; and to Dr L. Barnett, Keeper of the Oriental Manuscripts and Printed Books in the British Museum, for his valuable Note' printed on pp. lviii and lix and for many helpful suggestions.

It is my pleasant duty to put on record here the fact that the publication of this work has been made possible by a contribution towards the expenses of printing from a generous friend.

E. A. WALLIS BUDGE.

BRITISH MUSEUM,
Aug. 13, 1923.

[ix]

CONTENTS

LIST OF PLATES

INTRODUCTION

I

THE BOOK OF BARLAAM AND IÔASAPH, OR JOSAPHAT

THE Book of Barlaam and Iôasaph is a Christianized version of a very ancient "spiritual romance," which was composed in India and first written down in an Indian language by Buddhist propagandists in one of the centuries that immediately preceded or followed the beginning of the Christian Era. It is written in Greek and has been commonly thought to be the work of St John Damascene. Like the Fables of Bidpai, with which it appears to be contemporaneous, the Book of Barlaam and Iôasaph has for at least fifteen hundred years been a popular work in the West as well as in the East. More than sixty translations, versions or paraphrases of it have been enumerated. Wherever it has appeared it has been warmly welcomed by men of every great creed for untold generations. Its aesthetic, moral and religious teachings have won the approval of Indians, Chinese, Persians, Arabs, Syrians, Armenians, Jews, Egyptians, Ethiopians, and other Oriental peoples. And the manuscripts and versions of it in Greek, Latin, German, Italian, Slavonic, Servian, Czech, French, Spanish, Portuguese, Swedish, Danish, Icelandic, English, Irish, etc., testify to the esteem with which the Book was regarded among European peoples. As it stands now it is a strange mixture of parable and fable, and folklore and history, and romance, in which shrewd worldly wisdom is mingled with the highest and greatest religious truths in such a way that the perusal thereof will increase the piety of the godly, the wisdom of the wise, and the pleasure of those who seek amusement and instruction in the writings of teachers of olden time.

The contents of the Book of Barlaam and Iôasaph in the form in which it captivated the learned of Europe may be briefly summarized thus:

After the preaching of the Gospel of Christ in India by St Thomas the Apostle, many monasteries were established in that country and as the result of the example and teaching of the monks who lived in them the religion of Christ spread abroad in the land, and Christianity became established there so firmly that the native rulers were alarmed at its progress, and the priests of idols urged them to take steps to arrest it. A certain district had for its king one Abenner, or Avennir, a great and powerful ruler, who loved pleasure and hunting and pageants and amusements of every kind, and who possessed almost everything that health and wealth could give a man. But he had no son, and he lamented continually that his family consisted of daughters only; day and night he longed for a son, and it seems that the priests of idols suggested to him that if he persecuted the Christians and paid special honours to their own gods, a son would be given to him. Therefore he began to persecute the Christians, and to torture them and burn them alive, and to drive them out from among his people ; and the monks were obliged to forsake their monasteries, and to take refuge in the deserts and mountains, where large numbers of them perished from thirst and hunger and cold and wild beasts. Whilst the persecution was at its height a son was born to Abenner, and he celebrated his appearance with extravagant rejoicings. He heaped gifts upon the priests, and greatly enriched their temples, and sacrificed to the gods thousands of cattle and sheep. He called his son "Iôasaph," and among those who flocked to the birth ceremonies were great numbers of astrologers, diviners, soothsayers, and all kinds of men who were skilled in the art of working magic. In answer to the king's enquiries all but one of them declare that the boy will become a very great king, a king more powerful and richer than his father. The one exception was an aged astrologer who held quite a different opinion from that of his fellows, for he foretold that the young prince would become a Christian.

When Abenner heard these words he determined to prevent the fulfilment of this prophecy. He therefore had a palace specially built for his son in a remote part of his country, and he furnished it most luxuriously, and surrounded it with high walls, and then sent Iôasaph to live there. He set his trusty servants to watch over the child, and he had him surrounded with happy children, who rejoiced in games and amusements of all kinds. No sad or sick person was allowed to enter the palace, and no one was allowed to tell the child anything that would interfere with his happiness, and his guardians and teachers took care that he should have no knowledge whatsoever of the want, misery, pain, sickness, disease and death that were in the world. When Iôasaph was grown up he persisted in begging his father to allow him to go outside the palace and see the world. Abenner at length consented, and the prince with a suitable escort rode out into the city; but he was only allowed to ride through the streets that had been specially made ready to receive him. His outriders took care to clear out of his way all beggars and undesirable folk, but one day, by accident and in spite of all their care, he met a blind man, and a leper, and a dead man, and a very aged man who was infirm and helpless. His escort tried to hurry him on, but he insisted on stopping and asking them questions about these men, and he learned for the first time that there is disease in the world, and that the end of prolonged sickness and old age is death. His natural intelligence and shrewdness of mind enabled him to understand the fleeting character of all things in this world, and he was assailed by doubts and difficulties which no amusements or gay companions could drive out of his mind.

But the all-seeing Eye of God was watching him, and the Lord of the Universe decreed his salvation, and selected an agent to bring this about. This agent was a certain holy ascetic who lived in the desert of Sennaar and was called Barlaam. To him God revealed the state of Iôasaph's mind, and Barlaam made ready to go to India and win his soul for Christ. He marched to the coast, took ship, and in due course arrived in India, where he disguised himself as a merchant, and set out for the city where Iôasaph dwelt. He found means to make acquaintance with one of the prince's teachers in the palace, and he begged him to introduce him into his master's presence so that he might show him a most wonderful gem, the like of which had never been seen by man. This gem could only be seen by the man who had a pure heart and pure eyes. At length the teacher was persuaded to bring Barlaam into the presence of the prince, who listened with joy to all that the hermit had to say about the gem and its wonderful beauty. Barlaam paid many visits to Iôasaph, and little by little he unfolded to him the doctrines of ascetic Christianity. By degrees the prince fell under the influence of the hermit, who reasoned with him and showed him the futility of idolatry, and answered his questions, and Barlaam made his discourse both entertaining and instructive by means of ancient parables and fables. He showed him the beauty of the life which the saints of God led as monks and anchorites in the desert, and at the same time described to him the hardships which they must perforce endure, hunger and thirst, cold and heat, the attacks of wild beasts and, what was far worse, the temptations and assaults of the Devil and his fiends. Pointing to his own ragged apparel and to the marks that scores of years of fasting and exposure had left upon his emaciated body, he warned Iôasaph that he was not at that moment capable of enduring the strenuous life of the ascetic, but urged him to cast aside idolatry and to accept

Christ. In many long conversations Barlaam explained to him the doctrines of Christianity, the
Trinity, the Eucharist, Christian Baptism, etc. He
found Iôasaph a ready and willing convert, and
having taught him the Nicene Creed, and baptized
him, and lovingly admonished him as to his future
life Barlaam departed to his cell in the desert of
Sennaar.

When Abenner the king heard of the conversion
of his son to Christianity and of his baptism, he sent
out men to search for Barlaam so that he might
slay him, but the holy man had left India, and they
failed to find him. Abenner then took counsel with
one of his friends who advised him to summon a
general council, and to let representatives of the
Christians and of the idolaters hold a debate on
Christianity and paganism before them in public.
The king and his friend persuaded a pagan called
Nachor to personify Barlaam, and arranged with him
to pronounce an oration in favour of the worship
of idols, instead of an argument in which all the
beauties of the Christian Religion would be clearly
demonstrated. They hoped by this means to convince Iôasaph that Barlaam had apostatized, and
expected that he would abandon the Christian
Religion. On the day of the great debate Nachor
stood up, but instead of extolling the power and
glory of the heathen gods, he pronounced the wonderful discourse on behalf of Christianity which is
now known to be the famous "Apology of Aristides."
The king in his wrath would have slain Nachor, but
Iôasaph had him conveyed out of the city secretly

by night, and Nachor departed to the desert, where he repented and became a monk.

Abenner was in despair at the unlooked for result of the public debate, and he sent for Theudas. or Theodas, a great magician, and asked him to show him a way by which he could crush the obstinacy of Iôasaph, and bring him back to the worship of the gods. Theudas was greatly skilled in all that appertained to magic, and myriads of fiends and devils were believed to be under his authority and to perform his will. After hearing the king's wishes he recommended that Iôasaph's palace should be filled with women servants, and that a number of young and beautiful girls should be made his companions by day and by night. When the king had selected the loveliest maidens in the city and dressed them in splendid apparel, he sent them to Iôasaph with instructions to seduce him physically and mentally. As soon as they had begun their ministrations to the prince Theudas summoned the evil spirits and sent them into the maidens so that they might inflame their passions and overthrow the chastity of the prince. But all their efforts to this end were in vain, and Iôasaph triumphed over them and over the devils that Theudas had sent in them and with them. Abenner's grief at their failure was very great, and his chagrin was increased when he saw Theudas himself converted to Christianity; Theudas lost all faith in his devils and he went and burned all his books of magic.

Abenner's next act was to divide his kingdom, and half of it he gave to his son to rule over. Iôasaph promptly destroyed the temples, smashed the images that were in them, and built churches to which the people flocked from far and near. Under his enlightened rule his half of the kingdom flourished, whilst that of his father decayed. Abenner, seeing that he was powerless to stay the advance of the Christian faith, became a Christian and retired to a monastery where four years later he died. Iôasaph buried his father with all the pomp and ceremony that befitted his rank, and then having returned to his capital, where he was welcomed with great joy by all the people, he abdicated his kingdom, and appointed one Barachias, a man with whom he had been long on good terms, to be his successor. Free at last from the care of a kingdom, he stripped off his royal apparel, and in the garb of a mendicant monk made his escape to the desert, where he began to lead the life of an ascetic in real earnest. He fasted and prayed and suffered great tribulation, he resisted the attacks of devils in every shape and form, he fought with wild beasts and overcame them, and he conquered the Arch-Devil Satan, who attacked him under many forms. Meanwhile his wish was to find Barlaam, and he wandered about for two whole years before he found him. At length master and pupil met, and they lived together and fought the spiritual fight with great content. At length Barlaam fell sick, but before he died he urged Iôasaph to continue to live in the desert and work out his salvation. Barlaam died in the arms of Iôasaph, who buried him with great sorrow, and then lived alone for many years in that same desert.

He was found dead one day by a fellow monk, who buried him side by side with Barlaam. In due course the news of his death reached King Barachias, who came to the tomb and translated the bodies of Barlaam and Iôasaph to the church which Iôasaph had founded, and miracles were wrought at their tombs.

It is easy to understand that the "spiritual romance" summarized above would become very popular among Christians of every denomination, and that it would be read with great avidity by all who were occupied with the ascetic life. The author's main object was to exalt the life of the monk, and his work would be especially acceptable in monasteries, and would form one of the principal books chosen to be "read for edification" privately in the cells and at meal times in the refectories. But the Christian dogmas and homilies which fill so large a space in the narrative would not account for the great popularity of the Book of Barlaam and Iôasaph among the Chinese, the Persians, the Arabs and the Jews, and the reason for this must have been due to some other factor in the work. This factor is not far to seek. The universal popularity of the romance was due to the series of Fables, or Parables, or "Apologues" as they are generally called, which Barlaam quoted in the course of his conversations with Iôasaph. These are not of Christian but Indian origin, and may be enumerated thus:

1. THE PARABLE OF THE SOWER. A sower sows seed of which some is trodden under foot, some is eaten by the birds, some is blown away, some falls

among the rocks and withers after germination, some falls among thistles and its growth is choked, and a very little falls on good earth, where it grows and brings forth fruit. The Sower is the sage, and his seed is wisdom. There is a Buddhistic parallel for this Apologue, but the details in Barlaam are taken from the New Testament (Matt. xiii. 3; Mark iv. 3; Luke viii. 5). For the Greek text see *Barlaam*, VI. 39, and for Parallels see Jacobs, *Barlaam*, London, 1896, p. cxi; *Sutta Nihata*, translated by Fausböll, pp. 1–5; Carus, *Gospel of Buddha*, § 74.

2. THE GEM. (*Barlaam*, VI. 35 ff.) Barlaam, a hermit, inspired by heaven, leaves the desert of Sennaar, disguises himself as a merchant and sails to India. He tells Iôasaph's tutor that he has a marvellous gem which he wishes to show to the prince, for the sight of it will fill him with wisdom; but the sight of it can only be borne by one whose eyes are pure. The tutor was persuaded, and brought Barlaam into the palace and obtained for him an audience of the prince.

3. THE TRUMPET OF DOOM. (*Barlaam*, VI. 41, 42.) A great king driving in his chariot meets two hermits, and leaps down and makes obeisance to them. His escort are amazed and ask the king's brother to ask the king not to demean himself by such conduct. The brother rebukes the king for his unseemly conduct and returns to his house. When the king wanted to announce to any noble malefactor that he had condemned him to death he sent a herald to blow a special trumpet before the door of

his house, and when the wretched man heard it he prepared himself for death. On the evening of the day of the rebuke the king sent his herald to blow blasts of the trumpet before his brother's house; the brother understood and spent the night in tears and preparing for death. In the morning he appeared at the palace with his wife and children, all dressed in black, and the king received him and explained to him that he had only sent the herald with the trumpet of death to rebuke his folly in censuring him for greeting the heralds of God, the mere sight of whom warned him of his death and of the meeting to come with his Master Whom he had so greatly offended. He comforted his brother, gave him a gift and dismissed him, and then set to work to rebuke the nobles who had incited his brother to remonstrate with him. The original form of this Apologue is thought to be the legend of Asoka's brother Vitasoka. See Benfey, *Pantschatantra*, vol. I. p. 408; Liebrecht's Article in Ebert's *Jahrbuch für Romanische und Englische Litteratur*, vol. II. (part for April–June) Berlin, 1860, pp. 314–334; Braunholtz, *Die erste Nichtchristliche Parabel des Barlaam und Josaphat, ihre Herkunft und Verbreitung*, Halle, 1884; *Gesta Romanorum*, cap. 143; Ward, *Catalogue of Romances*, vol. II. 1893, p. 122; Jacobs, *Barlaam*, p. cviii.

4. THE FOUR CASKETS. (*Barlaam*, VI. 43.) The king had four wooden caskets made. In two of them he placed the bones of dead men, and in the other two gems and precious stones; the first two caskets he covered with gold and provided with gold fastenings,

and the second two he daubed over with pitch and tar and bound round with hair ropes. He then sent for the nobles who had incited his brother to rebuke him, and when they arrived he asked them to appraise the value of the caskets. They thought the caskets covered with gold were the more valuable, and those covered with tar of lesser value. The king ordered the gold caskets to be opened, and their contents presented a hideous sight and gave forth an evil smell; but when the tar-covered caskets were opened all present were amazed and delighted at the beauty of the gems contained therein. Then the king said that the dead men's bones symbolized the wicked nobles who were arrayed in spendid apparel, and that the gems were emblems of the humble and vilely dressed men, to whom he had bowed down, and the priceless beauty of their souls. See Benfey, *Pantschatantra*, vol. I. p. 408; Liebrecht in Ebert's *Jahrbuch*, pp. 329, 330; Braunholtz, *Parabel*, Halle, 1884; Burnouf, *Introduction*, p. 333; St Hilaire, *Bouddha*, p. 105; Oesterley, *Gesta Romanorum*, capp. 109 and 251. For the Derivatives see the list in Jacobs, *Barlaam*, p. cix. The Indian original is the tale of Yasas, Asoka's Minister, for which see Burnouf's *Introduction*.

5. THE NIGHTINGALE AND THE FOWLER. (*Barlaam*, x. 79.) A fowler caught a nightingale and took his knife to kill her, meaning to eat her. The bird said that she was too small to fill his belly, and promised to tell him three useful things if he spared her life. The fowler agreed to spare her and the bird said, 1. Never try to attain the unattainable. 2. Never

regret the thing past. 3. Never believe the word that is unbelievable. When the bird was set free she told the fowler that he was a fool to let her go because she had inside her a pearl as large as the egg of an ostrich. The fowler, being filled with grief that he had set her free, tried to recapture her but failed. Thereupon the nightingale told him he was a mighty fool, for he was regretting the past, and trying to attain the unattainable, and was believing that she had inside her a pearl as large as an ostrich egg, which was bigger than her whole body. See Benfey, *Pantschatantra*, vol. I. p. 380, vol. II. p. 543; Liebrecht, p. 332; *Gesta Romanorum*, cap. 167; Petrus Alfunsi, *Disciplina Clericalis*, quoted by Ward, *Catalogue*, p. 122.

6. THE STORY OF THE UNICORN. (*Barlaam*, XII. 112.) A man chased by a savage unicorn falls half way down a pit, and only saves himself by clinging to the branches of a shrub which was growing at the side. As he hangs there he sees two mice, one white and the other black, gnawing at the root of the branch, which they had almost gnawed through, and looking down he perceives an awful fire-breathing dragon at the bottom of the pit waiting for him to fall. From the side of the pit, quite close to him, he sees heads of four asps projecting. From the upper branches of the shrub honey drops down upon him, and in enjoying the sweetness of that honey he forgets all about the raging unicorn, which is death, the pit, which is the world, the tree, which is a man's life being eaten away by the two mice, which are day and night, the four asps, which typify the four

unstable elements of his body, and the fire-breathing dragon, which is hell. The honey, of course, typifies the fleeting pleasures of this life. For the Indian originals of this Apologue, see *Mahabharata*, XI.; *Avadanas*, vol. I. pp. 132, 191 ff.; Benfey, vol. I. p. 80 and p. 407; Liebrecht, pp. 330, 331; Ward, *Catalogue*, p. 123; Jacobs, *Barlaam*, p. cxiii; the Literature quoted by Jacobs and the table given by him on p. lxxiii.

7. THE MAN AND HIS THREE FRIENDS. (*Barlaam*, XIII. 114.) A man had three friends. Two of these he adored and flattered and hazarded his life for their sakes, and the third he treated with condescending arrogance. One day the man was arrested for a debt of 10,000 talents, and in his distress he applied to his friends for assistance. The first denied that he was the applicant's friend, and telling him that he was engaged to feast with friends gave him some old clothes and dismissed him; the second friend said that he himself was also in trouble, and could not help him; the third friend received him graciously and went to the king and pleaded his cause, and saved him from his enemies. For Derivatives and Literature, see Jacobs, *Barlaam*, p. cxiv.

8. THE KING FOR A YEAR. (*Barlaam*, XIV. 118.) The citizens of a certain state were in the habit of electing a stranger or a foreigner who knew not their customs, to be king for one year. During that year he had absolute power, and lived in a state of great luxury. At the end of a year the citizens deposed him and banished him to some island where, having made no provision since he was ignorant of what was to befall him, he lived a life of want

and died miserably. One man who was elected king discovered the custom of the citizens, and he secretly sent up to the island much gold and silver by the hands of trusty servants, and when he was banished to the island he was able to live as luxuriously as before. Moreover he had no state cares to trouble him. The kingdom is the vain world, and the citizens are the powers of the devils who rule this world. The wise counsellor who informed the king of the year of the custom of the citizens was some man like Barlaam. The Indian parallel to this Apologue is given in *Dhammapada*, 25, p. 235–8, and see Matt. vi. 19, 20. See also Liebrecht, *Die Quellen des Barlaam* (Ebert's *Jahrbuch*, p. 333); Kuhn in *Abhandlungen der König. Bayerischen Akad.* vol. xx, Munich, pp. 79, 80; Jacobs, *Barlaam*, p. cxv.

9. THE PAGAN KING AND HIS BELIEVING WAZÎR. (*Barlaam*, xvi. 135.) A king and his Wazîr went out into the city to see the sights and noticing a light shining through a shutter of an underground chamber they looked in. There they saw a man in rags and his wife mixing wine for him; whilst the man drank the woman sang and danced to him. The king thought the manner of life of the couple wretched and horrible, but the Wazîr told him that the manner of life even of the noblest and richest seemed to God like that of the man and woman. See Kuhn, *op. cit.*, p. 22, note.

10. THE RICH YOUNG MAN AND THE BEGGAR'S DAUGHTER. (*Barlaam*, xvi. 139.) A rich man wanted his son to marry a maiden of high rank and wealth, but the young man refused and went into exile.

On his way he stopped at the house of a poor man to rest and refresh himself during the hour of noon, and saw the man's daughter who, whilst engaged in some handicraft, praised God and gave thanks to Him. In answer to a question of the young man she told him that she blessed and thanked God for small mercies, and hoped for greater ones. Moreover she had learnt to know God, and the gate of Paradise was open to her. The young man was so charmed with her that he asked her father to give her to him in marriage, but the beggar objected, saying that a rich young man could not marry a beggar's daughter. The young man insisted that he wanted to marry her, and then the beggar said he could not let her leave him, for she was his only child. Then said the young man, I will abide here with you and live as ye live. When the beggar was convinced that the young man's love was genuine, he gave him his daughter, together with a sum of money that was larger than the young man had ever seen. Jacobs (p. cxx) quotes as a parallel *King Cophetua and the Beggar Maid*.

11. THE TAME GAZELLE. (*Barlaam*, XVIII. 157.) A certain man had a tame gazelle, which when grown up strayed frequently in the desert. One day she found a herd of gazelle grazing, and went off with them and grazed with them all day, but returned at night. This she did until at length her owner missed her and sent out men on horseback to seek her and bring her back. They found her and brought her back, but before they returned they killed several of her wild companions, and ill-treated the others.

12. Apologue of Theudas. THE PRINCE WHO HAD NEVER SEEN A WOMAN. (*Barlaam*, XXX. 268.) A son was born to a certain king, and the physicians told his father that the boy would lose his eyesight if he saw the sun or a fire before he was twelve years old. Thereupon the king made the child to live with his attendants in a rock-hewn house full of dark chambers, and for twelve years the boy never saw the light. At the end of this period the king ordered his servants to take the prince out into the town and to show him everything—men, women, gold, silver, precious stones, gorgeous apparel, splendid chariots and horses, golden bridles and purple harness, soldiers in armour, oxen, sheep, etc. In answer to his questions the servants told the prince the names of each of these, and when he asked what women were called, they said, " Devils that lead men astray." When the prince returned the king asked him which of the things he had seen pleased him most, and he replied, "The devils that lead men astray." For the Indian original Jacobs (p. cxxxi) quotes the story of Kshyasrnga in *Mahabharata*, III. 9999; and *Ramayana*, I. ix.; see also Kuhn, *op. cit.*, p. 80 and Ward, *Catalogue*, p. 123. Among the many Derivatives may be mentioned Boccaccio, *Decameron*, Day IV, Introduction, and the Exempla of Odo of Cheriton in Arundel 231, vol. I. fol. 203 b.

Now although the Book of Barlaam and Iôasaph in the form described above existed in manuscripts written in Greek (and perhaps also in Syriac and Pehlevi), in the VIIth century of our Era, and probably earlier, it did not gain the great popularity which it subsequently enjoyed until the Xth or XIth century. This popularity was due entirely to the Latin translation, which was carried rapidly into all the countries of Europe. The first Latin translation was made by Anastasius, a papal Librarian, in the second half of the IXth century, and the second by J. Billy (born 1535, died 1581), Abbot of St Michel in Brittany. Both have been printed in editions of the works of St John Damascene. The popularity of the Book of Barlaam was further increased by the abridgments of it which were printed in the XIIIth century by Vincent de Beauvais in his *Speculum Historiale* (Lib. xv. capp. 1–64), and Jacobus de Voragine in his *Legenda Aurea*. It is possible that here and there some scholar may have had doubts about the accuracy of its ascription to St John Damascene, and many, no doubt, hesitated about accepting it as a historical work. But copies of it were multiplied, as the extant manuscripts prove, and several translations of it were made into European languages other than Latin before the end of the XVth century. Barlaam and Iôasaph were treated as Saints in the *Legenda Aurea*, and likewise in the Catalogus Sanctorum of Peter de Natalibus (died about 1370). And they were so regarded during the rest of the Middle Ages, though it seems that they were not fully canonized until the time of Gregory XIII, when that Pope sanctioned a revised edition of the Martyrologium Romanum[1], in a licence

---

[1] See *The Roman Martyrology set forth by command of Pope Gregory XIII, and recised by the authority of Pope Urban VIII, translated out of Latin into English by G. K. of the Society of Jesus, and now re-edited by W. N. Skelly*, London, 1847.

dated 14 January 1584, or according to Cosquin[1] in 1583. Their day was fixed as the 27th November[2]. No one seems to have troubled to enquire who Barlaam and Iôasaph were, or when they lived. As their names had something of the sound of the old Hebrew names of Balaam and Jehosaphat, it is possible that readers of the Book of Barlaam believed them to have been natives of Palestine who were in India carrying on the work of the evangelization of India, which is said to have been begun by Thomas the Apostle.

Among the first to hear the narrative given in the Book of Barlaam when freed from its Christian additions and interpolations was Marco Polo, the great Venetian[3] traveller, who set out on his voyage to China in 1271. In the course of his travels he visited the Island of Seilan (Ceylon), and there on the top of a very high mountain (Adam's Peak) he saw a building which the Muslims regarded as the house or tomb of Adam, and the "Idolaters" (i.e. the Indians) believed to be the tomb of SAGAMONI BORCAN, who was "the best of men, a great saint in fact, according to their fashion, and the first in whose name idols were made." The natives told him that this saint was the son, as the story goes, of a great and wealthy king. "He was of such an holy temper that he would never listen to any worldly talk, nor would he consent to be king. And when the father saw that his son would not be king,

---

[1] *Revue des Questions Historiques*, tome xxviii. Paris, 1880, pp. 579–600.

[2] Ward, *Catalogue*, p. 119. In the Menology of the Greek Church the day of Iôasaph is given as August 26.

[3] See *The Book of Ser Marco Polo the Venetian concerning the Kingdoms of the East. Newly done into English by Henry Yule, C.B.* Two vols., London, 1874.

nor yet take any part in affairs, he took it sorely to heart. And first he tried to tempt him with great promises, offering to crown him king, and to surrender all authority into his hands. The son, however, would have none of his offers; so the father was in great trouble, and all the more that he had no other son but him, to whom he might bequeath the kingdom at his own death. So, after taking thought on the matter, the King caused a great palace to be built, and placed his son therein, and caused him to be waited on there by a number of maidens, the most beautiful that could anywhere be found. And he ordered them to divert themselves with the prince, night and day, and to sing and dance before him, so as to draw his heart towards worldly enjoyments. But 'twas all of no avail, for none of those maidens could ever tempt the king's son to any wantonness, and he only abode the firmer in his chastity, leading a most holy life, after their manner thereof. And I assure you he was so staid a youth that he had never gone out of the palace, and thus he had never seen a dead man, nor anyone who was not hale or sound; for the father never allowed any man that was aged or infirm to come into his presence. It came to pass however one day that the young gentleman took a ride, and by the roadside he beheld a dead man. The sight dismayed him greatly, as he had never seen such a sight before. Incontinently he demanded of those who were with him what thing that was? And then they told him that it was a dead man. 'How then,' quoth the king's son, 'do all men die?' 'Yea, forsooth,' said they.

Wherefore the young gentleman said never a word, but rode on right pensively. And after he had ridden a good way he fell in with a very aged man who could no longer walk, and had not a tooth in his head, having lost all because of his great age. And when the king's son beheld this old man, he asked what that might mean, and wherefore the man could not walk. Those who were with him replied that it was through old age the man could walk no longer, and had lost all his teeth. And so when the king's son had thus learned about the dead man and about the aged man he turned back to his palace and said to himself that he would abide no longer in this evil world, but would go in search of Him Who dieth not, and Who had created him.

"So what did he one night but take his departure from the palace privily, and betake himself to certain lofty and pathless mountains. And there he did abide, leading a life of great hardship and sanctity, and keeping great abstinence, just as if he had been a Christian. Indeed, an he had but been so, he would have been a great saint of Our Lord Jesus Christ, so good and pure was the life he led. And when he died they found his body and brought it to his father. And when the father saw dead before him that son whom he loved better than himself, he was near going distraught with sorrow. And he caused an image in the similitude of his son to be wrought in gold and precious stones, and caused all his people to adore it. And they all declared him to be a god; and so they still say. They tell moreover that he hath died fourscore and four times. The first time he died as a man, and came to life again as an ox; and then he died as an ox and came to life again as a horse, and so on until he had died fourscore and four times; and every time he became some kind of an animal. But when he died the eighty-fourth time they say he became a god. And they do hold him for the greatest of all their gods. And they tell that the aforesaid image of him was the first idol that the Idolaters ever had; and from that have originated all the other idols. And this befel in the Island of Seilan (Ceylon) in India.

"The Idolaters come thither on pilgrimage from very long distances and with great devotion, just as Christians go to the shrine of Messer Saint James in Gallicia. And they maintain that the monument on the mountain is that of the king's son, according to the story I have been telling you; and that the teeth, and the hair, and the dish[1] that are there were those of the same king's son, whose name was SAGAMONI BORCAN, or Sagamoni the Saint. But the Saracens (i.e. Muslims) also came thither on pilgrimage in great numbers and *they* say that it is the sepulchre of Adam our first father, and that the teeth, and the hair, and the dish were those of Adam[2]."

SAGAMONI, or more correctly SAKYA MUNI, or SAKIYA MUNI, means "the Sakiya sage," and BORCAN, or more correctly BURKHAN, means "divine," and was used by the Mongols as a synonym of the Buddha. It is almost incredible that some member of Marco

---

[1] This was of course the famous begging bowl of the Buddha which multiplied the food that was placed upon it.

[2] *The Book of Ser Marco Polo*, ed. Yule, vol. II. pp. 299 ff.

Polo's party did not tell him that the man, the narrative of whose life (which he describes so carefully) made such a great impression upon him, was the Buddha himself.

The next person who has written on the subject was the famous Portuguese traveller Diogo do Couto, who visited Ceylon in the second half of the XVIth century, about three hundred years after Marco Polo. He refers to Marco Polo's visit and mentions that the natives told him that the building on Adam's Peak was the tomb of our father Adam, and that they connected it with the son of a great king who once lived on the mountain. He calls this son "Sogomombarcão," who is, of course, the SAGAMONI BORCAN of Marco Polo. He goes on to say what he had heard, how a certain king who was married, but had no son, longed for a son, how God gave him a beautiful male child, how the astrologers declared that he would renounce the kingdom and become a hermit, how the king shut him up in a palace so that he could never see anything of the world, how he surrounded him with guardians who never let him go outside the palace gardens, how at length he allowed him to go forth with a strong escort, how on various occasions the prince met a blind man, a lame man, a paralytic, and a dead man, how when he learned that all men must die he was seized with melancholy, how a saint appeared to him in a vision and advised him to renounce the world, how he succeeded in escaping from the palace, how, disguised as a monk, he departed into the desert where he lived the life of a hermit, how at length, having wandered over several deserts, he came to Ceylon with many disciples, how he lived there for many years, how the people worshipped him like God, how, when he decided to depart from Ceylon, his disciples urged him to leave them some memorial of himself, and how, in answer to this petition, he left on a flat part of the mountain the impression of his foot, which is reverenced to this day. To this name the Gentiles in all India have built great and splendid pagodas.

Diogo do Couto then goes on to say that he asked some aged men there if their writings contained any account of Saint Josaphat who was converted by Barlaam, who is represented as the son of a great king of India, and who was brought up in the same way and of whom are told the same stories as he has been told of the life of the Buddha. When do Couto went to Salsette in the country of Bassein to see the famous Canará Pagoda (i.e. the Kânhari Caves, which he describes at length) he asked an old man there who had carried out the work. The old man told him that it was the father of Saint Josaphat, and that the Pagoda was intended to be the place where the prince was to be brought up in seclusion. As Josaphat was the son of a great king of India do Couto concludes that he may have been the Buddha, of whom such wonders are related—"E como nós temos della, que fora filho de hum grande Rey da India, bem póde ser, como ja dissemos, que fosse esto o Budão, de que elles contam tantas maravilhas." (Diogo do Couto, *Da Asia, Decada Quinta*, Pt. ii. Liv. vi. Cap. ii. p. 17.) Remembering the work of

Thomas the Apostle in India do Couto seems to suggest that the stories told of St Josaphat, or the Buddha, have a Christian origin[1].

[1] Dizem, que houve hum Rey, que reinava sobre todo este Oriente ; que havendo muitos annos que era casado sem ter filhos, lhe viera Deos no cabo de sua velhice a dar hum macho, a maior, e mais formosa creatura que podia ser ; e mandando-lhe tirar o nascimento por seus Astrologos, Acháram, que aquelle menino seria santo, e que desprezaria os Reynos do pai, e se faria peregrino (a que elles chaman Jogues) de que o pai posto em cuidados determinou de atalhar todas estas cousas com encerrar o filho que não visse cousa alguma. E assim como foi de sinco annos pera sima, o recolheo em huns Paços, que pera isso tinha mandado fazer, fechados, e cerrados, com grandes, e frescos jardins por dentro, onde o mandou crear em companhia de moços nobres de sua idade, com guardas, e vigias, pera que fóra daquelles ninguem mais fallasse com elle, nem visse, nem ouvir cousa, que lhe désse paixão, nem soubesse que havia outra cousa fóra dalli, pera que a não desejasse. Aqui se creou até idade de dezeoito annos, sem saber que havia doenças, mortes, nem outras miserias humanas.

Chegando á idade di entendimento, não deixou de saber que havia mais cousas que aquellas que via ; pelo que mandou pedir ao pai, que o deixasse sahir dalli, e ver as Cidades, e Villas do seu Reyno. Isto lhe concedeo El Rey, mandando-o tirar fóra, e levallo pela Cidade com grande resguardo ; e em huma rua encontrou hum homem manco, e enfermo, e perguntando aos que hiam com elle o que era, disseram-lhe que eram cousas da natureza mui ordinarias no Mundo, em que havia muitos mancos, cegos, e com outros defeitos. Outra vez que o tornáram a tirar fóra, vio hum velho muito decrepito encostado a hum bordão, tremendo-lhe o corpo todo. Espantado este Principe daquella visão, perguntou o que era, e disseram-lhe, que aquillo procedia dos muitos annos que vivêra, e que por isso se vinham da homens, que chegavam áquella idade, a debilitar muito. Outro dia encontrou com hum morto, que levavam a enterrar com grande pranto, e perguntando por aquillo, lho disseram ; ao que o Principe perguntou, como ? Eu, e todos havemos de morrer ? e dizendo-lhe que sim, ficou malencouizado, e triste.

Andando com aquella imaginação, dizem que lhe appareceo em visão hum santo em figura de peregrino, e que o persuadíra ao desprezo do Mundo, e á vida solitaria ; e como ella andava já abalado, e tinha mais largueza, teve modo com que desapparecêra em trajos de peregrino, e que se mettêra por essa terra dentro a fazer vida solitaria, e asperissima. E deixando muitas fabulas que contam, assim da fugida, como da peregrinação, depois de correr muitas terras, dizem que fora ter a Ceilão, levando já comsigo grande concurso de discipulos. Alli naquella serra fez tal vida tantos annos, que o adoravam os naturaes como a Deos ; e querendo-se partir dalli pera outras partes, os discipulos que alli ficavam lhe pedíram lhes deixasse alguma memoria sua, pera em seu nome a reverenciarem ; ao que fixando elle o pé naquella lagea, imprimíra aquella pégada, que ficou tida em tanta veneração, como temos dito. A este Principe nomeam suas historias por muitos nomes, o seu proprio era Dramá Rajo ; o porque foi conhecido, depois que o tiveram por santo, he o Budão, que quer dizer sabio.......A este nome tem dedicado os Gentios por toda a India grandes, e soberbos Pagodes. Vendo nós esta historia, estivemos cuidando se teriam os antigos Gentios destas partes em suas escrituras conhecimento do santo Josaphat, que foi convertido por

Thus it is clear that before the end of the XVIth century the relationship of the story of Josaphat to that of the Buddha was recognized, but it is equally clear that the recognition of this fact was not general. The popularity of the Book of Barlaam and Iôasaph in no way declined, and new translations and versions of it in European languages made it even more and more widely known. Thus the matter remained until Benfey was enabled to study the fine collection of Nepalese manuscripts, which had been brought to Paris early in the XIXth century, when he redis-covered the fact of the Oriental origin of the Book of Barlaam and Iôasaph, which Diogo do Couto published in 1612. In his Introduction to his work on the *Pantschatantra*, published in 1859, he pointed out the Buddhistic characteristics of the Apologue of the man pursued by a "Unicorn," and in his Appendix he stated that his views had just been

Barlão, que em sua lenda temos ser filho de hum Grande Rey do India, e que tivera a mesma creação, e todos os mais termos que temos contado da vida deste Budão. E como a historia de Josaphat havia de ficar escrita pelos naturaes, (que nado lhes fica por escrever,) perece que por tempos lhe vieram accrescentar muitas fabulas, como elles tem na vida do Budão, que nós deixámos, porque nem em dous Capitulos as concluiremos da maneira que as elles tem. E porque nos vem a proposito o que nos disse hum homem muito antigo das terras de Salsete em Baçaim do santo Josaphat, nos pareceo bem trazellu. Andando nós nesta Ilha de Salsete vendo aquelle raro, e admiravel Pagode, (que chamam do Canará), fabricado em huma serra, e talhadas em huma só pedra muitas salas, e huma dellas tamanha como a grande dos paços da Ribeira de Lisboa, e mais de trezentas cameras pela serra assima, quasi em caracol, cada huma com sua cisterna á porta, na mesma pedra viva, da mais fria, e excellente agua, que se póde desejar ; e nas portas de sala grande formosissimas figuras de vulto tamanhas como gigantes, de obra tão subtil, e prima, que nem em prata se podiam esculpir melhor; com outras muitas grandezas, que deixamos por não ser comprido.

E perguntando a este homem velho, que dissemos, por esta obra, e o que lhe parecia por quem fora feita, nos disse, que sem dúvida aquella obra se fizera por mandado do pai do Santo Josaphat, pera o recolher, e crear nella, como diz a sua lenda." Diogo do Couto, *Decada Quinta*, Part ii. Liv. vi. Cap. ii. pp. 13–17.

confirmed by two Chinese versions of the same Apologue, translated by Stanilas Julien in *Les Avadânas*, 3 vols., Paris, 1859 (see vol. I. pp. 132, 191). The eminent Hebraist Steinschneider had suspected that the Book of Barlaam was of Indian origin several years before[1], but he did not prove it. Five months after Benfey wrote his Preface (which is dated February 18, 1859) E. Laboulaye contributed two articles on *Les Avadânas* to the *Journal des Débats* (July 21 and 26), and in the second of these he mentioned the two Chinese versions of the Apologue concerning the man pursued by a Unicorn. And he went on to show that the framework of the Book of Barlaam and Josaphat is taken from the Legend of the Buddha, and finally declared that "cette histoire si caractéristique, ces rencontres si particulières, c'est le roman même de Josaphat." In the following year Saint-Hilaire published his work *Le Bouddha et sa Religion*, and the life of the Buddha which it contains is chiefly compiled from several versions of the LALITA VISTARA written in various Indian dialects, Chinese, etc. In the same year (1860) Liebrecht published his famous article[2] entitled *Die Quellen des Barlaam und Josaphat* (in Ebert's *Jahrbuch für Romanische und Englische Litteratur*, Bd. II. pp. 314–334), and he proved by quotations from Saint-Hilaire's work and the recension of the German version of Barlaam and Josaphat, which he had published in 1847, the truth of the

---

[1] See his article in *Zeitschrift der Deutschen Morgenländischen Gesellschaft*, v. 91.

[2] It is reprinted substantially in Liebrecht's *Buch zur Volkskunde*, Heilbronn, 1879, pp. 441, 460.

assertions made by Laboulaye and Saint-Hilaire. In 1880 M. E. Cosquin published a valuable article on the origin of the Book of Barlaam and Josaphat in the *Revue des Questions Historiques* (*La Légende des Saints Barlaam et Josaphat, son origine*), tom. XXVIII. pp. 579–600, and produced a few new facts[1] which supported Liebrecht's contentions. Finally must be mentioned Jacobs' excellent essay on the whole subject (*Barlaam and Josaphat*, London, 1896), in which the conclusions of the eminent Oriental scholars quoted above are cleverly and convincingly applied.

[1] See also his *Contes de Lorraine*, pp. xlix ff.

II

THE INDIAN SOURCES OF THE BOOK OF BARLAAM AND IÔASAPH, OR JEHOSAPHAT

It is now certain that the sources whence the author of the Greek version of the Book of Barlaam and Iôasaph drew the material for the framework of his story are not only of Indian but are of Buddhistic origin. And when we come to examine these sources in detail it is easy to see that Iôasaph, or Jehosaphat, the recipient of the wise counsels of Barlaam, is no other than the Buddha himself, and that Barlaam, his master, if we are to regard him as a human being, is a reflection of the Buddha. The Sanskrit word that has been turned into Iôasaph and Jehosaphat, through the mistakes of scribes and translators, is " Bodhisattva," meaning "he who is to become a Buddha," or "Buddha Elect." In the hands of Persian (Pehlevi) and Arab translators the initial *b* turned to *y*[1], the *dh* or *d* and *va* disappeared, and a termination in *af* (Persian?) being added, we obtain the form from which the Greek translator made "Iôasaph." Scribes familiar with Biblical names turned this into "Josaphat" (Matthew i. 8) for "Jehoshaphat" (1 Kings xv. 24), and thus the Sanskrit word with its meaning, obviously unsuitable in a Christian romance, was eliminated. Kuhn thought that ΙΩΑΑΣΑΦ was a mistake for ΙΩΔΑΣΑΦ[2] and Jacobs agrees with him[3].

---

[1] ﺏ=b, ﻱ=y ; there is just the difference of one dot.
[2] *Abhandlungen der König. Bayer. Akad.* vol. xx. Munich, 1897.
[3] *Barlaam*, p. xlvi.

About the name Barlaam there is more difficulty. The monk who adapted the Legend of the Buddha for the use of Christian readers was no doubt familiar with the story of the martyrdom of Barlaam, or Barlâhâ, who suffered during the reign of Diocletian, and as it was probably somewhat similar to the name of the hermit who converted the Bodhisattva, he applied it to him without hesitation. The name of the earthly father of the Bodhisattva was "Suddhodana" but it seems impossible to turn this into "Barlaam," or anything like it, by any conceivable confusion of letters. "Barlaam" must then represent some title or epithet which in the oldest Indian forms of the legend was used to describe the teacher of the Bodhisattva. The family name of the Bodhisattva was "Gautama," but in the legends he is always called "Bodhisattva." Some authorities[1] think that the name "Barlaam" represents the Sanskrit *bhikshu*, a "mendicant monk," but Kuhn and others regard it as a form of "Bilauhar," the name given to the hermit in an Arabic version of the story. Kuhn prefers to write "Balauhar" because the Georgian version gives "Balavari," which must, he thinks, have been derived from "Balavhari" or "Balahvari." And according to the same authority "Balauhar," بلوهر in passing through Pehlevi became "Bhagavân" بگوان. Now, according to Rájendralála Mitra "Bhagavân" is not an "arbitrary or superfluous, but the most appropriate title of the Buddha," and he says that it has been used by the Vedas to designate the Deity's self.

---

[1] For the literature see Kuhn, *op. cit.* p. 19.

"The essence of the Supreme is defined by the term 'Bhagavân'; it is the denomination of the primeval and eternal God....It is a convenient form to be used in the adoration of that Supreme Being, to Whom no term is applicable, and therefore 'Bhagavân' expresses that supreme spirit, which is individual, Almighty, and the cause of causes of all things. It is used in reference to the Supreme in a special signification[1]." Burnouf says that the epithet is primarily applied to absolute Buddhas, and secondly to Bodhisattvas, who have discharged all their religious obligations and are ready to become Buddhas[2]. If this be so both Balauhar and Iôasaph represent in a certain sense the Buddha, and Balauhar is only, as Hommel pointed out long ago, "eine nach echt indischer Weise vollzogene Repetition der (*sic*) des Buddha selbst[3]." Certainly the Buddha is commonly called "Bhagavân," i.e. the "Lord." And if the teacher of the Bodhisattva were in reality the Buddha himself we must assume that he took the form of a mendicant monk. I am told that from the Buddhist point of view there is nothing strange in the idea of one perfect Buddha advising and counselling another Buddha in the making. But it would be a stumblingblock to the Christian adapter of the story, so he made a human being, a monk, to go and visit the Prince and convert him to Christianity, as the result of instructions received from God, probably in dreams or visions.

[1] *Lalita Vistara*, p. 8.
[2] *Histoire du Buddhisme Indien*, p. 72.
[3] In Weisslowits, *Prinz und Derwisch*. Munich, 1890, p. 145.

The oldest Indian form of the Legend in which the perfect Buddha instructs a Buddha in the making probably came into existence within a comparatively short time after the death of Gautama the Buddha, but the Apologues, which form such an important section of the Book of Barlaam and Iôasaph, must be very much older. These "moral-comic tales," as Mr Rhys Davids calls literature of this kind[1], are undoubtedly of Indian origin, but their shrewd common sense and humour have appealed alike to Chinaman, Buddhist, Brahman, Arab, Persian, Jew and Christian, and made them universal favourites. The Apologues of Barlaam belong to the class of moral-comic tales which are found in the so-called "Aesop's Fables," and in the "Book of Kalîlah and Dimnah," or "The Fables of Pilpay, or Bidpai." Aesop apparently left no written works, but Plato[2], Aristophanes[3] and Aristotle[4] refer to his fables, and Herodotus (ii. 134) makes him a contemporary of Amasis II, a king of the XXVIth dynasty, who reigned in Egypt in the first half of the VIth century B.C. Few, if any, of the so-called Aesopic Fables known to us are older than the time of Planudes, who made his collection in the XIVth century of our era, but there is abundant evidence that most of them are of Indian origin, and that they are extremely old. The Book of Kalîlah and Dimnah had its origin in India and formed a part of Bud-

---

[1] *Buddhist Birth Stories or Jâtaka Tales.* London, 1880, p. xxix. (Reprint in Trübner's *Oriental Series.*)
[2] Bentley, *Dissertation on the Fables of Aesop*, p. 136.
[3] *Vespae*, 566, 1259, 1401 ff. and *Aves*, 651 ff.
[4] *De part. animal.* III. 2.

dhist literature. About 570 A.D. it passed into Persia and was translated into Pehlevi, and about the same time a Syriac translation of it was made by one Bôdh; about two hundred years later an Arabic translation of it was made by 'Abd Allâh Ibn al-Muḳaffa'[1]. It is probable that the Indian original of the Book of Barlaam had much the same history.

As to the remote origin of popular tales and fables in general Benfey thought that fables about animals in which animals act as animals are Western or Aesopic, and that the tales in which animals act as men in the form of animals are Indian. At a very early period, certainly not later than the Ist or IInd century A.D., Indian stories passed with Buddhism into China, Tibet and Mongolia[2]. They must have passed westward as well as eastward, especially after the departure of Alexander the Great from India. And a considerable knowledge of India and Indian matters must have found its way into Eastern Europe through the writings of Megasthenes, who was sent as an ambassador to the court of Chandragupta by Seleucus Nicator during the last years of the IVth century B.C.

Before referring to the actual Indian works still extant which prove that the framework of the Book of Barlaam and Iôasaph is derived from the Indian Birth Stories about the Buddha, the main facts of the life of that great religious reformer may be briefly set forth. GAUTAMA, later known as the

---

[1] Keith-Falconer, *Kalilah.* Cambridge, 1885, p. xiv.
[2] Benfey, *Einleitung zur Pantschatantra*, pp. xii–xxvi.

Buddha, was the son of Suddhodana, a Sâkya Chief,
who reigned over a district round about Kapila-
vastu, on the Rohini river, 27° 37′ N. lat. by 83° 11′ E.
long., about 130 miles due north of the city of
Benares[1]. His mother was called Mâyâ, and she
was the daughter of a Râja of Koli; both she and
her sister Gautami were wives of Suddhodana, their
cousin. When she was about forty-five years old,
she dreamed a dream, in which she saw the future
Buddha entering her womb in the form of an elephant, and she afterwards conceived. When the
time for the birth of her child drew near, she told
the king her husband that she wished to go to her
father's estate, but the pains of labour came upon
her suddenly when she was in the Lumbini Grove,
and she brought forth her son there—about the
year 557 B.C. The exact site of the Lumbini Grove
(Rummindei) was fixed in 1895 by the discovery of
the pillar and inscription[2] which king Asoka set up
there to mark the birthplace of the Buddha, when
he made his religious tour in the Nepalese Tarai
about 249 B.C.[3] The Lumbini Grove is between nine
and sixteen miles from Kapila-vastu. Mâyâ died
seven days after her child was born, and the boy
was given into the care of her sister Gautami. At
the age of sixteen Gautama married Yasodharâ, the
daughter of Suprabuddha, by whom he had a son
called Râhula; a common name for Yasodharâ is
Râhulamâtâ, i.e. "Mother of Râhula." The *Lalita*

---

[1] Rhys Davids, *Buddhism*. London, 1920.
[2] See Bühler, *Epigraphia Indica*, v. 1; and Smith, V. A., *Asoka*,
p. 144 ff.
[3] According to the calculation of Mr V. A. Smith.

PLATE I

The Bodhisattva in the form of a young elephant entering his mother's womb. From Foucaux's *Le Lalita Vistara.*

Vistara calls his wife Gopâ. The Chinese legend
says that Gautama had three wives, Yasodharâ,
Gotamî, and Manoharâ, and another authority mentions four, Yasodharâ, Mrigaja or Gopâ, Utpalavarṇâ
and Gotamî. There is no evidence, however, that
any wife except Yasodharâ existed.

When Gautama reached his twenty-ninth year a
god appeared unto him in a vision, or visions, in the
form of a man helpless through old age, a man sick
unto death, a putrefying corpse, and a calm and
dignified hermit. The meaning of each appearance
was explained to him by his charioteer Channa, or
Chhandaka, who showed him that sickness, old age
and death were the inheritance of every man and
that there was no means of escaping from them.
Realizing the truth of his charioteer's words Gautama
became filled with despair. When he saw the quiet
dignified hermit, and heard how remote he was from
the joys and troubles of this world, his mind told
him that true peace and happiness in this world
could only be obtained by becoming a monk and
following the ascetic life in the desert far removed
from the affairs of men. There is no doubt that
Gautama had become dissatisfied with the life he
led some years before he saw the four visions, and
that he had been trying to find some course of
action which would silence his doubts and satisfy
his aspirations. He was sated with the pleasures of
life, tired of the palace ceremonial, and wearied with
the unsatisfying character of his daily life and its
pursuits and occupations. Whilst he was pondering
on the four visions, his son Râhula was born to him,

ten years (*sic*) after his marriage, but the event caused him little joy because he felt that his love for the child would bind him more tightly to the life of which he was exceedingly tired. As he returned to Kapila-vastu, among all the plaudits which greeted his arrival, he caught the words of the maiden Kisâ Gotami, who cried out "Blessed indeed is that mother, blessed indeed is that father, blessed indeed is that wife, who owns this Lord so glorious[1]." These words, having to him a special meaning, comforted him and encouraged him to pursue the course of action which he was meditating upon, and he sent the maiden, his cousin, his necklace of pearls as her fee for teaching him. She thought that Siddhârtha was falling in love with her, but such was not the case, for he took no further notice of her, although her words had comforted him.

That night he sent for Channa, his charioteer, and ordered him to saddle his horse Kanṭhaka and to bring it to him, as he intended to flee from his palace. Whilst Channa was bringing the horse, Gautama went into his wife's room and looked at her and his child, and suppressing his desire to take the boy in his arms, because it would waken his wife, he left the room, and went out, and mounted his horse and rode away to take up the life of a mendicant monk. This was the Great Renunciation, which has stirred the imagination of untold thousands of men. Channa urged his lord against taking this step, and Mâra, or the Devil, appeared to him and

---

[1] Rhys Davids, *Jâtakas, Buddhist Birth Stories*, vol. I. p. 80; *Hibbert Lectures*, 1881, pp. 149, 150; and *Buddhism*, p. 31.

PLATE II

The Bodhisattva in the form of a young elephant entering his mother's womb. From Foucaux's *Le Lalita Vistara*.

offered him the sovereignty of the world if he would
abandon his flight. Gautama rode far that night,
and when outside the boundaries of Koli he gave
his horse to Channa, and sent him back to Kapila-
vastu, and having persuaded a stranger to exchange
apparel with him, he set out for Râjagriha, the
capital of Maghada[1]. Here he joined the society of
hermits who lived there, and became a disciple of
Âlâra and Uddaka. Soon, however, being dissatisfied with his progress, he left them, and went to
Buddha Gayâ, where he stayed for six years with a
few disciples of his own. He almost killed himself
with the severity of his ascetic labours, but finding
that they brought him no peace, he abandoned
them, and returned to a normal course of life. When
his disciples saw him eating and drinking like an
ordinary man they lost their belief in him, and left
him alone to carry on his quest for peace. He then
departed from that place and wandered along the
side of a great river, until at length he came to a
spot where there was a very large tree (*ficus religiosa*); there he sat down and began the series of
meditations by which he attained to Buddhahood.
This tree was the famous Bo-tree[2], the Tree of
Wisdom, or the Tree of Intelligence. During the
weeks which he sat at the foot of this tree he was

---

[1] See Cunningham, *Ancient Geography of India*, p. 462 ff.

[2] Rhys Davids says that the Bo-tree was to the Buddhists what the Cross
is to the Christians; the Indians worshipped it. The original Bo-tree grew
at Bodh Gâyâ, near Rajgir, and a cutting from it is still growing among the
ruins of the old temple. A branch of it planted at Anurâdhapura in Ceylon,
B.C. 245, by the lady Sanghamittâ is still growing, and is the oldest historical
tree in the world, being about 2167 years old. Tennent, *Ceylon*, vol. II.
pp. 613 ff.; Cunningham, *Arch. Report*, vol. I. p. 6; Rhys Davids, *Buddhism*, p. 39.

fed day by day by Sujâtâ, a maiden who was born
in the house of Senâni the landowner, in the village
of Senâni in Uruvela. It was at this time that
the Bodhisattva had to endure temptations of all
kinds, and the attacks of Mâra and all his hellish
brood, which assumed various forms and colours.
The angels who tried to protect him were defeated,
and Mâra and his devils attacked him on three sides,
but in vain. Then the Evil One created a whirlwind
to destroy him, but when it reached him it failed to
ruffle the hem of his garment. Mâra created mighty
storms of rain, stones, deadly weapons, charcoal,
ashes, sand, and mud, but when these things came
to where the Bodhisattva was, they turned to
flowers, perfume, etc. Mâra cast his javelin at him,
but it became a garland of flowers, and the rocks
which Mâra's devils hurled on him became nosegays.
In a final encounter with Mâra, when a witness was
required to prove that the Bodhisattva had given
alms, the Earth herself opened her mouth and
testified on his behalf. Mâra's elephant, which was
250 leagues high, dropped on its knees, and his
army was overwhelmed, and broke and fled. This
was the Great Victory over the Tempter which
the Bodhisattva gained under the Bo-tree, and he
obtained peace and great confidence in himself
thereby.

The Bodhisattva set out for Benâres, and on his
way thither met one Upaka, with whom he conversed,
but when he told him that he was going to Benâres
to turn the Wheel of the good Law[1] and to take

[1] See Alabaster, *The Wheel of the Law*. London, 1871.

PLATE III

Asoka Pillar at Rummindei in the Nepal Tarai.

light, and to open the gate of immortality to the
people there, Upaka lost his temper and parted
from him. The Bodhisattva went on his way and
came to Benâres, and took up his abode in the place
now called Dhamek[1]. Here he made his first public
declaration of his system, which is preserved in
the "Sutra of the Kingdom of Righteousness." He
preached the necessity of the "Middle Path" with
its Eight Principles[2], and stated that he had arrived
at his convictions "by the light of reason and intui-
tion alone." He continued to live in the Migadaya,
or "Deer-Park," where he taught his disciples, and
after three months he sent forth sixty of them to
preach his doctrines. Later he visited his father
Suddhodana, and converted his wife Yasodharâ to
his doctrines, and she become one of the first
Buddhist nuns. The Buddha passed nearly forty-five
years in preaching his religion, but as a description
of the work which he accomplished does not fall
within the scope of this summary, I pass on to the
forty-fourth year of his preaching, when he crossed
the Ganges and went to Ambapali, where he accepted the hospitality of the leading courtesan of
the town. A year later he fell ill at Belu-gâmaka,
and told his followers that his life was drawing to a
close; a little later he announced that he would die
in three months' time. He then went on to Kusi-
nagara, where he rested in a grove, and knowing
that his death was near he began to talk to his

[1] See Cunningham, *Archaeological Report*, 1862, vol. i. pp. 103 ff.; and
Purna Chandra Mukherji, *Antiquities in the Tarai Nepal* (*Arch. Survey
of India*), No. xxvi., Part 1, Calcutta, 1901.
[2] See Rhys Davids on the *Angas* in his *American Lectures*, 1896, p. 134.

faithful Ānanda about his burial, and matters connected with the Order. He was sufficiently strong
to expound his system to Subhadra, a Brahmin
philosopher who, it is said, became converted to
Buddhism. He addressed some words of admonition to the "Mendicants," urging them to work out
their salvation with diligence. After this he did not
speak again, and having fallen into a state of un-
consciousness he passed away about B.C. 477[1], being
about eighty years of age. On the eighth day after
his death his body was taken outside the city and
cremated, and the ashes were divided into eight
portions by Droṇa, a Brahmin. The recipients were:
Ajâtasatru, king of Magadha, the Lichchhavis of
Vaisâlî, the Sâkyas of Kapila-vastu, the Bulis of
Allakappa, the Koliyas of Râmagrâma, a native of
Vethadîpa, the Mallas of Pâvâ, and the Mallas of
Kusanagara. The earthen vessel in which the body
was cremated was given to Droṇa, the Brahmin, and
the charcoal ashes were given to the Mauryas of
Pipphalîvana. A stûpa, or funerary monument, was
built over each portion of the relics, and these
stûpas were for centuries visited by pilgrims from
all parts of India and from foreign countries.

Authorities have found it very difficult to ascertain
the exact extent of the influence of Gautama's
teaching and religion at the time of his death. It
must have been considerable but was not paramount,

---

[1] The tradition of South India and Ceylon makes him die in 544 or
543 B.C., but Mukherji makes it nearly half a century earlier. The above
date is that of Cunningham (*Bhilsa Topes*, pp. 20 ff.), which was accepted
by Max Müller and Dr Bühler. Dr Fleet gives the exact day—Oct. 13,
483 B.C.; see *Journal Royal Asiatic Society*, 1909, pp. 1–34.

PLATE IV

Asoka Pillar (excavated) in the Nepal Tarai.

and many other ascetic orders must have flourished side by side at that period. It is possible that accounts of Gautama's system were taken to the West by the followers of the army of Alexander the Great, but facts on this point are wanting until we come to the time of Chandragupta Maurya, the first king of all India, who reigned about B.C. 322-298. When he was a young man Chandragupta was among the rebels who were captured by the troops of Alexander the Great in the year B.C. 325, but he somehow escaped the fate which was meted out to many of his fellows, and returned safely to his native district. How much he had seen of Greek methods of fighting cannot be said, but he set to work to form an army, and a few years later he became a formidable chief. In B.C. 315 he seized the throne of Nanda, Râja of Magadha, who had been murdered, and assumed the title of "Chandragupta." He it was who defeated Seleucus Nicator, governor of the provinces which Alexander had conquered in India, and drove out the Greeks from his country. The rise of Chandragupta to power synchronized with a great development of Buddhist influence in the country, which was due to the radical views about caste that were held by the followers of Gautama. The Buddhists held that every man, no matter how low his caste, had a right to hope to attain to Nirvâna. Asoka (B.C. 273-231), son of Bindusâra and grandson of Chandragupta, became converted to Buddhism in the tenth year of his reign (B.C. 263), and he devoted himself whole-heartedly to its interests. He spent money freely in building monasteries and hospitals,

and he endowed the monks liberally, and he tried
to rule his great kingdom with humanity and justice. He respected the Law himself and expected
everyone else to do the same. He adopted the title
of "Piyadasi," the "kind-hearted," and his works
proved that it described him accurately. About the
year B.C. 249 he made a pilgrimage to all places
which were associated with the Buddha when on
earth, and he visited the Lumbini Grove, where the
Buddha was born[1], and Kapila-vastu, Bodh Gâyâ,
Sârnâth, Sravâsti, Kusanagara, etc., and at each place
he set up a Stûpa, or pillar, to commemorate his
visit and the event in the Buddha's life which made it
famous. Under Asoka's protection Buddhism reached
the summit of its power, and the Council of Patna
decreed that missionaries should be sent to teach it
in the principal countries of India[2]. Asoka sent his
son Mahinda to Ceylon during the reign of Devânam
Piya Tissa (B.C. 250–230) to introduce Buddhism
into the Island, and with him the sacred books
(Piṭakas) and commentaries upon them. Tissa became a Buddhist and built the famous Thûpârâma
Dâgaba at Anurâdhapura, and several of his female
relations became nuns in the house of Sanghamittâ,
sister of Mahinda, who brought over to Ceylon a company of nuns and a branch of the sacred Bo-tree at
Buddha Gâyâ, under which the Buddha obtained
Buddhahood. This branch was planted near Thûpârâma Dâgaba, and as said above (p. xlvii) still
grows.

[1] For the inscription which he set up there see Smith, V. A., *Asoka*.
Oxford, 1901, pp. 145 ff.
[2] For a list of the missionaries see Rhys Davids, *Buddhism*, p. 227.

PLATE V

Piprava, Basti district. General view of Gautama Buddha's relic-stupa outside Kapila-vastu.

Buddhism was carried into Syria and Egypt by the envoys of Chandragupta and his grandson Asoka in the third century B.C., and there is no doubt that it made its way into China before the Christian Era. Professor Rhys Davids says that it penetrated to China "along the fixed route from India to that country, round the north-west corner of the Himâlayas and across Eastern Turkestan. Already in the second year B.C. an embassy, perhaps sent by Huvishka, took Buddhist books to the then Emperor of China, A-ili; and the Emperor Ming-Ti, 62 A.D., guided by a dream, is said to have sent to Tartary and Central India, and brought Buddhist books to China. From this time Buddhism rapidly spread there. Monks from Central and North-Western India frequently travelled to China; and the Chinese themselves made many journeys to the older Buddhist countries to collect the sacred writings, which they diligently translated into Chinese. In the fourth century Buddhism became the State religion" (*Buddhism*, p. 241). Again, "It is clear from the coins of Huvishka and Kanishka that Buddhism became the State religion of the north-westerly parts of India at about the commencement of our era" (*Buddhism*, p. 238). From these parts the knowledge of Buddha and Buddhism would pass into Afghanistan and Persia, and the Christians who lived eastward of the Tigris must have heard the Fables and Parables, which were even then associated with the Birth Stories of the Buddha.

The evidence available is not sufficient to show

which collection of the Birth Stories of the Buddha was used by the Christian monks who compiled Barlaam and Iôsaphat, but the Indian work that most probably supplied the framework of his narrative was the LALITA VISTARA. This view is shared by many scholars as we have already seen. This book was unknown in Europe until 1807, when Major W. D. Knox, having obtained a copy of it in Nepal, sent it to H. T. Colebrooke, and a description of its contents by R. Lenz was published in the *Bulletin der Akademie von St Petersburg* for 1836. In 1837 another copy of it was sent by Mr B. H. Hodgson to Paris among a large collection of Indian MSS., where it was carefully studied by Burnouf. The Sanskrit text was first published in *Bibliotheca Indica*, Calcutta, 1853–77. Another edition, the result of many years arduous labour, was published by S. Lefmann, entitled *Leben und Lehre des Çâkya-Beddha*, Halle, vol. I. 1902, vol. II. 1908. There is a complete French translation by Ed. Foucaux, entitled LE LALITA VISTARA—*"Développement des Jeux"*—Contenant *L'Histoire du Bouddha Çakya-mouni depuis sa naissance jusqu'à sa prédication*, Paris, Part I. 1874, Part II. 1892. This work forms vol. VI. of the ANNALES DU MUSÉE GUIMET. And an English translation of the first fifteen sections of the *Lalita Vistara*, with elaborate notes, was published by Râjendralâla Mitra in BIBLIOTHECA INDICA (New Series, No. 455, vol. XC. Calcutta, 1881–86), entitled "Memoirs of the Early Life of Sâkya Siñha." According to Lefmann *Lalita* means "natürliche ungesuchte Handlung," and *Vistara* "Ausbreitung,

PLATE VI

The Buddha Sàkya-muni. From Foucaux's *Le Lalita Vistara*.

ausführliche umständliche Darstellung," and the
two words taken together = "Geschichte des Vor-
gänge oder Handlungen" im Leben Çâkya-Siñha,
des Tathâgata oder Buddha. Mitra renders the
title "exposition of recreations," and Foucaux,
following the Tibetan, "développement des jeux."

The *Lalita Vistara* is one of the Nine Dharmas
(the Eighth), or Books of Excellence of the Law,
that the Nepalese place in a different category from
their collection of sacred books, which are two hundred in number. When the book was written is not
known, and authorities differ in assigning a date to
its composition. According to Burnouf (p. 356) it
was in existence in the second century after the
death of Buddha, and La Gomme (*Le Bouddhisme*,
p. 176) says it was translated into Chinese in A.D. 65.
On the other hand, Rhys Davids thinks that it was
composed in Nepal by some Buddhist who lived
600 or 1000 years after the Buddha (*Hibbert Lectures*, 1881, p. 199). In the last edition of his excellent
manual, *Buddhism*, published in 1920, he says the
Lalita Vistara "is partly in prose and partly in
verse, the poetical passages being older than the
others. M. Foucaux has published a translation
into French of a translation of this work into
Tibetan. He holds the Tibetan version to have
existed in the VIth century A.D. How much older
the present form of the Sanskrit work may be is
quite uncertain[1]. The *Lalita Vistara* is full of extravagant poetical fictions in honour of Gautama,

[1] Thus rejecting Foucaux's view which assigns the Sanskrit original to
Kanishka's Council of 500 learned monks. Kanishka began to reign A.D. 10.

some of which are not without literary value; and
it is just as much a poem on the birth and temptation of Gautama, based on earlier lives of the
Teacher, as Milton's *Paradise Regained* is a poem
on the birth and temptation of Christ based on the
accounts found in the Gospels. Such historical
value as it possesses is derived therefore from the
comparison which it enables us to draw between the
later Sanskrit[1] and the earlier Pali traditions, and
from the light which it throws on the development of the religious beliefs which sprang up regarding the person of the Buddha." But whether the
Lalita Vistara was compiled in the IIIrd century
B.C. or the IInd century A.D. matters little for our
purpose, for our chief authority, Rhys Davids, is
convinced that it is "based on earlier lives of the
Teacher." And this means that the Birth Stories of
the Buddha or, as they have been called, "Legends
of the Romantic Life of Buddha," were in existence
and were well known all over India, and in many
parts of China, some centuries before the Greek
"spiritual romance" of Barlaam and Iôsaphat, at
least in the form in which we now know it, was
compiled. It is impossible to gather from the Greek
text any adequate idea of the style and scope and
contents of the *Lalita Vistara*, and I have therefore
drawn up a short summary of it, based as far as the
first fifteen sections, or Chapters, are concerned,
upon the English version of them by Râjendralâla
Mitra, and for the other Chapters on the French
translation published by Foucaux in 1874 and 1892.

[1] For the earlier Sanskrit accounts see Senart's edition of the Mahâvastu.

PLATE VIII

Facsimile of the last leaf in the Royal Asiatic Society's MS. of the *Lalita Vistara*, containing the conclusion of the narrative, concluding title, the Buddhist Confession of Faith, the scribe's colophon giving the name of the scribe (Vimarānanda) and his father, the date (Samvat 785 Nepali era, the 14th of the waxing fortnight of the month Kārttika), and a final blessing.

On the accompanying plates are given facsimiles of the first and last palm leaf of the Codex in the Library of the Royal Asiatic Society which contains the Sanskrit text that forms the principal authority for Dr S. Lefmann's edition. The Colophon of the Codex, which is comparatively modern, offers some interesting difficulties, and on these my friend, Dr L. Barnett, Keeper of the Oriental Books and Manuscripts in the British Museum, has most kindly written for me the following learned note.

III

NOTE ON A MANUSCRIPT OF THE *LALITA VISTARA*
IN THE LIBRARY OF THE ROYAL ASIATIC SOCIETY

This manuscript of the Sanskrit text of the *Lalita Vistara*, which is the one on which S. Lefmann has mainly based his edition, consists of a series of folios of brownish native paper, measuring on the average 15 inches in width and 3⅞ inches in height. The character is a Nepali form of the Northern Indian type of writing, clearly written in a free style. The text is followed by a colophon in debased Sanskrit, written by the scribe. It is as follows: *śrī-vidyā-nandakasa praniti kēsāōti gyānāōti tasya putra śrīvimarānandaḥ* || || *samvat* 875 *kārttika śukla* 14 *śubham astu savaddā*. The first sentence of this is somewhat puzzling. Apparently *-vimarānandaḥ* should be corrected to *-vimalānandaḥ*, which gives a fairly common name. But *praniti* is mysterious; possibly it is a mistake for either *praṇati* ("obeisance") or *praṇīti* ("guidance" or "composition"), but it may be something quite different. The words *kēsāōti gyānāōti* are still more obscure: the first looks like the familiar name Kēśava misspelt, with a particle *ti* tacked on, and in *gyānāōti* one is tempted to see the word *jñāna* ("knowledge") in some derivative form. On the other hand, it is conceivable that *praniti kēsāōti gyānāōti* is a compound phrase forming a sort of clan-name, or other kind of

Plate VIII

Facsimile of the last leaf in the Royal Asiatic Society's MS. of the *Lalita Vistara*, containing the conclusion of the narrative, concluding title, the Buddhist Confession of Faith, the scribe's colophon giving the name of the scribe (Vimarānanda) and his father, the date (Samvat 785 Nepali era, the 14th of the waxing fortnight of the month Kārttika), and a final blessing.

description, which for the present may be left un-explained. The rest of the sentence, then, is: "of the fortunate Vidyānanda...his son the fortunate Vima-lānanda" [wrote or caused to be written this book?]. The rest is clear, if we correct the blunder *savaddā* to *sarvadā*: "the year 875, the 14th [lunar day] of the waxing fortnight of [the month] Kārttika. May there be welfare everywhere!" The Nepali *samvat* year 875 would correspond to A.D. 1753.

IV

SUMMARY OF THE LALITA VISTARA

Chap. I. INTRODUCTION. Begins with OM, the symbol of the Deity, and describes how Bhagavân, i.e. the Deity, vouchsafes to grant the request of the sons of gods, etc. about Him to recite the LALITA VISTARA.

Chap. II. The Exhortation to Buddha Siñha to descend to earth, for "time is come, tarry thou not."

Chap. III. Describes the Dynasty from which the mother of the Buddha is to be chosen. Contains the prophecy "twelve years hence will the Bodhisattva (i.e. the individual who was to descend to earth and acquire Buddhahood) be conceived in his mother's womb."

Chap. IV. Bodhisattva takes his seat on the throne in the pavilion of Uchchadhvaja, and lectures on 108 subjects, before his descent from Tushita, or Heaven.

Chap. V. Bodhisattva appoints Maitreya to be Vicegerent in Tushita. The form in which he should enter his mother's womb discussed; the form of a huge elephant with six tusks is decided upon. The eight auspicious signs appear in the palace of Suddhodana, the father of the Buddha, and his mother Mâyâ declares her determination to fast. The nymphs visit her in the palace of Dhṛitaráshṭra in the city of Kapila. The gods carry forth the Bodhisattva on their shoulders.

Chap. VI. In the day of full moon, in the month of Vaiśâkha, in the spring of the year, the Bodhisattva left the mansion of Tushita and entered his mother's womb in the form of a yellowish-white elephant, having six tusks, crimson veins, golden teeth and perfect members. Thus he acknowledged sonship to Suddhodana. Mâyâ, his mother, had a dream, which the Brâhmans interpret satisfactorily. The gods build habitations for Mâyâ, and in them she receives visitors from morning till evening, and the unborn Buddha offered them welcome, whilst his mother performed miracles. He remained in Mâyâ's body 10 months.

Chap. VII. When the time for his birth drew nigh Mâyâ requested permission to go to the Lumbini Garden, which was a beautiful park full of scented waters and flowers, and when she arrived there she left her chariot and walked about from tree to tree. This Garden was in the country of Dewah, or Koli, and was the property of Mâyâ's father. As she approached the fig-tree Plaksha (*ficus religiosa*), it felt the glory of her child in her and bowed its head and saluted her. In this Garden the Buddha was born. He alighted on the earth and took his seat on a lotus flower. His father Suddhodana named him "Sarvârthasiddha," i.e. one through whom every object has been obtained. After the Buddha was born Mâyâ's flank became unbroken and scarless; but seven days after his birth she died, and the child was handed over to the care of his mother's sister Gautamî. Then the king consulted his counsellors as to whether the boy would become an imperial sovereign or a houseless hermit. At this time a great sage called Asita was informed supernaturally that a wonderful prince was born in the house of Suddhodana at Kapila, and he told his nephew Naradatta that he must go and see him. When he arrived there and was taken into the king's presence, he prophesied the future greatness of the prince as a holy man and declared that he would be a Buddha.

Chap. VIII. The Prince is taken to the temple, but before he went the streets and roads were cleansed and decorated, trumpets were blown, bells were rung, the nobles and the wealthy were assembled, and all maimed, and lame, and blind, and deformed persons were cleared out of the streets.

Chap. IX. Describes the ornaments that were prepared for the Prince, and ends with an address to the king and his nobles by the goddess Vimalâ who said that all ornaments were as a lump of ink compared with the resplendent virtues of the Prince.

Chap. X. Deals with the education of the Prince. His schoolmaster Visuâmitra, as soon as the Bodhisattva entered the school, felt his marvellous powers, and fell prostrate on the ground before him. When asked to write the alphabet by the schoolmaster, the Prince asked him "which?" and then enumerated sixty-four different kinds of writing.

Chap. XI. The Prince went to a village with other boys, and sat under a Jambu tree, and fell into a state of meditation.

Chap. XII. The king and his council decide that the Prince must be married, and a messenger is sent to Kapila-vastu to find a bride. The maiden chosen is Gopâ, who in the Chinese text is called Yasodharâ, the daughter of Daṇḍapáṇi, who objects that the

Prince is not an athlete, and that he is ignorant of the art of swordsmanship, and the use of the bow, and the driving of elephants. Thereupon a species of tournament is arranged, and Gopâ plants a flag of victory, saying that it shall be awarded to the bravest competitor. The elephant being brought for the Prince is killed at the city gate by Devadatta, and when the Prince comes and sees the carcase, he puts out one foot from his chariot, and seizing the tail of the animal with the great toe only, whirls the carcase across the seven walls and seven moats of the city, and casts it two miles away in the outskirts. The Prince then shows his great skill in calligraphy, in arithmetic, astrological calculations, leaping, jumping, running, wrestling, archery, riding, driving, etc. and so he obtained Gopâ to wife.

Chap. XIII. Palace of the Prince described and his life therein. The celestial powers make exhortations to him.

Chap. XIV. The king dreams a dream in which he sees his son leaving the palace and putting on the ochre-coloured garb of an ascetic. When he awoke he determined that the Prince should no longer visit the garden but remain in the zenana. He built three palaces, providing them with ladders, and fitted heavy doors to the Lucky Gate, or Gate of Mars, through which he thought the Prince might try to escape, and filled the palaces with everything necessary, and kept musicians and dancers in attendance. With the permission of his father the Prince set out with his charioteer to visit the garden by the eastern gate, and as he drove out he saw a broken down, decrepit, toothless, and grey-haired old man leaning on a stick. When he learned from the charioteer that all men came to this state he turned back to his palace. On the second visit to the garden he saw at the northern gate a sick man on the point of death, and again instructed by his charioteer he turned back. On the third visit he saw by the western gate a dead man, and realizing the transience of life he turned back. On the fourth visit he saw by the northern gate a Bhikshus, or mendicant hermit, with his begging bowl. This calm, quiet, and self-possessed man impressed him greatly, and he approved of the charioteer's explanation, and subsequently turned back. The king, seeing the effect which these four men had upon him, had the Prince watched more closely. He raised the walls, broadened the moat, increased the armed guards, stationed bodies of troops at the four gateways, and had strict guard kept over his son day and night. And in the palace he ordered that amusements of every kind should be continued at all times, and the women were bidden to display themselves and to employ every enticing allurement known to them.

Chap. XV. The Prince goes to Suddhodana and begs his permission to depart, but offers to remain if he can promise him immunity from decay, disease and death, together with unmeasured life; this being impossible for him to grant, he gave the Prince permission to go. The precautions taken by the king and Gautami were in vain, for the gods assisted the Prince. At midnight he ordered Chandaka to bring him his horse Kaṇṭhaka ready for riding, and going through the women's apartments for the last time, he left his palace, and departed from Kapila-vastu. He passed through the country of the Mallas, and in the city of Anumainêya he dismounted and, giving his horse Kaṇṭhaka and trappings to Chandaka his charioteer, he sent him back alone to the palace. Suitable apparel having been provided by the gods, he dressed himself therein and set out on his wanderings. When his departure was discovered in the palace, the king had the city gates closed—but too late—the Prince had escaped.

Chap. XVI. The Prince visits various learned hermits, goes to Magadha and then to the river Nâirañjanâ.

Chap. XVII. Describes the austerities which the Prince practised for the next six years, and the attacks, unsuccessful, which the demon Pâpîyân made upon him.

Chap. XVIII. Describes the food which he ate, and how his body assumed the form and colour which it had before he began his ascetic practices, and how the 32 marks of a great man and the 80 secondary signs appeared in him.

Chap. XIX. Having bathed in the river Nâirañjanâ, and eaten and restored the strength of his body, the Prince sets out to go to the great tree of Intelligence at Bôdhimaṇḍa, and the efforts of millions of demons could not drive him away from that tree.

Chap. XX. Describes the arrangements made on behalf of the Prince by the Bôdhisattvas at Bôdhimaṇḍa.

Chap. XXI. Describes the temptations and attacks of the devils upon the Prince, Mâra Pâpîyân sent him a dream in 32 terrifying forms, and surrounded him with multitudes of terrible animal forms and devil-like monsters of loathsome and awful appearance. In fact the whole district was packed with demons and fiends, and the world seemed to be full of them. Pâpîyân next sent his daughters to tempt the Prince, but he resisted all their 32 modes of attack, and drove them off defeated.

Chap. XXII. The Prince, the Bodhisattva, seated under the Tree of Intelligence (i.e. the Bo-tree) becomes arrayed in the perfect intelligence of a Buddha or Tathâgata.

Chap. XXIII. A chapter of praisings of the Tathâgata by the gods of heaven and of earth, and every other being.

Chap. XXIV. The Prince, having become a perfect Buddha, or Tathâgata, continued to set cross-legged under the Tree of Intelligence for a week. During the second week he made a journey among the thousands of worlds. During the third week he looked at Bôdhimanda without blinking an eye, having made an end of sorrow, birth, old age and death. During the fourth week he made a journey from the Eastern to the Western Sea. Then the arch-devil Pâpîyân visits him and suggests that the Tathâgata should go into Parinirvâna, but he refused, saying that he would not go there until the works of the Buddha were completed. The arch-devil retired in grief and sorrow, but his three daughters, Rati, Arati and Trîchnâ, went to tempt the Tathâgata, who promptly turned them into decrepit old women. During the fifth week the Tathâgata dwelt in the house of Mutchilenda, the king of the Nâgas, who wrapped a seven-fold garment about him. This act was repeated by other kings of the Nâgas, who saluted his feet with their heads, walked round him three times and departed. During the sixth week he went to the fig-tree of the goat-herd, and during the seventh he lived at the foot of the tree Tarâyaṇa. Two merchants, Trapucha and Bhallika, salute him and bring him food.

Chap. XXV. A Chapter of exhortation to the Tathâgata to turn the Wheel of the Law.

Chap. XXVI. Describes how the Tathâgata turned the Wheel of the Law, i.e. to preach and to teach Buddhism. With this Chapter the *Lalita Vistara* comes to an end.

V

THE JÂTAKAS, OR BIRTH STORIES OF THE BUDDHA

THE authorities generally agree that the *Lalita Vistara* is the principal source of the main portions of the Book of Barlaam and Iôasaph, but the Life of the Buddha, which is included among the Jâtakas, or Birth Stories of the Buddha, contains a considerable number of supplementary statements that are of importance for the elucidation of the work. Orthodox Buddhists believe that the Buddha in the course of his years of teaching illustrated his arguments with stories, fables and fairy tales which explained events that had happened either at the time when he was speaking or during his previous lives. These stories were carefully learned by his disciples, who immediately after his death compiled a work containing the best known of them and called it the "Book of the 550 Jâtakas," or Birth Stories. In other words, the orthodox Buddhists believe that this Collection of Birth Stories was in existence some three or four centuries before the Christian Era. Professor Rhys Davids says that this "orthodox Buddhist belief" rests on a "foundation of quicksand," but attaches great value to the Stories themselves, and believes that a Book of Birth Stories " existed at a very early date " (*Buddhist Birth Stories*, vol. I. p. lviii). At the end of the IIIrd century B.C. they were held to be so sacred that they were chosen as the subjects to be repre-

sented round the most sacred Buddhist buildings,
e.g. the relic shrines at Sânchi, Amaravati and
Bharhut, and they were popularly known under the
technical name of "Jâtakas." With the Birth Stories
as a whole we are not here concerned, and so we
pass on to note the facts about the life of the
Buddha which are contained in the Commentary
prefixed to them. The following abstract is made
from the translation of Avidûre Nidâna made by
Professor Rhys Davids and published by him in his
*Buddhist Birth Stories; or, Jâtaka Tales. Being
the Jâtakatthavaṇṇanâ...edited by V. Fausböll and
translated by T. W. Rhys Davids.* Translation,
vol. I. London, 1880 (Trübner's Oriental Series).

The deities of the ten thousand world systems
assembled, and the archangels in each world-system
with them, and they went to the future Buddha in
the Heaven of Delight, and informed him that the
time for his Buddhahood had arrived. This Great
Being reflected on:—(1) the TIME of his advent;
(2) the CONTINENT and COUNTRY where he should
appear; (3) the TRIBE in which he should be born;
(4) the MOTHER who should bear him; (5) the time
when her life should be complete. He decided that
the time had come; that he would appear in the
continent of Jambudvîpa, in the town of Kapila-
vastu in the Middle Country; of the Kthatriya
caste; that his father should be Suddhodana and
his mother Mahâ Mâyâ, and that her life should last
ten months and seven days. So the Great Being
decided to appear on the earth. During the mid-
summer festival the lady Mahâ Mâyâ dreamed a

dream. The Four Archangels carried her in her couch to the Himâlaya Mountains, and set her down under the Sâla-tree. Then queens came and took her to the Lake of Anotatta, washed every human stain from her, arrayed her in heavenly apparel, anointed her with perfumes and decked her with heavenly flowers. They took her into a house of gold on Silver Hill close by and laid her on a heavenly couch with its head towards the East. The future Buddha, in the form of a superb white elephant came to Silver Hill from the north and entered the house of gold. In his trunk was a white lotus flower, and uttering a far-reaching cry, he came to the couch, made obeisance thrice to it, then gently struck the side of Mahâ Mâyâ and "seemed to enter her womb" (p. 63 note).

When on the following day Mahâ Mâyâ had related her dream to Suddhodana, he summoned sixty-four Brâhmans and asked them to interpret the dream. They told the king that he would have a son who, if he adopted a householder's life would become a king, and that if he forsook his home and embraced the religious life he would become a Buddha. When the future Buddha became incarnate in his mother's womb the elements of the 10,000 world-systems quaked, and light appeared in them. The blind saw, the deaf heard, the dumb spake, the crooked became straight, the lame walked, and all prisoners were set free. The fire of hell was extinguished, the hungry ghosts were fed, the pains of the sick were alleviated. These and many other wonderful signs appeared. Four angels armed with swords kept guard over the Bodisat and his mother. When the time drew nigh Mahâ Mâyâ told the king that she wished to go to Devadaha, her native city, and he caused her to be placed in a golden palanquin and escorted thither by one thousand attendants. When she came to the Lumbini Grove she was carried into the flower-laden wood of Sâla trees, and when she put out her hand to take hold of a branch of the monarch Sâla tree in it, the branch bent down to meet her and when she touched it her pains came upon her. The attendants drew a curtain round her, and standing upright and holding the branch of the tree she brought forth the Bodisat, and the four Mahâ Brahma angels received him in a golden net, and four kings received him from them on a cloth made of antelope skins. The Bodisat dwelt in his mother's womb ten months, and seven days after his birth Mahâ Mâyâ died, and was reborn in the City of Delight. At the time of his birth his future wife and mother of his son Râhula, Channa the attendant, Kâḷudâyi the minister, Kaṇṭhaka the royal horse, the great Bo-tree, and the four vases of treasure all came into being. As the Bodisat was being taken to Kapila-vastu all the people rejoiced and the choirs of angels in the Tâvatiṇsa heaven sang. An ascetic called Kâḷa Devala, who was a confidential adviser of the king, went to see the Bodisat. When he came into his presence, the child planted his feet in his matted hair, and the holy man did homage to him and declared that he would become a Buddha.

On the fifth day they performed the ceremony of choosing a name for the Bodisat, and the king summoned one hundred and eight Brâhmans and asked eight of them to declare from their observation of the signs what the child would be. Seven of the eight held up two fingers and prophesied that he would be either a Universal Monarch or a Buddha, but one of them, Kondanya by name, beholding the perfection of the marks on the Bodisat, held up only one finger and prophesied boldly that he would become a Buddha. Then the king asked, "After seeing what, will my son forsake the world?" And the answer was, "After the Four Omens, that is to say, a man worn out by age, a sick man, a dead body and a monk." The king determined that the Bodisat should not see these Omens, and placed guards two miles apart in the four directions that he should not do so. He appointed nurses to rear the Bodisat, who grew up in great splendour. When the Ploughing Festival came the king went out to plough, and the child was placed by his nurses under a Jambu tree, and they went to see the ceremonies performed. When the Bodisat saw that he was alone, he got up, seated himself cross-legged, and sank into the first religious meditation ; and the shadow of the Jambu tree remained where it was and did not move round like the shadows of the other trees.

When the Bodisat grew up to manhood the king had three mansions built, nine, seven and five stories high respectively, one for each of the three seasons, and he provided him with 40,000 dancing girls. The

mother of his son Râhula was his chief queen. When
the clansmen murmured, saying that Siddhattha
was living a life of pleasure which unfitted him for
war, the Bodisat caused his relatives to be assembled and performed in their sight wonderful feats
of skill in archery.

One day the Bodisat had his chariot prepared
and drove out into his gardens, and the angels
caused him to see a man wasted with age, broken
in body and walking by the help of a stick. This
was the First Omen. When he realized that living
beings decayed, he was troubled and returned to
his palace. When driving out on another occasion
he saw a sick man (the Second Omen) and was
troubled and returned to his palace. The sight, a
little later, of a dead man (the Third Omen) drove
him again troubled to his palace. Last of all he saw
a mendicant friar (the Fourth Omen), and his charioteer explained to him the advantages of retiring
from the world. The sight of the hermit made the
Bodisat decide to forsake the world. Thus the Four
Omens were seen by the Bodisat in spite of all the
precautions taken by the king. At that time his son
Râhula was born, and seeing that love for his child
would become an "impediment," he determined to
effect the Great Renunciation that night. As he
passed through the city a noble virgin called Kisâ
Gotamî sang to him a song in which she proclaimed
the blessedness of the mother, father and wife who
owned a Lord so glorious. These words pleased the
Bodisat, who interpreted them as having reference
to the Nirvâna of Peace for which he longed, and

he sent her a string of pearls, which caused her to think that he was in love with her.

When he returned to his palace singing and dancing women ranged themselves about him, and sang and danced before him, but he fell asleep, and they too lay down to sleep. When he awoke, just as the lamps were burning out, he saw the women lying about him in various attitudes of abandon, and the sight of them disgusted him. And the splendid chamber in which they were became to him as a charnel house full of loathsome corpses. Deeply moved, he cried out, " It all oppresses me! It is intolerable," and he resolved to accomplish the Great Renunciation that very day. He ordered his charioteer Channa, who was sleeping with his head on the threshold, to saddle his horse, saying that he was going to accomplish the Great Renunciation forthwith, and Channa went and saddled Kaṇṭhaka, who knew of his master's resolve and neighed a mighty neigh. The Bodisat went to his wife's chamber and looked a farewell to his son Râhula, and then he went to his horse and called upon him to save him, so that he might become a Buddha and save the world of men and angels. The horse Kaṇṭhaka was 18 cubits long, and he was white all over like a chank shell. The Bodisat leaped on the horse and, telling Channa to lay hold of his tail, set out for the city gate, which opened of its own accord and let him pass. In that night the Bodisat passed beyond three kingdoms, and travelled thirty leagues and reached the bank of the river Anomâ, which was five or six hundred yards wide. This the horse sprang over, and stood on the opposite bank.

The Bodisat then gave his ornaments and the horse to Channa, telling him to go back to the city as he was going to become a hermit. Channa said that he would become a hermit too, but the Bodisat thrice refused to allow him to become one and told him to depart. The Bodisat then cut off his own hair with his sword, and the archangel Ghaṭikâra, having given him the three robes, the alms bowl, razor, needle, girdle and water strainer, he dressed himself in the "sacred garb of Renunciation" with the outward signs of an Arahat. Meanwhile the horse Kaṇṭhaka realized that he would never see his master again, and he went away and died of a broken heart. He was reborn in the Tâvatiṇsa heaven as an angel with the name of Kaṇṭhaka; Channa, rent with sorrow for the loss of his lord and the horse, returned to the city with weeping and lamentation.

Thus the Bodisat renounced the world. He spent seven days in a mango grove called Anûpiya, and then went on foot to Râjagaha, a distance of thirty leagues, in one day, and begged his bread from door to door. He joined himself to Âḷâra Kâḷâma, and to Uddaka, son of Râma, but being dissatisfied with the results of their ecstatic trance, he went to Uruvela to carry out the Great Struggle. For six years he lived a life of self-abnegation and toil and carried on the Great Struggle. He became a mere skeleton through over-fasting, his body became dark in colour and the thirty-two signs of a Great Being disappeared, and one day he collapsed through pain and exhaustion, and some thought that he was dead. He recovered his consciousness and, perceiving that penance was not the way to Wisdom, went about and collected food and ate it, and his body returned to its former condition, and the thirty-two signs of a Great Being reappeared upon him. When his five mendicant attendants saw this, they concluded that there was no further advantage to be got from him; and each taking his robe and begging-bowl departed to Isipatana.

One night the Bodisat had five dreams, and on considering their purport he came to the conclusion, "Verily this day I shall become a Buddha." And having washed and dressed himself he went and sat under the Tree of Wisdom (Bo-tree). Here he remained for forty-nine days and he was fed by a girl called Sujâtâ, a native of the village of Senâni at Uruvela. He seated himself with his back to the Tree of Wisdom and his face towards the East, and he resolved to remain there until he received complete insight. Then Mâra, thinking that the Bodisat desired to free himself from his dominion, determined that he should not escape from him and he told his intention to his hosts of angels. And sounding the drum called "Satan's War-cry," he led forth the army of Satan. Mâra mounted his elephant, which was two hundred and fifty leagues high, and created a thousand arms, and his hosts, taking various colours and forms, set out to overwhelm the Great Being. As the army advanced against the Bodisat, all the angels who were proclaiming his praises fled, and the Great Being was left alone. When Mâra and his hosts attacked him on three sides, he smote them with the sword of his virtue and overthrew them, and he sat meditating on the Ten Perfections—namely, Almsgiving, Goodness, Renunciation, Wisdom, Resolution, Patience, Truth, Good Will, Equanimity, Firmness in duty[1]. Mâra first hurled a whirlwind of the four winds upon him, but they failed to ruffle the hem of his robe; then a flood of water, which failed to wet his robe; then a shower of rocks, which when they reached him had changed into bouquets of flowers; then a shower of swords, spears and arrows, which also turned into flowers; then a storm of red-hot charcoal, which also became flowers; then a storm of ashes, which fell at his feet in the form of sandal wood; then a storm of sand, which fell as flowers; then a storm of mud which fell as perfume; then a four-fold thick darkness, which was entirely dissipated when it reached the Bodisat. All these things failed to dislodge the Bodisat, and Mâra then mounted his monster elephant, and riding up to him said, "Get up, Siddhattha, from that seat! It is not thine, but is intended for me." When the Bodisat refused to do this Mâra hurled at him his Sceptre-javelin, the barb of which was in the form of a wheel; but this turned into a garland of flowers, and remained as a canopy over him. Mâra's hosts hurled rocks also, but these turned into flowers, and the Bodisat continued to sit on the "throne on which sit the

---

[1] Or Charity, Goodness, Self-sacrifice, Wisdom, Exertion, Longsuffering, Truth, Resolution, Kindness and Equanimity.

Buddhas-to-be when they are perfect in all goodness, on that day when they shall reach Enlighten-
ment." Then the Bodisat asked Mâra for proofs
that he had given alms, and all the hosts of the
Evil One testified that he had. On this Mâra demanded testimony that the Bodisat had given alms,
and the Great Being appealed to the "great and
solid Earth" to testify that in addition to the alms
which he had given in other births he had given
great alms seven hundredfold when he was born as
Wessantara. And the earth said, "I am witness of
that." Then Mâra's elephant fell down on his knees
before the Bodisat, and Mâra's army fled away defeated. On this the hosts of heaven cried out,
"The Tempter is overcome! Siddhattha hath prevailed!" And the gods of the 10,000 world-systems
offered garlands, perfumes, and praises, and the
Bo-tree paid him homage. During the First, Middle,
and Third Watches of the night he acquired respectively the Knowledge of the Past, the Knowledge
of the Present, and the Knowledge of the Chain of
Causation which leads to the Origin of Evil. At
break of day he attained to complete Enlighten-
ment and Omniscience, and the Bodisat became
Buddha and reached Nirvâna. He decided not to
leave his seat, which was his throne of triumph, and
he sat there motionless for seven days, realizing the
bliss of Nirvâna.

When the angels saw this certain of them thought
that the Buddha sat there because there was still
something which he had to do. And he, knowing
their thoughts, rose up and performed the miracle

of making another appearance like unto himself.
Then he stood a little to the north-east of the
throne, and gazed at it for seven days; hence that
spot was called the "Dâgaba of the Steadfast Gaze."
Other seven days he spent in walking up and down
between the throne and the place where he had stood,
and this walk was called the "Dâgaba of the
Jewelled Cloister." And other seven days he spent
in sitting cross-legged in a house of gems which the
angels built to the north-west of the Bo-tree. During
the fifth week he went to the Shepherd's Nigrodha-
tree and sat there meditating on the Truth and
enjoying the sweetness of Nirvâna.

At this time Mâra lamented that he had found
no sin in the Buddha, and that he was beyond his
power, and he sat down in sorrow on the highway.
When his three daughters, Taṇhâ (Craving), Aratî
(Discontent) and Ragâ (Lust), found him there they
asked him the reason, and when Mâra told them
they said that they would go to him and bring him
to subjection. They went to the Buddha seven
times, and assuming the forms of virgins, young
married women, mature women, and middle-aged
women, offered themselves to him; but he admonished
them and sent them away, disappointed and dis-
comfited. The Buddha next spent seven days under
the Mucalinda-tree, where Mucalinda, the Snake-
king, shielded him with seven folds of his hood
during a storm. Then he went on to the Râjâya-
tana-tree, where he remained for seven days. Thus
for seven weeks he had no bodily wants, but fed on
the joy of Meditation and Nirvâna. When the seven

weeks were ended two merchants, Tapassu and Bhalluka, who were travelling from Orissa to Central India with 500 carts, offered food to the Master, who received it in a bowl which the angels made for him, and ate it. These merchants became his professed disciples.

The Buddha next returned to the Nigrodha-tree, and doubts arose in his mind about his ability to explain the Truth to others. But, encouraged by the angels, he set out to inaugurate the kingdom of Righteousness in Benares, begging his food as he went. When half-way there he met the mendicant Upaka, and the Five Elders received him, and many other disciples followed him. He sent out sixty disciples to preach and to teach his doctrines. Going on to Uruvela he met the three Hindu ascetics, brothers, Uruvela Kassapa and the rest, and overcame them by performing three thousand five hundred miracles, and he received their thousand disciples into the Order with the words "Follow me." He then went on to the Palm-grove near Râjagaha, accompanied by these thousand Arahats, intending to pay a visit to king Bimbisâra, for he had promised him that after he had attained to Buddhahood he would visit his kingdom first. When the king heard of his arrival, he and innumerable priests and nobles fell down at the feet of the Buddha, and at this time Uruvela Kassapa, who was formerly a "mighty infidel," bowed his head at Buddha's feet, saying, "The Blessed Lord is my master, and I am the disciple." Buddha was then in the Grove of Reeds, six miles from Râjagaha, and the press of people was so great on the road that Sakka the archangel took the form of a young Brâhman, and came down on the earth, and made a path among the people by which the Buddha walked into the town accompanied by one thousand mendicants. When he arrived there the king poured scented water over Buddha's head and told him that he could not live without the Three Gems, i.e. the Buddha, the Order, and the Faith. And, he added, "In season and out of season I would visit the Blessed One. Now the Grove of Reeds is far away; but this Grove of mine, called the Bambu Grove, is close by, is easy of resort, and is a fit dwelling-place for a Buddha. Let the Blessed One accept it of me." The Master accepted the Monastery of the Bambu Grove, and he and his disciples went and lived there. And the broad earth shook, as if it said, "Now the Religion of Buddha has taken root."

About this time the two ascetics Sâriputta and Moggallâna took orders under Buddha, who made them Chief Disciples, and established the "Corporation of the Disciples." Meanwhile Suddhodana had heard about his son who had become the Buddha, and he wished to see him. He summoned one of his courtiers and told him to take one thousand men and to go to Râjagaha and bring his son to him. The courtier departed with his men, and when they arrived at the place where the Sage was, they stood by his disciples and listened to his discourse, and became converted and joined the Order; forgetting all earthly things they did not deliver the king's message. The king sent eight other envoys, one after the other, each with his thousand attendants, with his message, but they all became absorbed in the teaching of the Master, and forgot to deliver it. Then the king remembered his faithful servant Kâla Udâyin, who was born on the same day as the future Buddha, and had been his play-fellow and companion, and he sent him with his message to his son. When Udâyin arrived at Râjagaha he stood close to the disciples at the time of the Master's instruction, and heard the Gospel and joined the Order. In due course he delivered the king's message, and the Master said that he would go to his father. When he arrived at Kapilavatthu the Buddha begged his bread from door to door, and when he came to the palace he ate the food prepared for him; and all the women, except the mother of his son Râhula, came and did obeisance to him. Whilst there, in the apartments of the king's daughter, he told the story of his Birth as the Moonsprite, and Râhula his son went to him and claimed his inheritance as a son. The child followed the Buddha to his Grove, and Sâriputta received him into the Order.

The Buddha then went to Sâvatthi and accepted from Anâtha Piṇḍika, a wealthy householder, the gift of the Jetavana monastery, which covered thirty acres. In that place the Blessed One lived from the attainment of omniscience under the Bo-tree till his death.

PLATE IX

The Buddha in the Moon in the form of a hare.

VI

THE PEHLEVI VERSION OF THE BOOK OF BARLAAM AND IÔASAPH

IT seems tolerably certain that long before the Buddha was born there was considerable intercourse for trading purposes between India and Western Europe, Syria, Egypt and neighbouring countries. The products of India were sent westwards by various routes, but the two most important were those which led by way of the Persian Gulf to Syria, and by way of the Red Sea to Egypt. The existence of the old Egyptian Canal from the Nile to the Red Sea suggests that traffic was considerable and markets were brisk, and that caravans and ships were in constant use. Whether the Indians cared much about the information that camel-men and sailors gave them about the countries of the West, or whether the Egyptians and Syrians were greatly interested in the news which reached them from India cannot be said, but it seems certain that Syrians, Egyptians and Indians knew more of each other than is commonly supposed. The men who accompanied the envoys of Asoka to Syria, Egypt and Greece must have brought with them a good deal of authoritative information about their country and religion, and as propagandists of the Buddha's teaching they must have proclaimed the glory of his religion. As the successors of Asoka maintained communication between India, Syria and Egypt, it is probable that when the Christian Era began the Syrians and Egyptians in the West were as familiar with the parables and fables which the Master employed in his teaching as were the Chinese in the East. It is possible that even in the early centuries of our Era versions of these and lives of the Buddha existed in Syria and Egypt in the native languages of these countries.

Now the knowledge of Buddha and his religion spread northwards as well as eastwards and westwards, and the caravan of the merchant contributed largely to this result. There was much trading between Iran and China in the early centuries of our Era, and long before the close of the VIth century the religion of the Buddha was accepted by many in Parthia and the neighbouring countries[1]. Buddhist envoys and missionaries preached the doctrine of their founder in these countries, and there is no doubt that many books, both of Buddhist and Brâhman origin, were translated into Pehlevi, and that the translations were well known and greatly appreciated. The date when the earliest translations into Pehlevi were made is unknown, but it is certain that many were in existence in the IInd century of the Hijrah. The chief authority for this statement is the famous " Kitâb al-Fihrist," كتاب الفهرست, a very fine Bibliography of Persian and Arabic books, which was written by Abu'l Faraj Muḥammad bin Isḥâḳ al-Warrâḳ, al-Bagdâdî, com-

---

[1] See Hirth, *China and the Roman Orient*, pp. 140 ff.; Gutschmid, *Geschichte Irans*, pp. 63 ff.; Saint Martin, *Mémoire sur l'Arménie*, vol. II. p. 54; Beal, *Buddhist Records*, I. 19, pp. 44 ff.; and Kern, *Der Buddhismus*, vol. II. p. 543.

monly known as "Ibn Abî Ya'ḳûb an-Nadîm," who composed this famous work in the year 987 (A.H. 377)[1]. From this we learn that Ruzbah, روزبه, a Persian, better known as 'Abd-Allâh ibn Al-Muḳaffa', who lived at the court of the Khalîfah Maṇṣûr and died in the third quarter of the VIIIth century A.D., translated a number of Persian books into Arabic, among them being the famous work "Kalîlah wa Dimnah," كتاب كليه ود منه. A portion of the Arabic text of this book was published by Schultens[2], and the complete text by de Sacy[3]. From the Pehlevi a Syriac version of Kalîlah wa Dimnah was made by one Bûd, or Bôd, in the second half of the VIth century, and the text of this has been published by Bickell and Benfey[4]. Another completely independent Syriac translation was made about four or five centuries later, and the text of it was published by Wright[5] and an English translation by Keith Falconer[6].

[1] For the text see Flügel (G) and Roediger, *Kitab al-Fihrist*. Vol. I. Leipzig, 1871, page ١١٨. A second vol. containing "Anmerkungen" was published in the following year.

[2] *Pars versionis Arabicæ libri Calailah wa Dimnah sive fabularum Bidpai philosophi Indi*, Lugd. Bat. 1786, 4°.

[3] *Calila et Dimna, ou Fables de Bidpai, en Arabe, précédées d'un mémoire sur l'origine de ce livre, et sur les diverses traductions qui en ont été faites dans l'orient, etc.*, Paris, 1816. See also Guidi, *Studii sul testo arabo del libro di Calila e Dimna*, Rome, 1873, and Nöldeke, *Die Erzählung vom Mäusekönig und seinen Ministern*, Göttingen, 1879. There is an English translation of the whole work by Knatchbull, *Kalila and Dimna, or the Fables of Bidpai*, Oxford, 1819, and there are German translations by Holmboe (*Calila und Dimna*, Christiania, 1832), and Wolff (*Das Buch des Weisen in lust- und lehrreichen Erzählungen des indischen Philosophen Bidpai*, 2 vols. Stuttgart, 1837).

[4] *Kalilag und Damnag. Alte Syrische Uebersetzung des indischen Fürstenspiegels.* Leipzig, 1876.

[5] *The Book of Kalilah and Dimnah translated from Arabic into Syriac.* Oxford, 1884.

[6] *Kalîlah and Dimnah or the Fables of Bidpai.* Cambridge, 1885.

In another section of the Kitâb al-Fihrist (page
٣٠٥) we find it stated that another Persian translated
several Pehlevi books into Arabic for Hishâm ibn
Al-Kalbî in the second half of the IInd century of
the Hijrah. This translator was called Gabalah ibn
Sâlim, جبلة بن سالم, and the works translated by him
were "Rustum and Asfandiyâr," "Bahram Shûs,"
"Shahrîzâd ma' Abrawîz," " Kârnâmag fisîrat Anu-
shirwân," etc. In the section following the names
of several Indian books are given, among them being:
1, Kalîlah wa Dimnah; 2, The Great Sindibâd Book;
3, The Little Sindibâd Book; 4, The Book of Budd
(i.e. Buddha), كتاب البد (بد or بد. Pers. بُت); 5, Kitâb
Bûdâsaf and Bilauhar كتاب بوداسف وبلوهر (varr. يداسف,
بوداسف. Bûdâsf or Bûdâsp); 6, The Book of Bûdâsaf
alone, كتاب بوداسف مفرد; 7, Book of the Learning of
India and China, etc. Another translator of Pehlevi
books into Arabic was 'Abd al-Ḥumêdah ibn Al-
Lâḥiḳ Ar-Raḳâshî, who flourished in the IInd century
of the Hijrah ; among the works which he translated
is the Kitâb Bilauhar wa Bûdâsif, but the latter
name is wrongly written بردانه and بردانه (Kitâb al-
Fihrist, p. 119).

Thus we have clear proof that in the VIIIth
century of our Era there existed in Pehlevi three
books relating to the Buddha, the Bodisat, or the
" Buddha in the making," and the Bodisat and the
sage Bilauhar, and that they were of such interest
to Muḥammadans that translations of them were
made into Arabic. But it is difficult to believe
that the Arabic-speaking peoples waited until the
VIIIth century for Arabic translations of books of

such general interest, and it seems only reasonable
to assume that Arabic or Syriac and even Greek
versions of them were made before this period.
There is also to be considered the great population
of Christians who lived to the west of Persia, and
who were scattered all over Parthia and the moun-
tainous districts east of the Tigris, to say nothing
of the Nestorian Christians who were established in
Khorasan in the Vth century. The general teaching
of the Buddha must have been well known to Arabs
and Christians, and the sources of their information
lay in the Pehlevi works described above. There is
no reason to believe that the Pehlevi Books of the
Buddha and the Book of Bûdâsif, or the Book of
Bûdâsif and Bilauhar, were *translations* of Buddhist
originals. On the contrary, the writers of them must
have edited their material with great care and discretion, or they would never have been popular
among the Persians. But be this as it may it is impossible not to agree with Hommel[1] and Kuhn[2] that
the Pehlevi Version, through an Arabic translation,
is the foundation of the "spiritual Romance" of
Barlaam and Iôasaph. Some authorities[3] would
derive the Greek and the Georgian Versions from
a Palestinian original written in a "Christian-Pales-
tinian" dialect, but the forms of the proper names
that occur in them proclaim their Pehlevi origin.
The common title for the prince who is destined to be-

[1] *Die älteste arabische Barlaam Version* in the *Verhandlungen* of the
VIIth International Oriental Congress, Vienna, 1888 (Semitische Section),
p. 119.
[2] *Barlaam und Joasaph*, pp. 34 ff.
[3] E.g. Nöldeke in *Zeitschrift D.M.G.*, vol. xxii. pp. 443 ff.

come a Buddha in the original Indian texts is "Bodhisattva," and this as we have seen above became
"Bûdâsaf," بوداسف, or, "Bûdâsif" in Pehlevi. But the
form "Yûdâsaf," يوداسف, occurs frequently in the works
of Arabic writers as a variant, and it is clear either
that the letters b and y must have been similar in
form, and that the copyist of some authoritative
codex mistook the one for the other, or that in
Pehlevi b and y are interchangeable[1]. In Arabic
the change could be accounted for very easily, being
caused by the addition of a single dot, thus بـ $= b$
and يـ $= y$. Some Arabic MSS. give instead of بوداسف
Bûdâsaf, the variant يواسف Yûâsaf, or Yawâsaf, which
shows that the scribes mistook the د for و and read
يواسف instead of يداسف. And it is this form, which
is due to a scribe's mistake, that has been per-
petuated in the Greek 'Ιωάσαφ and in the Ethiopic
(through the Arabic) "Yĕwâsĕf."

In the southern Indian texts the Bodisattva's
charioteer is called "Channa[2]," and in the northern,
Chanda(ka) (or, Chhandaka)[3]. The Pehlevi text
probably had, as the equivalent of this word, "Zadani"
or "Zandani," which by the interchange of r and n
in Pehlevi, became in Greek "Ζαρδὰν." This form
"Zardan" is important, for it proves that the redactor
of the Pehlevi Version used documents which were
common in Eastern Persia and the districts to the
north of it, and shows how the d of the Pehlevi
"Zadani" has passed, probably through the Arabic,

[1] On this point see Kuhn, *op. cit.* p. 35.
[2] Rhys Davids, *Jâtakas*, pp. 81 ff.
[3] Râjendralâla Mitra, *Lalita Vistara*, p. 280.

into Greek. Kuhn goes so far as to say that it shows that Eastern Iran and the district northwards are the home of the Iôasaph Romance, and he points out that in this region Zoroastrianism, Bactrian and Chinese Buddhism and Christianity flourished side by side for centuries[1]. Christianity made its way into this country at a very early period, and the list of East-Syrian Bishops and dioceses published by Guidi[2] proves that the Christian communities there were large and numerous.

The name "Barlaam" has also been shown by Hommel and Kuhn to be a faulty transcription of the name "Balauhar," بلوهر. The scribe had before him the name indistinctly written, and being un-familiar with it he read hastily برلام Barlâm, the Greek Βαρλαάμ. On the other hand the writer of the Greek Version, being probably familiar with the name of the well-known martyr Βαρλαάμ, may have confounded it with Bilauhar, or he may have used it intentionally with the view of adding to the Christian character of his work. It seems quite certain that this is what he did in other cases. Thus he calls the father of Iôa-saph Ἀβεννὴρ, having in his mind the name of Abner (1 Samuel xiv. 50), the cousin of Saul and captain of his army. To the hermit who was supposed to be able to bring Iôasaph back to the worship of idols, he gives the name of Ναχωρ, having in mind Nahor (נָחוֹר), the idolater and grandfather of Abraham mentioned in Genesis xi. vv. 22-25; Luke iii. 34. The Christian redactor by introducing him into the

---

[1] *Op. cit.* p. 36.
[2] *Zeitschrift D.M.G.*, vol. 43, pp. 388 ff.

story seems to have personified some characteristic
of the prime mover of the king's actions, who was
called 'Αραχῆς. And again the name of the magician
who advises king Abennêr to corrupt his son by
means of young and beautiful women is given in the
Greek version as Θευδᾶς. What the Pehlevi original
of this name was is not known, but in the Arabic
text of the "Book of Bilauhar [1] and Bûḍâsaf" he is
called "Al-Bahûn," البهون. It is easy to confound ز with
ي and د with و, and therefore Kuhn would read this
name التهدن " At-Tahdan [2]," which probably suggested
to the Christian redactor the name of Θευδᾶς, with
which he was familiar from the Acts of the Apostles
(v. 36), if not from the writings of Josephus (Antiquities of the Jews, xx. 5, 97 ff.). Theudas the false
prophet or Messiah was a magician, and deluded
many, and there was much in his character which
resembled that of At-Tahdan. If, as Kuhn suggests,
the name At-Tahdan represents the Pehlevi equivalent of Udâyin, the name of one of the friends of
Iôasaph's youth, it is difficult to put forward an
adequate explanation. Nor is it easy to explain the
occurrence of the name of Βαραχίας as applied to
the man whom Iôasaph appointed to be king over
his country in his stead. He is represented as being
a friend and supporter of Iôasaph during his conflict
with his father and the pagan priests, and it is quite
possible that his native name is given in one or other
of the original Indian texts. As the Book of Bilauhar
and Bûḍâsaf contains no mention of the appoint-

---

[1] See the edition printed by Nûr ad-Dîn Ibn Jîwâkhân the bookseller at
Bombay A.H. 1306 (= A.D. 1888–9), page 251, last line but one.
[2] The Georgian Version actually has T'edam (Kuhn, op. cit. p. 29).

ment of a king in the place of Iôasaph, we can get no help in solving the difficulty from the Arabic text. The adoption of Bible names wherever possible in the Christian version by its redactor was no doubt intentional, for he felt that it would add to the verisimilitude of his narrative and make it more acceptable to his Christian readers. He and they were acquainted with the tradition of St Thomas's preaching and teaching in India, and the survival of Biblical names in that country might from their point of view be regarded as a necessary consequence.

THE SYRIAC VERSION

The Syriac Version, which I am assuming existed, is lost, and so far I have been unable to find any remains of it. When, nearly thirty years ago, I copied the Ethiopic Version from the two manuscripts in the British Museum I wrote to friends in Môṣul and Al-Ḵôsh, and asked them to make enquiries among the Nestorians in the Ṭiyârî country, but though many priests and others knew the book in Arabic, none had ever seen or heard of a Version in Syriac. The answers to my letters to friends in Mardîn who had access to the MSS. in the Dêr Az-Zaʻafarân, and to friends in Urmî who were able to speak with authority, were always in the negative, and few of them had ever heard of the Syriac Version of the Book of Barlaam. Kuhn thought[1] that the Greek and Georgian Versions might have been made from a Syriac or Pehlevi Version, as did both Huet and Nöldeke, but he was

---

[1] *Op. cit.* p. 34.

B.   *g*

on the whole in favour of regarding the Pehlevi
Version as their original. Jacobs believed that the
Georgian Version was made from the Arabic Version
and the Greek from the Syriac[1], and says, rightly,
"Syriac was the main conduit pipe through which
the treasures of Greek literature debouched on to
the Orient, and inversely, it was mainly through
Syriac versions that Oriental treasures were added
to Graeco-Byzantine literature." Krumbacher was
convinced that a Syriac Version existed, and believed
that the Armenian Version was derived from it, but
then he goes on to say that the Syriac Version itself
was made from an old Greek original, which is now
lost, and that the published Greek text is an ampli-
fied and reworked form of it[2]. It is possible that the
Greek Version was made from the Syriac, but it
seems wholly impossible to me that the Syriac
Version, at least in its earliest form, can have been
made from the Greek. The testimony of the Kitâb
al-Fihrist makes it quite certain that the Book of
the Buddha, the Book of Bûdâsaf, and the Book of
Bilauhar and Bûdâsaf existed in Pehlevi and that
they were translated into Arabic. And it is tolerably
certain that some parts, if not all, of them were
translated into Syriac for the use of the Nestorian
Christians who in large numbers were settled in
Persia in the Vth century. We know that the Book
of Kalîlah wa Dimnah was translated into Syriac in
the VIth century, and to this instance we should

[1] *Barlaam*, p. xxxi.
[2] "Der syrische Text selbst ist vielleicht die Übersetzung eines älteren
verlorenen griechischen Originals, von welchem der edierte griechische Text
eine erweiterte Umarbeitung darstellt." *Byzantinische Litteratur*, p. 889.

add the Book of Sindibân (Sinbad the Sailor), the Book of Bilauhar (i.e. Barlaam) and the Bûdâsaf, and the History of Alexander the Great. The Syriac text of this last-named work contains many proofs that it was translated from the Pehlevi in the VIIth century, although the recension of it that I published[1] is probably not older than the VIIIth century[2]. If the Syrians caused a Syriac Version of Kalîlah wa Dimnah to be made, it seems to me to follow of necessity that a Version of the Book of Bilauhar was made also; for the former represented Brâhman and the latter Buddhist propaganda. We know of at least two independent Syriac translations of Kalîlah wa Dimnah, and it is probable that the Book of Bilauhar was translated into Syriac more than once. It goes without saying that the Syriac Version, which was, of course, intended for the use of the Nestorian clergy and laity, would contain a Christianized version of the original Indian story.

THE ARABIC VERSIONS

The greater number of the Arabic Versions of the Book of Barlaam that have come down to us contain the Story in a Christianized form, and it is clear that they cannot have been made direct from Pehlevi originals. The translators appear to have been acquainted with the translations that were

---

[1] *The History of Alexander the Great, being the Syriac Version of the Pseudo-Callisthenes*, with an English Translation, Introduction, etc. Cambridge, 1889.

[2] See Nöldeke in *Beiträge zur Geschichte des Alexanderromans* (Denkschriften der Wiener Akad. phil.-hist. Cl. 38 (1890)), who thinks that the Syriac Version was made in the VIIIth century from a Pehlevi original written in the VIIth century by an Eastern Syrian.

made direct from the Pehlevi, but they found it necessary to abridge and paraphrase and modify the texts before them so as to produce a work that would appeal to Christians and the dwellers in Christian monasteries. The principal source of their information was the "Book of Bilauhar and Bûdâsaf," though they were probably acquainted with the contents of the lost Kitâb al-Budd, or "Book of the Buddha." Fortunately one of the Arabic translations that were made direct from the Pehlevi has come down to us in a precious manuscript preserved at Halle, and we owe it to Professer Hommel that its text is available for study[1]. The great value of this translation lies in the fact that the text has not been tampered with by any Christian scribe or editor, and it therefore enables us to obtain a very clear idea of the general character of its Pehlevi original, and to realize what kind of treatment the original Indian texts received at the hands of the man who translated them into Pehlevi. The reader will find a good English translation of the Halle text by Mr E. Rehatsek in the *Journal of the Royal Asiatic Society*, New Series, vol. XXII. pp. 119 ff. (1890). A perusal of the text shows that the object of the translator was to provide for his readers a "good story," with a plot just sufficiently good to give him the opportunity of introducing those Fables and Parables that have interested and amused the educated world in India, China, Western and Northern Asia and Europe for two thousand years.

[1] See the *Verhandlungen* of the VIIth International Congress of Orientalists, Semitic Section, p. 113, "Die älteste arabische Barlaam-Version."

The general teaching of the book is highly moral, and all the Fables and Parables (or "Apologues") tend to edification; there is no dogma whatsoever in it, and nothing to offend the beliefs or religious susceptibilities of any man.

Another important Arabic Version is contained in the "Book of Bilauhar and Bûdâsaf," with exhortations and wise Parables, which was issued under the care of Al-Ḥagg, the Shêkh Nûr ad-Dîn ibn Jîwâkhân, the merchant in books, and proprietor of the Hêdarian and Ṣafdarian Printing Press. It was printed in the Ṣafdarian Printing Press in Bombay, in the year 1306 (= A.D. 1888–9)[1]. The contents of this book have been summarized by Kuhn and compared by him with those of the Greek, Georgian, and other versions[2]; they are free from every trace of Christian dogma. The name of the king is given as جنيسر, which is very difficult to derive from Suddhodana, as the king is called in the *Lalita Vistara*. How the Greek redactor obtained 'Αβεννὴρ from this also cannot be explained. Kuhn thinks that 'Αβεννὴρ may have been suggested to his mind by the remembrance of Abner, Saul's commander-in-chief (2 Sam. iii. 6 ff.). And جنيسر he thinks may be a misreading of جبنس, whence the Georgian Jabenes-

<hr/>

[1] كتاب بلوهر وبوذاسف فى المواعظ والامثال الحكمية على ذمة
الحاج الشيخ نور الدين بن جيواخان تاخر الكتب ومالك المطبع
الحيدرى والصفدرى. طبع فى المطبع الصّفدرى بمبيٌ في سنه ١٣٠٦

The British Museum Press-mark is 14579. c. 34.

[2] See *Barlaam und Joasaph* in the *Abhandlungen der Königlich Bayerischen Akad. der Wissenschaften*, Phil.-Hist. Classe. Bd. xx. Munich, 1897.

Abenes. In the Bombay edition the king's son is called Bûdâsaf, بوداسف (p. 18, l. 3). The country over which the king reigns is called شولابط (p. 284, last line), which Hommel vocalizes Shawilabaṭṭ, but this is very unlike the name Kapila-vastu, or Kapilavatthu, of the Indian texts. This Version contains many passages that were borrowed direct from the *Lalita Vistara* and the Jâtaka Birth Stories but are omitted entirely in the Christianized Recensions.

Another important Arabic version of the Book of Barlaam is contained in the "Kamâl ad-Dîn wa tamâm an-ni'mat," كمال الدين وتمام النعمة, by Abu Ja'far Muḥammad ibn 'Alî ibn Bâbawaih, commonly called "Al-Kummî," who died about 381 A.H. (= A.D. 991)[1]. According to the summaries of the contents of this version published by Rosen and Hommel[2], the beginning and the end of it agree with the opening and closing chapters of the Book of Bilauhar and Bûdâsaf in all essentials, but the middle of it is treated in an independent manner, and the equivalent of 135 pages of the text of the Bombay edition is wanting. As the story of Barlaam and Iôasaph forms only a small episode in the large theological treatise of Bâbawaih this need not surprise us.

The date when the Christianized Version of the Book of Barlaam was made is unknown. According to Zotenberg it is mentioned for the first time in the Ecclesiastical Encyclopaedia of Abu 'l-Barakât, a Christian writer at the end of the XIIIth century,

---

[1] See Ahlwardt, *Verzeichniss der arabischen Handschriften der Königlichen Bibliothek zu Berlin* (No. 2721), vol. II. p. 656.

[2] See pages 166–175 of Weisslowits, *Prinz und Derwisch*. Munich, 1890.

but it is, in his opinion, much older[1]. This Version is extant in several manuscripts, and the Bibliothèque Nationale possesses seven codices of it, the oldest (No. 169) belonging to the XIIIth century. Another copy, made in the XVth century, is in the Vatican (see Mai, *Script. Vet. nova Collectio*, tom. IV. p. 597) and Dorn has published an account of another in St Petersburg (see *Bulletin* de l'Académie impériale des sciences de St Pétersbourg, tom. IX. (1852), col. 305)[2].

THE HEBREW VERSION

The Hebrew Version of the Book of Barlaam was made by the Spanish Rabbi Abraham bar Samuel Halevi ibn Chisdai, who was born in the second half of the XIIth century and died about 1220. The title given to it by its author is "The Son of the King and the Ascetic," בן המלך והנזיר, the "son of the king" being no other than the Bodhisattva, the son of Suddhodana, king of Kapila-vastu, the "ascetic" being Bilauhar or Barlaam. The first to discover that Ibn Chisdai's work was derived from the Book of Bilauhar and Bûdâsaf was Steinschneider; see Busch, *Kalendar und Jahrbuch für Israeliten*, Year 4, Vienna, 1845, pp. 219 ff. The correctness of the discovery was clearly proved by his papers in the *Zeitschrift der D. M. G.*, vol. V. pp. 89–93 and vol. VIII. p. 552. Two translations of the Hebrew text into German by Meisel appeared, the first at Stettin in 1847, and the second at Pest in 1860.

---

[1] *Notice sur le Livre de Barlaam*, p. 83.
[2] Zotenberg, *op. cit.* p. 81.

Zotenberg gave a short account of the Version in his *Notice sur le Livre de Barlaam*, pp. 84 ff. A handy edition of the Hebrew text appeared in Constantinople in 1518 and another in Mantua in 1557 ; there have been several editions since. The manuscript authorities are summarized by Kuhn (*op. cit.* p. 44). The great value of the Hebrew Version by Ibn Chisdai is due to the fact that it was made from an Arabic translation of the original Pehlevi text, and not from a Christianized Arabic Version. Whether this Arabic translation was made from the Book of Bilauhar and Bûdâsaf or from a work bearing some title like the "Prince and the Ascetic" matters little, for it is certain that it was made from the Pehlevi. This question has been discussed by Hommel in the introduction to the old Arabic Version which he discovered and printed in the "Verhandlungen" of the Seventh International Congress of Orientalists.

The general scope and contents of the Hebrew Version are discussed with thoroughness and skill in the excellent work of Dr N. Weisslowits entitled *Prinz und Derwisch, ein Indischer Roman enthaltend die Jugendgeschichte Buddha's in Hebräischer Darstellung aus dem Mittelalter, mit einem Anhang von Dr F. Hommel*, Munich, 1890. Ibn Chisdai was a translator of Greek and Arabic works rather than an independent author, and the Book of the Son of the King and the Ascetic, كتاب ابن الملك والناسك or ספר בן המלך והנזיר, is one of the seven works of his which are enumerated by Weisslowits. By some kind of mistake Ibn Chisdai uses these words אמר מעתיק מלשון יון אל לשון ערב, "the translator from the

Greek to the Arabic language says," and some have
tried to argue from this that Ibn Chisdai's Arabic
text was translated from the Greek and not from
the Pehlevi. Hommel has shown the fallacy of this
argument, and Kuhn thinks that the word in the
Arabic text was "Indian," هندية, and not "Greek,"
يونانية. The connection between the non-Christian
Arabic and the Hebrew Versions is proved by the
fact that the order and succession of the Apologues
are almost identical, that the texts of the Apologues
are fuller in these Versions than in the Greek, and
that the Greek lacks many Fables and Parables
that are found in the Arabic and Hebrew Versions.
Proofs of these facts are given by Weisslowits, p. 21,
and Jacobs, *Barlaam*, p. xxxviii. The following
Fables, etc., are only found in the Hebrew Version:

1. The Bird that swallowed a fish with a hook
   in it and died of hunger. (Door IX.)
2. A number of dogs quarrel over some carrion,
   but when they see a stranger passing they
   attack him, though he has made no attempt
   to interfere with them.
3. A king flees before his enemy with his Queen
   and children; on the road a child dies and
   they are forced to eat him. Necessity not
   greed is the cause of their cannibalism.
4. The Sun of Wisdom. Wisdom is like the sun
   —always shining on everyone; the weak-
   sighted cannot bear to look at it and the
   blind cannot see it at all.
5. The King and the Shepherd. A king invites
   a shepherd to eat today and fast tomorrow,

but the shepherd will not do so unless the king guarantees that he will see tomorrow.

6. The Bird and the Prophet. The preaching of a prophet is compared to the cry of the mother bird to her young.

7. A boorish and ill-bred prince is reformed by a girl with whom he has fallen in love.

8. The king and the servant who upset the tureen of soup.

9. The Man who was taught the language of animals by Solomon.

10. The Merchant and the two nobles who poisoned each other.

11. The greedy Dog that tried to get two breakfasts.

Thus it is quite evident that it was no theological matter but the Fables and Stories of the Arabic Version that induced Ibn Chisdai to make his metrical Hebrew Version.

The Hebrew Version contains thirty-five sections, or "doors," but the last four are, unlike the preceding thirty-one, in prose, and contain a dissertation on philosophical matters by Ibn Chisdai himself.

THE PERSIAN VERSION

A manuscript of the Persian Version of the Book of Bilauhar and Yûdâsaf was acquired by the Trustees of the British Museum in October 1887, and a description of it was sent by von Oldenberg to Baron Rosen, who identified it as a translation made from the Arabic Version of Bâbawaih, which has already been described (see p. xcvi). Baron Rosen sent a copy of about one-quarter of the text and a full list of the contents of the manuscript to Hommel in 1889, and a comparison of the Arabic and Persian texts convinced him that Rosen's identification was correct. The descriptions by Rosen and Oldenberg will be found in the *Zapiska* of the Archaeological Society, vol. III. pp. 273-276, vol. IV. pp. 229-265, and Hommel's account of the Version will be found in his *Anhang* to Weisslowits' *Prinz und Derwisch*, pp. 131-134. For an account of the British Museum MS. (Oriental 3529), see Rieu, *Supplement* to the *Catalogue of the Persian Manuscripts in the British Museum*, No. 230, London, 1895, p. 238. Dr Rieu points out that another copy of the Persian Version is included in the *Zubdat at-Tawárîkh*, No. 36, foll. 226-249. This was extracted from the 'Ain ul-Ḥayât of Aḳâ Muḥammad Bâḳir, who gives it on the authority of Ibn Bâba. Thus it seems that the translator of Bâbawaih's Arabic text into Persian was Aḳâ Muḥammad Bâḳir.

THE ARMENIAN VERSION

The Armenian Version of the Book of Barlaam and Iôasaph was first described by Brosset in his *Rapports* on his archaeological researches in Georgia and Armenia, published at St Petersburg in 1849. An Armenian Abridgment was described in the *Catalogue* of the MSS. preserved in the convent of Etschmiatzin in 1863. In 1896 Mr F. C. Conybeare, M.A., published a translation into English of the first half of the Armenian Version and of the last paragraph in *Folklore*, London, 1896, vol. VII.

pp. 111 ff. His translation is made from the Bodleian Codex 438, which was written about A.D. 1550. He compared this MS. with a similar MS. (dated 1603) obtained by himself from Tiflis, and now in the British Museum. The Armenian Version is contained in the Menologion, i.e., the collection of lives of martyrs, homilies, etc., a part of which is appointed to be read on every day in the year. The Story of Barlaam comes at the end of the Menologion and is probably a later addition to the main collection, which was made as early as the IXth century. A notice or Colophon mentioned by Mr Conybeare (p. 112) says that the Story of Barlaam was translated into Armenian by one Asat, under the king Bagratuni, whose dynasty reigned from 850 A.D. to 1050. Thus the Armenian Version was probably made in the IXth or Xth century. Mr Conybeare thinks that it was made from a Syriac original. For a list of the Armenian codices see Kuhn, *Barlaam*, p. 52; Zotenberg, *Notice*, p. 95; and Conybeare, *op. cit.* p. 113. A Metrical Version in 24 chapters (see Brosset, *Mélanges Asiatiques*, tom. VIII. pp. 541 f.) was made in 1433 by Aṛaqel, or Arhaqel, Archbishop of Siuni, and a copy of this will be found in Brit. Mus. Orient. 4580, fol. 164 b. See Conybeare, *Catalogue of the Armenian MS. in the British Museum*, London, 1913, p. 278. An edition of the text was printed at Amsterdam in 1668, as is proved by the copy which was formerly in the library of Dulaurier (Zotenberg, p. 166).

THE GEORGIAN VERSION

Extracts from the Georgian Version of the Book of Barlaam were published by Professor N. Marr under the title of "MUDROST' BALAVARA" in the *Zapiska* of the Archaeological Society, tom. III. pp. 223-260. This title may be translated "The Wisdom of Bilauhar," and in the title the book is attributed to Isaac, son of Sophron of Palestine. The authorities who possess knowledge of the Georgian language and Version of the Book of Bilauhar are convinced that this work was translated from some old-Arabic, non-Christian Version, and not from the Greek. The order of the Apologues, or Parables and Fables, follows closely that which obtains in the old-Arabic and Hebrew Versions. On the other hand, the Georgian Version agrees with the Greek Version in a very large number of important passages for which the Arabic and Hebrew have no equivalents. Professor Marr was convinced that the language used in the Georgian Version was very old and pure, and that the quotations from the New Testament that occur in it were derived from a very old form of the Georgian Bible. For a discussion on the ancient forms of the proper names see Kuhn, *Barlaam*, pp. 10 ff., and for translations of passages from the Georgian Version see Hommel, in Weisslowits, pp. 146 ff., and Conybeare, *Folklore*, vol. VII. pp. 102 ff.

THE GREEK BOOK OF BARLAAM AND IÔASAPH

The Greek text of Barlaam and Iôasaph is found in a large number of manuscripts, the earliest being of the XIth and the latest of the XVIth century. According to Zotenberg (*Notice sur le Livre de Barlaam et Joasaph*, p. 3) there are six in Vienna, four in Munich, ten in Oxford, and single copies in the British Museum, Heidelberg, Rome, Florence, Venice, Turin, Madrid, the Escurial, Moscow, Cairo, and the monasteries of St Sâba and Mount Athos. To these places Kuhn adds (*Barlaam*, p. 48) Athens, Constantinople, Jerusalem, Lesbos, Messina, Modena and Patmos. In the oldest MSS. the title of the work is given by Zotenberg thus: "Ἱστορία ψυχωφελὴς ἐκ τῆς ἐνδοτέρας τῶν Αἰθιόπων χώρας, τῆς Ἰνδῶν λεγομένης, πρὸς τὴν ἁγίαν πόλιν μετενεχθεῖσα διὰ Ἰωάννου μοναχοῦ, ἀνδρὸς τιμίου καὶ ἐναρέτου μονῆς τοῦ ἁγίου Σάβα." Some MSS. add ἐν ᾗ ὁ βίος Βαρλαὰμ καὶ Ἰωάσαφ τῶν ἀοιδίμων καὶ μακαρίων. According to this title the work was brought by John the monk of Saint Sâba from that inner region of the Ethiopians which is called that of the Indians. In one manuscript *Sâba* is written σάνα, which, owing to a misunderstanding, some copyists in other MSS. changed into σινᾶ, and others into σιναῖτου or συναῖτου. According to these forms John belonged to the Monastery of Sinai.

In a group of manuscripts of more recent date the title reads: "Ἱστορία ψυχωφελὴς ἐκ τῆς τῶν Αἰθιόπων χώρας τῆς Ἰνδῶν λεγομένης ἀπελθόντων (τῶν) τιμίον ἀνδρῶν πρὸς τὴν ἁγίαν πόλιν ἐν τῇ μονῇ τοῦ ἁγίου

Σάββα καὶ ἀπαγγειλάντων συγγραφεῖσα παρὰ τοῦ ἁγίου Ἰωάννου τοῦ Δαμασκηνοῦ." According to this title the story was brought by certain godly men to Jerusalem, to the monastery of Saint Sâba, and was redacted by Saint John of Damascus. The titles of two other manuscripts state that the story was translated into Greek from Iberian, or from Ethiopic, by Euthymius an Iberian, the one reading "μετενεγθεῖσ[α] διὰ ἰωάννου μοναχοῦ μονῆς τοῦ ἁγίου σάββα [ἑρμηνευθεῖσα] ἀπὸ τῆς ἰβήρων πρὸς τὴν ἐλλάδα γλῶσσαν ὑπὲρ εὐθυμί[ου] ἀνδρὸς τιμίου καὶ εὐσεβοῦς τοῦ λεγομένου ἰβηρος" and the other "καὶ μεταβληθῆσα ἀπὸ τῆς τῶν ἐθίοπων διαλέκτου ἐπὶ τὴν ἐλληνίδα γλῶσαν παρὰ εὐθημίου τοῦ ἁγιοτάτου μοναχοῦ τοῦ ἤβυρος." Now Euthymius was the second Abbot of the monastery of Mount Athos, and he flourished in the latter half of the Xth century; he is famous as the translator of the Bible and other works into Georgian, the knowledge of which language was restored to him miraculously by the Virgin Mary. For reasons which most scholars accept as satisfactory, Zotenberg has shown (pp. 10, 11) that this statement is not to be accepted literally, and that it is due to a monkish scribe of Mount Athos who wished to magnify the glory of Euthymius and the monastery of Iberen.

The Greek text of the Book of Barlaam remained in manuscript until the beginning of the last century. Schmidt published the text of five of the Apologues in vol. XXVI of the *Wiener Jahrbücher* (1824, pp. 25 ff.), but the first complete edition of the Greek text was that of Boissonade, which appeared in Paris in 1832 as vol. IV. of his *Anecdota Graeca.* Boissonade

accepted the statement in the title given by the
later group of manuscripts, and regarded the Book
of Barlaam as the work of St John of Damascus.
As such it has been included in editions of the collected works of John of Damascus, e.g. in Migne's
Patrologiae cursus completus, Ser. Graeca, tom. XCVI.
where Boissonade's text is printed side by side with
the Latin translation of Billius (cols. 857–1250)[1].
An edition of the Greek text by Sophronios Kechajoglus appeared at Athens in 1884 with the title
"Ἱστορία συγγραφεῖσα παρὰ τοῦ ἐν ἁγίοις Ἰωάννου τοῦ
Δαμασκηνοῦ διαλαμβάνουσα τὸν βίον τῶν ὁσίων πατέρων
ἡμῶν Βαρλαὰμ καὶ Ἰωάσαφ ἀνέκδοτος οὖσα ἐκδίδοται
ἤδη ἑλληνιστὶ ὑπὸ Σωφρονίου μοναχοῦ Ἁγιορείτου ἐκ
Ῥαιδεστοῦ Κεχαγιόγλου ἐπὶ τῇ βάσει μεμβραΐνων χειρο
γράφων τῆς ἐν τῷ ἁγιωνύμῳ ὄρει ἱερᾶς σκήτεως τῆς
Θεοπρομήτορος Ἄννης. Ἐν Ἀθήναις Σπυριδ. Κουσουλίνου
τυπογράφειον καὶ βιβλιοπώλειον 1884." The text is based
upon vellum manuscripts preserved in the Skete of
Saint Anne on Mount Athos.

The questions of the authorship of the Greek
Book of Barlaam and the date of its composition
have been discussed by several authorities, with
varying results. If we follow the title of the oldest
Greek MSS. of the work we must believe that the
story was brought from the inner region of the
Ethiopians, which is called the region of the Indians,
to the holy city (Jerusalem), by John, a monk of
St Sâba, a monastery near Jerusalem. This state-

---

[1] Boissonade's text has also been reprinted in *St John Damascene
Barlaam and Ioasaph, with an English translation*, by the Rev. G. R.
Woodward, M.A. and H. Mattingly, M.A. London, 1914.

ment is valuable as indicating the source of the Story, but where was the ἐνδοτέρα τῶν Αἰθιόπων χώρα ἡ Ἰνδῶν λεγομένη? The nature and contents of the Story make it quite certain that the words can contain no allusion to the Ethiopians, i.e. Abyssinians, of Africa, and the region must clearly be sought for in Asia. It is now known[1] that the original home of the Iôasaph Story was either in eastern Iran, or in the neighbouring countries, which could include Bactria, Parthia, and the whole region between Egypt and Persia, and Ethiopia (Abyssinia) and Arabia need not therefore be considered in connection with the "inner region of the Ethiopians called that of the Indians." The title of the oldest Greek MSS. does not say what language the Story was written in, or in what language it was related to John the monk of Sâba, or whether he brought the Story with him in manuscript form. He gives us further information in the concluding lines of his Preface, in which he says, "I will in no wise pass over in silence the edifying story that hath come to me, the which devout men from the inner land of the Ethiopians, whom our tale calleth Indians, delivered unto me, translated from trustworthy records," ἐξήγησιν ψυχωφελὴ ἕως ἐμοῦ καταντήσασαν οὐδαμῶς σιωπήσομαι· ἥνπερ μοι ἀφηγήσαντο ἄνδρες εὐλαβεῖς τῆς ἐνδοτέρας τῶν Αἰθιόπων χώρας, οὕστινας Ἰνδοὺς οἶδεν ὁ λόγος καλεῖν ἐξ ὑπομνημάτων ταύτην ἀψευδῶν μεταφράσαντας. And at the end of the work John says, "Here endeth this history, which I have

---

[1] See Kuhn, *op. cit.* p. 38. Conybeare places the home of the Story in Bactria.

written to the best of my ability, even as I heard it from the truthful lips of worthy men who delivered it unto me." Ἕως ὧδε τὸ πέρας τοῦ παρόντος λόγου, ὃν κατὰ δύναμιν ἐμὴν γεγράφηκα, καθὼς ἀκήκοα παρὰ τῶν ἀψευδῶς παραδεδωκότων μοι τιμίων ἀνδρῶν. Thus there is no doubt that John the monk heard the Story in conversation with certain godly men who had obtained their information from authoritative manuscripts.

The statement made in the titles of the later group of manuscripts to the effect that the Story was brought to Jerusalem, to the monastery of Saint Sâba, by certain godly men, and that it was written down [in Greek] by John of Damascus, must now be considered. John of Damascus was born in the latter half of the VIIth century, and died in the Monastery of Saint Sâba (?) soon after 760 A.D. For centuries no one seems to have seriously doubted that John of Damascus composed the Book of Barlaam, and the earliest edition of his works included the Book of Barlaam among them. Lequien, however, had doubts, and in his edition of the works of John Damascenus, which appeared in Paris in 1712 (reprinted at Venice in 1748), the Book of Barlaam is placed in a kind of Appendix. In 1886 Zotenberg published his monograph *Notice sur le Livre de Barlaam et Ioasaph*, and brought forward a number of cogent arguments in which he maintained that John of Damascus was not the author of this work. He attributed the ascription of the work to him in the titles of the later manuscripts to blunders on the part of scribes, who had confounded

John the monk of St Sâba with John of Damascus. He held the Greek text was not a translation, but the original text, which was drawn up in Syria in the first half of the VIIth century, and that John of Damascus lived nearly a century too late to have written it. Zotenberg then examined portions of the Greek Book of Barlaam very carefully and compared the general style of it with the style of John Damascenus in his works of certain authenticity, and concluded that in every respect it was its superior. The supporters of the claims of John Damascenus said that the quotations from the writings of St Gregory of Nazianzus, St Basil and others, found in the Book of Barlaam proved that he was its author, but Zotenberg showed that John the Monk and John Damascenus quoted from common sources. And he showed that in eloquence, phraseology, argumentative skill, idiomatic usage, and readiness of quotation, the former was superior to the latter. The fact that the Arabs were not mentioned convinced him that the Book of Barlaam was composed before the rise to power of Muḥammad, and, judging by the reflections of the religious controversies that he recognized in it, he felt justified in asserting that it was not written later than the first half of the VIIth century. This view has been accepted by Krumbacher (*Byzant. Litteraturgeschichte*, p. 888), and Jacobs (*Barlaam*, p. xx), and Kuhn thinks (*op. cit.* p. 47) that the Book of Barlaam was written before the downfall of the Sasanid kingdom. On the other hand, Messrs Woodward and Mattingly find Zotenberg's arguments "insufficient," and maintain

that it was written either by John Damascenus himself or by another monk called John, who *inter alia*
took the same side in the Iconoclastic Controversy
(*St John Damascene, Barlaam and Ioasaph*, Preface,
p. xii).

But whether the Book of Barlaam was written by
John Damascenus or John the monk of St Sâba
seems to me to be of small importance; the all-
important point is *When* it was written. The Greek
text published by Boissonade is undoubtedly, as
Zotenberg says, not a translation of any Version of
the Story of Barlaam and Iôasaph, but a Christianized
form of the Story which was current in Greek after,
say, the VIIth or VIIIth century. In reading it one
feels that the composition is too perfect, the language
too eloquent, the quotations too pertinent and
numerous, and the summaries of Christian theology
too complete for the first edition of a Story of this
kind. An earlier form in Greek (probably more
than one) must have existed before Boissonade's
text, and there is no reason why it should not have
been current in the early centuries of the Christian
Era. The main facts of the life of the Buddha must
have been well known among the *literati* of Syria
and Egypt, and short and simple versions of them
in Greek and Syriac must have appeared as a
matter of course. Mr Conybeare's remarks (*Folklore*, vol. VII. pp. 140 ff.) on the Armenian Version
show this to have been absolutely certain. This
short and simple form of so edifying a story was
enlarged perhaps in the Vth or VIth century, and
the author of this enlargement probably added the

Apology of Aristides[1], the mention of St Anthony
of Egypt, who died about A.D. 360, the Passion of
St Perpetua[2], and extracts from the works of several
ecclesiastical writers. It has been pointed out by
Jacobs, Krumbacher and others[3] that there are
passages in the Greek Barlaam that have their
source in the so-called "Mirror of Princes" of
Agapetos, a deacon of the Church of Saint Sophia
in Constantinople. This work consists of 72 short
chapters which treat of the moral, religious and
political conduct of a prince, and was dedicated by
its author to the Emperor Justinian I. It has been
thought by some that the author of the Greek
Barlaam borrowed his extracts directly from the
Ἔκθεσις of Agapetos, but Krumbacher thinks that
the passages concerned were derived from a source
whence both he and Agapetos drew[4].

The last redaction of the Book of Barlaam was
probably written in the VIIth or VIIIth century,
when the work became neither more nor less than
a glorification of Christian asceticism and the life of
the monk. Its author must have been a scholar and
have possessed great literary skill and imagination.

---

[1] See *The Apology of Aristides on behalf of the Christians from a
Syriac manuscript preserved on Mount Sinai, with an introduction and
translation*, by J. Rendel Harris, *and an Appendix containing the main
portion of the original Greek text*, by J. Armitage Robinson, Cambridge,
1891. See also Hennecke, *Die Apologie des Aristides*, Leipzig, 1893; and
Seeberg, *Die Apologie des Aristides untersucht und wiederhergestellt*,
1893, pp. 159–214.

[2] See Robinson, J. A., *The Passion of St Perpetua* (*Texts and Studies*,
Part II.), Cambridge, 1891. Dean Robinson was the first to recognize in the
Greek Barlaam the borrowings which its compiler made from the *Apology
of Aristides*.

[3] See Prächter, *Der Roman Barlaam und Joasaph in seinen Ver-
hältniss zu Agapets Königsspiegel* in *Byzant. Zeit.*, vol. II. pp. 444–460.

[4] *Byzantinische Litteraturgeschichte*, pp. 456, 457, and 887.

He was well acquainted with the Scriptures, and the works of the Fathers, and Christian apocryphal literature, and he was familiar with the history of all the great disputes that had convulsed the Church from time to time. He drew upon the literature dealing with the life of the Buddha for many important sections of his romance, but it is quite clear that he followed the generally received traditions about that great Teacher, rather than any detailed history contained in a single book. The document most used by him was probably that which is now known as the Book of Bilauhar and Bûḍâsaf, or Yûḍâsaf. He accepted the Christian tradition of the conversion of the Indians by St Thomas, and so found reason for the existence in India of the Christian official who explained Christianity to Abenner. It is possible that the name Abenner may be derived from Ḥabban, the name of the Indian merchant to whom St Thomas sold himself. When necessary the writer of the Greek Barlaam modified the old Indian story to suit his purpose, and suppressed details in it that were inconvenient. Thus he represents Prince Iôasaph as a young man weary of court ceremonials and the luxury of his father's palace, but he never mentions the fact that the original Indian prince was a married man, who had for many years before he became an ascetic indulged in the delights of the *ḥarîm*. And he altered the order of the Fables and Parables to suit his convenience, and many of them he suppressed entirely. Yet his literary skill enabled him to preserve the atmosphere of the native Indian lives of the Buddha with great success, and at the same time to treat the facts essential for his narrative in a manner that rendered them acceptable to every Christian ascetic in the world. There seems to me to be no doubt that the last form of the Greek Barlaam Story, i.e. that which we now have, is as different from the earliest form of it as are the latest from the earliest forms of Kalīlah and Dimnah and the Alexander-Story. The latest forms of all three works I believe to have been compiled from earlier Versions in the VIIIth or the early part of the IXth century.

THE LATIN AND WESTERN EUROPEAN VERSIONS OF THE BOOK OF BARLAAM AND IÔASAPH

The popularity of this work is due entirely to the LATIN TRANSLATIONS of it which appeared in the Middle Ages, and all the Western European Versions, abridgments and paraphrases of it, whether in prose or in verse, are founded upon them. The first Latin translation is said to have been made by Anastasius, a librarian of the Vatican in the IXth century, but no manuscript of any Latin translation older than the XIIth century seems to exist (see Ward, *Catalogue of Romances*, vol. II. p. 119). This translation was printed at least twice in the XVth century, and the two incunabula in which it appears are described by Kuhn (p. 54)[1]. Another translation into Latin was made by George Trape-

---

[1] A copy of each of these is in the British Museum, press-marks Grenville 11741 and IB. 8428; see Pollard, *Catalogue of the XVth century Printed Books in the British Museum*, pp. 73, 483.

zuntius (born 1396, died 1485) and printed at Antwerp[1], and the Latin translation by Billy (born in Paris 1535, died 1581) of Guise, Abbot of St Michael, was made and printed in the XVIth century in the editions of the collected works of St John of Damascus[2]. Billy's translation was included in both editions of Rosweyde's *Vitae Patrum* (Antwerp, 1615 and 1628), and it is reprinted in Migne's *Patrologiae*, Series Latina, tom. 73, coll. 443–606. Abridgments of the earliest Latin version appeared in Vincent de Beauvais (about 1250), *Speculum Historiale*, Lib. XV. capp. 1–64; and in Jacobus de Voragine (about 1270–1280), *Legenda Aurea*. Both these abridgments were very popular, and copies of them were widely circulated.

Among FRENCH TRANSLATIONS may be mentioned : 1. The metrical version of Gui de Cambrai (12352 verses when complete) which was made in the first half of the XIIIth century. It was published by Paul Meyer and Zotenberg in vol. LXXV. of the Bibliothek des Litterarischen Vereins in Stuttgart under the title, *Barlaam und Josaphat Französische Gedicht des dreizehnten Jahrhunderts von Gui de Cambrai*, etc. Stuttgart, 1864. 2. The metrical version (abridged) of Chardry (3000 verses), written in Anglo-Norman in the beginning of the XIIIth century. It is edited by Koch, *Chardry's*

---

[1] See *S. Joannis Damasceni historia de vitis et rebus gestis Sanctorum Barlaam Eremitae, et Iosaphat Regis Indorum, Georgio Trapezuntio interprete*, Antwerp, 12° (no date). His translation was also printed in the editions of the collected works of John of Damascus which appeared at Basel in 1535, 1539, 1548, 1559 and 1575.

[2] See the editions of Paris, 1577 fol., 1603 fol., 1619 fol. His translation was printed separately at Cologne (1593 and 1643).

Josaphaz, Set Dormanz und Petit Plat Dichtungen in der Anglo-normanischen Mundart des XIII *Jahrhunderts zum ersten Mal vollständig mit Einleitung, Anmerkungen, und Glossar*, Heilbronn, 1879. Three specimens of a prose translation of the XIIIth century were edited by Meyer and Zotenberg (*op. cit.* pp. 335–352). A French translation of Abbot Billy's Latin translation by Jean de Billy, the brother of the Abbot, was published at Paris in 1578. Jean de Billy corrected many of his brother's mistakes and mistranslations. This translation was often reprinted. For later French translations see Kuhn, *op. cit.* p. 60. Specimens of a PROVENÇAL TRANSLATION have been printed by Meyer and Zotenberg (pp. 352–356), and by Bartsch in his *Chrestomathie Provençale*, pp. 353–360.

The ITALIAN TRANSLATIONS may be divided into two classes, i.e. complete texts and abridgments; the former may be grouped under the heading "Storia," and the latter under the heading "Vita." The complete text is printed in *Storia de' SS. Barlaam e Giosafatte Ridotta alla sua antica purita di favella, coll' ajuto degli antichi testi e penna. In Roma appresso Giovanni Maria Salvioni Stampator Vaticano* M.DCC.XXXIV. Many of the editions of the "Vita" are enumerated by Kuhn (p. 63) and among them may be mentioned *La Vita di San Giosaphat convertito per Barlaam*, printed by Bindoni in Venice, 1539; *Vita del glorioso S. Giosafat*, Florence, 1582; Remondini, *Vita di san Giosafat convertito da Barlaam*, Venice, about 1600. The "Vita" treated poetically will be found in Opezzinghi, D. A., *Della Vita di San Giosafat convertito da San Barlaam Eremita*

Canti v., Palermo, 1584; Pagliaresi, Landoccio, *Leggenda di Sancto Giosafa figliuolo del Re Avenire dindia* (MS. in the Bodleian; see Kuhn, p. 65); the dramatized versions of Colomb de Batines (printed at Florence in 1852) and Bernardo Pulci (printed at Florence in 1872); and the modern work *Maggio di San Giosaffat*, Volterra, 1867.

For SPANISH TRANSLATIONS see Solorzano, Juan de Arce, *Historia de los dos soldados de Christo Barlaan y Josaphat*, Madrid, 1608; Baltazar, Fr. *Verdad nada amarga, hermosa bondad; honesta, util, y delectable, grata, y moral historia, de la rara vida de los famosos, y singulares Sanctos Barlaan, y Josaphat*, Con las licencias necessarias impresso en Manila, MDCXCII. From this text Antonio Borja's Tagolic translation, which was printed in Manila in 1712, seems to have been made. For a Spanish dramatized version see Lope de Vega, " Barlan y Josafa" (analysed in Schaeffer's *Geschichte d. Span. National dramas*, Leipzig, 1890).

A PORTUGUESE TRANSLATION, edited from a manuscript, was announced by G. de Vasconcellos Abreu, with the help of F. A. Coelho, who proposed to add a preface discussing the philological and palaeographical importance of the work, and Buddhism and its influence on Christianity. I cannot find that this work was published.

An IRISH TRANSLATION, said to have been written about A.D. 1600, exists in manuscript; see Nettlau, Irish Texts in Dublin and London MSS. (*Revue Celtique*, tom. x. p. 460) where O'Curry's Catalogue is quoted.

The oldest GERMAN TRANSLATIONS are poetical, and were written by Rudolf von Ems and Bishop Otto in the first half of the XIIIth century. For the text of Rudolf von Ems see Köpke, F. K., *Barlaam und Josaphat von Rudolf von Montfort herausgegeben*, Königsberg, 1818. The text of Bishop Otto is unpublished, but see Diefenbach, L., *Mittheilungen über eine noch ungedruckte mittelhochdeutsche Bearbeitung des Barlaam und Josaphat*, Giessen, 1836. Fragments of a third poetical version are described by Kuhn (p. 69).

A shortened prose form of the work, which resembles the Latin Text of Jacobus de Voragine, was current in the XVth century; four printed editions of this are known, two incunabula and two editions which appeared in the XVIIth century. The British Museum possesses copies of the two incunabula, one illustrated with woodcuts (Grenville Library, press mark 11766) and one without (Grenville Library, press mark 11767). The latter, according to a note in the volume, is thought by Ebert to be the earliest Latin edition, and to date from 1476. It has no title page and begins, Cum cepissent monasteria. The preface to the former reads:

HIe vahet an eyn gar loblich vnd | heylsam allen christglaubigen cro | nica. Sagend von eynem hey-ligen | kúnig mit namen Iosaphat. wie | der ward bekeret von eynem heyli- | gen vatter vnnd aynsideln genant | Barlaam. Vnd wie diss kúnigs va | ter vil vnd manig grausam peyn die lieben heyligen| marterer christi angeleget hat. Vnd doch am letzstẽ| von dem sun den er geboren håtte leiblich· geystlich |

widerumb geboren warde ñit dem sacrament der |
heyligen tauff. Darinn auch eyn yeder mensch· er
sei | in was stand er wôlle· volkommenlich vindet·
wie er | fliehen soll· den leibe· die welt· vnnd den
teufel· vnnd | sich in rechtem wàren gelauben· in
státter hoffnung | vnnd heyliger liebe czǔ gott keren
durch vil manig | der neúwen vnnd alten ce auss
der heyligen geschrift | exempel vnd lere. Auch
wirdt er gantz vnderweisst | von allem vngelauben
vnnd abgôtterei der kriechen | chaldeischen egip-
cyschen vnd hebreischen· vnnd von | dem rechten
glauben der christen wie d auff den rech- | ten fôlsen
der do ist christus grunduôstet vnd gebau-|wen
seie Dariñ auch der andechtig mensch sein heyl |
sǔchen vnd allen anfechtungen des bôsen wider-
steen | mag· weib vnd kind vnd alles zeitlichs gǔt
verlas-|sent vnd alleyn in rechter armǔt des geystz
nackend | vnd bloss dĕ blossen christum nachuolge.
vnd durch | sôllichs múge werdĕ wirdig des ewigen
lebens vñ | erbschafft christi amen. Vnd ist diss
bǔch geteylet in | vierundsechtzig capitel mit iren
figuren. |

Eyn ende hat die vorred. Vnd vahet an das bǔch
der heyligen christenlichen lere.

The opening words of Chap. I are: Es schreibet
der hoch lerer und meyster der hystori Damascenus
in seinem bǔch der geschicht· Das nach der geburd
unsers herrn ihesu christi dreihundert und achtzig
iar. Vñ von anfang der welt· fúnfftausend fúnff-
hundert achtundsibentzig iar ist gewesen eyn kúnig
in dĕ kúnigkreych india mit namen auennir. The
volume was produced by Günther Zainer at Augs-

burg in 1470; see Pollard, *Catalogue of XVth century printed books*. It is important to note the statement here made that Avennir was King of India in the year 380 A.D.

A modernized German version of Barlaam and Josaphat for the use of children was written by Christoph von Schmid; it appeared first in the edition of his collected works (vol. XV. pp. 3–194 Augsburg, 1843). Many reprints of it have since been issued. The story was also dramatized by San Marte (A. Schulz), and this "Glaubenstragödie" was entitled "Des Kreuzes Prüfung," and was published at Magdeburg in 1845.

ENGLISH TRANSLATIONS. According to Kuhn (p. 71) the Story of Barlaam exists in English in four abbreviated Recensions, three in verse and one in prose. The oldest and most complete versified form, in 1250 verses, and the two shorter forms are published by Horstmann, *Altenglische Legenden Kindheit Jesu, Geburt Jesu, Barlaam und Josaphat, St Patrik's Fegefeuer*, Paderborn, 1875, pp. 113–148, 215–225, and 226–240. A version of the prose Recension was published also by Horstmann in the *Programm* of the Königliche Katholisch Gymnasium zu Sagan, 1877. In 1895 Dr K. S. Macdonald published in his *Story of Barlaam and Joasaph: Buddhism and Christianity*, Calcutta, 1895, several English versions, viz. *The History of the Five Wise Philosophers*, by H. P. Gent, London, 1732; *The Hystorye of the Hermyte Balaam* (from *The Golden Legend of Master William Caxton done anew*, Kelmscott Press, London, 1892, pp. 1152–1166); *Bar-

laam and Josaphat from the Vernon MS.; *De Santis Berlam et Josaphat* from the Harley MS. 4196; *Barlaam and Josaphat* from the Bodleian MS. 779. Mr J. Jacobs has also published the *Lyf of Saynt Balaam* from Caxton's *Golden Legend*; and the *Life of Prince Jehosaphat, the son of King Avenerio, of Burma in India*, London, 1783, in his *Barlaam and Josaphat*, pp. 3–56.

DUTCH TRANSLATION. See *Het leven en bedryf van Barlaäm den heremijt, en Josaphat koning van Indien, Beschreven door den H. Oudvader Ioannes Damascenus, En nu in Nederduits vertaelt door F. v. H.*, Rotterdam, 1672.

OLD NORWEGIAN TRANSLATION. See R. Keyser and C. R. Unger, *Barlaams ok Josaphats Saga. En religiös romantisk Fortaelling om Barlaam og Josaphat, oprindelig forfattet paa Graesk i det 8de Aarhundrede, senere oversat paa Latin, og herfra igjen i fri Bearbeidelse ved Aar 1200 overfört paa Norsk af Kong Haakon Sverressön*, Christiania, 1851.

MODERN DANISH TRANSLATION. See *Barlaam og Josaphat. En religiös Roman. Oversat fra oldnorsk af H. E. Kinck*, Christiania, 1852.

OLD SWEDISH TRANSLATION. See Klemming, G.E., *Samlingar utgifna af Svenska Fornskrift-Sällskapet. Prosadikter från Medeltiden. Första Häftet [Barlaam och Josaphat]*, Stockholm, 1887. For details of the Scandinavian Versions see Kuhn, *op. cit.*, p. 72.

The RUSSIAN and other cognate Versions are described by Kuhn, *op. cit.* (*Kirchenslavisch-Russische und Rumanische Bearbeitungen*) p. 53, and (*Westslavische Bearbeitungen*) p. 73. See also Kirpiš-

nikov, *Griechische Romane in der neueren Litteratur,*
2. Theil, Charkov, 1876; St Novakovič, *Barlaam
und Joasaph,* Belgrad, 1881 (*Glasnik Srpskog Ušenog
Društva,* Bd. 50, Servian); Gaster, M., *Literatura
populara Romana,* Bukarest, 1883, S. 32–53 and
Greeko-Slavonic, London, 1887, S. 111 ff.; Franko,
Barlaam und Joasaph, Zeichnungen und Textpro-
ben aus einer Ms. des 16 Jahrh. *Zapiski der wiss.
Gesellsch.,* Sevšenko, vol. 7, Lemberg, 1895.

At the Annual Meeting of the British Academy held in the Rooms of the Royal Society, Burlington House, on the 11th of July, Sir Frederic Kenyon gave an account of a Greek manuscript, recently acquired by the British Museum, which contains a portion of the famous "Apology of Aristides." This Apology, which is a defence of Christianity addressed to the Emperor Hadrian, was unknown, except for a few references, until Prof. Rendel Harris discovered a Syriac translation of it in a Monastery on Mount Sinai. On reading it Dean Armitage Robinson recognized at once that it had been incorporated almost completely in the famous "Spiritual Romance" of Barlaam and Josaphat, which was commonly regarded as the work of St John of Damascus. In this Romance it is put in the mouth of Nâkôr, the magician whom King Abenner expected to curse the Christians. The recently acquired papyrus consists of two attached leaves, the text of which deals with the contents of Chapters XVI and XVII of Prof. Rendel Harris's Syriac text. I understand from Sir Frederic Kenyon that the Greek text will be published by Mr Milne in the *Journal of Theological Studies* in the autumn, and it would seem from Sir Frederic's account of its contents published in *The Times* of July 12 that it must have much in common with the Ethiopic text, at any rate as far as the description of the virtues of the Christians is concerned. See *infra* pp. 186 and 187.

[THE BOOK OF] BARALÂM[1] AND YĔWÂSĔF[2] BELONGING TO THE CHURCH OF THE SAVIOUR OF THE WORLD[3].

IN THE NAME OF GOD, THE COMPASSIONATE, AND THE MERCIFUL, IN WHOM IS OUR HELP! WITH THE HELP OF GOD AND HIS FAIR FAVOUR, WE BEGIN TO WRITE A HISTORY THAT IS PROFITABLE BOTH TO SOUL AND BODY, WHICH A CERTAIN HOLY MONK FROM GÊTÊSÊMÂNÎ (GETHSEMANE), WHOSE NAME WAS JOHN[4], BROUGHT FROM THE COUNTRY OF HĔNDĔ (INDIA) TO BÊT MAḲDAS (JERUSALEM). MAY HIS PRAYER AND INTERCESSION BE WITH HIS BELOVED...FOR EVER AND EVER. AMEN.

[*Preface*]

The Apostle and Evangelist saith, "All those who perform the work of the Holy Spirit are the sons of God[5]." And the saints are those whom He holdeth worthy to find the work of virtues, that is to say, the gift (or, grace) that is above nature, and is perfect among the things that are to be desired. Some of the saints became martyrs through many spiritual fights, and they waged war against sin until they fought it down. And some of them fought against hunger and thirst as they entered in through the strait gate and became martyrs of their own good will. And now we will begin to relate the history of the conquests and of the bravery of the hearts of those who possessed the strength to become martyrs, even to the shedding of their blood, and who by reason of their excessive toil resembled the angels in their lives, and became an example to the generations who were to come after. And the example that they received from the Apostles was the

---

[1] A name suggested by Bar-Allâhâ, and substituted for Balauhar = the Sanskrit Bhagavan, a being who had attained Buddhahood.

[2] = Iôasaph, a corruption of Yôdâsaf, from the Pehlevi Bôdâsaf = Sanskrit Bodhisattva "one who is destined to become a Buddha."

[3] The name of the Church which King Theodore intended to build at Maḳdalâ.

[4] See the Introduction (Greek Version). [5] Romans viii. 14.

B.   1

likeness of Christ which they proclaimed by the Holy Spirit, and also from the blessed Fathers who had set themselves to effect the salvation of our race. [p. 2] Now the path that leadeth unto spiritual excellence is rugged, and it is hard for men to walk therein. It is high and cannot be travelled over, and it is exceedingly difficult to journey therein for those who have not put their trust in God with their whole hearts. But before they began to fight against the might of the passions it was meet for them, because of their hearing about it, to enquire carefully into the history of the journeyings of those who had travelled by this path without experiencing sorrow, and to seek [to know about] the journeys of those who had given up in despair. The difficulty of the way is light, and there is joy therein to the man who shall press on his way along that narrow, rugged road, provided that he discovereth that the word of his doctrine maketh him bold and vigilant, and he will peradventure profit thereby. For a very little will be sufficient to make such a man vigilant, and if he seeth many who have already travelled over that road, and who have succeeded in the attainment of much riches, he will therefore certainly be emboldened to continue his journey. Now, the consideration of this maketh me eager [to travel over that road], but besides this there is another thing that moveth me, namely that I have myself seen the destruction of that servant who took the talent of his lord and buried it in the ground ; his lord had given it unto him to obtain interest thereon, but he hid it in the ground where it lay unused in trafficking and without gaining interest[1].

[The History of Baralâm and Yĕwâsĕf.]

Behold now, there hath come to me a glorious story, one that is profitable both to the soul and to the body, and I will not keep silence concerning it, but will publish it abroad openly. Certain rich men of the country of India have related it unto me, and have interpreted to me the hidden things of a memorial that is true. Now the country of India is very far

---

[1] See Matthew xxv. 18.

away from the land of Egypt[1], and it is a very large country, and the population thereof is very great, and rivers and great streams of water go round about through it, and men travel thither in ships from the country of Egypt ; and the desert part of it lieth near the borders of Agam[2] and Fârs[3]. In these countries from of old have dwelt people with the love of the worship of idols, and the manners and customs of their lives were exceedingly corrupt ; moreover their speech was not understood. And when the Only-begotten Son of God, Who lived in the bosom of His Father, willed the salvation of those people who lived in those regions, and was graciously pleased not to endure the sight of His creatures [p. 3] in the service of sin, He compassionated us with His customary compassion, and He appeared unto us in our own form, sin alone excepted, without being deprived of His Father's throne. And He took up His abode in the womb of the pure Virgin MARYÂM (MARY) MÂRÎHÂM for our sakes so that He might make us to dwell in heaven, and deliver us from sin, and receive divine birth. And in the operation of His wisdom He experienced to the full the exhaustion of the flesh for our sakes, and He suffered crucifixion and death. And He made the beings of earth to become one with the beings of heaven in a union that cannot be described ; and He rose from the dead, and ascended in His glory to heaven, and sat down at the right hand of His Father. And He sent His Spirit, the Comforter, in the form of tongues of fire to His followers, and to the men of His mystery, even as He promised them[4]. And He sent them unto all peoples so that they might lighten with their light those who were dwelling in the darkness of destruction, and make them to be baptized in the Name of the Father, and of the Son, and of the Holy Spirit. On some of them the lot fell to go to the East, and some of them were sent to the West, and some of them journeyed to the regions of the South and of the North, but all of them were perfect in their work.

---

[1] ⲅⲏⲝⲓ = Arab. قبط = Copt. ⲉⲕⲉⲛ†ⲁ.   [2] Arab. العَجَمِ Al-'Ajam.

[3] Arab. الفَارِس Al-Fâris.   [4] John xiv. 16; Acts ii. 3, 4.

[The preaching of St Thomas in India and the conversion of the Indians.]

At that time Thomas, great in holiness, one of the Company of the Twelve Apostles, was sent to the country of India[1], and he preached unto the Indians the preaching of salvation. And he made them to understand the voice of the miracles[2] which he caused to follow it, and which said, "Behold, the darkness of the worship of idols hath come to an end ! Behold, it hath been removed as a thing of no account!" And Thomas destroyed and made to be forsaken the country that had been wont to offer up sacrifices to graven images, and he converted the people thereof from their error; and the country was sanctified and saved, and the people thereof waxed strong in the Faith which is without deceit. And having been created a second time by the apostolic hand through receiving the garment of baptism, the people were then called by the Name of Christ, and they increased in numbers everywhere and grew up in the perfect Faith. And many large churches were built there.

And when the Rule of the monks began to flourish in the land of Egypt, and when there had gathered together in the [p. 4] monasteries numerous companies of monks who resembled the angels in their dispositions, the report of them was noised abroad, and it reached even unto the ends of the earth. And the report of the abstinence of these monks reached also the country of India, and at length the Indians made themselves like unto the [monks of Egypt] in the beauty of their life and works. And many of them abandoned everything and took up their abodes in the deserts, and they became possessed in their mortal bodies of the appearance of those who have not flesh. And when in this manner the fairness of their actions grew ever more beautiful, many of them flew up on golden pinions to heaven, even as it is written[3].

[1] See Lipsius, *Apostelgeschichten*, vol. I. p. 249 ff., and Budge, *The Contendings of the Apostles*, vol. II. p. 319 ff.
[2] One of the governors in India had flayed Thomas, but the Apostle survived, and carried about his skin for many days and worked many miracles by means of it. Budge, *Contendings*, vol. II. p. 346.
[3] Compare Isaiah xl. 31.

[How Wadâgôs, King of India, led a life of luxury and wantonness, and how he yearned for a son.]

And in those days there reigned over the country [of India] a certain king whose name was Wadâgôs[1] (?), and his riches were great and his power was mighty, and he conquered all those who set themselves in opposition to him. And he was victorious in war. His face and features were handsome, his stature was noble and awe-inspiring, and he was renowned and admired for his riches in every kind of possession of this fleeting world. He was thoughtful in mind, but incurably lazy, and his thoughts were very evil; by race he was descended from the nation of the Greeks. And he held in very high honour the demons who seduced him to worship idols, and made him hold them to be gods, and to obey their behests. And this king used to lead a life that was full of scandalous pleasures and debaucheries. He would gather together a crowd of men and waste his time and squander money with them in the useless and frivolous amusements of this world, and in the gratification of wanton lusts. And he never missed an opportunity of satisfying his heart's desire, or in gratifying his passions in the smallest matter. One thing alone held him in restraint in these matters, and one thing alone caused him trouble, that is to say, the want of children, for he never had a son. And he took the greatest pains possible in order that this fetter which bound him might be loosed, and that he might get a son, and with this idea in his mind he used to give away much money in alms and oblations. And thus was the king's desire.

[How the Indians of all classes rejected the things of this world and embraced the Christian Religion.]

And the Christian people who were arrayed in splendour did not ascribe the smallest glory to the gods of the king, and the object of his worship did not in the least degree make them afraid, but they treated his gods as contemptible graven

---

[1] This is a corruption of a Greek form of some Oriental name; the Greek version has 'Αβεννερ, or 'Αβεννὴρ.

images, and their hearts were carried away ever more and more by the love of God. And for this reason those who had chosen the ladder of monasticism rejected all the desirable things of this world, even unto death, for the sake of Christ our Lord. And they crucified their hearts [p. 5] in respect of the gifts of this world. And they loved the Name of Christ our Redeemer so fearlessly and so boldly that at length they delivered up their souls therefor. And there was nothing whatsoever in their mouths except the mention of the Name of Christ [which they uttered] boldly before all those who were of weak disposition and who were to be blotted out speedily, for the sake of the hope of the life which is to come and shall have no end, even as it is said, They rejected riches and despised them, so that they might become in truth the sons of God Most High, and might find life in Christ our Lord. And through this very many were illumined by His glorious doctrine, and they turned from the bitterness of error to the sweetness of the light, and they increased [in numbers], until at length many of the nobles and royal councillors forsook everything in the world and became solitary dwellers in the desert.

[*How King Wadágós issued a decree ordering the persecution and slaughter of the Christians, especially the monks.*]

And when the king heard about this he was filled with exceedingly great wrath, and his indignation burst into flame, and straightway he commanded that a decree should be sent forth from him ordering [his officers] to compel the Christians to deny the True Faith, and to make ready the instruments which were used to inflict punishment and agonizing tortures. And he sent out letters to all the cities that were under his dominion, and to all princes and governors, ordering them to torture and slay with a sharp sword those who believed on Christ, more especially the excellent and understanding men who were in the communities of the monks. And because of these [commands] the minds of many of the believers were greatly disturbed, and the others who [knew] that they could not endure torture submitted to the commandment of the king, which was altogether darkness. And as concerning the princes, and the great men, and the various orders of the monks, some of them rejected the king's command and suffered death and became martyrs, and they attained the state of the beatified which never passeth away. And some of them hid themselves from his face in the mountains, and in deserts, and in holes in the ground, but this was not due to their fear of punishment but to the divine wisdom [that was in them]. And whilst this darkness, wherein there was no profit, was spread over the country of India, the believers were persecuted everywhere, and cruelly treated and oppressed. [p. 6] And the priests of those who denied the Faith revelled in the blood of their sacrifices, and the air was darkened by the smoke of their unclean offerings.

[*How an Indian nobleman who was a great friend of King Wadâgôs embraced the Christian Religion, and retired to a cell in the desert.*]

And it came to pass that when one of the king's nobles, who was held in high honour by the king, and was renowned above all [the other nobles] for his execution of judgement and his victory [in battle] and his greatness, saw these things and heard of the beauty and the strength of the Faith (now it happened that he had been one of those who denied [Christ] and had been a doubter, and was living in this state of error, and in the splendour of the deceitful luxury which passeth away), he joined himself unto the monks of his own good will and pleasure, and he withdrew himself to a desert place, and served there as a servant. And he fought a good fight, and fasted, and prayed, and kept vigil continually, and he read the Divine Books, and he purified his soul and the thoughts of his rational mind, and he delivered himself from all the things that trouble and from all the desire of the passions, and he shone with the light of one in whom the passions of sin were lacking.

[How the desert hunters tracked the nobleman to his cell and brought him back bound to King Wadâgôs.]

Now the king loved this nobleman greatly, and he had heaped honours upon him, and when he heard the story of what had happened to him, his heart was pained because of his defection, and his wrath blazed up fiercely against the monks. And the king sent out messengers to seek for him everywhere, and behold, the nobleman had made his abode in a desert place and the messengers tracked him by means of hunters of the beasts of the desert, and they seized him and [brought him back] and set him up before the throne of the king with [his arms] tied behind [him]. And when the king saw in this state of disgrace, and humility and utter dejection the nobleman who had been in the habit of dressing himself in splendid attire and adorning his person elaborately, and who had led a life of luxurious pleasure and enjoyment, when, I say, the king perceived his beggarly state, and his dire poverty, and his famished condition, and his absolute destitution, which were made known by the expression on his face, the heart of the king was filled with mingled sorrow and anger.

[How King Wadâgôs and the nobleman held converse.]

And the king and the nobleman talked together after the manner of old friends, and the king said unto him, "O thou man who art lacking in understanding, O thou who art of evil disposition, O thou who art astute and art instructed in the doing of evil, what is it that thou wishest for in bringing thyself from riches to poverty, and from a position of greatness and dignity to the state of dishonour wherein I see thee? Once thou wast a prince in my kingdom, and the commander-in-chief of my armies, and behold, thou hast made thyself to be at this moment an object of cursing to [thy] children, for thou hast shown no pity for thy sons. Riches, and all the glory of knowledge [p. 7] are imagined by thee to be as nothing, and thou hast chosen for thyself this contemptible position. And what, prithee, shall become of thy posterity (or end)? And in what way wilt thou gain rest through these things? Thou hast behaved evilly towards all the gods and towards men in paying honour to this Being Who is called Jesus. And thou hast chosen this hard life, and this path of misery rather than a life of pleasure and luxury, with its abundance of dainty food and rich meats and honours."

And when the man of God Most High heard this he made answer unto him with words of wisdom, and quietness, and humility. And he spake unto him thus: "If, O king, thou wishest to enter into an argument with me in words, cast out every enemy which is inside thee, and I will forthwith make answer unto thee concerning everything that thou wishest to know from me; but if thou keepest within thee these enemies I shall be unable to speak one word to thee. And after I have made my speech to thee, pass judgement on me, and do whatsoever thou wishest to do to me. Whatsoever is pleasing to thee that do, for behold, The world is crucified unto me, and I am crucified unto the world, even as my Teacher saith[1]."

And the king answered and said unto him, "Who are these enemies whom ye command me to drive forth from inside my palace?" And the man of God answered and said unto him, "They are [called] wrath and passion (or, lust). All the weaknesses of human nature were sent forth from God at the beginning, and they are in being at the present time, not in those whom the Holy Spirit directeth in the body, but in thee. Thou hast not in thee the Spirit, and thou art wholly and entirely a creature of the flesh, and thou hast in thee nothing whatsoever of the Spirit. And they (i.e. wrath and passion) are become enemies, and shall work in thee the work of hatred and destruction. When passion worketh in thee it exalteth itself arrogantly, and it maketh itself appear as a pleasing thing, and when it ceaseth it produceth wrath. Put thou then away from thee this day these enemies, and let us draw nigh unto the place where the company is gathered together to hear the decision of the word, the decision of the

---

[1] Galatians vi. 14.

judge, and that which is right. [p. 8] And if it be that thou
wilt remove from inside thee wrath and passion, and wilt of
thine own freewill arrive at righteousness and a right judgement, I will then discourse to thee concerning everything."

And the king made answer concerning this and said unto
him, "Speak without fear. Where didst thou find the astuteness whereby thou wast able to set the honouring of a vain
hope before that which we actually have in our hands[1]?"

*[How the nobleman discoursed to King Wadâgôs and de-
scribed to him the vanity of the things that are seen, and
the beauty of the religion of Christ.]*

And the man of God answered and said unto him, "O king,
I would not have abandoned the fleeting things of this world
unless I had secured for myself the things that abide for
ever. Hearken now. Many years ago when I was a little
boy I heard a beautiful and saving word (or, voice), and the
power thereof took possession of me entirely, and there was
sown in my heart the similitude of divine seed, and after
much time it hath sprung up and blossomed ; and behold
thou canst see the fruit thereof with thine own eyes. And
the power of that word (or, voice) is now [directed] to those
who lack knowledge, and who prefer to reject the things that
endure as though they were things that did not endure, and
who take transitory things and treat them as if they were
things that endure. And it is exceedingly difficult for a man
to know how to regard as infirm (or, weak) that which is the
perfection of strength, but he who doth understand their
perfection how can he reject them ? Behold, the Book calleth
the things that are not transitory 'things that endure for
ever[2].' Now the things that are transitory and are poured
out like water belong to this present time and to the day

---

[1] I.e. Whence didst thou obtain the cunning that enabled thee to set the
hypothetical heaven of the Christians above the material joys and pleasures
and riches of which thou wast actually the master ?

[2] Compare "While we look not at the things which are seen, but at the
things which are not seen : for the things which are seen *are* temporal ; but
the things which are not seen *are* eternal." 2 Cor. iv. 18.

which thou seest, and are planted in thy heart. Behold, moreover, in past years I used to look lovingly upon them, and preferred them. But although that power[1] helped me, and stirred up my heart to wakefulness, and guided me to the choice of that which was good and that which was honourable, the law of sin nevertheless overcame my heart, and bound me in fetters of iron, and I became a fettered man, because the affection for things transitory which I had gave me a little excuse. And when I set out on my good and profitable course, and I was baptized in the Name of our Lord Jesus Christ, my God, that very same day, I say, He was pleased to redeem me from that [p. 9] cruel captivity. And immediately He had taken possession of my heart He vanquished the rule of sin, and He opened mine eyes to the full when as yet they were half-closed over a vision of shame and disgrace, and I was able to see. And behold, everything that was apparent to me was vanity, even according to the word of Solomon in his Book[2]. And at that moment the veil of sin wherein I was wrapped was withdrawn from my heart, and the curtain of sin which covered my soul was rent asunder, and the error of the flesh was removed from me, and I knew Him Whom I had found.

"And behold, it was meet for me to follow after the Creator (exalted be His praise!) by performing [His] commandments, and for this reason I forsook everything and followed Him. I give thanks unto God in Jesus Christ Who hath guided me, and hath delivered me from the hand of him that is dense of heart, the Destroyer, the angel of darkness of this transitory world. And He hath shown me a paved path, which is quickly found, whereon I can walk in confidence, and so I am able to choose ignominy in this body which groweth old, for the sake of the divine wisdom which I seek, if only I may find Him by travelling on the road that is straight and sorrow-compelling. And I have chosen the things that are enduring, and have rejected the things that are tran-

---

[1] I.e. the power of the beautiful and saving word.
[2] Ecclesiastes i. 2.

sient, with their risings up wherein there is no permanence, and their revolutions wherein there are many changes and overthrowings. And I have not followed on to acquire any other thing that is true except the True Faith, wherefrom thou hast separated thyself, O king; and it is because thou hast done this that we ourselves are separated from thee at this moment. Behold, thou art fallen into the destruction which is manifest and is well-known, and thou wishest to destroy us, and to bring us into disgrace because of that destruction and worldly cunning. Thou thyself art my witness that I have hidden nothing from thee. And wishing to fight against us, and to carry away the chief thing of our possessions, that is to say, our Beautiful Faith and to cut us off from God, which would be absolute destruction, thou dost hold out to us the offer of honours, and the reward of much-coveted positions of high rank! Why now should I not say that thy riches lack understanding and reasoning thought? [p. 10] For thou rejectest the Elect and Beautiful Faith of God, and dost declare to be righteous the honour that is of the flesh, and that is poured out like water.

"And behold, more especially we see thee, O King, denying God Who permitteth thee to possess thy glory, that is to say, Jesus Christ, the Lord of the Universe, Who is without beginning, Who before the world was existed with the Father, the Creator by His Word of the heavens, and of the earth, and of everything that is therein. And in His wisdom He fashioned man with His own hands, whom He honoured and made king over the earth and of everything that is therein. And He set apart for Him a region that was greater than any kingdom, that is to say, the Garden of Delight, and food grew up for him out of it, and he was seduced by the lust of his body through the envy of the Envious One. And His Creator had mercy upon him, and had compassion upon his tears because of the broken state wherein He found him, saying, 'We fashioned him, and We created him.' He looked with His eyes lovingly upon the children of men because they were the work of His hands; He descended [to earth], the Godhead of His Nature (or, Being) unchanged ; He became a man for our sakes, sin alone being non-existent in Him ; and He was like unto us in His bodily form. And of His own free will He suffered crucifixion and death, and He crushed the crafty designs of the Enemy which he had hitherto worked in our race, and He delivered us from our bitter captivity a second time, and restored unto us our pristine freedom after we had fallen through eating of the tree of evil. And because of His love for man He brought us back, and made us to be worthy of honour that was greater than that which we had aforetime. And although He suffered for our sakes and hath made us worthy of so great glory, thou dost rebel against Him, and dost deny Him, and dost blaspheme the Lifegiving Cross. Behold, the whole of thee is penetrated by the sharp goads of envy, and thou art filled with the passion that destroyeth. And thou givest the name of gods to those miserable and contemptible idols which cannot hear, and cannot see, and cannot speak. But be thou a man of knowledge and discernment.

"I will not submit myself unto thee, and I will not consent to do thy bidding in this matter, and I will not deny Him Who hath done good unto me and delivered me. Supposing thou dost give me to the wild beasts, or dost hack me in pieces with swords, or dost hurl me headlong from the rocks, [p. 11] or dost cast me into the fire over which thou hast power, I am not afraid of death. My heart doth not desire the things that pass away, the worthlessness and transient character of which I know well. What profit is there in them at this present ? Is there any one of them about which a man would care to think uninterruptedly ? And their profitless character is not the only thing, for besides this there are the things that appertain to them, that is to say, much misery, great sorrow, and grief that is endless. The riches of this world are poverty (or, beggary), and the glory thereof is shame. Who can count the unforeseen troubles that may happen through them ? Tell them to me, and recount them to me, O thou who dost dispute with me on the subject of the Godhead. It saith in the Epistle of John, 'Love not the world, nor that which is in the world, for it standeth in wickedness. And all that is therein tendeth to lead astray the body and the eye, and to the increase of sorrow and grief. And the world also passeth away, and the desire thereof, but he who doeth the good pleasure of God abideth for ever[1].' And because of this I myself seek the good pleasure of God which is profitable. And because of this I have forsaken everything and have made myself a companion of those who have gotten possession of this love, and who have sought for this God, and who are neither avaricious nor envious, and who neither sorrow nor grieve. He who travelleth the divine road shall find the habitation that is for ever, which the Father of Light hath prepared for those who love Him. And because of this I have withdrawn myself from the world, and have taken up my abode in the desert, and I await my Lord God, unto Whom I have fled, Who shall deliver me from the oppression of the breast[2] and from iniquity. He is God, and Him will I praise until the departure of my soul [from me]. Amen." With such words did the man of God speak as he stood, fearing only God.

[*How the king in his wrath reviled the Indian convert and bade him flee to the desert lest he should forget his promise to respect his life and should kill him.*]

And the king was filled with anger and fury, and he said unto him, "O accursed man, thou hast forgotten death, and hast made long thy tongue. Had it not been that I promised thee at the beginning of [our] talk that I would expel from within me my wrath and my passion, I would this moment give thee over to the flame of fire. But inasmuch as thou hast set thyself boldly before me, and hast [p. 12] placed confidence in my word, I have endured thine audacity in respect of myself; and besides this thou didst at one time entertain affection for us. Rise up now, and betake thyself to flight from before my face, and if thou refusest to do so I will

---

[1] 1 John ii. 15–17.   [2] I.e. anxiety or, anxious care.

destroy thee with a terrible destruction, and will blot thee out." And the man of God went out into the desert and exiled himself and he continued to fight against the powers of darkness who hold the world of darkness, even as the Apostle Paul describeth them[1].

[*How a son was born to King Wadâgôs.*]

And the king greatly increased the intensity of his persecutions of the company of the monks, and he beautified the temples of the idols with many glorious decorations. And it came to pass that whilst he was living in this state of absolute destruction, and evil error, and bitter cruelty, there was born unto him a man child who was exceedingly handsome in his appearance, and because of the abundance of the grace which surrounded the boy his father rejoiced very greatly. And this was because of the marks of grace that appeared in him, and at length people said concerning him, "There never hath appeared on this earth so gladsome a boy, and never one who was superior to him in beauty." And the king was filled with great joy because of the birth of the child.

[*How King Wadâgôs thanked his gods for his son and consulted the magicians and astrologers as to his future.*]

And he called his name Yĕwâsĕf. And the father of the child, who was lacking in understanding, went into the temple of graven images and offered up offerings to them because of the birth of his son, and he paid honour unto those things that had no heart and that were worse than he was in their lack of understanding. And he ascribed unto them glory, and gave them thanks, and refused to acknowledge Him Who is truly the source (or, cause) of every benefit. It would have been far more seemly for him to have offered up spiritual offerings according to his desire, but instead of doing this he attributed the birth of his son to the idols in which there is no soul. And then he sent messengers into every place so that a great multitude of people might be gathered together

[1] 1 Ephesians vi. 12.

there from his cities, and he made a great and royal feast for all of them, and he paid honours unto them all. And they came and vied with each other in the amount of the offerings that they made ready, and they brought many gifts in honour of the birth of the boy. And there came unto the king [p. 13] a great assembly of men who knew how to make calculations by the stars, and the king had them brought into his presence, and he asked them to inform him what would be the future of the boy who had just been born. And they enquired into the matter very carefully and most thoroughly, and they said unto him, "He shall become great, and renowned, and mighty, and powerful, and he shall be more exalted than any of the kings who have been before him." And one of the learned astrologers, who was most honourable among all those who had come with him, said unto the king, "O king, all the stars make me to know that this child shall never be king in the same way in which thou art king. But he shall be the king of another kingdom which shall be higher in glory than thine own kingdom, nay his kingdom shall, in my opinion, be far more exalted than thine, and I think that he will raise up on high the Religion of the Messiah, which thou art this day driving out from thee. Moreover, according to my opinion it seemeth that his appearance shall be like unto that of a star which shooteth out light[1], and in his word and mind there shall be no false-hood." Now this man did as Bâlâk the king did in times of old. This man did not derive this information by enquiring of the stars, for God (may His memorial be exalted !) by another way and by another means of enquiry revealeth knowledge to His servants, so that He may cut off from them the devices of those who doubt.

---

[1] An old comparison in north-east Africa. Thus Usertsen I is called "Star of the South lighting up the Two Lands" (Champollion, *Monuments*, I. 34, 36) and Thothmes III is likened by the god Amen-Râ to a "revolving star scat-

tering its flame in fire."

(Mariette, *Karnak*, pl. 11, § 15). And Balaam prophesied " there shall come a Star out of Jacob." Numbers xxiv. 17.

[How King Wadâgôs took precautions to seclude his son and to keep him in ignorance of worldly affairs.]

And when the king heard this pronouncement from the astrologer, he received it unwillingly, and by it that astrologer brought sorrow upon his joy. And then he commanded his people to build a beautiful royal palace in his city, and it was to stand alone and away from [other buildings], in one of the most beautiful quarters of the habitable part of the city, and there he placed the habitation of the child ; and when it was finished he commanded the builders to build a strong wall round it. And he appointed a teacher for the child, and attendants who belonged to honourable families ; and their persons were comely and pleasant to look upon. And he commanded them not to make known to the boy anything whatsoever about the trials of life and the sorrows thereof, and they were not to make mention to him of death, or wickedness, or suffering, or poverty, in short, nothing whatsoever that could cut away joy from him. On the contrary, they were to bring to him the things that would amuse and please him, and would help him to pass his time happily, and would bring rejoicing to his heart and mind. And they were to make [p. 14] songs for him, and perform music for him, and they were to do for him whatsoever he wished, so that his heart and mind might rejoice. And they were to make him to enjoy their jokes and merry converse, so that he might never think at all about the last things, and he was never to hear a word of the praise of Christ. And the king commanded especially that the things that the astrologers had foretold concerning him should be carefully concealed from him [as being likely] to frighten him. And he also commanded that if the servants who ministered about his person met with accidents, or fell sick, they were to be sent away from that place, and that others, young men who were sound and healthy in body, should be established in their room, so that the boy might have no experience of sorrowful things and know only of joy. And thus was the king's intention continually, and he was as one who although he had eyes did not see, and although he had a

B.   2

heart (i.e. intelligence) did not understand. Quite well he knew that some of the monks were left [in his country], yet he feigned to think that there were none of them left; and his wrath burned and his indignation against them stirred him. And he sent for the heralds that they might go out into every city and country and make proclamation, saying, "If the people find any kind of monk in our dominions after [the date of] this proclamation, they shall burn them in the fire, for it is they who teach the people to commit themselves to the God Who was crucified." And after this [proclamation] a great commotion, which I remember, took place, for behold, the king's wrath against the monks was bitter, and his anger and indignation waxed greater and greater.

[*How an Indian nobleman who was a Christian succoured a wounded man in the desert, and how his enemies accused him falsely to King Wadâgôs.*]

And there was in the palace a certain man of most exalted station and most honourable rank, and he lived a life of simplicity and faith, and believed in the Blessed Faith, and preserved himself from all impurity; and because of his fear of the king he used to keep himself hidden. And certain men were envious of him, and they laid false charges against him before the king. And one day the king went out to hunt with great pomp and ceremony, according to his wont, and this good man went with him dressed in the garb of one of the huntsmen. And as he was going along by himself at the turn of the day he found a man lying upon [p. 15] the ground, and, behold, one of his feet had been wounded by the bite of a wild animal. And when the wounded man saw that good man he asked him not to leave him [there], but to have compassion upon him and to take him to his abode. And he said unto him, "Thou shalt not lack a reward from me." And the good man answered and said unto him, "I belong to an honourable family. Behold, I will carry thee with thy kinsfolk to the place where I rest. But what is the reward of which thou tellest me?" And that wretched man said unto him, "I am a man who maketh good the voice if it becometh feeble in a man when he is talking. And when because he is unable to draw it forth from himself, [his adversary] revileth him, and he is overcome by him, at that moment, I say, I can heal that man with a profitable healing so that he will no more suffer defeat and reviling." And the nobleman commanded [his servants] to take him to his abode because of the command from on high.

And those envious men whom we have already mentioned proclaimed publicly the words which they had strung together with the help of fraud, and they made accusations to the king against that nobleman, and said unto him, "Not only hath he forgotten thy friendship, but he hath also disgraced thy honour and the honour of the gods. He inclineth towards the belief of the followers of the Messiah, and he stirreth up strife against thy sovereignty, and he draweth men to his Faith. And if, O king, thou desirest to know of a certainty that this is so, have him brought unto thee secretly when thou art alone, and speak unto him cunningly and say unto him, 'O holy man, I wish to abandon the Faith of my fathers and the glory of my kingdom, and I wish to become a Christian, and to put on the garb of the monks, whom in times past I have persecuted, and it was not good that it should have happened through me '."

[How King Wadâgôs feigned to be wishful to become a Christian and deceived his friend.]

Now these men who made false accusations against that good man knew the desire and the beauty of his mind, and for this reason they counselled the king with this counsel so that his deeds might be tested by this ; and these crafty ones joined themselves in a league to overcome that man. Now the king had not forgotten his affection for that excellent man, and he held all that was [p. 16] said about him to be false and unjust. And then he pondered whether the accusations were true, and whether their words were to be accepted without testing them. And because of this he wished to find out the truth of the matter concerning which they had accused him, and he therefore summoned him to a private audience so that he might put him to the test. And he said unto him, "Thou knowest well, O holy man, what I have done in respect of the men who are called 'monks,' and all those who are followers of Christ. Now, behold, I have repented of that, and I wish to become one of these who are waiting for the things that are to be hoped for, concerning which I have heard. They say that that kingdom shall last for ever, and that there is no death in it, and that there is another life which is to come and which hath no end, whereas the present life is put an end to by death. Now, according to what I think, I cannot attain to this life unless I become a Christian, and abandon the pomp of my kingdom, and forsake the desirable things of this world. What hast thou to say to me concerning this? Tell me the truth. With what counsel wilt thou counsel me? I know the truth of thy words, and the good disposition of thy mind towards me, and that in truth thou dost love me more than all [my other friends]."

[*How the nobleman encouraged King Wadâgôs to become a Christian.*]

And when the excellent man heard this from him he did not perceive the deceit that was hidden in the king's heart, and with his pure soul he encouraged him, and with many tears flowing from his eyes he made answer to the king, saying, "O king, live for ever[1]! Behold, thou art now seeking after the counsel that is good. Behold, there doth exist a Good Being, the Redeemer, the heavenly King, and even if the place where He is to be found were remote it would be meet for thee to seek Him with all thy might. Behold, it is said that he who seeketh God shall find Him[2]. And even if the joy and pleasure of revelling in the things of the present world, which are transient, were evident, it is still better to forsake that which is transient and which doth not abide for ever, and to obtain possession of Him Who abideth for ever and in Whom there is no end. Those who rejoice in this world shall sorrow for it with a sevenfold sorrow in the next. The tribulations of

---

[1] For ትየሙ፡ read ሕየሙ፡
[2] 2 Chronicles vii. 14; Matthew vi. 33.

this world are fleeter than the shadow that passeth ; like the
track of a ship sailing through [p. 17] the waves of the sea,
and the track of the bird which flieth through the air, even
so do they pass quickly away. But the hope which is to come,
and for which the Christians wait, is enduring, and those who
suffer in this transient world are rewarded therewith. And
something that is like unto this existeth in thine own kingdom.
If thou, O king, hadst a general who had served thee loyally,
and had helped thee in war, wouldst thou not honour him
more than the other officers, and increase his pay ? Even so
is the hope of the world which is to come ; each man shall be
rewarded according to his work. The sorrows of this world
endure only for a time, and the pleasure thereof lasteth but a
moment, and the sufferings of the followers of the Messiah are
for a few days only, and afterwards there cometh everlasting
pleasure, and death is their reward. And now, O king, be strong
in thy good resolution, and endure patiently, for it is most
pleasing so to do, and exchange the things that are transient,
and lay hold on the things that endure."

[*How the nobleman knowing that he had offended the king,
summoned the man whom he had found wounded in the
desert to help him.*]

And when the king heard these words from him he was
filled with great wrath against him, but he set aside his soul
from indignation, and spake never a word to him at that
moment. And the man whose actions were excellent, was
a man of keen understanding and very wise, and he knew
straightway that his speech was grievous to the king, and he
was very sure that the king had only been trying him with
words; and he returned to his abode pained in heart. And
he pondered in his mind by what means he could soften the
heart of the king, and how he could attain his mercy and
escape from his wrath ; and he passed the whole night in
sleeplessness. And it came to pass that he suddenly remembered the words of the wounded man, and he summoned
him quickly, and said unto him, "I remember thy words and

how thou didst say unto me, that thou couldst set right the word (or, matter) which had gone awry." And the wounded man answered and said unto him, "Yes, I can set it right. Hast thou any wish in respect of this matter that I should show thee my skill in setting right the matter [which is awry]?" Then the excellent man began to tell him how the king formerly had affection for him and had paid him honour, and how he had lately been trying him craftily. Then the sick man collected his senses and said unto him, "Dost thou wish to know, O man [p. 18] who hast been honoured so greatly? The king entertained an evil opinion of thee, and he hath spoken to thee to test thee. Rise up, however, at once, shave off thy hair, take off thy rich apparel, and in its stead put on a garb of sackcloth, and go to the king at the time of daybreak. And when he shall ask thee, saying, 'Why dost thou come into my presence dressed in the garb wherein I see thee?' thou shalt answer and say unto him, 'I have come unto thee in this garb because of what thou didst say unto me yesterday. I have taken the opportunity of coming to thee because it was meet for me to follow thee on the road whereon thou wishest to travel. If it were a matter of re- nouncing something that was very pleasant I should not like to do it without thee; but this path of virtues whereon thou wishest to travel, even were it difficult, if I am with thee it will become smooth and easy. Inasmuch as thou didst make me a partner with thee in the great things of this world, it assuredly is incumbent upon me to become thy partner in the sorrows that are to be'." And the good man accepted the words of the wounded man and did as he had counselled him.

[*How the nobleman shaved off his beard, and went to the king at daybreak dressed in sackcloth, and how the king restored him to his favour.*]

Now when it was dawn the man of God went to the city of the king, and when the king saw him in that garb he said unto him, "What hath happened unto thee?" And the man of God replied according to the instructions which he had received from the wounded man. When the king heard his words he rejoiced exceedingly thereat, and he marvelled at his affection for him, and he knew that those who had made accusations against him had done so falsely and through envy. And he appointed him to many high dignities, and bestowed upon him honours which were greater than any that he had held before.

[How the king met two monks in the desert and burnt them alive.]

And the king waxed wroth with the monks, because, he said, "It is they who teach men to make themselves remote from the pleasures of this world, and they wait for things that they hope for and that will never appear." One day the king went out to hunt wild animals, and he saw two monks walking about in the desert. And he commanded his servants to seize them and set them before him, and he looked at them in wrath, and his heart waxed hot like fire, and he said unto them angrily, [p. 19] "O ye crafty and evil men, did ye not hear the words of the heralds who made a proclamation unto all people, saying that three days after this day none like unto you, who are filthy and disgusting in your garb and appearance, shall dare to appear in the city, or in the country, or in the borders of my dominions, and that if there was any man of them who did so they were to burn him in the fire?" And forthwith the monks answered and said unto him, "According as thou didst command we went forth from thy city and from thy dominions, and we are setting out on the road to our brethren, for we lack food, and we wish to obtain some so as not to die of hunger." And the king answered and said unto them, "He who is hoping for death doth not take the trouble to collect things to eat." And they said unto him, "Thou sayest truth, O king. We are not afraid of death. Why should those who have rejected useless desire flee from death? But it is those who oppress unjustly and who devote themselves ever more and more to the laying up of the things that are transient who do not hope for death, and who accept the good things of this world rather than those that endure for ever. And these same men only acquire with difficulty the things that are transient, and for this reason they fear death. As for us, we are those who hate this transient world, and we travel the road of tribulation and hardship for Christ's sake. We neither fear death nor do we desire the things that are transient, but rather the things that endure and that come afterwards. And the death that will come upon us from you is that which shall bring us to life everlasting."

And the king answered and said unto them, "Why did ye tell me just now that ye are travelling because of my words, and because of my command, if ye were not afraid of death and were not taking to flight? Behold, ye have lied to the king so that ye might vaunt yourselves over his command and say it is nothing." And they answered and said unto him, "We are not afraid [to die], and we are not betaking ourselves to flight, but travel away through pity for thee, so that we may not be the cause of increasing the severity of the punishment and judgement which shall befall thee; and it is for this reason that we have chosen to withdraw ourselves from thy city; as for the tortures which thou couldst inflict upon us [p. 20], it is not because of these that we flee."

And forthwith the king was wroth, and he commanded [his servants] to beat them, and to pile up heaps of wood, and to kindle it, and to make it burn with great flames; and they did even as he commanded, and the monks became martyrs boldly in the True Faith, according to the command of the Most High. Then straightway the king issued an imperial decree, saying, "If any man shall find a monk he shall kill him without obtaining from me permission [to do so] and without taking counsel with any man." And as the king continued in this error no monk of any sort or kind was left in his dominions, with the exception of those who were hidden in the mountains and caves in the hills. Thus was it in those days.

[How Yĕwâsĕf the prince wished to be free from the restraints of his life in the palace, and how Wadâgôs tried to keep from him the knowledge of the existence of death.]

Now the son of the king, of whom we have already spoken, was kept immured in the royal palace which the king had built for him. And when he arrived at the fullness of his powers[1] he had learned all the teaching of the countries of India, and 'Êwĕlâtôn, and Nûbâ (Nubia) and Fars (Persia), and understood [it]. His natural intelligence was not little. On the contrary, it was very great. In person he was exceedingly handsome, and his intellect was bright, and he persevered in his desire to acquire the good qualities that do not pass away. He inclined to the making of experiments, and he tested in his own mind, with great eagerness, the investigations made concerning natural objects, and he asked his teacher such deep questions that everyone marvelled at the acuteness of the young man's mind. As for the king, he used to marvel at the beauty of his person and the wisdom of his mind. And the king commanded those who were with him never to talk to the young prince of anything connected with the troubles of this world, and he even wished to keep hidden from him the coming of death, by making him to see the joys only of this world; but his expectation was a vain hope, and that which happened to those of whom it was said, "And they set their faces towards heaven," came to pass on him. How was it possible to hide from him the knowledge of death as one can hide a human being of flesh? Now it was quite impossible to hide the knowledge of death from the youth's intelligence, for his mind was filled with knowledge. And he used to ponder in his mind what reason his father had when he commanded that he should be kept hidden, and why he would never allow to be brought to him any of those whom he wished to come to him. And the youth pondered over it and said, "If I ask [p. 21] my father to inform me as to the reason of my being kept unseen by the people he will not tell me"; and he sought to find out the reason from others than his father.

[1] I.e. at early manhood.

[How the prince found out why he was kept in the palace.]

And there was one of his teachers who was beloved by him far more than the other instructors whom his father had chosen for him, and because of the greatness of his love for him he used to give him gifts and pay him very great honour. And the king's son called him, and said unto him privily, "Why doth the king wish to keep me imprisoned here? Tell me the explanation of this matter. Thou hast been chosen by me as my friend, from among my nobles, and I would make a covenant with thee, and will love thee for ever." And this teacher was a man of intelligence and understanding, and he knew the youth's ability, and knew that his intellect was perfect, and he said [in his heart], "If I do not tell him [my refusal] will be the cause of my ruin." And straightway he told the boy everything which had been done, and how his father had driven out the followers of Christ, and how they had fled from his cities, and especially the monks who fought the spiritual fight and lived ascetic lives. And he told him also what the astrologers had said at the time of his birth, and he said unto him, "I counsel thee when thou hearest their doctrine not to embrace it in the place of our own Faith. It is for this reason that thy father hath commanded that none of the people about thee shall tell thee of this; and he hath commanded us not to tell thee about the tribulations of this world and the trials thereof."

[How the prince entreated his father King Wadâgôs to allow him to go and see the world outside the gates of his palace.]

And when the king's son heard these things from his friend he began to study them most carefully and seriously, and he laid up his health-giving words in his heart; and from that day he regarded that teacher as a father who comforted him. Now the prince's father used to come frequently to his son's palace to inspect his servants, for he loved him with very deep affection. And one day the prince said unto his father, "O my lord the king, I wish thee to inform me why it is that

I am troubled with a sorrow. It is a never-ceasing sorrow, and it crusheth me and consumeth my soul." And when the king heard these words from him his heart suffered the pain of sorrow, and he said unto him, "Tell me, O my son, my perfect joy, What is the sorrow that overwhelmeth thee? and what is the cause thereof? I will quickly turn it into gladness." And his son answered him, saying, What is the reason for keeping me hidden in a house of restraint, and within walls, and [behind] closed gates? For [p. 22] thou keepest me concealed from the eyes of everyone." And the king said unto him, "O my son, I did not wish thee to see that which would distress thy soul and would carry away joy and gladness from it. I desire thee to live in the pleasure (or, enjoyment) of the world, and to enjoy thyself in every possible way with the things that please the appetite." And the son answered and said unto his father, "It is right that thou shouldst know, O my father, that under my present conditions I do not lead a life of pleasure and joy, but one of sorrow and great sadness. All my food and my drink are exceedingly bitter, and there is no taste therein. I want to see everything that is outside these gates. If thou wishest me not to lead a life of sorrow, give the command that I may go outside, and let my mind be expanded by the sight of the things that I have not seen."

[How the king granted his son's request.]

And the king was sorrowful when he heard these words, and he pondered, saying, "If I prevent him from this it will become the cause of increase in his sorrow"; and the king answered and said, "O my beloved son, I will do everything that thou desirest." And the king commanded his servants to make ready some fine, well-chosen horses, and to put in order armour suitable for the royal use, and [when they had done so] he commanded them to bring the prince out and to escort him wheresoever he wished to ride. And he commanded those who were to accompany him never to permit him to come across anything of a bad or disagreeable character on the road, on the contrary, everything which they were to let him see was to make him to have and to feel pleasure in it. Furthermore, on his journeys there were to be musical entertainments, and exhibitions of gymnasts which excite the clapping of hands, and athletic sports, and various kinds of games, and singing, and dancing and acrobatic feats, so that his heart might flourish by means of these things and so that he might enjoy himself.

[*How the prince set out from his palace with his escort, and how for the first time in his life he saw lepers, and the halt and the blind.*]

And it came to pass that during the days when the prince was taking his pleasure and amusing himself, he saw his soldiers driving away from before them as they were journeying along the road certain men who were sick with the sickness of zĕlgâsê (leprosy or elephantiasis); and among them was one with sores on his body, and another who was blind, and when he saw them his soul loathed them. And he said unto those who were with him, "What are these? What is the matter with them?" Now they were unable to hide the matter from him, for he had seen them with his own eyes. And they answered and said unto him, "These are [p. 23] things wherewith beings of flesh are afflicted, and in this way they happen to come upon men in this corruptible world, and they also come upon the body that possesseth the evil phlegmatic temperament." And the young prince answered and said unto them, "Is it customary for these diseases to happen to all men?" And they answered and said unto him, "It is not usual for these diseases to happen to all men, but only to a few." And he said unto them, "Do men know beforehand when such things will come upon them, or do these diseases come upon them unexpectedly?" And they answered and said unto him, "What man is there who can know what will come upon him? Only the angels who are immortal know this." Then the son of the king ceased to ask them further questions. And the heart of the king's son was sore because of what he had seen, and the beauty of his countenance was changed, and lines of care furrowed his face; and he perceived that he had never seen all there was to be seen.

[*How the prince learned that death is the natural fate of every man.*]

And then after some days as the king's son was passing along the road he met a very aged man whose face was furrowed by care and was very unpleasing to see, and the bones of his legs and feet shook through weakness, and his back was bent, and his teeth had dropped out, and his voice was querulous, and his whole appearance showed timidity and stupidity. And the king's son asked those who were with him, "What is the matter with this man?" And they said unto him, "The years of this man are very many, and his departure is nigh; [his life] is like the lives of the fathers. His strength hath failed and exhausted itself until he hath arrived at the incurable condition wherein thou now seest him, and with every morrow which cometh his limbs will become more and more weak." And the king's son said unto them, "What will be his end?" And they said unto him, "There is left for him nothing except death." And the king's son answered and said unto them, "Doth this death come upon every man or doth it find a few only?" And they answered and said unto him, "Death is ordained for every man, and it is by its means that the end cometh to their lives." And the young man said unto them, "After how many years doth this death come upon a man? Or doth it happen that the coming thereof is not permitted for every man? If there be any pretext which can be found for escaping from this death, why doth not a man escape from it before it cometh?" And they answered and said unto him, "After eighty years a man [p. 24] arriveth at this state of old age, and at that time he dieth; death is the natural penalty that was ordered for all the world from the beginning."

[*How the knowledge of the existence of death affected the prince and how he returned in sorrow to his palace.*]

And when the wise and understanding young man heard this, he groaned from the depth of his heart, and said, "How bitter indeed is this life, being filled as it is throughout with pain and tribulation! If this be the condition attached [to life] sorrow cannot be wanting. Who is there among these who wait for the death which is hidden who would not escape from its coming?" And he departed debating in his mind concerning the transient world, and concerning that which is not transient, and also concerning death. And after this he led a life of pain and sorrow, and he made his soul to remember the coming of death. And he said, "Who will renew like the eagle the memory of me after death if it be that time bringeth oblivion over all men, and if it happen that when I die I shall decay and be no more found? Is there another life? Is there another world?"

And he continued at all times to ponder upon this matter and upon matters that were like unto it, until his countenance became marred and his flesh fell away. And it came to pass that when he appeared before his father he forced himself to assume cheerfulness and to behave like one who was without a sorrow, and he spake to his father never a word about these things; but he longed greatly in his heart to find a wise man unto whom he could declare his thoughts, and who would drop into his ear the word of truth. And he asked him that was over his teachers if he knew of a wise man who would give comfort to his mind, and who would fulfil for him his heart's desire, and he said unto him, "I cannot cast out of my mind anxious thought about this matter." And his teacher answered and reminded him of the words which he had already spoken to him concerning his father, and how he had killed the wise men who were devoted to the truth. And he said unto him, "Like thyself they were always pondering upon this thought and they philosophized upon it in all wisdom, and thy father drove them away in wrath, and I know not where to find one who is like unto them, for not one of them is left in this city." And great sorrow filled the heart of the young man [p. 25], and his mind was sorely pained when he understood this.

[*How the wise man Baralâm, instructed by Divine Providence, disguised himself as a merchant in precious stones,
and went to the country of the king of India to seek an
interview with the prince.*]

And there lived in that city a certain man who had amassed
vast riches, and he made his heart to cling to the place where
his stores of wealth were. For this reason he made his life a
life of sorrow and trouble, and every worldly pleasure was
contemned and renounced by him, and he continued to exist
in a state of tribulation, even whilst he was seeking for things
that were good and excellent. And that Eye which seeth
everything having seen him, the Sustainer of the Universe
was not unmindful to save him, for His wont is to show
lovingkindness unto man, and He revealed unto him the way
wherein he should walk. [Now there was a certain man who]
was exceedingly wise in Divine wisdom and he was adorned
with the glorious excellences of the monks. I cannot declare
unto thee whence he came, or to what race he was akin, but
he lived in a most terrifying desert in the land of Sîlâ (?), and
there he had set his abode. He had attained to the perfection
of divine grace and of his priestly office, and the name of this
old man of God was Baralâm. And when this old man knew
through a divine vision which appeared to him that the king's
son would enter the True Faith, he went forth from the desert
and entered the world. And he changed his appearance, and
put on the apparel which men in the world wear, and he went
to the chief city of the kingdom of India, and he disguised
himself as a rich merchant, and entered into the city wherein
was the palace of the king's son.

[*How Baralâm became the friend of the prince's tutor and
guardian, and how he revealed to him his wish to give a
pearl of great price to the prince.*]

And he passed many days in asking who of all nobles of
the king's son was most intimate with him, and certain men
told him that the teacher of the king's son, whom we have

already mentioned, was his closest friend. And Baralâm went to that teacher when he was alone and spake unto him, saying, "O beloved, I have a matter which I would tell thee. I am a merchant and I have come hither from a far country. I have with me a pearl of great price, the like of which to this day hath never been found, and I have shown it to no one. And behold, I am telling thee of it for I perceive that thou art a man of understanding and discretion and intelligence, and I wish to give it to the son of the king. I ask thee to bring me [p. 26] into his presence, and I will give it to him, and it will be prized by him far more than all the possessions of glorious beauty which he hath. That pearl hath the power to give unto the blind the light of wisdom. It will open the ears of the deaf, and it will make those who are dumb to speak, it will drive away suffering from those who are sick, and restore them completely to health, and it will make fools wise, and will drive out devils, and it will give unto those who gain possession of it all the choicest riches that are to be desired, without deprivation and without greedy desire."

And the teacher answered, saying, "I see that thou art a man of sound wisdom and of healthy understanding, never-theless thy speech maketh it evident that thou vauntest [thy pearl] with vauntings that exceed the limit [of truth]. I tell thee that I myself have seen the royal gems, and with them various pearls of priceless value, and that among them there was not a gem that would warrant the description that thou givest me of thy pearl; and I have never seen or even heard of such a pearl. However, show me the pearl, and if thy speech be true I will bring thee speedily to the king's son, and then thou shalt receive from him forthwith great honours, and, more than this, gifts also. Before thou hast given unto me full knowledge concerning this pearl, and before mine eye hath seen it, it is impossible for me to describe to my lord and king a thing that hath not been seen by me. If thy words of praise of it be true it must indeed be a great and wonderful pearl."

[How Baralâm described the pearl to the prince's tutor.]

And Baralâm answered and said unto him, "True is what thou sayest that thou hast never seen the like of it nor heard of the like of the pearl which I describe, but it is not unworthy of my praise of it, and it is a great and marvellous pearl. As concerning thy wish to see it hearken first of all unto what I am about to say unto thee. Of this glorious and priceless pearl, it used to be said that it worked mighty deeds, and that no man could look at it, more especially a man who was not clear in his vision and pure in his heart, and whose whole being was not free from uncleanness. And if a man who did not possess these [p. 27] two qualities were to look at this gem he would not be able to see it with the sight of his heart. I have not become a fool through the exercise of wisdom, but I am afraid [to show the pearl to thee] lest I become the cause of the destruction of thy sight. But I have heard very much about the delight of the king's son in the exercise of purity, and I have heard that his eyes are clear, and that they consider the doing of righteousness and goodness (?), and therefore I shall make bold to show him this stone. Be not thou jealous then, and do not thou cause thy beloved one to miss this great gift."

And the teacher answered and said unto him, "If this property existeth in the pearl, even as thou sayest, do not show it to me, for from my childhood up to this day I have lived in much sin, and mine eyes, even as thou sayest, are not clear (or, innocent). But I will obey thy voice and I will not be slow in making known to the son of the king, my beloved one, this matter, for he is perfect in his vision, and his power to see is good, even as thou thyself hast said concerning him." And then the teacher departed and came to the son of the king, and related unto him in true order and in all detail the various things which had been told him [by Baralâm].

[*How the tutor introduced Baralâm into the prince's presence.*]

And when Yĕwâsĕf heard the words of his teacher he received them with gladness and with the spiritual enjoyment of his heart, for he found that they were eagerly desired in his soul ; and he commanded the teacher to bring in the wise man quickly. And when Baralâm stood before him he saluted him after the manner that befitted his honour ; and straightway Yĕwâsĕf commanded him to sit down, and his teacher withdrew.

[*The Doctrine of Baralâm.*]

And Yĕwâsĕf said unto the old man Baralâm, "Show me the precious stone concerning the many marvellous qualities of which, according to what my teacher hath related to me of thee, thou dost boast so extravagantly." And Baralâm began to speak in answer and said unto him, "It would be unseemly for me to utter the least word of falsehood before thy Highness, O King. But when thou hast searched out, and enquired into everything that they have told thee concerning me, [thou wilt find] that it is true beyond all doubt. However, without putting to the test thy patience it would not be right for me to show thee [p. 28] the pearl. My Lord spake what I am now going to tell thee : A sower went forth to sow. Some [seed] fell on the road, and the birds came and ate it. And some fell on the stony ground where there was no depth of earth, and when the sun rose upon it, it dried up because it had no root. And some fell among the thorns, and they crowded it and choked it. And some fell upon good ground, and it increased a hundredfold[1]. So I, if I find in thine heart ground that will bear good fruit, shall not be slow in sowing in thee divine seed, and I shall declare unto thee clearly a great mystery. But if the ground is stiff and pebbly, and hath been trodden hard by everyone, it is not meet to sow this seed of salvation in it, lest it become food for the birds and beasts ; for we are commanded before everything not to cast away the pearl to

[1] Matthew xiii. 3; Mark iv. 3; Luke viii. 5.

waste[1]. But it is meet for thee because of the virtues of thy works, which are nigh unto salvation, to see the precious stone, the price whereof cannot be estimated ; and it is meet for thee to see the splendour of its brilliance so that it may shine in thine heart. For thy sake I have come from afar, and I have toiled along a rugged road so that I might shew thee that which thine eyes have never seen, and so that I might make thee to know Him of Whom thou hast never heard."

And Yĕwâsĕf answered and said unto him, "O noble master, with fervent desire, and with longing which hath no limit, I am eager to hear the words that are new and have salvation in them, and are good, and because of this there is a blazing fire in my belly, but I have never before told any one about it. Art thou able in any way to give consolation to my heart in respect of these things ? As for me, if only I could find a man wise of speech, and could hear from his mouth the word of salvation, I would treasure it and would not leave it to the birds, and the beasts, and the rocky ground, and I would not allow the thorns to choke it, according to thine own words. If thou thyself art one who knoweth anything [p. 29] concerning this matter, make me acquainted therewith, and hide it not from me. When I heard that thou hadst come from a far country my soul rejoiced exceedingly, and the beauty of the hope that in thee I should find my desire took possession of me. Thou didst send a messenger unto me speedily, and for this reason I expect that my hope will not be put to shame."

[*The parable of the king who displeased his court by alighting from his chariot and paying homage to two hermits.*]

And Baralâm said unto him, "Thou hast done well in respect of what befitteth the glory of thy kingdom in paying no attention to the material things of this world which are apparent and are transient, and in taking good heed to the hope which is everlasting ; hearken unto what I shall say unto thee. A certain glorious and famous king was once driving a

[1] Matthew vii. 6.

3–2

chariot, plated with gold and inlaid with precious stones, which befitted his great majesty, when he met by chance two men who were wearing mean apparel, and whose faces were thin and pinched. Now the king knew that their bodies had wasted away through their ascetic labours in their wish to gain possession of that which was good, and he alighted from his chariot and cast himself down upon the ground, and he did homage to them, and rose up, and embraced them, and began to kiss them with sincere affection. And the nobles and great officers of his kingdom were vexed with him, and the matter was serious in their eyes because he had done that which it was unnecessary for him to do ; but they hid this in their hearts, and they did not venture to declare their displeasure openly. And they asked his brother to speak to him privily, and to tell him that he must not lower the dignity of the royal crown. And his brother spake unto him even as the nobles of the kingdom commanded him, and when the king had heard him he was wroth with him because of the smallness of his intelligence.

[*The parable of the Trumpet of Death.*]

Now it was the custom of that king when he passed the sentence of death upon a man to send word concerning it by a herald who blew a blast of a trumpet before the door of the house of the condemned man, and this blast was a sign of death, so that all men might know that the penalty of death was meet for him. And when the evening had come the king sent the herald who blew the trumpet to blow a blast before the door of [the house of] his brother, and when his brother heard the blast of the trumpet which was the sign of death, he abandoned all hope of saving his life. And during the whole night he set his affairs in order, and when the morning came he dressed himself in black raiment, the sign of sorrow, and together with [p. 30] his wife and children came to the courtyard of the royal palace ; and he wept and uttered cries of lamentation. And the king had them brought into his presence. And when he saw that the face of his brother was furrowed with care and grief he said unto him, "O thou fool, thou man devoid of understanding more than every [other] man ! If thou art in such a state of fear as this at the mere sound of the blast of the trumpet of the herald, whose nature is the same as thine own, and at the command of thy brother and fellow man who is thine equal in honour and who hath never sinned against thee, why didst thou revile and abuse me for receiving with humility the word of the divine herald, which is more honourable than the blast of a trumpet of this world ? As for me, I believe that I shall die and that I shall meet my Lord Who created me, and against Whom, as I believe in my heart, I have transgressed and committed great sin. And this that I have done unto thee I only did to rebuke thy folly, and to reprove the stupidity of those who urged thee on to rebuke me and to make me to abandon [my good work]." And when the king had rebuked his brother and stabbed him with these words, profit accrued to him [through the rebuke] ; and the king sent him to his house.

[*The parable of the Four Coffers.*]

And straightway the king commanded [his servants] to make four coffers of wood, and to overlay two of them with gold in every part, and to put in them the bones of dead men who were in a very advanced state of decay, and to bind the coffers with bands of gold. And he commanded [his servants] to daub over the other two coffers with pitch and bitumen, and then to place in them precious stones and gems and pearls of great price, and sweet unguents and perfumes, and to tie them round with hair ropes. Then the king commanded his servants to summon those honourable men who had reviled him because he had welcomed the two wretched hermits, [and when they came] they placed before them the four coffers, and the king commanded that they should estimate values to [the contents of] each two of the coffers, and declare them unto him. And the nobles said unto him, "Open for us these two golden coffers, the value of which must exceed very greatly that of the other two coffers"; for their thought was that there must be inside them kingly crowns and girdles of gold, and thus they underestimated the value of [the contents of] the coffers that were daubed over with pitch and bitumen.

And the king answered and said unto them, "Behold, I knew well that ye would speak thus, [p. 31] for your eyes are set upon material things, and they lack discernment. As for us it is not meet that we should be even as ye are, but we desire to see with the inner eyes of our mind what is inside these coffers, whether it be something that is precious or whether it be something that is useless." Then straightway he commanded his servants to open the coffers that were overlaid with gold, and there came forth from them at once a most foul odour of corruption and decay. And the king said unto the nobles, "This is an indication of the similitude of those who array themselves in splendid and costly apparel and boast themselves of their magnificence, but whose inner parts are a mass of corruption which stinketh like the bodies of the dead." And the king commanded his servants to open also the coffers that were daubed all over with pitch and bitumen, so that all those who were present might rejoice in the splendour and beauty of the things that were inside them, and in the sweetness of the perfumes and unguents. And the king said unto the nobles, "Do ye know of what things these coffers are similitudes? They are like unto those humble men who were arrayed in the glorious apparel which is hidden, and whose outward (or, visible) appearance ye yourselves have seen; yet when ye saw that I fell upon my face and did homage unto them, and paid them honour ye thought that it was a disgrace to me. As for me, I with the eye of my heart discerned their great honourableness and the praise that they merited, and I yearned therefor with lowliness of heart, and embraced them and held them in honour far higher than that of my crowns and kingly apparel." With these words did the king rebuke the nobles and put them to shame, and he made them to know that they must not be seduced by the visible and material things of this world, but [be guided] by the hidden things of the unseen world.

[How Baralâm taught the prince the knowledge of God and expounded to him the Parable of the Sower.]

And [Baralâm said unto the prince], "Thou thyself hast done this same thing, O wise king. Since thou hast received me graciously I expect that thou wilt make me to know thy mind, so that thou mayest not be put to shame thereby." And Yĕwâsĕf said unto him, "This word which thou hast spoken unto me is exceedingly good, and it would be pleasant to discuss it, but I wish to know Who is this God of thine Whom thou didst mention a little time ago, and who is the sower that soweth the seed." [p. 32.]

And Baralâm took up his parable and said unto him, "If thou dost in truth wish to know Who my God is, know that He is Christ, the Son of God, the One to Whom alone belong praise, and majesty, and power, the King of kings, the Lord of lords, the Living One Who dieth not, Who dwelleth in light, Whom none can approach, the One Who is the equal in praise (or, glory) of the Father and the Holy Spirit. I am not one of those who believe in gods who have no Law (or, Religion), and I am not one of those who worship them; on the contrary, I hold them to be graven images which have no soul in them. But I worship One God, and I believe that He is glorious with a glory that exceedeth that of the angels of light, and that He hath Three Persons, Father, and Son, and Holy Spirit, and One Nature, and One Substance, and One Praise, and One indivisible Kingdom, Three in His Persons and One God, without beginning and without end; Who existed before the world was, and Who shall exist for ever, Who is uncreate, Who cannot be encompassed (or, contained), Who cannot be touched, Who cannot be seen, Who cannot come to an end, Who cannot be comprehended by the mind, Who alone is Good and Just. He is the Creator Who brought forth the universe from a state of non-existence, both those things which are visible and those which are invisible, and the numerous hosts of the heavens which are invisible, and are without number, and are immortal, and are incorporeal, and are beings of the spirit, who minister unto the Majesty of God the Most High. And He created this visible world, and the heavens, and the earth, and the sea. And He made His own great light to illumine them, and He adorned them. The Heavens He adorned with the sun, and the moon, and the stars; and the earth He adorned with plants of every kind, and with beasts and creeping things; and He set bounds to the seas and placed in them everything which is created in the water, even as it is said, 'They were; He commanded and they were created[1].'

"And man He created with His own hands. He took [some] dust from the ground and created flesh [p. 33] and He gave unto him a rational and understanding soul by means of His own breath, even as it is written, 'He created man in the image of God and [in] His likeness[2].' And as regardeth what it saith, 'In the image of God,' these words refer to his knowledge and his understanding, which is vast, and to his power which dwelleth in him. And as regardeth the words 'in His likeness,' these refer to the exceedingly great power and glory, and dominion which were given to man, and to his mortal nature, and to his being set over everything that is upon the earth, and to his being made king over the same. And God brought forth to him a woman from his side to be his helper. And He planted the Garden of Êdôm in the East and He filled it with all kinds of things that caused joy and gladness, and gave pleasure to the taste. And He set therein the man whom He had created, and He gave him permission to eat of all the divine plants with the exception of one, and He laid down the commandment that he should never eat of one tree at all, whereof the name was '[the tree] of the knowledge of good and evil'; and He said unto him, 'The day wherein ye eat therefrom ye shall die.'

"And one of those angelic Powers whom we have already mentioned, the chief of one order [of angels] wherein no trace of natural evil had been created, but only good, by his own desire, and by his own authority departed from good to

---

[1] Psalm cxlviii. 5.   [2] Genesis i. 27.

evil, and magnified himself and rebelled against his Lord. And because of this he fell from his rank, and he exchanged honour and riches [for disgrace and poverty], and instead of being called 'angelic one' was called 'rebel.' And God cast down him that had been deemed worthy of the highest honour, and those who were under his dominion and whose wills and desires were evil fell down also, and they were called 'corrupt' and 'erring' ones; and they denied utterly life and salvation, and they gained possession of an evil and corrupt freedom. And the chief of these angels, when he saw the greatness and the glory that had been given to the man, was jealous of him, he himself having fallen from this state of glory, and he wove crafty schemes whereby he might cast the man forth from that blessed life which he was leading. And he made the [p. 34] serpent a weapon which would act craftily for him, and he went to the woman and seduced her, and she ate of that tree concerning which God had commanded them that they should not eat. Now Adam and his wife ate thereof through their desire to possess the nature of God, and through the seduction of Satan. And the first plasma, that is to say the first man, having turned aside and eaten of the tree of wickedness, became hateful to his Creator, and he was driven out of the Garden of Joy, and he fell from the blessed state of life and existence, wherein there was no corruption, into the wretched and miserable life of this world, and God passed upon him the decree of death for his end. And thereupon Satan obtained the power of the conqueror, and he boasted himself of his victory, and when the race of man multiplied on the earth, he made easy for them every path of wickedness.

"And because of this God, the Most High, wished to abate the growth and the increase of sin, and He brought a flood upon the earth, and destroyed every soul of life. And in those days God found only one righteous man, and He saved in a ship him, and his sons, and his wife alone on the earth. And when the children of men multiplied on the earth they forgot God, and they turned aside to apostasy and wickedness, and they worked the works of sin of every kind to their utmost ability and they made themselves slaves thereto. And they polluted themselves with works of abomination, and they divided themselves into tribes according to their races (?), and they acted towards God with the deceit that engendereth destruction. Some of them believed that all created things were made by their own will and power, and that they had neither Creator nor God Who commanded them to come into being. And some of them worshipped evil gods, who multiplied diseases so that men might obtain knowledge of them through the sicknesses which they inflicted, and they became helpers of these gods in their evil works. And they took to the making of images for themselves in their own forms and likenesses, [that is to say] idols in wood and in stone, deaf things which could not move; and these they worshipped in the place of the Creator, and they bowed down to them and sacrificed offerings [p. 35] unto them. And other men worshipped the sun, and the moon, and the stars, which God appointed to illumine this world; they have no souls and cannot breathe, but by the wisdom of God the Creator they maintain their strength, and they are incapable of doing anything of their own free will. And some men worshipped trees, and were unashamed, and although they were rational beings who possessed a soul capable of reasoning, they paid divine honours unto these objects. And other men worshipped wild beasts, and hyenas (or, wolves), and animals that go on four feet, and they offered service and gifts unto them, although they knew well that they possessed wholly different natures from those who worshipped them.

"And others called the statues of unclean and abominable human beings 'gods,' some of them being statues of men and some of them statues of women. And they openly declared that certain of these human beings had been whoremongers, and murderers, and men of wrath, and seekers of vengeance, and men who hated (or, were jealous of) their fathers and brethren, and thieves and robbers, and men who were lame, and decrepit, and infirm and paralytic. And of these some died, and some became mad whilst they were worshipping men, and they continued in their error, and they mourned and lamented in their tribulation. And because of the abomination of their perverse and unclean works the darkness of evil spread itself over our race during those years, and there existed no wise man who sought after God.

"And in those days there was found a perfect man whose name was Abraham, and the thoughts of his soul were good, and healthy, and strong. He it was who learned to know the Wise Artificer through the observation of His creations, which he saw in examining the heavens, and the earth, and the sea, and the sun, and the moon, and all the things which had been created, and the places wherein they existed. And when he looked upon this world, and everything that is therein, he knew and understood that all these works had a Creator, and that they were not created by themselves; and he knew that their subsistence was due neither to terrestrial beings nor to the graven images wherein was no soul. And he knew that this Wise Being was God indeed, and that He was the Creator [p. 36] of the Universe, and that his Essence (or, Being) existed in all the Universe, and that He had brought it into being from a state of non-existence. And God accepted his good thoughts, and his right understanding, and He revealed unto him that He Himself was God in His Being (or, Essence or, Nature). Now even the holy beings are not able to look upon the most high Being of God, but by the wisdom of His Godhead it is revealed unto them according as He wisheth. And He placed in his heart perfect knowledge, and He appointed him to be His messenger, because the faith that had sprung from him was good, having been tried in the balance, and He taught him to know God, and God was pleased to make for him a multitudinous seed, which could neither be numbered nor limited. And God called them a weighty (or, solid) and a peculiar nation.

"And the Egyptian people, and Pharaoh, their mighty, powerful, and oppressing king, made them their servants, but God brought them out from Egypt by the hands of Moses and Aaron, who were holy men, and whose faces were illumined with the splendour of prophecy, with a bringing out which was bold and awe-inspiring, and with signs and wonders, and deeds which struck [the Egyptians] with amazement. And He drowned the Egyptians, as their wickedness merited, and He made the Israelites, the seed of Abraham, to pass through that awful sea, the waters whereof were divided and became a wall on the right hand and a wall on the left. And when Pharaoh, and his horsemen, together with the Egyptians, willed to follow after them, the waters flowed back over them, and destroyed them altogether. And this people dwelt in the desert, seeing signs and wonders, for forty years, and God fed them with heavenly bread. And He gave them the Law on tablets of stone which was written by His own fingers, and He delivered it to Moses on the top of the mountain. And that became a sign and a symbol unto those who wished to withdraw themselves from the worship of idols, and from all evil works, to teach them the worship of God, the Righteous God, Who is for ever, and to enable them to acquire excellence in their works. And with such signs as these He [p. 37] brought them out, and [led them] until He brought them to the land of beautiful and bright things, which in days of old He had promised to that Patriarch Abraham to give unto his seed. Now, if we wished to inform [thee] concerning everything that happened to the seed of Abraham, that is to say, the innumerable miracles and stupefying things, we should make our narrative too long, but in spite of all this we desire to tell the story of God's will. It was the good pleasure of God to raise up the race of the children of men from serving under the slavery of wickedness and from the commission of sin, and He wished to restore them to the position that they had formerly occupied. But the beings of our nature found that they were involved in the cunning of the Law, and that they were under the compulsion of Satan, who ruled over them and made them to serve him in every way, and who carried them off to Sheol, where he took vengeance upon them.

"But although we had fallen into the most abject state of misery and tribulation, our Creator was not unmindful of us,

and He brought us forth out of a state of lacking everything
into one of being well provided. And He did not reject the
creature He had fashioned, and the work of His hands, and
He took care that we should not perish utterly. On the contrary, by the good pleasure of God the Father, there came
down the Only Son, the Word of God Who is from everlasting, from the bosom of the heavenly Father, Who is
co-equal with the Holy Spirit in His Nature, Whose existence
preceded times, Whose Essence (or, Being) was before the
world, Who is equal with the Father, Who is without beginning, God for ever. He came down to His servants, a marvellous descent! which cannot be comprehended. The God
Who is for ever, the First One, became a man in every
respect by the Holy Spirit and MARY, the holy Virgin, the
God-bearer, not by means of human seed or by human will.
He was not conceived by carnal union in the womb of the
Virgin, whose purity was perfect, but by the Holy Spirit
according [to the words] of one of the Archangels whom He
sent and who announced to the Virgin this unusual conception [and] this bringing forth which is indescribable. And she
conceived the Son of God by the Holy Spirit without the seed
of man. His own seed was in the womb of the Virgin, and
a living Man with a rational and understanding soul was
brought forth, and He preserved the virginity of His mother
[p. 38] unopened (or, unbroken). And He was like unto us,
with the exception only of sin, and He became the Redeemer,
and He bore our suffering, and through His coming into the
world we received freedom. And He was pleased in His compassion to redeem us from death by His own death.

"Little by little He grew up among men. In His thirtieth
year he was baptized in the river Jordan by the hand of
John, who was perfect in holiness, and a Voice came from
heaven, from God the Father, saying, This is My Son, Whom
I love, in Whom I am well-pleased[1]; and the Holy Spirit
descended upon Him in the form of a dove. And from that
time He began to work mighty miracles, and astounding

[1] Matthew iii. 17.

wonders: He raised the dead. He made the eyes of the blind to see the light. He cast out devils. He healed those who were diseased. Those who were leprous He cleansed and restored them wholly (?). Also He changed our nature, and admonished our souls with His commandments. He taught us the path of excellences, and removed us far from corruption, and guided us to the life which is for ever. Then He chose for Himself disciples, twelve men, whom He called 'Apostles,' and He commanded them to preach unto all men the heavenly life, which He came upon the earth to reveal, and by His wisdom we have become perfect. He graciously granted unto us earthly beings baptism, and [so] made us heavenly beings.

"And the chief priests and the leaders among the Jews envied Him, because He held authority among them. And they were angry with the signs and wonders, which we have already mentioned, and which He used to perform before them; all these things they forgot and they passed sentence of death upon Him. And having taken one of His disciples, who betrayed Him unto them, they seized Him forthwith and they brought Him, the Life of the Universe, to the people by His own good pleasure, as He Himself had wished aforetime. For our sakes He came and bore all our sufferings, so that He might release us from suffering. And they perpetrated many wickednesses upon Him, and finally they condemned Him to death on the Cross, and He endured everything in His human body, which He had taken from us. They crucified the [human] body of Him who was without [p. 39] sin, our Lord Jesus Christ, Who was innocent of sin, and falsehood was not found in the mouth of Him Who did not deserve death. As I said before, because of sin death entered the world, and it was therefore meet that the Redeemer of the world should be without sin. He died in the [human] body for our sakes, so that he might set us free and redeem us from the slavery of death and sin. He went down into Sheol and shattered the bolts thereof, and He set free the souls of the prisoners who had been there before times [were]. They laid Him in a grave, and on the third day He arose. He conquered death and gave unto us an incorruptible inheritance. And He appeared unto His innocent disciples and bestowed upon them 'Peace!' And He deputed to them the guidance of every man into the path of righteousness. After forty days He went up into heaven, and sat on the right hand of the Father, and He shall come again in glory to judge the living and the dead, and He shall reward every man according to his work.

"And after His Ascension into heaven in glory He sent the Holy Spirit unto His disciples in the form of tongues of fire, and they began to speak each in his own language according as the Holy Spirit gave them power. And then, by His grace, they were sent out among all nations, and they preached unto them the True Faith, and baptized them in the Name of the Father, and of the Son, and of the Holy Spirit; and they gave at all times strength and encouragement to the nations, which had been led into error by their own teaching, so that they might keep the Commandments of salvation. And they made powerless the fear of devils and the error of idols; nevertheless, even at the present time Satan seduceth the simple in heart and those void of understanding, so that he may yoke them to the worship of idols. But his power is not what it was formerly, and by the might of Christ, our God for ever, it is becoming very much weaker.

"And behold, I have now made thee to know [Him], and I have revealed unto thee the compassion of our Lord and Redeemer Christ, to Whom be praise to time of time (i.e. for ever). Amen. And behold, from this time onward thou knowest Him, and thou must devote thyself to this work, even as thy soul hath received His exalted grace, and even as it is meet for thee to be His servant."

[*How the prince received Baralâm's doctrine, and besought him to instruct him in the other mysteries of the Christian Religion.*]

[p. 40] And when Yĕwâsĕf, the king's son, heard these words, divine light sprang up in his heart, and he rose up from his

throne rejoicing and glad, and he embraced Baralâm, saying,
"O most honourable of all men, by my faith, thou hast not
lied in one word concerning that precious stone, that pearl of
great price which is in thy possession. Behold, a mystery is
hidden with thee; reveal it now to those in whom the thought
of their souls is healthy and right. As for myself, behold,
I accepted this word as soon as I heard it, and there flashed
upon me a great light, which was exceedingly pleasant, and
it took up its abode in my heart, and it tore aside and destroyed
quickly the veil of heavy sorrow which enveloped my mind.
If there be any other thing that thou knowest do not refuse
to reveal it unto me, but make me to know it."

[*How Baralâm emphasized the importance of baptism, and
how the prince entreated him to prepare him for baptism.*]

And Baralâm answered him, saying, "Yea, my lord the king,
this is a great mystery which was hidden before the generations
of men and times were, but in the last days it hath appeared
to the race of the children of men; and the Prophets prophesied concerning it by the grace of the Holy Spirit. Many
have had knowledge of this in different ways, and by signs
each of which was different in kind, but it is only this last
generation that hath been held worthy to have salvation committed to it. He who hath believed and hath been baptized
shall be saved, and he who believeth not shall be condemned
in the Judgement[1]."

And Yĕwâsĕf answered and said unto him, "I believe everything that thou sayest unto me, and I will worship the God
of Whom thou tellest me, and about Whom thou givest me
knowledge. But reveal unto me unsparingly everything, and
teach me what is right for me [to do] that I may be baptized.
And what is this baptism which thou hast mentioned unto me?
Explain to me this baptism very thoroughly."

And Baralâm said unto him, "[Baptism] is the foundation
of the holy Faith of the followers of the Messiah wherein
there is no blemish, and divine baptism is a sure foundation,

[1] Mark xvi. 16.

and it purifieth from sin, and it washeth away impurity of
long standing. Our Redeemer commanded thus: Men shall
be born again of water and of spirit, and they shall return to
their [p. 41] former position by prayer and supplication. And
it is called saving (or, redeeming) through the descent of the
Holy Spirit upon the water. And for this reason they baptize
with Christian baptism, even as our Lord, to Whom be glory!
saith, 'When ye baptize them say, In the Name of the Father,
and of the Son, and of the Holy Spirit[1].' In this manner it
maketh the grace of God to take up its abode in his soul, and
to illumine it, and it shall make him an equal in inheriting
the inheritance which is incorruptible, and he shall find everlasting life, for he shall be born again. And without Christian
baptism no man shall find that profitable hope, even though
his works were better than those of men who are wholly devoted to God. Thus saith the Word of God, Who was made
man for our salvation, 'Verily, verily, I say unto you, he who
is not born again of water and of spirit cannot enter into the
kingdom of God[2].' As for me, I wish before everything that
faith may be transmitted to thy soul, and that thou wouldst
draw nigh to Christian baptism. There is no man to prevent
thee; he who would prevent thee is a great sinner. [The hour
of] Death is a hidden mystery."

[*How the prince asked Baralâm to explain to him the profitable hope, and the kingdom of heaven, and Death, and the
Other World.*]

And Yĕwâsĕf answered and said unto him, "What is this
profitable hope of which thou tellest me, and which a man
cannot attain to without Christian baptism? And what is
this kingdom of heaven which thou hast named unto me?
And where didst thou hear the story of this God Who became
man? And what is this hidden hour of Death which is planted
in my heart, and maketh me to think overmuch, and burneth
up my body with pain, and devoureth my strength and my
bones? If it be that we are mortal men who must be destroyed,

[1] Matthew xxviii. 19.　　　　　[2] John iii. 5.

and there is no other world after we have departed from this world, in justice there cannot exist another world which He hath ordered for Himself [alone]."

And Baralâm said unto him, "The profitable hope about which I tell thee is the hope of the kingdom of heaven, concerning which the Book saith, 'Eye hath not seen, and the ear hath not heard, and it is impossible for the heart of man to imagine what God hath prepared for those who love Him[1].' If we are worthy [p. 42] to abandon the weight of this body and we find that blessed state, then He will teach us to make ourselves worthy to find that hope, and He will make us to understand those beautiful things, and the glory that is exalted above all imagining, and the light that cannot be comprehended, and the life that never endeth, so far as the nature of man hath the ability; then thou wilt know what thou canst not know now. And this teaching which I declare is [derived] from the Books of the Spirit, and if one is unable to make known concerning the glory, and the light, and the good things, and to describe them, it is not a matter to wonder at. If it happened that we could comprehend them with our minds, and that we, who are beings of earth who grow old and who are clothed with this heavy, and infirm, and suffering flesh, were able to praise them with our words, would it not be a glorious and wonderful thing? And as for Him Whom we know because of these glorious things, the belief in Him thou shalt receive for its own sake, without any doubt, and thou shalt make haste to do good works whereby thou shalt obtain a kingdom which is lasting, wherein there is no death, and wherein thou shalt, if thou art worthy thereof, enjoy perfect knowledge.

"And as concerning that which thou didst say unto me, 'Where didst thou hear the story of God Who became incarnate?' know thou of a certainty that we have obtained our knowledge of all His works from the words of the honourable Gospel. And the name of this holy Book [is] 'Announcer of good news.' He proclaimed for us mortal beings of dust when

[1] Isaiah lxiv. 4 ; 1 Cor. ii. 9.

He was here upon this earth not death, and not corruption, but life for ever in the kingdom of the heavens. Those who wrote the Book were messengers of the God Whom they saw with their own eyes, and I have already told thee that Christ our Redeemer chose them, and made them His Disciples and Apostles. It is they who have delivered unto us the Gospel after His Ascension into heaven, and they who have declared unto us His wise words, and His teachings, and His wonders. No man is able to tell His history and describe His teachings [adequately], neither by writing nor by word of mouth, even as saith John, the glory of the Evangelists, whose excellences in the perfection of speech of his Gospel surpass all the other Evangelists, 'This did [p. 43] Jesus, and there are many other things which He did, and if each and every one of them were to be written down the world would not suffice to hold the great number of the books about Him which would have to be written[1].' And in this holy Gospel there are written down, by the wisdom of the Holy Spirit, His pure work in the flesh, and the manifestation of His wisdom, and His wonders, and the ordering of His commandments, and also the story of His sufferings which He endured for our sakes, and of His Resurrection on the third day, and of His Ascension into heaven, and concerning His second coming in glory and great majesty. For the Son of God shall come in glory indescribable with a multitude of heavenly hosts to judge our race, and to reward each man according to his works.

"For in the beginning God created man from the dust of the earth, as I have already told thee, and He breathed into him the breath of life, and it is that breath which is called the rational and understanding soul. And then He rebuked us by the judgement of death which was to kill us, and this cup cannot pass from us, and it is for every man alike. And this death is the separation of the soul from the body, and this flesh (or body), which was created from the earth, returneth to the earth whence it was taken, and it perisheth and falleth into corruption. And the soul, which is immortal,

[1] John xxi. 25.

goeth to the place to which it is ordered by the Creator, which He prepared for it whilst it was in its body; there every man is rewarded according to the work that he doeth here. And our Lord Christ shall come again after many years in glory which is indescribable, and which is as strange as is its exceedingly terrible awfulness. And the powers of heaven shall be shaken, and all the hosts of the angels shall stand before Him, and the dead shall rise up at the sound of a blast from the trumpet of God and shall stand up before His awful throne. This is the Resurrection. The soul shall return again to its body, and the body shall be in a state of great fear and terror, and shall be exceedingly sorrowful, and the word of doom shall go forth against it and against the soul also, and at length He shall raise it up again [p. 44], turning it from one state of being to another, just as He did when he created it at the beginning; for its creation for the first time was better than its non-existence. And now those states of being are separated, and He bringeth them back to what they were originally. And the bringing together by the Creator of the creatures which He fashioned is a small matter, in respect of difficulty, in comparison with the bringing of them out of a state of non-existence when they were not. And if thou wilt consider very carefully how God created and brought into being the things that were not in being, and set them for thyself as a similitude, this careful consideration shall be a light unto thee, which shall be sufficient [to inform] thee.

"For at the beginning He took the dust of the earth and created therefrom a rational man, but inasmuch as the earth did not exist in the earliest time, how was it that the earth became a rational man? And how did it send forth out of itself the families of the beasts, and the multitudes of wild beasts and creeping things, and the multitudes of trees and plants which bear fruit? And moreover, consider and understand the creation of us children of men. A little drop of seed is poured into a womb, but whence doth the womb which receiveth it obtain the power to fashion [from it] the bones of the living being which resulteth? And since we know that He

created before the Universe was, and we can see that from
the beginning to the end He hath created in this manner, is it
impossible for Him to raise up from the earth him that
sleepeth? The two of them (i.e. the body and the soul) are
separate things by His own commandment, therefore the
bringing of them back is an easy matter for Him. If it were
too difficult for Him to perform this, seeing that that which
is material and that which is immaterial join together, how
could that which hath weight and that which hath no weight
become associated? And in like manner He bringeth to the
bodies which are mortal their souls which are immortal, after
the manner of deposits which men have laid up in safety until
the time when they return to their houses; and the house
shall be raised up at the time of His coming to reward in
righteousness every man according to his work.

"And behold it is said that this present world produceth
the opportunity, and that the world which is to come rewardeth
the same, for it (the opportunity) did not exist before, and the
integrity of God is justice. Behold, many righteous men have
toiled in this world and God hath punished them heavily and
slain them; and again there have been many half-hearted
men who have transgressed the Law of God, and yet they have
ended their lives in pleasure [p. 45] and restfulness, although
they lived in great comfort and luxury. And God, the Most
High, the Good and Just, hath ordained the day of the Resurrection so that He may make manifest His compassion, and
bestow rewards. Behold, sinners have received in this world
the good things thereof, and behold, in the next world they
will suffer torment for their transgressions and sins. Behold,
those who are good suffer more torture than sinners in this
world, but they depart to the things that are good, and they
inherit the pleasure that is everlasting. Our Lord saith[1]:
Those who are in the graves shall hear His voice, and those
who have done good shall go forth to the Resurrection of Life,
and those who have done evil shall go forth to the Resurrection
of the Judgement. The throne shall be set, and the Creator of

[1] Compare Matt. xxv. 31–46.

the Universe shall sit upon it, and what is written in the
Books, that is to say, our works, and our words, and our
thoughts, shall be revealed. And the River of Fire shall flow
forth, and all the things that are [now] hidden shall become
manifest. At that time there will be nothing that can help a
man, neither the words of an oath, nor the answer with words
of falsehood, and riches and money will avail a man nothing.
He will have regard neither for rank and dignities, nor for the
giving of gifts, for He is the Judge Who doth not accept
bribes, but He will judge every man in His balance of justice,
and He will give unto those who have done good everlasting
life, and never-ending pleasure, which cannot be described.
And they shall rejoice with the angels, being worthy of the
enjoyment of the good things which are of such varied kinds
that they cannot be described. And they shall stand boldly
before the Holy Trinity.

"And those who have done evil things shall [go] unto [the
place of] everlasting torture, which is called Jahânam, and
they shall depart to the uttermost limit of darkness, and to
the gnashing of teeth, and to woe, and, what is far worse than
all these things, to remoteness from God, and exile from before
His face, and the lack of indescribable glory, and shame and
disgrace before all created beings. And their shame and their
casting away shall have no end. When the time of the punishment of the awful Judgement hath passed, every creature shall
live without change and alteration, and the life of the Righteous
shall be without end. And the punishment of the sinner shall
be unending, for there is no other Judge who is more exalted
than this Judge to come after this One. [p. 46] There will
therefore be no performance of deeds a second time, and there
will be no reconsideration of what He hath done, and there
are no excuses that can be accepted from those who suffer
torture, and they shall endure the judgement of torture for
ever.

"Since then the matter is thus it is meet that our lives
should be [passed] in holy wisdom and sincere piety, so that
we may be worthy of salvation and of the hope that is to

come. And may He make us to share the standing place on
the right hand of the Son of God where shall stand those
righteous ones whom God hath called, saying, 'Come, ye blessed
of My Father, and inherit the kingdom which is [without]
end[1].' Amen."

*[How the prince asked Baralâm to give him more definite
proofs for his belief.]*

And when Yĕwâsĕf heard these words he answered, saying,
"Behold, O man, thou hast related unto me exceedingly great
and wonderful things which are meet to be received with fear
and much trembling. Even supposing the matter be thus, and
there follow after death and corruption the Resurrection, and
a second life, and punishment for the deeds that we have
committed during life in this world, by what means is this
known? Where didst thou obtain thy knowledge about these
things which thou hast not seen? What maketh thee certain
that they are thus? Why dost thou hold them to be true and
believe them without doubt? Hath any of these things appeared unto thee, and hast thou seen them, or hast thou heard
about them through the words of those who praise them?
And as for these invisible things which thou proclaimest,
seeing that they are of such limitless greatness, why dost thou
believe concerning them with firm faith?"

*[How Baralâm adduced proofs of the Resurrection from the
Old and New Testaments.]*

And Baralâm answered, saying, "We have received this
faith from the preachers of righteousness who have not added
anything to the true word, but who have performed signs and
marvellous wonders, and have made [men] to know and have
confirmed the words that have been said about the things that
are to come. And as they did not do in this world anything
wherein was error, but in everything which they said and did
there sprang up a shining brilliance which is brighter than the
light of the sun, even so did they lay down as laws for them-

1 Matt. xxv. 34.

selves the things which are to be believed. These our Lord Jesus Christ [p. 47] strengthened by word and deed, saying thus, 'Verily, verily, I say unto you that the hour shall come and now is, that the dead shall hear the voice of the Son of God, and those who hear it shall live[1].' And He also saith, 'Behold, the time shall come, and all those who are in the grave shall hear His voice, and those who have done good things shall go forth to the Resurrection of Life, and those who have done evil to the resurrection of punishment[2].' And again He saith concerning the resurrection of the dead, 'Have ye not read what is written, how God saith, I am the God of Abraham, and of Isaac, and of Jacob? He is not the God of the dead, but the God of the living[3].' And as [men] gather together the tares and burn them in the fire, even so shall it be at the end of the world. The Son of Man shall send His angels, and they shall gather together the doers of sin, and cast them into a red-hot furnace, where there shall be weeping and gnashing of teeth. Then shall the righteous shine in the kingdom of their Father like the sun[4]. And He saith thus, 'He that hath ears that hear let him hear[5].' With words like unto these and many others did our Lord Jesus Christ reveal unto us the resurrection of our bodies.

"And He made us to know His words, for He Himself raised up many dead persons when He finished the work of His glorious Will upon earth. And besides these He summoned from the belly of the grave His friend, whose name was Lazarus, after he had suffered corruption, on the fourth day, and He raised him up a living man[6]. And moreover, He Himself being God was the beginning of the resurrection of the dead, and He was the first-fruits of our resurrection also[7], and did not come under the dominion of death, but He tasted death in His body which He made the curtain for our rest, and He rose from the dead and became unto them the first-fruits of the resurrection for them all. And thus He fulfilled the words

---

[1] John v. 25. [2] John v. 28, 29. [3] Matt. xxii. 32.
[4] Matt. xiii. 38–43. [5] Matt. xiii. 9, 43. [6] John xi. 39, 44.
[7] 1 Cor. xv. 20.

of the Prophets of old who proclaimed the glad tidings of the resurrection to the dead and to all created beings. Paul the Apostle saith ; 'My call was not from men but from heaven[1].' This he saith rebukingly, making known unto you, O our brethren, that the story which I have handed on, and which ye yourselves have handed on was received by me in the beginning. [p. 48] Christ died for us sinners, even as the Scriptures say[2]. And if they preach concerning Christ, there being no resurrection of the dead, and if the dead rise not, Christ Himself hath not risen from the dead, and if Christ hath not risen, an empty thing is our death in this life. Hath not Christ redeemed us by Himself, and tasted that cup for the sake of man? And behold, Christ did rise [from the dead] and He became a type for us. For through one man death came, and through another the resurrection of the dead came, and as because of Adam they shall all die ; so in Christ they shall all live[3]. And a little further on St Paul saith, This which is old shall put on that which is not old, and this mortal shall put on that which shall not die. Then shall be fulfilled the word of the Book which saith, Death is swallowed up in victory. Where is thy sting, O death? Where is thy victory, O Sheol[4]? At that time death shall be wholly annulled, and its power shall be destroyed, and its operation shall cease for ever, and men shall find immortality and incorruptibility. And beyond doubt resurrection shall be given to the dead.

"And this we believe unhesitatingly, but it is meet for us to know and to be sure that there will be reward and punishment according to what we have done in this transitory life, on the day of the coming of our Lord Christ, when the heavens shall melt, and the corners of the world shall burn and flow away[5], even as the theologians say. Behold, we shall see new heavens, and a new earth. There shall [men] be rewarded for the good and the evil which have been wrought [by them], and for their words and the thoughts, with the reward which befitteth them. Our Lord, to Him be glory ! saith, 'Whosoever

---

[1] Gal. i. 1, 12.   [2] Romans v. 8.   [3] 1 Cor. xv. 12–22.
[4] 1 Cor. xv. 53–55.   [5] 2 Peter iii. 12.

shall give, if it be only a cup of cold water, to one of these little ones, his reward shall not be destroyed.' And He saith also, 'When the Son of Man shall come in His glory and all the holy ones His angels with Him, and when all the nations shall be gathered together before Him, He shall separate each kind of them even as a shepherd separateth the sheep from the goats, and He shall set [p. 49] the sheep on His right hand, but the goats on His left. Then the King shall say unto those who are on His right hand, Come, O ye blessed of My Father, inherit the kingdom which was prepared before the world was created. For I was hungry, and ye gave Me to eat; I was thirsty, and ye gave Me to drink ; I was a stranger, and ye provided Me with an abode; I was naked, and ye clothed Me ; I was sick, and ye visited Me ; I was in prison, and ye comforted Me[1].' And in another place He saith, 'Whosoever shall confess Me before men him will I confess before My Father Who is in the heavens[2].'

"Behold, He hath revealed unto us all these things concerning the reward for good works which shall abide for ever. And He hath also told us concerning the punishment of the Judgement which shall come upon the wicked by means of the marvellous parable, in the narrative of which is a fountain of wisdom: 'There was a certain rich man who arrayed himself in apparel of scarlet *bîsôs* (byssus), and who enjoyed himself every day, and in whom there was no compassion for the wretched. And there was a beggar whose name was Lazarus lying in his courtyard, and there was none to give him anything, not even the crumbs of his table. And both of them died, and they took the beggar [who was covered with] sores to the bosom of Abraham, which is the abode of the righteous, and the rich man they took to the torture of Jahânam, and to him Abraham saith, Behold, thou didst enjoy thyself during thy life, and so also Lazarus suffered misery [during his life] ; and behold, he shall enjoy himself here and thou shalt suffer[3].'

[1] Matt. xxv. 31–35.   [2] Matt. x. 32.
[3] Luke xvi. 19–25.

"And in another place it saith, 'The kingdom of heaven is like unto a king who made a marriage feast for his son[1].' Now by [the expression] marriage feast is meant the joy and gladness which arose; for He was talking with men who were earthly friends, and He spake unto them using familiar similitudes which each of them understood. God did not indicate by this similitude that there were marriages and suppers in the next world, but He abased Himself and spake these words because of the denseness of their hearts, and He uttered these words so that He might make them to know last things. And He said that the king, by the voice of a herald, invited every one to come to his marriage feast, so that they might enjoy these good things which cannot be described. And of the many who were bidden [p. 50] there were some who were lazy, and would not come; and there were some whose hearts were wearied with the perishable affairs of this fleeting world [and would not come]; and some made the affairs of their estates the excuse, and some the need for making profit on their trafficking, and some the marrying of wives, and they shut themselves out from the beauty of the heavenly palace, and from the pleasures thereof. And of their own free will they became strangers to joy and pleasure. And then [the king] summoned others and filled the house with those who sat at meat. And his servants, who had to inspect those who sat at meat, came and there was found a man who had not on the wedding garment, and one said unto him publicly, How didst thou come hither seeing that thou hast not on the wedding garment? And he held his peace and was sad. And straightway the king said unto his ministers, Bind his hands and his feet, and cast him forth into outer darkness, where there is weeping and gnashing of teeth. These who have not hearkened to the voice of the herald with all their hearts are those who reject Christ; and they remain in the worship of idols or in some other worship. And the man who hath not put on the wedding garment is he who hath believed in unclean faith and works, and hath defiled his honourable apparel, that is to say,

[1] Matt. xxii. 2.

the garment of baptism, which consisteth of right judgement, and hath gone forth from the joy of the palace.

"And He put forth also another parable, that of the ten virgins, five of whom were wise and five foolish. And at the time of midnight there was an outcry, 'The bridegroom hath come, go ye out to meet him.' By the word 'midnight' He indicated the day which was hidden. Then those virgins who were ready woke up and went to meet the bridegroom, and he went in with them to the marriage feast, and the doors were closed. And those virgins who were not ready and who are called 'foolish,' when they saw that their lamps were gone out departed to buy oil, and when they came later, the doors having been shut, they said, 'Lord, Lord, open to us, we would come in.' And he answered and said unto them, 'Verily I say unto you, I do not know you.' By these words He indicateth that there is a reward for deeds and thoughts[1].

"And He also saith [p. 51] 'That every idle word which a man shall speak he shall be questioned thereof on the Day of Judgement[2].' And again He saith '[Every] hair of thy head is numbered[3].' Now hair is a symbol of our thoughts which are as fine as hair. And likewise the blessed Paul taught with words which resemble these, saying, 'The word of God is living, and worketh, and is sharper than a two-edged sword, and cutteth through the nerves of the soul, and the spirit, and the limbs, and the brain; and it separateth the thoughts of the heart, and there is nothing hidden before it, but everything is revealed and known[4].' And concerning this He made known of old to the Prophets by the grace of the Holy Spirit. Thus Isaiah saith, 'I know their works, and their thoughts, and I will reward them, saith God. And behold, I will come and will gather together all tongues, and they shall come and shall see My glory. And there shall be a new heaven and a new earth which I will make before Me for ever, and everything which is living shall come and shall bow down in worship before Me, saith God. And behold, they shall see the dead

---

[1] Matt. xxv. 1–12. [2] Matt. xii. 36.
[3] Matt. x. 30. [4] Hebrews iv. 12, 13.

bodies of the men who have sinned against Me, for needs must that the time shall come and their day draw near; their worm is one that shall not die, and their fire is a fire that shall not be quenched[1].'

"And he also saith concerning that day, 'I will roll up the heavens like a roll of paper, and the stars shall fall even as fall the leaves of a vine. Behold, the day of God shall come, without sparing (or, pity), to root out and to put to the trial, that it may make the whole world a ruin, and blot out sinners from it. The stars of heaven and all the planets shall not give their light, and the light of the sun and moon shall become dark, and the memorial of men shall be destroyed, and the might of the mighty shall be made weakness[2].' And he also saith, 'Woe unto those who draw together their sins like a long rope, and make them like unto the bind-rope of a yoke which is equal to their depravity. Woe unto those who make evil good and good evil, and those who make darkness light, and light [p. 52] darkness, and those who esteem bitter sweet, and sweet bitter. Woe be to those who make themselves strong for evil, and to those who take bribes, and who turn aside the right judgement of the poor, and to those who snatch away the money of those who are in misery and rob the widow and plunder the orphan. What will they leave for those whom they have plundered when they die? And to whom can they give gifts to be helped? Or to whom will they leave it? They shall be like unto the man who setteth light to reeds with a flame of fire, and their flesh shall consume in a whirlwind of flame and they shall become like the dust. For they did not wish for the Law of the God of Hosts, and they stirred to wrath the word of the Holy One of Israel[3].'

"And he also saith, 'That day of God is nigh, and it shall be a hard day, a day of fierce anger, a day of sorrow and tribulation, a day of cloud and darkness, a day of lightning and thunder. Woe be unto the wicked, for they shall go along groping their way because they have transgressed against

---

[1] Isaiah lxvi. 18, 22–24.   [2] Isaiah xxxiv. 4; xiii. 9, 11.
[3] Isaiah v. 18–23; x. 1–3; vi. 24.

God. Their gold and their silver shall not be able to save
them on the day of the anger of God, for in His jealousy He
shall blot out the earth[1].' And David the prophet and king
saith thus: 'God shall come boldly and our God shall not
keep silence, a fire shall blaze before Him, and round about
Him shall be many storm-winds. He shall summon the heavens
from above and the earth that He may judge the nations[2].'
And again he saith, 'Rise up, O God, and judge the earth; for
the mind of man shall give Thee thanks, and Thou shalt judge
every man according to his work[3].' And this singer proclaimeth
many good things in the Psalter, and all the Prophets by the
Holy Spirit have preached concerning the world which is to
come, and concerning the coming of the Saviour Who was to
fulfil the words of their prophecy, which hath commanded us
to believe in the Resurrection of the dead, and in the wages
and the reward [which we shall receive] for what we have done
during our life, so that we may inherit the life that hath no
end in the world that is to come. Amen."

[*How the prince entreated Baralâm to tell him how to escape
from the punishment which is reserved for sinners, and how
to become fit for heaven.*]

And the soul of Yĕwâsĕf was filled with good thoughts (or,
happiness), and his whole being rejoiced. And he said unto
the sage Baralâm, "Behold, thou hast told me [p. 53] about
everything, and thou hast made me to know it plainly, and
thou hast brought before me and hast made perfectly clear
before me this awful matter. Since then this happeneth to
men dwelling here what ought we ourselves to do, so that we
may escape from the punishment which is prepared for sinners
in the world to come, and may become fit for the joy of the
righteous?"

And Baralâm answered, saying, "It is written that when
Peter, the chief of the Apostles, knew the fear of the hearts
of the people, who were like thee this day, and who said unto
him, 'What shall we do?' he answered and said unto them,

[1] Isaiah xiii. 9–13.   [2] Psalm l. 3.   [3] Psalm lxxxii. 8; lxii. 12.

'Repent ye, and be baptized, each and every one of you, for
the remission of your sins, and ye shall receive the gift of the
Holy Spirit, for it hath been promised to you and to your children,
and to all those who are afar off and who call upon the Lord
our God[1].' Now behold, at this time, [O Yĕwâsĕf,] He hath
poured out upon thee His mercy and the riches of His grace,
and He hath called thee who wast in thy mind far from Him,
and wast worshipping strange objects which are not gods, but
destroying devils. Therefore before everything draw nigh unto
Him Who hath called thee to receive from Him the wisdom
of His knowledge, wherein is no falsehood, and to the other
hidden things which are invisible. Behold, He hath called
thee, tarry not until thou becomest free from thy transgression
by the judgement of the just God. And behold, thus did Paul
[Peter?] the Apostle say unto one of the believing disciples,
We trust thee for thou didst submit to our calling, and thou
art able exceedingly, and thou shalt bear the cross, and shalt
follow God Who called thee, Who called thee out of death
into life, and out of darkness into light. He who knoweth not
God dwelleth in darkness and in death of the soul. And whosoever ministereth to devils destroyeth his nature, for the
whole power of his knowledge becometh lacking, and their
apostasy taketh possession of those who resemble them, and
they go on in their apostasy.

[The parable of the Hunter and the Bird.]

"But behold, I will give thee a sign that shall last for ever,
which a certain wise man related unto me. The works of
these men who worship idols resemble the action of a certain
hunter [p. 54] who snared in a net a little bird, the name of
which is 'shâḥrûr,' and he seized a butcher's knife that he
might kill it and eat it. And the 'shâḥrûr' opened his mouth
and spake unto him in a clear voice, saying, 'O man, what will
the slaughter of me benefit thee, for thou canst not fill thy
belly with me? If thou wilt permit me I will tell thee three

[1] Acts ii. 37–39.

counsels, and if thou wilt observe them they will benefit thee
more than every other thing in thy life.' And the hunter was
amazed, and he waited to hear the truth of his words, and he
set the bird free quickly from his cords. And the 'shâhrûr'
opened his mouth and said unto the man, 'Never dare to
undertake anything that thou art not able to obtain; regret
not anything that hath been snatched away from thee; and
believe not a word that is untrue. Observe these three commands and every affair of thine shall be good and peacegiving.'
And the man marvelled at the bird and let him go free, and
he flew up into the air. And the 'shâhrûr' wished to know if
the hunter had understood the import of the words which he
had spoken to him, and if he had obtained benefit therefrom.
And the bird said unto him whilst he was in the air, 'O man,
by thine own free will a great treasure hath been snatched
away out of thine hand, for there is in my belly a gem, a pearl,
which is as large as the egg of an ostrich.' And when the
hunter heard these words he lost his senses wholly, and his
members were loosened through sorrow, and he lamented
because of this thing. And he wanted to catch the bird again
for making a mock of him and he said unto it, 'Come to my
dwelling, and I will devote myself to caring for thee well, just
as I would for my friend, and I will send thee away with
honour.' And the 'shâhrûr' answered, saying, 'Behold, now I
know and am certain that thy folly is absolute, for thou didst
hear and accept with attention everything which I spake unto
thee, and didst approve of the same, but thou hast not obtained
therefrom a single advantage. Did I not say unto thee, Thou
shalt not regret anything that hath been snatched away from
thee? And behold, thou art sorrowing bitterly because of my
escape from thine hand, and art regretting a matter which is
past. And again I said unto thee, Do not seek after anything
[p. 55] that thou art not able to obtain. And behold, thou
didst seek the opportunity of catching me in a net, but thou
wast not able to do so, nor to follow my flight. Moreover, I
commanded thee not to believe a word that is not true, but
behold thou didst just now believe that there was in my belly

a gem, a pearl, which was as large as myself. Dost thou not
know and dost thou not understand that if thou didst weigh
the whole of me in a pair of scales I should not balance even
the shell of an egg of the ostrich? How then could I possibly
contain within me a thing as large as myself?'

"Even so are foolish those who put their trust in idols which
they have made with their own hands, and say, 'These have
created us'; and they guard them carefully from theft so that
men may not steal them. And they call them guardians who
save them, but this is folly, and error, and lack of understanding. Therefore did David the prophet cry out concerning
them, saying, 'May all those who made them be like unto
them, and all those who put their confidence in them[1].' And
it is also said concerning these men, 'They shall be disgraced
and ashamed who worship a graven image, and those who put
their trust in their gods[2].' And again he saith, 'Ye sacrifice
to devils and not to God; they are a perverse generation and
there is no faith in them[3].' And concerning the race which is
thus wicked and which believeth not, he saith, 'Go out from
among them and separate yourselves from them that ye may
be saved from this perverse generation; flee and depart ye[4],'
and other words like these. Now we have not like them many
gods and lords, but we worship one God, God the Father, from
Whom is everything, and we are in Him; and one Lord
Jesus Christ, in Whom is everything, and we exist because of
Him, Who is the form of the Person of God most High, the
Firstborn of all creation and of all times, for in Him He
created everything, that which is in the heavens, and that
which is in the earth, likewise that which is visible, and that
which is invisible, and everything existeth in Him, and
without Him nothing that is came into being; and the Holy
Spirit, Who is One, Whom everything awaiteth, the right
Spirit, the Spirit the Comforter, Who made the Prophets to
prophesy, and the praise (?) of God. And these Three Names
[p. 56] have one Nature, and each of these is known in His

---

[1] Psalms cxv. 8 ; cxxxv. 18.   [2] Psalm xcvii. 7.
[3] Deut. xxxii. 17, 20.   [4] Acts ii. 40; 2 Cor. vi. 17.

Person, and they are equal, Father, and Son, and Holy Spirit, the Three of These have one Godhead, and one Substance, and one sovereignty, one honour, and one power, and They only differ in the names whereby They are called.

"One is the Father in operation, the unbegotten Begetter ; One is the Son in operation, the Being begotten ; and One is the Holy Spirit in the operation of proceeding [from the Father and Son]. And similarly for us from the light of the Father and the Son light hath risen upon us in the splendour of the Holy Spirit. And of the Three Persons One became incarnate, He Who is God indeed, by Himself, concerning Whom it is known in the Trinity that through Him everything [cometh], and everything is because of Him, and in Him everything existeth. And by His grace I myself had knowledge of thy work, and I have been sent to teach thee, and I understood Him from of old. And the end of this matter is that if thou believest and art baptized thou wilt be saved, and if thou believest not thou wilt be condemned in the Judgement. For as thou thyself seest this day, the glory, and the riches, and all the deceitfulness of this world, which is a thing of nothing, shall be changed and pass away. And they will indeed carry thee out from this world, and as for thy body, they will shut it up in a little chamber, and thou wilt be closed in by thyself. And it will fail to find its men (or, servants), and its friends, for the luxury of this world will be blotted out speedily, and instead of sweet scents and perfumed odours and beauty an odour of foulness and foetor will emanate therefrom. And as for thy soul, they will suspend it below the earth in the punishment of Sheol until the day of the Resurrection of the dead. And when the soul shall put on its body on that day, they will drive it forth from before the face of God, and they will carry it into the fire of Jahânam which burneth and blazeth continually and unceasingly. And worse than this shall befall thee if thou continuest in denial [of Christ], if thou dost not follow me with confidence to this to which I invite thee, to salvation, and dost not awake with desire to be covered by His splendour, and dost not follow Him without turning aside, and dost not deny every [other god], and dost not believe in Him alone.

"And as for Him Whom thou shalt find, thou shalt go to Him to rest and joy. Hear what I say unto thee and hear Him. Then when thou sittest down thou shalt be [p. 57] without dismay, and when thou sleepest thou shalt find sleep pleasant and without fear, and where thou walkest stumbling shall not overtake thee, and the rising up of Satans shall not appear unto thee. But thou shalt journey in confident assurance like a lion, and thou shalt live in joy and gladness for ever, and upon thy head shall be beauty and glory and thou shalt find joy; and sorrow, and suffering, and the cry of grief shall flee from thee. Then shall thy light be sent before thee, rising like the sun, and thine integrity shall go before thee, and the glory of God shall cover thee. At that time when thou criest out God shall hear thee, and when thou callest upon Him, He shall say 'Here am I, I am thy Saviour Who hath destroyed thy sin, and it shall not be remembered [against] thee. Confess thou thy sin that it may be remitted to thee, and although thy sin be black I will make it white like snow, and although it be red like scarlet I will make it to be as white as clean wool. For the mouth of God hath spoken thus[1].'"

[*How the prince declared that he abominated idolatry, and how he decided to accept Christian baptism and how he asked Baralâm if baptism would secure for him complete salvation.*]

And Yĕwâsĕf said unto him, "My lord, thy words are good and wonderful. Indeed I do believe, and I wholly hate with all my heart the worship of idols. Before thy coming to me my soul loathed them and was in great doubt concerning them, and now I loathe them, and I loathe them wholly because of what I have learned from thee, the error of them and the madness of their dominion. And now, I long to be the servant of the God of righteousness, provided that He will not reject me because of my manifold transgressions, because

---

[1] Isaiah i. 16–20.

I can never be worthy of being so. But He Himself shall forgive me all my sins, for He is a lover of the children of men, and He is compassionate of heart, even as thou thyself hast taught me ; and it is meet that He should forgive me, so that I may become His servant. I intend to receive Christian baptism, but shall it be by faith only ? And is Christian baptism complete salvation, or is it meet for men to add something else thereto ? "

[Baralâm's Doctrine of Christian Baptism.]

[p. 58.] And Baralâm answered, saying, "Hear thou what is meet after the reception of Christian baptism, which is, that a man must make himself to be remote from all sins, and from every taint of evil. And the foundation of thy true faith must be built upon the performance of works of virtue, for the faith that is without works is a dead thing, as are works without faith. The Apostle Paul saith, 'Walk ye in the Spirit. Trouble not yourselves with the lusts of the flesh, for the works of the flesh are clearly visible, which are fornication, unclean marriages, fraud, the worship of idols, magic, contention, strife, murder, the love of money, blasphemy, drunkenness, pride, and such like things, even as I have already told thee. Those who do these things shall not inherit the kingdom of heaven. And the fruits of the Spirit are love, joy, peace, patience, spiritual excellence and good qualities, faith, gentleness, devotion, purity of soul and body, humility of heart with exceedingly great contrition, compassion, the forsaking of evil, watching, true repentance for what is past, that is to say, sins and transgressions, and lapses into sin and error, [coupled] with many tears, the fear of God, lamentation for sin, neighbourly love and such like things[1].' And these works shall be unto him that believeth like steps to the man who ascendeth a ladder, and if thou followest from one step to another they will when taken together make the soul to ascend to heaven. He commanded us to enter in at the strait gate and to keep away from those things which are opposed thereto, and if after

[1] Galatians v. 16, 19–23.

we know righteousness we go back and do works that are
abominable and bring on death, once again do we become like
unto the dog that returneth to his vomit, and what the Lord
spake shall be fulfilled on us. 'When the unclean spirit hath
gone out of a man he goeth about to a place wherein is no
water, seeking rest and finding none, and he saith, I will go
back to the place whence I came forth, and he cometh and
findeth it empty of dirt and adorned, and there come with
him seven other spirits worse than himself, and they go in and
dwell there, [p. 59] and the last state of that man is worse
than the first[1].'

"For holy Christian baptism submergeth in the water all
the past sins which have been registered by the hand of the
Most High, and it destroyeth them with a destruction which
is absolute, and it becometh a strong wall, and a solid fortress,
and strong armour before the face of the Enemy. It doth not
root out the power of the flesh, but it doth destroy the working of sin in the past. And we must not submerge ourselves
in the tank of water only, but we must [also] believe in one
baptism for the forgiveness of sins. And it is meet that we
should purify ourselves, and that we should take good heed
not to fall again into any committing of sins, but we should
perform the commandments of God, the Most High. For He
said unto His holy Apostles, 'Go ye and preach to all nations,
and baptize them in the Name of the Father, and of the Son,
and of the Holy Spirit[2].' And not this only did He say, but
He added, 'and teach them everything which I Myself have
taught you.' And as concerneth His honourable commandments the Holy Spirit resteth upon us, and as for His Apostles
to whom He ascribed blessedness, He called them His brethren
who were fit for the kingdom of heaven[3].

"And He commanded us also that we should weep in this
world, and we should become worthy of the joy which is to
come ; and that we should be meek, and that we should
hunger and thirst for righteousness ; that we should be com-

[1] Matt. xii. 43–45.   [2] Matt. xxviii. 19, 20.
[3] Compare Matt. xii. 49.

passionate and addict ourselves to giving; that we should be pure in heart, and be remote from all impurity, with soundness of heart, working peace with our neighbour; that we should suffer patiently sorrow and hatred for righteousness' sake, and for His holy Name, and everything which shall come upon us, so that we may receive the gift of grace, and the joy and gladness which are for ever[1]. And He commanded us that our light should shine in this world, as He saith, 'that [men] may see your good works and glorify your Father which is in heaven[2].'

"The Law of Moses which was given in times of old to the children of Israel saith thus: 'Thou shalt do no murder. Thou shalt not commit fornication. Thou shalt not steal. Thou shalt not become a witness of falsehood[3].' And Christ [p. 60] saith, 'He who shall be wroth with his brother without a cause, for him is ready the punishment of the Judgement, and he who saith to his brother, Rag, for him is ready the fire of Jahânam. If when thou bringest thy gift thou rememberest that thy brother is sorrowing over thee, set down thy gift on the altar, and go, first of all make friends with thy brother[4].' And He saith, 'Whosoever hath looked upon a woman and desired her hath already committed fornication with her in his heart[5]'; the longing of the soul and the impulse to sinful passion He calleth 'fornication.' Now the Law prohibiteth swearing falsely, but Christ commanded men not to swear oaths at all, but that they should say Yea at the time [for saying] Yea, and Nay at the time [for saying] Nay[6]. The Law saith, 'An eye for an eye, and a tooth for a tooth,' but Christ saith, 'To him that hath smitten thy cheek turn the other also, and to him that hath taken thy cloak give thy shirt also, and with him that hath forced thee to go one stade go two, to him that asketh give, and him that wisheth to take from thee prevent him not[7].' And He saith also, 'Love those who hate you, bless those who curse you, do good to those who do

[1] Matt. v. 3–12. [2] Matt. v. 16. [3] Exodus xx. 13–16.
[4] Matt. v. 22–24. [5] Matt. v. 28. [6] Matt. v. 33–37.
[7] Matt. v. 38–42.

harm to you, pray for those who cheat you ; that ye may be children of your Father which is in heaven, for He maketh the sun to rise on the good and on the wicked, and He maketh the rain to fall on the righteous and on those who oppress[1].'

"And He saith also, 'Judge not that ye be not judged, forgive ye, and men shall forgive you. Lay not up for yourselves treasure on the earth where there is moth, and where thieves dig through [the wall] and steal, but lay up for yourselves treasure in the heavens where there is no moth and where are no thieves. Where your treasures are there will your hearts be. Think not about your lives, what ye will eat, or what ye will drink, nor about your bodies as to what ye shall wear, for your Father which is in heaven knoweth about all the things which ye need. It is true, without falsehood, that the Creator of the soul and the body will give food to everyone, and He giveth food to the birds of the heavens, and He adorneth the earth with the beauty of flowers. Seek ye first of all the kingdom of heaven and all these shall be added unto you. Take no anxious thought for the morrow, for the morrow will take thought for itself[2]. As ye wish men to do unto you [p. 61] even so do ye yourselves do unto them. Enter in at the strait gate, for narrow is the path that leadeth unto life, and few are those who wish for it ; but very broad and spacious is the road that carrieth [a man] to destruction, and those who travel thereon are many. Not all those who say unto Me, Lord, Lord, shall enter into the kingdom of heaven, but he that doeth the will of My Father which is in heaven. He who loveth father or mother more than Me is not worthy of Me ; he who loveth son or daughter more than Me is not worthy of Me ; he who doth not bear his cross and doth not follow Me is not worthy of Me[3].'

"As our Lord commanded the holy Apostles [to do] these and such like things, even so do they teach them to those who believe on Him. And it is meet for us to take heed to the observance of all these things if we wish to arrive at the

[1] Matt. v. 44, 45.   [2] Matt. vii. 1, 2 ; vi. 19 ff.
[3] Matt. vii. 12, 13, 21 ; x. 37.

end, and to receive the incorruptible crowns which God, the Righteous Judge, shall give on that day to those who will love His appearance."

[*How the prince feared that backsliding would induce despair and how Baralâm discoursed on the greatness of the mercy of God and His knowledge of our frailty.*]

And Yĕwâsĕf said unto him, "If these things be laid down by the Law it is necessary to observe them with exceedingly great care and exactness. But if after [receiving] Christian baptism I happen to fall into sin must I of necessity become without hope, and will all my expectation be in vain?"

And Baralâm answered him, saying, "Think not thus, for the Word of God, Who became man for our salvation, knoweth well how great is our frailty, and He will not allow us to fall sick of the state of suffering wherein is no hope, but like a very wise and skilful physician He hath prepared for us the wise healing by repentance, and He hath proclaimed thereby the remission of sin which He ordained when He appeared. For after we have acquired the knowledge of righteousness, and have been baptized in water and in the spirit, we are purified by the Sign of the Cross from all sin; and if it happen that we fall into [p. 62] sin it is not necessary for us to be baptized again, for this gift is given once and for all. And we are saved by making repentance, which is given unto us by our Creator, that is to say by fasting, and prayer, and scalding tears, and these by the grace of God are called 'baptism.' But it is meet for men to fast for a few days so that they may escape especially from a great falling into sin, and as the path is thus there is no sin therein, for it is vanquished by the love of God. But it is meet for us to follow repentance before the coming of death, so that we may not depart from this world in a state of impurity, for there is no repentance in Sheol. And for this reason He hath commanded us not to despair when we transgress, for we know the goodness of God, and we know that the Lover of men Who hath shed His blood for us hath ordained remission of sin because of it. Glory be to Him for ever and ever! Amen.

"And the power of repentance is made known by many passages, and especially from the commandments and similitudes of our Lord and Redeemer Jesus Christ. In the beginning of His teaching He saith, 'Repent, the kingdom of heaven hath drawn nigh[1].' And He spake the parable of the son who took his father's riches, and journeyed into a far country, and squandered all his money therein in dissolute living, and when he was in that country ever sinking deeper and deeper into sin, he became hungry, and he went and made friends with a certain wicked man of that country, and it is said that this man sent him into his field to herd his pigs, and that he was not able to fill his belly with the crushed tamarinds(?) on which they fed the pigs. And at the time of the close of his life he returned from that state of disgrace, and he lamented over himself, saying, 'How many hirelings are there in my father's house who leave food whilst I am here suffering the tribulation of hunger! I will go to my father, and I will say unto him, O father, I have sinned against heaven and before thee. I am not fit to be called thy son, but make me as one of thy hirelings.' And he rose [p. 63] up and went to his father, and when his father saw him afar off, he had compassion upon him and made haste to embrace him. And he made a feast with joy because he had found him, and he slew the fatted calf[2].

"This parable [our Lord] made concerning those who return from their sins to penitence. And He indicateth [the remission of sins] by a clear sign [in the parable of] the good shepherd who had a hundred sheep. When one of them was cast away he left the ninety and nine and went and sought after that which was lost until he found it, and he carried it on his shoulder, and set it with those sheep which had not strayed, and he cried out [the news] to his friends and neighbours. Thus saith our Redeemer, 'There shall be great joy in heaven over one sinner that repenteth, more than over ninety and

---

[1] Matt. iv. 17.   [2] Luke xv. 11, 23.

nine righteous men who need not repentance[1].' And similarly
the chief of the Apostles, Peter, the Rock of the Faith, by the
operation of His wisdom, fell into the sin of denying [Christ][2]
at the time of the Passion of our Redeemer so that He might
make him to know the weakness of the children of men. And
when he remembered our Lord's words straightway he wept a
bitter weeping, and by the shedding of scalding tears he saved
himself from dismay, for he was instructed in conflict. And
even though he fell he neither became weak nor did he
despair, and this man became a master by his deeds and a
pattern for all the world in respect of working repentance.
And after our Lord Jesus Christ rose by the power of His
Godhead, He asked him, saying, 'O Peter, lovest thou Me?'
and He strengthened the three denials with three questions.
And Peter answered, saying, 'O Lord, Thou knowest that I
love Thee[3],' and with all this and with many other things he
strengthened the number three, and the power of his tears is
well known.

"Let us then love the casting away of sin and the driving it
afar off, and the flight from it through the flow of tears, even
as David saith, 'I suffered tribulation and I bathed my couch
[with tears], and I defiled my bed with my tears[4].' It is meet
for a man after he hath known righteousness, and the second
birth, and the taste of the Divine Mystery, to take good heed
with all his might, and to be afraid lest he fall, for falling is
not a good thing for [p. 64] those who fight the spiritual fight.
Now those who have fallen and have not been able to rise
up again are many. Some of them have opened the doors of
passion and remained therein, and some of them were unable
to flee from it; moreover they were unable to turn to repentance and could not raise themselves up by confessing that
they would wash away the impurity of their sins. And because
of this suddenly cometh a fall, and when once a fall hath come
lust [followeth] quickly. Men shall rise up and shall fight the
good fight[5], and to those to whom it happeneth thus, let them

---

[1] Luke xv. 4–7. [2] Matt. xxvi. 70, 72, 74, 75.
[3] John xxi. 15, 16, 17. [4] Psalm vi. 6. [5] 1 Timothy vi. 12.

rise up and fight the fight until the end ; for our Lord saith, 'Turn ye unto Me and I will turn unto you[1].'"

[How the prince wished to be preserved from backsliding after his baptism, and how Baralâm taught him how to avoid falling into sin.]

And Yĕwâsĕf answered and said unto him, "How can a man after he hath been baptized keep himself pure from every sin ? I wish to find the way of God with certainty, and not to be rejected therefrom, and I do not want to fall again after the remission of my sins is effected."

And Baralâm said unto him, "Exceedingly good is what thou sayest, O king ; this is my own wish and my own desire, but it is a difficult matter. It is impossible for men to walk about in the fire and not be burnt, and it is difficult to stand on the fire [and not be scorched]. And it is very hard for a man when he is fettered with the things of the world and the cares thereof, and when he is toiling to heap up riches and to find pleasure whilst he is alive, to walk without a turning aside from the commandment of God, and to save himself [from sin] entirely. For God saith, 'A man cannot serve two masters, on the contrary, he will hate the one and love the other, and will honour the one and despise the other ; ye cannot serve God and mammon[2].' John the Evangelist, His friend, the theologian, wrote in his Epistle saying, 'Love not the world nor the things that are in the world, for the love of the world is the lust of the flesh and of the eyes. And the world shall pass away, and the lusts thereof with it, but he who doeth the Will of God [p. 65] shall abide for ever and ever[3].'

"Consider then our fathers, who were inspired and who heard these things from the mouth of Christ. They commanded that after Christian baptism men should possess their souls undefiled. And some of them were ready to receive the second baptism, that is to say, to become a witness (i.e. martyr), even to the shedding of blood. For this martyrdom also is called

---

[1] Zechariah i. 3.   [2] Matt. vi. 24.   [3] 1 John ii. 15-17.

'baptism,' and it is exceedingly honourable and sublime, for thou canst never again be defiled by the impurity of sin. For those (i.e. the martyrs) gave themselves up to kings and governors, who were wicked men, for Christ's sake, and they endured their tortures of every kind—now they cast them to the lions, and into the fire, and to the swords—and they confessed a good confession, and they finished their course, and they kept their faith. And they were rewarded with the wages of righteousness, and they became participators with the angels, and became the heirs of Christ, Who had made splendid their excellences, and made them to shine until the riches of their grace went forth into all the earth, and the splendour of their teaching into all the ends of the world. And this not only through their condition, but through their works, and the shedding of their blood, and through their bones which are full of sanctification of every kind, and their putting of Satans to flight, and their healing of those who were sick with grievous sicknesses. And they have told me many things—if we were wishful to make known their excellences, and how they destroyed evil men and destroyers. And they reigned in all the world [as] believing kings, and they contemplated at that time the fathers with such a right mind that they offered their bodies and their souls to God, the Most High, without reward. And they cut away every deed of passion, and they withdrew themselves from the reward of the body and the soul ; and they understood that they could not preserve this state without keeping the commandments of God. And they have taught us also that we must acquire these things and keep the commandments, and perform them during the tribulation and misery which shall come upon us, and worldly persecution ; and they acquired another and a strange habit, according to the Divine [p. 66] Word.

"And they rejected everything, and they forsook their parents, and their brothers, and their children, and their friends, and their kinsfolk, and their possessions, and their pleasure. And they forgot everything that is in the world, and they fled like the men who flee to wretched, miserable, and dangerous deserts, and who make their habitations in the caves and holes of the earth. And they made themselves to be remote from all the joys that are in this world, and from [rich] apparel, and [dainty] food, and from cities, and from travelling about in them. And in this [state of life] they found two resting-places. One of these [consisted of] the consideration of this transitory world and the pains thereof so that they might cut off lust at its root, and blot out the memory thereof, in order that they might plant in their hearts the desire of heaven and the acquisition thereof. And the other was that they might destroy the work of the flesh and become martyrs in their wills, and that they might become like unto Christ in their sufferings, in so far as it lay in their power, and that they might become partakers with Him of his never-ending kingdom. And when they discerned that this intention was good, they left their abodes and hid themselves in caves and caverns. And in this manner they lived, and they acquired spiritual excellences and maintained them, and they renounced everything, so that they might find joy and peace. And they chose to make unboiled herbs their food, and on this insufficient (or, lowering) food they fed the life of their bodies. And there were some of them who passed the whole week without eating, and there were some who ate twice only during the week, and there were others who merely tasted food each evening; and their prayers and vigils were very little fewer than those of the angels. And they renounced gold, and silver, and possessions with an absolute renunciation, and they forgot everything that passeth between the folk who sell and buy. And there was no room for jealousy and pride in them, but they made themselves to benefit by humility of heart, not doing anything perfectly, but they were men who took good heed to themselves, even as our Lord saith, 'Even if ye perform all the commandments say ye, We are idle servants, for we have only done [p. 67] what we were commanded to do[1].' And some of them judged concerning

---

[1] Luke xvii. 10.

themselves that they did nothing unless they were commanded
to do so.

"And similarly each and every one of them acquired the
good mind, and there was no empty boasting in them, and
they did not disfigure(?) the face because of the things for
which they forsook the world and dwelt in the deserts. They
awaited their reward from God and not from man, and they
believed in their minds that the toil which is performed for
empty praise is without reward, inasmuch as it is performed
in the sight of men. And those who crave for the glory that
is celestial, and long for the same renounced the things of
earth, and they struggled until each [virtue] was perfected in
them, and they withdrew themselves from the habitation of
men all the days of their life; and because of this they
became nigh unto God. And there were some of them who
set their habitation far from those of their companions, and
each one [lived] by himself. And on the First Day of the
Week they assembled in the holy church to receive the
Divine Mystery, which is the Offering of the Body and holy
Blood of Christ, the Honourable One, which He bestowed on
believers for the remission of their sins, to illumine and to
sanctify soul and body, each being strengthened by the other
by exercising himself in divine words. And they revealed [to
each other] their methods of fighting against invisible opponents, so that [Satan] might not snare among them any one
of those who did not know how to enter into the fight. And
then they went back again into their places, laying up the
honeycomb of their spiritual excellences in rags, the honey
which encourageth to perfect longings, and they made from
this the sweet fruit which is profitable for the heavenly table.

"And others walked in the living ordinances which made
[them] companions and caused to gather together a numerous
company into a single community. And they cast aside their
own wills by the command of all the believers, and they slew
their desires with the knives of command, and they counted
themselves as slaves who were sold of their own free will.
I say then that those men lived not their own lives but the

life of Christ, Who dwelt in them, Whom they followed, and for Whom they [p. 68] denied [themselves] everything when they withdrew from the world. Among the various grades of these men healings were granted, with them men took refuge from death and they denied the inferior nature through a longing for that which was more sublime than the earthy nature. There were some who walked upon the earth after the manner of angels, singing and praising God, and they were strong men like the martyrs, who made [their] confession by striving [to do] what was commanded. And then was fulfilled the Divine word, 'Wheresoever two or three are gathered together in My Name I will be in their midst[1].' Now by 'two or three' He meaneth the whole assembly which is without number, and the single or double places wherein few or many are gathered together for the sake of His holy Name and where they worship Him in lowliness of heart. We believe and we confess that there He will be with His servants and that He will be in them. And by these signs beings made of dust shall emulate the work of heavenly beings, with fasting, and vigil, and prayer, and scalding tears, and remembrance of death, and withdrawal from anger, and silence of the lips, and toil boldly performed in purity, and with humility, and patience, and with perfect love of God and love of our neighbour. And in this wise they finished their days like the angels. And because of this God adorned them with signs and wonders, and He made the grace of their marvellous manner of life to be noised abroad and to resound in all the world.

"And if I were to describe to thee the course of one of them [whose name] is preserved in my mouth, and who is called Anthony[2], thou wouldst understand and wouldst wonder how it came about that a tree with such dense foliage (?) and such sweet fruit, and such well-grown luxuriant branches,

[1] Matt. xviii. 20.
[2] He was born about 250 A.D. and died about 355. The Syriac version of his "Life" by Athanasius, Archbishop of Alexandria, gives a complete account of his ascetic labours and triumphs. See my *Paradise of the Fathers*, vol. I. p. 1 ff.

had made its foundation upon tranquillity, and how it was that the height thereof reached unto the firmament which is raised on high. It is meet for him to receive blessings from our Redeemer. And others also fought the spiritual fight in the same way as did he, and found heavenly crowns; blessed are those who loved God. And because of love of Him they renounced everything. They continued to weep day and night, so that they might find everlasting joy, and they subdued the thoughts [p. 69] of their own good pleasure, so that they might be exalted in the next world. And they reduced their bodies by hunger, and thirst, and vigil, so that they might receive the freedom of spiritual beings and the pleasure of the Garden of Joy, and the kingdom which is for ever; and they became pure in heart and habitations of the Holy Spirit. They crucified themselves in this world, so that they might stand on the right hand of Him Who was crucified for them. They girded up their loins and kept their lamps ready at all times, and waited for the coming of the immortal Bridegroom. They acquired two bright eyes of the understanding, whereof the vision was keen, and they kept themselves always on the watch for that terrifying hour; and they kept their gaze fixed on those good things which will not pass away, and upon the punishment and torture which is for ever. And it was graven in their hearts and they longed with great anxiety to find that glory which endureth for ever. And now they go about among those who resemble them in their course, and who are blessed even as they are, for with the eye of their heart which cannot be deceived they have removed the weight of the things that are transitory and that do not endure. And they denied [themselves] of all this for treasure laid up, namely, the good things that neither pass away nor die, and they were strong thereby. Such were these holy and strange men!

"And as for us who are feeble it is not right for us to compare ourselves with them, for we have not attained to the celestial wisdom which dwelleth in heaven. But as far as it is possible for our feebleness and the shattered condition of our fleeting strength, let us imitate their course and array

ourselves in this outward garb. And if we have transgressed
in our actions, behold, there is divine hope [left for us]. We
know that He will give us help in the sin of the depravity
which hath been planted in us, when we receive divine baptism.
Let us follow the words of these blessed men, and let us
understand thoroughly the fleeting nature of the things of
the world, which are fleeting things wherein is no profit, and
are lighter than dreams, and the shadow that vanisheth, and
the breath in the air. Even so are the things [p. 70] of this
world which they have taught us not to love at all, nay, we
must hate them with a perfect hatred, for it is meet for a man
to hate them, because they waste in wrath all his friendship
which is given unto them, and they bring him continually to
sorrow, and we become emptied of all goodness. And love of
the things of the world layeth a heavy burden upon men, and
it casteth down those who have raised themselves up. Thus
is its appearance and thus are its gifts. It hateth its friends
and it heapeth disgrace upon those who do not perform its
good pleasure. It maketh evil to descend upon all those
who trust it, and it cutteth the roots of those who put
confidence in it. It maketh a covenant with the foolish, and
it maketh false promises to them, so that it may drag them
to itself. And when they fulfil their desires from it, they
know straightway that the world is a liar and is evil. And it
never fulfilleth what it hath promised in anything whatsoever,
for to-day it inclineth favourably to their desires, and causeth
to enjoy food, and to-morrow it will assign food to their enemy.
To-day it maketh one of them a king, and to-morrow it will
bring him back to evil things and disgrace. To-day it giveth
him a thousand good things, and to-morrow it will set him in
want and misery. To-day it setteth a crown of glory on his
head, and to-morrow it will bring him down to the earth, and
he will fall on his face. To-day it adorneth his neck with
glory and with a state of boasting, and to-morrow it will bind
iron fetters about his neck. It maketh him to be beloved by
everyone for a moment, and after a little while it will make
him to be hated excessively. To-day it giveth him pleasure

and maketh him to enjoy himself, and to-morrow it saddeneth him with tears and groaning and lamentation.

"And what is the end which shall be theirs? Hearken now. It setteth the abode of those who love it in the fire of Jahân-nam, the place of wailing and destruction. The form of its manner is always thus, and its attribute is thus: It spareth not those who are dead, and it hath no compassion on those who live, for it hath seduced with evil the former and snared them in its nets, and as for the latter, it wisheth to hasten its own work, [p. 71] and it hath no desire that anyone should escape from his own evil net. And these forsooth serve God ! Behold, by the depravity of their hearts they make themselves remote from glory, but they themselves fall whilst expecting their dissolution, through the love of transitory things, never thinking at all about Him Who shall come [to] the world. And they prepare for the pleasure of fleshly things, and they cast away their soul to be dissolved by hunger and sated by thousands of evil things.

[The parable of the man who fell into a well.]

"And these seem to me to resemble the man who fled before the face of the rhinoceros in great fear. He was unable to endure the hearing of the sound of its grunting, and its awful-ness, and he fled with all his might, so that it might not make him its food; and as he fled precipitately, being sorely afraid of it, he fell into the depths of a very deep well. And as he was falling he stretched out his hands and laid hold of a tree which had two branches. These he grasped firmly with both his hands, and his feet stood on the sides of the tree, and he thought that in this manner he had found safety, and that he could not be shaken off. And as he was looking he saw two locusts, the one white and the other black, which were all the time eating through the branches that he was grasping with great firmness; and he dared not cling to them until they were eaten through by the locusts. And he looked down the well and saw a serpent of terrifying appearance which breathed out fire, and its eyes emitted flashes of fire with fierce anger,

and it opened its mouth towards him and wanted to swallow
him up. And he turned his gaze to the support whereon his
feet rested, and saw four serpents putting out their heads
from the cleft of the tree wherein was their nest on which he
was supporting himself. And he lifted up his eyes and saw a
bee making honey, which was dropping down from the top of
the tree with the two branches, and he licked the honey with
his tongue, and enjoyed the taste thereof; and he rejoiced
therein, and his heart was relieved from anxiety about his
condition. And he ceased to occupy his mind with thoughts
of the trouble that surrounded him, and he paid no heed to
the fact that the rhinoceros was at the top of the well snorting
and seeking to devour him, and that below in the depths of
the well there was also the serpent which [p. 72] was opening
its mouth to swallow him up, and that the branches which
he was grasping were well-nigh eaten through [by the locusts],
and that his feet were resting on a place which had no strength
in it, and that he was unable to save himself from the four
serpents. And that man forgot all those troubles and their
difficulties, and gave his heart relief by the enjoyment of the
taste of a little honey. Now those who are dissolved in the
seductive love of the world are like unto this man.

"Behold, I now come to explain this parable unto thee. The
rhinoceros is the commandment of death which is always impelling a man to run so that he may come to the kin of Adam.
The well is the world, which is full of every kind of suffering
and evil, and it symbolizeth the grave. The tree with two
branches, which was always being devoured by locusts, is our
appointed span of life which is [always being] consumed and
passing away. The black locust is the night and the white
locust is the day. The four serpents are the four transitory
and unstable natures in the children of men, which, if they
be withdrawn from their grade or are set in a state of commotion, destroy the man through this natural constitution of
the body. And the serpent [in the well] may be likened unto
the belly of Sheol, the fire of which burneth to receive those
who have chosen this commotion of transient things in pre-

ference to the good things which are to come. And the honey is the enjoyment and desire of the world, which deceiveth those who are its friends, and doth not permit them to occupy themselves with the salvation of their souls."

And Yĕwâsĕf answered and said, "Verily, this is indeed truth, and it agreeth with thy words. Delay not in making clear to me such similitudes and examples as these, always instructing me so that I may know thoroughly well what the life in this transitory world is, and what shall come upon us at the end thereof."

[The parable of the Three Friends.]

And the honourable sage Baralâm answered him, saying, "Behold, those who love the joy of this transitory life and the love of the world [p. 73] and those who appreciate the savour of the desires thereof, and who choose transitory things in preference to those which do not pass away, are like unto the man who had three friends. To two of these he paid honour, and he fought for them, and he multiplied exceedingly the trouble which he took on their behalf; but he utterly despised the third, and paid him no honour whatsoever. Now he did not love him truly, as was meet, though outwardly he showed him some little affection. One day there came to him soldiers, whose appearance was terrifying and alarming, and they had ridden fast and hard. And they made many enquiries and asked many questions, and they had been ordered to take that man to the king; and he was to bring with him the amount of a debt which he owed, [some] thousands of talents. Now as the matter was a serious one for him, and he called to mind the terrifying judgement hall of the king, he wished that there was some one who would help him.

"And early the following morning he went to his chief friend whom he loved dearly, and said unto him, 'Thou knowest, O my friend, how at all times I have devoted myself to thy welfare. Behold, I want thee now, this very day, to help me, and to deliver me from the great tribulation which encompasseth me. With what wilt thou help me now? And for what may

I hope from thee, O my friend?' And that friend answered
him, saying, 'I have never been a friend of thine, and I know
not whence thou comest. I have other friends with whom it
is meet for me to rejoice this day, and henceforth I shall make
them my friends. But behold, I will now give thee two ragged
garments which thou mayest wear on the road which thou
art to travel, but in the matter of the debt they will benefit
thee in no way whatsoever. Do not hope for anything else
from me.'

"And when [the debtor] heard this he gave up all hope of
the help which he had expected to receive from him, and he
departed straightway to another friend of his. And he said
unto him, 'Remember, O my friend, how many benefits I
have bestowed upon thee, and how great is the beauty of the
affection which I have manifested towards thee. Behold, this
day I have fallen into great sorrow and tribulation, and I need
a helper who will help me. Tell me how much assistance thou
canst afford me.' And this friend answered and said unto him,
'I am unable [p. 74] to mix myself up in this affair to-day;
besides this I am much occupied, and I am hard-worked, and
sorely perplexed. Now I will walk a little way on the road
with thee, for I cannot be of benefit to thee in anything
[else]; but I must come back to my place quickly and be at
my work and attend to my business about transitory things.'
And [the debtor] came back empty from that man also, and
was sorrowful all the way. And he ascribed woe to his false
expectation, and to his evil-minded friends to whom formerly
he had given pleasure, and whom he had loved, and who were
now useless to him.

"And he went to his third friend, to whom he had never
given any cause for satisfaction, and whom he had never
accepted as a participator in his pleasure, and said unto him
with a face of shame, and with constraint and trepidation,
'It ill beseemeth me to show my face before thee and to lift
up mine eyes to thee, for I know full well that I have never
performed for thee one good deed, and that I have never
turned to thee in friendship. But I have come unto thee

now because of the trouble that hath overtaken me, and I have not obtained either help or assistance from my other friends. And if thou hast the power, and thou canst afford me a little help, I pray thee withhold it not from me and do not thrust me aside because of my wicked disposition which I have shown towards thee.' And that friend answered him with a bright and glad face [saying], 'I, O my friend, have indeed remembered thee often, and few indeed are the good deeds which thou hast done for me. Behold, I will reward thee for them this day, and will add to their reward that which is due; be neither afraid nor alarmed. I will go before thy face and will petition the king on thy behalf, and he will not deliver thee over into the hand of thine enemies; be of good courage now, O my friend, and fear not.' At that moment [the debtor] was afraid, and he shed tears with burning anguish of heart, and said, 'Woe is me! On whom shall I rely for comfort? On what hath passed or what is yet to come? I will weep then for my wasted kindness and compassion on my lying friends who would not remember my goodness [to them]. Woe be to my heart and to my folly that I did not make friends with this healing friend!'"

[p. 75] And this story pleased Yĕwâsĕf and he demanded an explanation thereof from the sage. And Baralâm answered, saying, "The first friend is riches, and the love of money which is in them [i.e. in men] casteth a man down into thousands of troubles, and in that love he findeth much misery. And when the time of his death cometh he can take with him nothing but useless rags, that is to say, only the cloths in which his body is wrapped. And the second friend is a man's wife, and his children, and the rest of his kinsfolk to whom his mind inclineth, and he neglecteth his soul through his affection for them. But in the hour of death we obtain no benefit from them, and he can only go to the grave alone; sometimes even they go back [from his grave] to their laughter and pleasure. And the third friend, whom he neglecteth and maketh to see that he is nothing [to him], is the chief works of spiritual excellence, namely faith, hope, love, truth of word,

alms and oblations, and the rest of the company of virtues of
all kinds, which will go before our face when we depart from
this world. And they petition God on our behalf, and they
deliver us from the hand of our evil enemies by their voices
which they lift up over us in the air, which is the abode of
those who wish to pass a severe sentence of judgement upon
us. This is the third friend—the beautiful love which setteth
in its mind only the beauty of our works; and it rewardeth
us with an increased reward."

And Yĕwâsĕf answered and said unto him, "O the splendid
reward that thou shalt have from thy God, O thou wisest of
all men of understanding! Behold now, my soul rejoiceth
more and more with each utterance in the desirable words
which thou utterest. Make me to know also the manner of
the transitory character of this world, and by what means a
man may go through it in safety and confidence."

[The parable of the man who was made king for one year.]

And the excellent Baralâm answered, saying, "Certain men
have told me that there was a very great city the inhabitants
of which were in the habit [p. 76] of taking a man who was a
stranger, one whom they did not know, one who knew nothing
whatsoever of the laws of this city, and who was wholly un-
acquainted with their ways and customs, and appointing him
king. And it is said that he ruled over them and had absolute
power over them, according to his own good will and pleasure,
for the period of one whole year. And at the end of the year,
during which he had lived in a state of pleasure unmixed with
sorrow, and in satiety and gladness, he imagined that the
kingdom would remain to him for ever. At that moment [the
people] rose up against him suddenly, and despoiled him of
the royal purple apparel, and made him to appear in the city
naked before the whole community. And then they drove
him out and settled him on a large island, which was a long
way off and was very rugged and barren. And it was impossible for him to obtain food to satisfy his need, and he could
get nothing to wear, and he remained hungry and naked.

And he was always sorrowful in mind, and [wondered] why his former glory, which he had never thought or expected would pass away, had departed from him.

"And according to the custom of the men of [that] city they chose in his room for the sovereignty a man whom they found. And he was [by chance] a man of very great knowledge, and full [of wisdom], and his understanding did not change because of the glory and power which surrounded him, and it did not diminish by reason of his royal position, as did that of those who had gone forth in difficulty and in much sorrow. And he used to meditate anxiously how he could improve the state of his mind, and he kept a strict watch over himself. And at that time he studied and investigated matters like a man who is wise in counsel, and he considered the behaviour of the men of that city in respect of his predecessors; and he knew the places of exile, and he learned of a certainty that it was right for him to choose [one of them] for himself. And when he knew of a certainty that after a short time the people would exile him to that island, and that he would have to leave the possessions which were stored up for others, straightway he opened unrestrainedly his treasure stores, over which he had been appointed, and he took out much money, and gold, and silver, and gems of great price. And he sent them away time after time by the hands of faithful [p. 77] servants, and they took them to that island to which the people would exile him a [little] later. And when the year was completed the men of the city rose up, and stripped him of the royal apparel, and drove him out to live with those kings whom they had expelled. Now these kings, each of whom had been king in his period, lived in tribulation and poverty. And that king who was wise in his counsel, and who had taken care to provide the means beforehand by sending on riches before his face, lived on food in good health, and had money always and pleasure which was never ending. And he put away from his soul the fear of the men of that city who were treacherous and not to be trusted; and he lived in riches through that excellent counsel which was full of all wisdom.

"And now [O king], do thou understand the following explanation of this story. The city is this world, which is deceitful and transient. And the people thereof are the chiefs and nobles who have gotten possession of the world of dark things of this transitory time, and who seduce us with the taste of its things which are to be desired for a moment only, and who force us to occupy ourselves with agreeable things which grow old, and which we imagine to be without corruption. And in this way we are seduced, and there doth not enter into us even one thought of the things that abide for ever, and we do not lay up any treasure at all for the life in the next world, which endureth for ever. And suddenly cometh the Angel of Death, and [the angels] will separate us from this world, and from the men of the city who are oppressors and evil ones, and we shall be naked like the man who hath consumed all his days, and they will take us into the land of darkness, and we shall be in the land wherein the moon doth not appear nor life in the flesh. And the good and trustworthy counsel which is well known in all generations, and which saved that wise king, is the diminutiveness and contemptibleness of myself who came to thee to show thee the path of goodness and the benefit wherein there is no deceit. This shall give thee the life [p. 78] everlasting whereof there is no end, and shall counsel thee to acquire and to lay up for thyself here treasure which shall be all glory; and it shall make thee to be remote from the error of this transitory world.

"At one time I was its vessel (?), and because of its promptings I observed carefully with the two eyes which were not led astray how they themselves were tempted all their days by the things which passed from men; some of them went beforehand, and some of them followed after; there was nothing among them which was enduring and which did not pass away. Among the things that make riches there was nothing enduring, the strength of the strong did not endure, the wisdom of the wise did not endure, nor the repose of those who dwelt in confident security, nor the pleasure of those who enjoyed themselves. And in the belaudings that belong to this world there was found to be neither cause for boasting nor support. Moreover, their work resembleth the passage of the water of the rivers which floweth into the depths of the sea; even so are all their transitory things. And for this reason I understood that they are all vanity and are profitless. Like all those who have gone before [us], and who are forgotten and have disappeared, even so shall glory be forgotten, whether it be that of a king, or that of a nobleman, or that of a mighty man of war, or that of any one like unto these; and likewise even if time maketh a treaty with these transitory things they will perish and decay. And I myself who am one of them shall fall (now there is no mistake about this) into a state of change and agedness according to unfailing custom ; and as those who have gone before me were not permitted to enjoy themselves with the things that pass away, even so shall it be with me. And as it is evident in the case of men that He assigneth ever to them movement, and removeth them from this world to the next, so one half of them He removeth from riches to poverty, and some of them He removeth from poverty to riches. Some He taketh out of the world and bringeth others in their places, and some of the men of understanding He reduceth to disgrace; and He heapeth honour upon those who are silly and upon those who play the fool, and He setteth upon thrones of honour those who have no wisdom.

"And the human race find it very difficult to see that they have not in them the strength which would enable them to stand up before the face of its spoiler. Moreover it is like the dove which [p. 79] fleeth before the face of the vulture and the hawk. The dove goeth from place to place, at one time taking shelter in a tree or in a cave, and at another in a hole in the rocks, and it casteth itself about hither and thither uttering many cries, and it findeth no place whereto it can flee and feel safe ; and it wandereth about continually in agitation and fear. Even so are those who love fleeting things; it is a bestial love and they suffer therein the suffering of misery. And they have no strength in them, and they know not what will happen to them at their end because of this, nor where will lead them this deceitful world, to which they have dedicated themselves so devotedly even after they have known it, and they have preferred evil to good, and have travelled the path of evil instead of the path of good. And they do not know who shall inherit the fruit of their difficult and painful toil, or whether the inheritors will be of their own kinsfolk or people whom they themselves have chosen. And who knoweth whether they will not be without friends and neighbours, and have only enemies who will oppose [their wishes]? All these things and the things that follow them shall come into the hall of the soul.

"I myself straightway hated this, and the whole period of my transitory life, and all the vain work which draggeth it (the soul) into fleeting things that dissolve it with earthly suffering. And straightway I cast off from my soul this tribulation, and I removed from myself everything, and I followed righteousness and the good that is good indeed, which is to be loved and which maketh its foundation. And I knew that this is the beginning of all good things, and one calleth [it] the 'beginning of wisdom.' Moreover it is itself perfect wisdom, and is itself the life which sorrow shall not reach, and it is remote from causing shame to those who acquire it, and men become strong thereby and place confidence in God. And I made strong my mind on this path, the path of the commandments of God wherein is no error. And I knew well that there was in it no stumbling, and no crookedness, and no rugged place, and no pit, and no terror, and that it was a well-paved path without a stumbling-block, and without thorn-bushes and noxious growth. On the contrary, [I knew] that it was a straight and a good path, which maketh to rejoice by the fairness of [p. 80] its appearance the eyes of those who travel thereon in purity, and especially of those who look out for it, and who await the good tidings of salvation [or, safety], so that they may hasten to travel on it with the feelings of pleasure which are everlasting. And because of my error in former times, and my seduction which was due to my madness, I devoted myself to the travelling upon it with vigour. And rightly did I choose it and prefer it to every [other road], and I began to build the habitation for my soul which had fallen down and was in ruins. And thus I made plans for myself. And I made wrath to withdraw from within my heart, and I heard the sound of the words of the wise man teaching and crying out to me, saying, 'O all ye who desire salvation, get ye out, and separate ye yourselves from the error of the world which changeth its appearance, and which after a very little [time] will not exist. Get ye out, turning not back, and ye shall carry [with you] the provision for the life which is for ever, and the taste of the pleasure thereof. For ye will have to travel over a road which reacheth afar and which will require many necessary things and many provisions, and ye shall find a place of rest for ever, a place wherein there are two cities that contain many habitations. One of these God hath prepared for those who love Him and perform His commandments, and it is full of every kind of beautiful thing. And those who are worthy of it shall live therein for ever, without corruption and without becoming old, where, as they have heard, there is no suffering, and no sorrow, and no lamentation. And the second [city] is full of darkness and suffering and sadness, and it is prepared for Satan and his hosts. Therein shall be cast those who do evil things, and those who have loved transitory things instead of the things that abide and pass not away ; and there they shall fall into corruption quickly and there [the angels who punish] shall make them food for everlasting fire.'

"And when I heard these words and knew the truth thereof, I appointed me a work whereby I might attain to that habitation, which is free from hunger and sorrow, and is full of every kind of good thing, and of which I now have the knowledge that it is for ever. [p. 81] And behold, I have attained to a part of the knowledge thereof, like a child who is growing up little by little in the spiritual life, and I see, as in a mirror, the things that are there, but when the full time hath arrived and I shall see Him face to face[1], then He will do away my shame and disgrace. And now I give thanks to God, in Jesus Christ our Lord, for, behold, the Law of the Holy Spirit in the spirit of life hath carried away from me the Law of sin and death, and hath opened mine eyes to the sight of the vision wherein is no error. The mind of the flesh is death, and the mind of the spirit is life and peace, even as I myself know the deceitfulness of transient things and the manner in which they lead astray, and I hate them with a perfect hatred.

"And I give thee likewise this same counsel so that thou mayest understand quickly, and mayest learn and know in thy heart the transitoriness of the world which is nigh unto thee. And thou must receive in this world all the things thereof, and mayest lay up for thyself the treasure of liberty, which is for ever, and which neither passeth away nor cometh to an end, the riches that poverty cannot find. When these riches are thine thou wilt go to Him without hindrance. And when thou departest thou wilt not be a man needy and destitute, but the possessor of the necessary means which it is meet to possess, the which thou wilt have laid up beforehand for thyself."

[*How the prince asked Baralâm how he could lay up treasure in heaven, and how Baralâm explained to him the efficacy of almsgiving.*]

And Yĕwâsĕf answered, saying, "How is it possible for me to send on for myself before-hand treasure of money and possessions in this world, so that when I depart to that world I shall find pleasure unending and incorruptible? And how can I hate that which is visible and choose that that which is invisible shall come? Explain also this to me openly with goodness and sincerity."

And the excellent Baralâm answered and said, "Thy sending money and riches on to that place which is for ever is an easy matter. If thou wilt give it to the needy, it will be

[1] 1 Cor. xiii. 11 12.

doubled for thee and thou wilt lay up treasure in the other world. One of the prophets, that is to say, Daniel, whose words are true, said unto King Nebuchadnezzar, 'O king, let my counsel be pleasing unto thee [p. 82] so that God may pardon thee thy sins caused by thy abundant injustice because of thy showing compassion on the poor[1].' And there is the word of our Redeemer Who said, 'Acquire for yourselves friends by the mammon of injustice, so that when ye depart they may receive you into their houses which are for ever[2].' And behold, well did our Lord lay down, both in the beginning and at the end, many precepts concerning the giving of alms, and in His saying, 'Blessed are the merciful, for to them mercy shall be shown[3].' Likewise everything which is given into the hand of the poor and needy shall be increased very greatly, and it is laid up as treasure in the other world with the usury thereon, for everything which shall be done to them, provided that it is something which pleaseth God, shall be rewarded twofold, even as He Himself said, 'He shall be rewarded a hundredfold, and he shall inherit life everlasting[4].' For He knoweth the benefactions and the gifts that are sublime and that give life. For this reason renounce the treasure of this world in the desires whereof thou hast been submerged for many days, and set thyself free to turn away from the attraction thereof. By these gifts of transitory things thou shalt buy the things that endure for ever, and by this help of God thou wilt be able to examine closely the destruction of the state of this world and to hold it lightly. And thou shalt journey on without sorrow for transitory things, and thou shalt depart to the abiding things that shall exist for ever. Thou wilt have removed the apparel of darkness and the works of death, and thou wilt have renounced this world, and that which is closely bound up with this world. And as for the flesh which groweth old, treat it as if it were thine enemy, and commit thyself to the care of the light which is not to be met with in the [present] manner of

---

[1] Dan. iv. 27.
[2] Luke xvi. 9.
[3] Matt. v. 7.
[4] Matt. xix. 21, 29.

thy journeying. Take upon thy shoulders the life-giving Cross, and follow Him without any turning back, so that thou mayest be praised with Him, and mayest become heir of the life which is unending, wherein is no deception."

[*How the prince enquired whether the commandments order-ing self-abnegation and the renunciation of the world were laid down by the Apostles and others in ancient times, or whether they were of recent origin.*]

And Yĕwâsĕf answered, saying, "Now as concerning the renunciation of everything, the abandonment of everything, and the acquisition of a life as difficult as that which thou hast already described to me : Did ye learn these things of old? Did ye receive them traditionally [p. 83] from the commandments of the Apostles? Or were they ordained in recent times? Or were these ordinances laid down thus by thyself, or didst thou choose them thyself?"

And the honourable Baralâm made answer to these questions and said unto him, "It is not a Law which I have fashioned newly that I declare unto thee—far be it from me to do such a thing—but it is that which I have received from olden time. The Lord said unto the man who asked Him, 'O Master, what shall I do that I may inherit the life which is everlasting?' (Now that man boasted himself, saying, 'I have kept everything which is written in the Law.') And the Lord answered and said unto him, 'One thing is left for thee [to do]; go and sell everything that thou hast and give [it] to the poor, and lay up for thyself the treasure which is in the heavens, and take up thy cross, and come, follow Me.' And when he heard this the man departed being sorrowful, for he was very rich. And when the Lord Jesus saw him thus sorrowful, He said, 'Assuredly it is difficult for those who have treasure to enter into the kingdom of heaven; it is easier for a camel to go through the hole of the needle than for the rich man to enter into the kingdom of heaven[1].' And all the saints heard this commandment, and they were ready

[1] Matt. xix. 16 ff.

forthwith to separate themselves from riches, seeing that the
difficulty caused by them was so great. And they cut themselves off completely from them, and they distributed all
they had among the poor, and prepared for themselves the
riches that are everlasting and indestructible. And they took
up of their own free will the lifegiving Cross, and followed
Him in the love of Christ God. Some of them died by
martyrdom, and some of them fought the fight in silent contemplation, but they let drop nothing of this work. This
then is the true philosophy, the knowledge whereof it is
necessary for thee to know well, namely, that this commandment that we must turn away from transitory things, and
make ourselves partners with the things that are abiding, is
from Christ our King and God."

*[How the prince enquired why these ancient commandments
were not universally observed at that time, and how Baralâm
showed him that it was due to the wilful blindness of men.]*

And Yĕwâsĕf answered and said unto him, "If this philosophy be so honourable and so ancient why doth not the
multitude practise this wisdom to-day?"

[p. 84] And Baralâm said unto him, "Behold, those who
have found it and acquired it are many, but many are lazy
and have held themselves back from it, even as our Lord
said, 'Those who travel on the road that maketh sorrowful
and is difficult are few, and those who travel on the road
that is broad are many[1].' Those who travel possessed entirely
by the love of money and by the counsel thereof seek the
love of desirable things and the love of vain glory which
leadeth astray. Behold, they become aliens from God, and
they are fettered. For the soul which is in absolute despair
cannot do the works of excellence ; behold, it is ready to
be dragged into bestial lusts, even as David the prophet
lamented concerning the folly (or madness) which is poured
out on souls like these, and concerning the gloom and darkness that covereth them over. And he lamented over the

---

[1] Matt. vii. 13, 14.

crassness of their hearts and the stubbornness of their minds, saying, 'O ye sons of the children of men, how long will ye make heavy your hearts? Why do ye love vanity? Why do ye follow falsehood[1]?' Why do ye imagine that this present world and the pleasure thereof are a great matter? And why do ye esteem vain praise, which is a naked thing and abideth in disgrace? The work that they do because of it is vain, that is to say, those who travel on that road are of more [importance] than the things which they send before. And the way is superior to [all] these, because it doth not act deceitfully. Vain praise is a mass of dust; one might call it a marriage of four [wives], seeing that it changeth and dismisseth them, one by one, to the last of them. And it is dissolved like vapour which is intangible, nay, it departeth like the shadow.

"And our Lord, to Whom be praise! commanded the Prophets, and the Apostles, and all the Saints to preach in the strongest terms, and to work to their utmost for the rousing up of everyone to the way of spiritual excellences, wherein there is no error. And because of this those who travel thereon are few, whilst those who choose the broad road which leadeth [p. 85] to destruction are many. And because of this it is not meet for us to belittle wisdom and the divine course, but we should regard them like the bright sun which shineth upon all, and sendeth forth its splendour, showing compassion, under command, to everyone and illumining all. And there are some who cover over their eyes, it being their wish not to see its light; now the darkness of the sun is because of their pride. And it is not meet that all men should neglect and renounce the praise of its excellence because of the folly of these others, for these others deprive themselves of the light which illumineth, for those are blind who dash themselves against a wall and who fall into many pits. And the shining sun is permanent in its constitution, and in the splendour of its beauty, and it illumineth these when shining with its light. And with this, a sublime simili-

---

[1] Psalm iv. 2.

tude! may be compared the light of Christ, which illumineth every man abundantly. He hath bestowed upon us the splendour of His light, and hath made every man a partner therein in proportion to his desire and vigilance ; His is the sun of righteousness Who never letteth Himself be lacking to any one of those who desire to see Him. And He never compelleth any one of those who chose darkness of their own free will, but every one ruleth the good pleasure of his heart with his own permission as long as he liveth in this visible world."

[*How the prince asked Baralâm for explanations of the terms " Free will " (αὐτεξούσιον) and " Choice " (προαίρεσις) and how the sage defined the same.*]

And Yĕwâsĕf wished him to make known [to him] what is [the meaning of] "permission of self," and what is [the meaning of] "power of good pleasure" (or, "power of the will ").

And the honourable sage Baralâm answered, saying, "' Permission of self' is the rational will (or wish) of the soul which is given unto thee without any restraint on him that wisheth, whether the wish be to perform works of excellence, or to do things that are to be rejected, and thus was it made by the Creator, may His Name be magnified ! 'Permission of self' is the faculty of movement in the understanding soul which ruleth itself. And the 'doing of [one's] will (or, good pleasure)' is the lesser wish which is in us, and what the counsel of the desires counselleth within us ; what we have already decided upon in our mind we wish for [and that is] [p. 86] our good pleasure. And the thought becometh a desire through the workings which are inside us, for a man will sometimes take counsel with himself as to whether it is desirable (or, necessary) to do a certain thing, and also he will decide as to what it is best [to do], and that cometh to pass ; and then he will think and approve of what his mind hath decided upon, and this is called 'the will.' But if he hath decided, and still maketh [himself] to question what he hath decided, and hath not thought it out completely, this is not called 'the will.' Moreover, if after his thinking there groweth up in the decision his good pleasure, that is that which he hath already decided upon (?). And these two operations, willing and choosing, are manifest, and one [taketh place] before the other. And it is manifest and well-known that the thinking [cometh] after the decision hath sprung up, and that this is his choice. And by this passage may be known that the words (i.e. willing and choosing) are employed in correct order, for he who chooseth a thing first of all willeth it, one [following] on the other; for no man maketh a decision in his will, and there is no man who can choose a thing before this, and thou canst not make a decision before knowing the matter. Not all the things that thou thinkest and knowest are good, but thou wishest to proceed from them to the knowledge of the same, and then it happeneth that that which he thought first returneth, provided that the wish be acceptable, and then he putteth forward his choice, and his good pleasure is strengthened. And thus the germ that he chooseth returneth and becometh the desire of counsel, in that it existeth in us, and the counsel that we guard arriveth in our interior. That which we will first of all in the mind we wish for and choose, for the whole mind thinketh about doing so. And thus a man chooseth first what was first in the mind, and everything that he maketh first is the thing chosen first. And this doth not [p. 87] concern things done only, but the raising up of the things chosen, which come first, and which are thought in the mind, and they appear at that time as crowns or tortures. That which is in us maketh us to know that the beginning of sin and the commission of the act precede will (or, desire), but the acts thereof are in proportion to the [power of] action that is in us. For within us exist acts that are like virtues, and within us are the signs of all the spiritual virtues ; and because of the acts which are therein its dispositions either are belauded or they cause it suffering. Likewise men weep by their own permission, and they make their choice by their own will ; and according as each man chooseth, in proportion to his own longing, he becometh a partner in the divine light, and he gaineth the fellowship of wisdom, for in it are

choosings of various kinds. And as there are in the heart of
the earth fountains of various kinds, some of them pouring
out water on the face of the earth, and some of them are
not very deep, and some of them are very deep, and among
these springs some pour out an abundant flow of good, sweet
water, and of the water that cometh up from a depth some
of it is bitter, and some of it is sweet, and some of it cometh
up boiling hot by the force of the spring, and some of it
droppeth in little drops only, so must thou understand to be
the various kinds of the choosings of men and their joy.
Some of them are hurried because they are very hot, and
some of them are sluggish because they are very cold, and in
some of them the power of turning aside absolutely ruleth,
and they turn to the doing of what is good, and there are
some of them who with all their might are the contrary of
this, from whom, against their will, the fountain of their
actions bursteth forth."

*[How the prince asked Baralâm if this doctrine of free will
and choice was held by him alone, and how the sage im-
puted the iniquitous deeds of the king his father to the
wilful misuse of his free will.]*

[p. 88] And Yĕwâsĕf answered and said unto him, "Is there
to be found among men anyone who this day preacheth this
thy [doctrine]? Or art thou alone in admonishing [us] that
this world is transitory as thou sayest?"

And Baralâm answered, saying, "I know not whether there
be anyone in your city who faileth to accept this [doctrine].
Behold, the injustice of thy father condoned thousands and
tens of thousands of sins of divers kinds, and among them
was the sin of determining that no one among you should
ever hear the story of the grace of God, whilst by [men of]
other tongues He is praised and is lauded with words that
are right, even as the Apostles who told the story taught,
and the fathers, who were clothed with divinity. His light
shineth in the Holy Church, which existeth from one end of
the world to the other, with a light whereof the beauty is

greater than the light of the sun. It is through this same God that I have been sent unto thee as a preacher and teacher."

And Yĕwâsĕf answered and said unto him, "Did not my father ever know anything of this [doctrine]?"

And the honourable sage Baralâm answered, saying, "The thing the doing of which was necessary he did not know, for he closed his mind, and did not wish to accept the doing of good of his own free will, on the contrary, he acquired the faculty of doing evil, even as every man chooseth and pleaseth."

And Yĕwâsĕf said unto him, "I wish to know what this [thing] was."

And Baralâm answered him, saying, "The thing that is too difficult for man, and is impossible for him to do, is not too difficult for God. How knowest thou whether thou canst save thy father, and whether by some wonderful means thou canst become a father to thy begetter? I have heard that his kingdom is indeed in a good [p. 89] condition, and that he governeth the people who are under his dominion in sincerity, and love, and quietness."

[*The parable of the pagan King and the believing Wazîr, or the story of the wine-drinker and the dancing woman in a cellar.*]

Now the father of Yĕwâsĕf remained in crassness of heart because he did not know that God was the refuge of hearts; and he was devoted absolutely to errors, that is to say, to the error of idols. And he had only one counsellor who worshipped God; he was an excellent man, and was also well versed in the wisdom which is honourable; and he used to admonish the king and to urge him on to the doing of good deeds. And he was sorry because the king was led into error, and he wished to rebuke him because of this, but he omitted to do so, fearing the rising up of his wrath, and fearing lest it should be the means of bringing calamity upon himself and the loss of his exalted position, and lest it should cause the withdrawal of the benefit that accrued to many through him. And he sought for a time of peace and agreement when he might be able to draw him to that which would be profitable to him.

And one night the king said unto him, "Come, let us go out and walk about the city, peradventure we may see something in it which shall be profitable to us." And as they were walking about the city they saw a brilliant light which was emitted from a hole in the ground, and they steadied their gaze, and examined it carefully. And they saw in the ground a kind of cellar, and in it was sitting a man who was living there in great want, and he was wearing wretched apparel, and before him was a woman who was giving him wine to drink. And when the man received the cup from her hand the woman danced before him a dance to make him to rejoice, and she caused him to rejoice by the swift movement of her feet as she danced, and she flattered him by her praises which he received with ready willingness. And when the king had looked on this [scene] for some time he marvelled and said, "How can these people live in such a state of wretchedness, lacking as they do both house and apparel, and still rejoice in living out the full period of their days?" Then the king said unto the captain of his hosts, "O my friend, is not this a marvellous sight? Why should we not rejoice, I and thou, in this pleasure which we have? And why should we not be [p. 90] pleased that we live during a season of pleasure, and glory, and majesty? And why should not we enjoy ourselves for one day even as this wretched woman maketh merry and enjoyeth herself? These two people have not in them the knowledge that there existeth in this life enmity which they ought to fear, and they imagine that it is a right thing and they are well-pleased therewith."

[*How the Wazîr explained the scene which he and the King had witnessed.*]

And straightway the captain of the king's hosts found a manner of speech from which it would appear that he was agreeing with the king, and he said unto him, "What doth the manner of life of these people seem to be like unto thee?" And the king answered and said unto him, "It is worse and more terrible than anything I have ever seen since I was born." Then the captain of the hosts said unto him, "Truly, this is very bad, but our life, the life which we lead, will seem to be just the same to those who see us, that is to say, to those who lived in glory before the world was, and who will prevail for ever, and who [enjoy] the good things which are exalted above all wisdom and knowledge. And they [possess] habitations that are made of gold. And in like manner will appear contemptible the beautiful apparel and all the pleasure of this world in the sight of those who know the beauty of those habitations, which are in heaven, and which are not made with hands, and which we are unable to describe, for God is the maker thereof, and of the unfading Crowns which the Maker of the universe hath prepared for His friends, after the manner of double feast-chambers, and the anxiety concerning transient things. And as we ourselves think concerning these people who are lacking in understanding, even so shall we appear to those who live in glory. And we ourselves are bound to come to an end like those who are seduced by this useless and fleeting world, and who desecrate themselves with this present transient and false glory, and with the pleasure wherein there is no profit. And now weeping and lamentation are meet for us before the eyes of those who have tasted that pleasure that abideth for ever."

And when the king heard these words from him he was amazed and said unto him, "And who are these who have acquired the life of good things which is more excellent and more glorious than the life which we now are living?" And the captain of the hosts answered, saying, "These are they who have preferred the work of the gifts that abide for ever to the things that are transient." And again the king asked him to inform him what were these gifts which last for ever. And the captain of his hosts answered and said unto him, "These are they who have chosen [p. 91] the glory of the kingdom that shall never be destroyed, and the life that death shall never reach, and the riches to which exhaustion shall never come, and joy and gladness wherein sorrow shall never mingle. These are they who are exceedingly blessed, and they live a life that lasteth for ever, and they are provided with all the delights and with all the riches that make them happy, and that are in the kingdom of God, without toil and without fatigue; and with Christ they reign over a kingdom that shall never come to an end."

And the king answered and said unto him, "And who is fit to receive such enduring gifts as these?"

And the captain of his hosts answered and said unto him, "Those who travel that path which leadeth thither, for there is nothing that can prevent those who wish to enter from entering."

And the king said unto him, "Of what kind is the path which carrieth [a man] thither?"

And the captain of his hosts, whose soul was shining, said unto him, "The path is the knowledge of Him Who is God indeed, Who is God alone with His Son, Who is His Word, Jesus Christ, and His Holy Spirit, the Lifegiver."

And the king could not understand this, for the majesty of [his] sovereignty possessed him, and he answered and said unto him, "What hath prevented thee up to now from informing us about this matter? Whether it is true, or whether it is because there is a doubt in it it is meet for us to search out the matter very carefully until we come upon the truth, and to dispel all doubt about it."

And the captain of his hosts answered and said unto him, "It is not the smallest doubt whatsoever that hath prevented me from informing thee about it, for this thing is certain, and it is removed absolutely from doubt, and from all blemish (or, suspicion), but because of the glory of thy sovereignty I felt ashamed to be the one to reprove thee openly. Command me, however, to serve thee so that I may recount this matter to thee. For up to now I have been thy minister and I stand under thy command."

And the king answered him, saying, "Yea, renew the discussion of this matter for me [p. 92] continually, not once each day, but always, and on every occasion; for this is not a matter which it is meet for me to enquire about negligently, but with the deepest interest and urgency."

And Baralâm said also unto Yĕwâsĕf, "Behold, we have heard concerning this king that he is careless about the pursuit of the good things that are to come after, and that he fulfilleth the appointed time of his days in this world without troubling himself about them, and that he will not make himself miserable about the blessed things that are to come. And if thou wast to tell thy father this at a time of quietness peradventure he might understand how many evils surround him, and it might be that he would turn from this [manner of life] and choose for himself one that is better. For he who subjecteth himself to this present time, and believeth therein, is like unto a blind man who is groping about trying to find the light, but who is in truth turning his face towards the darkness of those who doubt with evil desire."

[*How the prince committed the direction of his father to God, and how he wished to renounce the world, and to end his days with Baralâm, and how Baralâm spake the parable of the young man and the maiden who made tents.*]

And Yĕwâsĕf said, "As for the actions of my father God directeth them according to His Will, for He is almighty, even as thou thyself sayest; and as for myself, I desire most earnestly to renounce these transitory things. And behold, I have it in mind to go away far from the world and finish my life with thee, so that I may not fall into the transitory things of this present time."

And Baralâm answered, saying, "If thou doest this thing actually thou wilt become like unto a certain young man of whom I have heard whose forefathers were believers, and they betrothed to him the daughter of a certain nobleman who was well known, and who might be compared to thyself in person and dignity and in [his] riches which were very great. And the young man enquired into this matter, and when he heard this thing he hated it in his heart, and he withdrew himself, and fled, and forsook his father. And it came to pass that during the time of his travel a certain poor old man received him, and he entered his house, so that he might rest from the fierce heat of the sun. And the old man had an only daughter who worked with her hands, and her mouth uttered praises ceaselessly, and she thanked [God] from the depth of her heart. And when the young man heard her [p. 93] praisings, he said unto her, 'O daughter, what is thy work, and in what consisteth the beauty of thy mode of life? I see that thou art a poor tentmaker, and that many noble gifts have been bestowed upon thee.' And she said unto him, 'Dost thou not know that a small amount of healing medicine will cure a man of great pain? Therefore we give thanks unto God for small matters, and for what is smaller than these, and this becometh a cause for [thanking God] for the things which are more precious than they. And behold, I am the daughter of a feeble old man, and I thank God for these small things, and I bless Him because there shall be praise to Him from every created thing for ever. And I know that it is He Himself Who giveth this [present world], and He Himself hath the power to give what is greater than this. And this present world, because it is external, and because it cometh not to us from within, hath no benefit to those who acquire it, I say (i.e. I mean) even if there be not in it destruction, for both of them (i.e. the external and the internal) travel together on one road and are thrust onwards. And of the things that are necessary and are evident, behold, there have been given unto me by God many great gifts which are innumerable, and my ability is unable to employ them for the best. I was created in the likeness of God, exalted be His praise! And behold, He hath graciously bestowed upon me the knowledge of Himself, and I have become a rational being more honourable than all the beasts. And behold, by the compassion of God I have been called from death to life everlasting, and He hath given unto me the power to become a partner in His Holy Mysteries.

And behold, He hath opened unto me the gates of the Garden of Pleasure without restraint, and He hath given me the power to enter whensoever I wish. And because of the greatness of these gifts, wherein the rich and the poor participate equally, it is impossible for me to thank Him sufficiently and in accordance with what is fitting. And if I did not offer to the Giver of this honour thanks and praise what excuse should I have, and what should I say before Him?'

[p. 94] "And the young man marvelled at the beauty of her faith and at the abundance of her wisdom, and he called to her father and said unto him, 'Give me thy daughter and let her be my wife, for I love her understanding.' And the old man answered and said unto him, 'O my son, this befitteth thee not—to take to wife the daughter of poor and needy folk, thou thyself being the son of famous people.' And the young man said unto him, 'It is good for me to take her if thou thyself art pleased thereat. For behold, my father hath betrothed to me the daughter of rich and noble parents and I fled from this thing; and as for this daughter of thine, behold, I love her and desire her for the sake of the beauty of her faith in God, and especially for her understanding; moreover, I have decided to take unto myself a wife.' And the old man answered and said unto him, 'I cannot give her to thee to take away from me to the house of thy father, and thou shalt not separate her from me for she is my only [child].' And the young man answered, saying, 'I will dwell with you and will acquire your habits.' And straightway he stripped off his beautiful apparel, and asked the old man for clothing and arrayed himself therein. And the old man tested him many times, and tested his mind in various kinds of ways. And when he knew that there was sense in him and strong and firm understanding, and that the thought caused by the lust of the flesh had not happened upon him, he gave him his daughter as he wished. But the young man had only chosen her for the sake of her faith and her beauty, and his wish did not remind him that he would have to live in tribulation and misery; and he forsook the majesty of his honourable estate and the honour of his family.

And at that moment the old man took his hand, and brought him into his treasure house, and showed him much riches which had been hidden there by himself, [and] money beyond count, whereof the like the young man had never seen since he was born. And the old man said unto him, 'O my son, all this which thou seest I have given unto thee because thou hast chosen to be the heir of my riches.' And the young man inherited those riches."

[*How the prince approved of the parable which, he thought, had some bearing on his own case, and how Baralâm encouraged him to have confidence in his own strength.*]

And Yĕwâsĕf answered and said unto Baralâm, "This story also [p. 95] it seemeth to me should stir me up to action, and I think that it hath been related by thee for my benefit, so that if I attempt the things which are [described] in it they ought to strengthen my mind."

And Baralâm said unto him, "I have tried thee, and I know that in thy mind and soul thou art strong, and that thy knowledge of the right is acute because of what thou hast said about this word and this thing. As for me, I bow my knees and I worship our God Who is glorious in His Trinity, the Maker of all things, both those that are visible and those that are invisible, Who existeth indeed, Who is indestructible, and Who liveth for ever in His Being. There is no beginning whatsoever and no ending to His awful praise, He is mighty over every good work, and He is compassionate and will illumine the eyes of thine heart, and will give thee Divine wisdom and the light of His understanding, so that thou mayest know what is the hope of His calling, and what are the riches of His praise which He maketh the righteous to inherit, and Who He is Who is exalted within us in the exaltation of His power in those who believe, and Who He is Who is built manifestly upon the foundation of the Apostles and the Blessed Prophets, the foundation which existed before the world, that is to say, Jesus Christ, the strong Stone at the top of the corner[1] of His holiness, the God Who will attach thee to Him firmly."

[How, in answer to the prince's request, Baralâm continued his explanation of the Christian Religion.]

And the fear of God entered into the heart of Yĕwâsĕf when he heard this, and he said, "I desire to know thoroughly all this matter, and I demand from thee that thou shalt make me to know the glory of God and the perfection of His Power."

And Baralâm said unto him, "I will pray to God and entreat Him to make [thee] to know this, and to set in thy heart a similitude of this thing. As for His glory and power, men are not able to describe them, neither the beginning nor the end thereof, even as the Holy Gospel of the great orator of God [p. 96] saith, 'No one hath ever seen God, the Only Son, Who is in the bosom of His Father[2].' He said this, and also that the greatness of His glory and honour cannot be comprehended. Who then among the beings of earth is able to comprehend His glory and honour, unless He Himself revealeth them to him according as He willeth, and according as He hath revealed [them] to the Prophets and Apostles? As for us, we can only know Him, according to the capacity of our ability, from the words of their preaching and from the manner of these things. The Book saith, 'The heavens declare the glory of God, and the firmament maketh known the work of His hands[3].' And what is invisible it hath been impossible [to describe] from the time when He created the world in His wisdom; and in this respect one cannot know the power of His Godhead, Which existed before the world. It is like a man who hath seen a beautiful habitation which hath been made with wisdom, or a building which hath been built with fine intelligence, and he straightway examineth carefully the structure thereof, and enquireth who was the builder. Similarly I myself also cannot make something out of what does not exist and make it to have being, and if I could (?) it would be impossible for me

---

[1] Psalm cxviii. 22; Ephesians ii. 20.
[2] John i. 18.   [3] Psalm xix. 1.

to consider great that which is put forth. But of Him Who made me to understand the beauty of His arrangement of creation, which is a beautiful marvel, I have deduced from that similitude the knowledge of His wisdom, so that I can imagine what it is, but only in proportion to my being able to understand [it]. I was created from a state of non-existence, and I did not come into being of myself when I was created. But He created me according to His Will and He commanded me to become the head over all His creatures, and He made me a little less than His angels[1]. And I shall be broken up in pieces again, and He shall give me strength, and He shall renew my created form according to what is best. And He shall also make me to go forth from this world by His divine commandment, and He shall translate me to another life, which shall endure for ever and shall have no end. And it is impossible for me to resist in any way what cometh from His wisdom. I cannot add anything to myself, and I can take nothing from my stature, nor anything from the goodliness of my person, and I cannot renew any of my members which have waxed old [p. 97], and I cannot restore any of them which have decayed. No man whatsoever is able to do any one of all these things, neither king, nor sage, nor rich man, nor strong man; none of these can deal successfully with operations that are connected with the body. For He Himself saith, 'No king and no nobleman will have a second birth, but to all of them there is one manner of entrance into this world, and they shall all go forth from the same in the same manner[2].'

"And from these [considerations] we are guided to the knowledge of the work of the Creator; to Him be praise! And together with this examine carefully the ordering of this beautifully ordained creation, and the Guardian of all created things, for He changeth them according to their natures and appearances. And of created beings with spiritual natures He changeth their minds, and directeth their counsel towards what is profitable and to the doing of what is good, and to

---

[1] Psalm viii. 5.　　[2] Compare Psalm xlix. 10; Eccles. ii. 16; ix. 2.

setting them far from evil. The things that are visible are brought forth and they wither away through what is bad, and through diminution, and through becoming changed, and through removal from place to place. And because of this they proclaim with loud voices, although [they utter] no word, that the God Who is uncreate is their Creator, the God Who is not subject to chance and to destruction.

"And now, how is it that the natural things which are absolutely opposed to each other have become one world (for their reconciliation and agreement are well known), unless there existeth in this world a mighty Power which maketh them to be at peace with each other in their well-ordered positions? And that same Power keepeth them together always without separation, and preserveth them from decay. And how is it that a thing abideth which hath no definite position? And if it doth not will this agreement and this ordered arrangement and doth not maintain it, how is it maintained? Even as the Book saith, 'If there be none who directeth the ship, and if there be none to strengthen it, it is sunk [in the sea']. For behold, when we look at a little house [we know that] it is unable to take care of itself, and that there is some one in it who taketh care of it; how then [p. 98] is it possible for this world, which is so great and beautiful, to have endured for so long a period of years without a strengthener, and a vivifier of the creatures thereof Who is wonderful? Is it possible for it to have existed without a sustainer and a glorious Governor, and without the care and protection of sublime wisdom? Behold, how many are the years which this heaven hath endured? And it hath not waxed old, nor hath it become dissolved. And the [fructifying] power of the earth hath not become sterile owing to length of times. And the fountains of water have not ceased to pour out their flow since the time when they were first created, and the sea receiveth such great rivers as these which [we see] without overflowing its boundary. And the courses of the luminaries, the sun and the moon, are unchanged, and the ordering of the night and the day is unaltered. And from all these things which cannot be described is known the power of Him concerning Whom the Prophets and Holy Apostles bore witness, but no man whatsoever is able to understand His glory, nor how adequately to ascribe to Him the ten thousand praises which are meet for Him.

"For the divine Apostle Paul, when he was proclaiming this same Christ to all spiritual and terrestrial beings in order to make them know Him, said, 'In one aspect we know Him in our minds, but when the perfection [of knowledge] cometh, then that will be done away[1].' He saith this because the track of His great wisdom which cannot be comprehended is wanting. And he cried out clearly and said, 'The depth of the wisdom of God cannot be sought out, and the track of His path cannot be known[2].' And if it was thus with the man who came to the third heaven, who heard words which he was unable to utter, and he could not [say] what these words were like, even so is it with me. He was by no manner of means able at all to enter into these depths thereof, [and he could not approach] the incomprehensible mysteries thereof. And so he could say nothing in his understanding and in his mind, and he was not able to think out the matter thereof with sure knowledge, unless this [faculty] had been given unto him from the Giver of wisdom, Who maketh wise those who possess not wisdom. For we are in His hand, and our speech also, and all wisdom and understanding are from Him. And it is He Who hath given unto us the knowledge of the things that exist, wherein is no falsehood, so that we may understand the foundation of the [p. 99] world, and the construction of natural objects, and their beginning and their end, and what will happen in times [to come], and the transformations and the changes which are affected by times and seasons. For He hath stablished everything by the scales and by calculation. For unto Him belongeth always the power to make the mighty things that exist, and no one is able to stand against the power of His arms; for like the tongue of the balance even so is the world before His face, and it is like unto a drop of dew upon

[1] 1 Cor. xiii. 10, 12. [2] Romans xi. 33.

the earth. He is the Mighty One Who is over everything, He payeth no heed to the sins of the world, and He putteth no man to shame, and He repelleth not those who come to Him. He alone is the Good One, the God Who loveth souls, may the name of His holy glory be blessed! He is above everyone who is praised, and He is exalted above all praise for ever."

[*How the prince enquired of Baralâm concerning his age, his place of abode, and his companions in his divine philosophy.*]

And Yĕwâsĕf answered and said unto him, "O thou who excellest in wisdom, who art heavily laden with grace, [who hast seen] many days, thou hast impressed so deeply on my mind what is sufficient for believing, and what is best for salvation, which we have sought out by our questionings, that I think thou hast never taught anything better than this. Thou sayest with thy voice that God, the Creator of the Universe, cannot be embraced or approached by fleshly minds, and thou hast proclaimed openly the majesty of His glory in words which cannot be overcome by argument, and that no one is able to comprehend Him, except those to whom He hath revealed [Himself], just as He Himself commandeth the tongue of the balance. And I marvel at thy wisdom, as thou reasonest, and at thy power of expressing the same. But tell me, O most blessed of men, how many years are the period of thy days? In what place didst thou set thy habitation? And who are thy companions in [thy] philosophy? For my soul is in a state of great suspense, and I do not wish to be separated from thee during the length of the period of my life."

And Baralâm answered, saying, "My years, as I count them, are five and forty, and my place of habitation is in the desert of Sanâ'ôr. And I have [p. 100] certain fighters of the spiritual fight who dwell with me, and they draw from the water which goeth up to heaven."

And Yĕwâsĕf answered and said unto him, "How canst thou tell me such a thing now? As it appeareth to me the length of thy days must be more than seventy years, and as for what thou sayest I think it is not true."

And Baralâm, the wise in counsel, answered and said unto him: "If thou wishest to know [the number of] the years [since] my birth, thy estimate of this is good, though it is more than seventy; but thou must not reckon to me [the years of] my life which I have lived in deceit, which is the custom of this transitory world, when I lived in serving the body and in sin. Behold, I am now arrayed in the garb of the inner man, and I do not call the years of sin life at all. And the world being crucified to me, and I also because of it, I have cast away the old man, which is corrupt with the desire of deceit, and shall never live again in my body; but Christ shall live in me. And now I live my life truly in the Son of God, Who loveth me, and hath given Himself for me. And these years rightly, and properly, and undoubtedly do I call years [of life], and days of salvation. Let this thought (or, mind) be with thee continually. And thou must never consider to be living those who are dead through the working of sin, and those who live committing sin, and who serve the life of this transitory world; but know thou that such as these are slain and dead to the operation of the life that is immortal, and this is understood by the rational and under- standing soul. For one of the wise men called sin 'death,' and Paul, the Apostle, saith thus: 'If ye continue to be the servants of sin ye are remote from righteousness and are separated therefrom. What kind of fruit shall ye have from this state of life wherein ye are now living? For the end thereof is death. And now, behold, ye are set free from sin and are made servants of God [p. 101] and ye shall bring forth the fruit of holiness, the end whereof is the life which is everlasting. For the fruit of sin is death, and the grace of God is the life which is for ever[1].' "

And Yĕwâsĕf answered and said unto him, "If [the years] of living according to the flesh are not reckoned by thee

---

[1] Romans vi. 20–23.

among the years of life, it is not meet that one should call them death, for everyone feareth death."

And Baralâm said unto him, "Thus do I believe without doubt: I am wholly unafraid of this death which is temporal, And if it cometh upon me whilst I am walking under the direction of God, I shall never call 'death' my departure from death into the glorious life in Christ, which the saints wished to receive when they were burdened with this world. And concerning this the Apostle saith, 'We know that if our earthly habitation is destroyed we have a building which God hath built in the heavens, which the hand of man hath not made. If we put on this [apparel] we shall not be found naked. And if we sorrow in this habitation [because of] this death we can depart to one which is more honourable, and which cannot be taken away from us. But let us clothe ourselves in this wise so that at length we may come through what is mortal to life[1].' And he saith also, 'I am a miserable man; who shall deliver me from the mortal body? I thank God through Jesus Christ our Lord[2].' And he saith moreover, 'I wish to dwell and to be with Christ[3].' And David also saith, 'How long shall it be before I come and appear before the face of God[4]?' And now, let it not be thought that I fear less than everyone, and that I do not fear the death of the body. And it is necessary for thee to know that of a certainty I do not esteem the wrath of thy father as a light matter, and that I have come to thee without fear that I may declare unto thee the word of salvation. For I have chosen the word of the Lord my God above everything, and I desire to depart to Him, and I am not terrified at death, which is only momentary, but I am subject to God's command. And I am not afraid of those who are not able [p. 102] to kill the soul, but I am afraid of Him who hath power to destroy both the soul and the body in the fire of Jahânnam[5]."

[1] 2 Cor. v. 1–4.
[2] Romans vii. 24.
[3] Philippians i. 23.
[4] Psalm xlii. 2.
[5] Matt. x. 28.

[*How the prince asked Baralâm for information about the food which he ate, the clothes which he wore, and the rules of the ascetic life which he and his fellows lived in the desert.*]

And Yĕwâsĕf answered, saying, "Mighty is the strength of thy true wisdom, which is exalted far above the nature of those beings of earth who are servants of [this] transitory life. With difficulty they drag themselves from it and forsake it, whilst ye blessed ones yourselves seek after the will which conquereth. Inform me now how thou and those who are with thee are able to feed yourselves in this desert, and whence ye obtain apparel, and explain to me your statutes and ordinances."

And Baralâm answered, saying, "Our food consisteth of the fruit of trees, and what we can obtain of herbs [and] grass, which are watered by the heavenly dew, and on account of which no one will quarrel [with us], and we find the means of our subsistence in the morning spread out and made ready for everyone. And a table [or, meal] is prepared forthwith without trouble and without great fatigue, and without anxiety (?). And as for that bread which one of our brethren who are our neighbours bringeth to us, we accept it as a blessing which is sent unto us by a Most High Providence, at the same time blessing him that offereth it to us in faith. As for our clothing, it consisteth of pieces of cloth made of hair. Sometimes it is made of old camels' hair which is sewn together in so many places that it maketh our flesh to melt, and this is our covering in summer and winter; and as for the apparel which it is meet for us to put on, we never take it off from us until it is worn out and is a mass of rags. And we wish that by means of these tribulations of cold and heat we may attain to that apparel which we shall wear hereafter and which never groweth old."

And Yĕwâsĕf said unto him, "Where dost thou obtain this apparel which thou art wearing?"

And Baralâm said unto him, "[I obtained it] from certain brethren who are believers when I wished to come to thee.

For it was not meet that I should come unto thee in that [ragged garb]. I was like the man who had kinsfolk who loved him more than all their other [p. 103] kinsfolk. Now he was living in exile by himself among an alien people, and he wished to take himself out of that place. And he put off his own apparel, which was [to them] like that of an alien, and put on apparel like that worn by those who were alien to him, so that he might enter into their city; and he freed himself from all the indications of the nobility of his family, and he acted the part of a servant with such astuteness that he saved himself by doing bitter violence to his feelings. Even thus have I done, for when I knew thy history I adorned myself with this apparel, and I came to sow in thy heart the seed of the Divine Story and to deliver thee from the works of the wicked possessor of the world. And now, behold, by the power of God I have finished my mission, and I have obtained my desire, in proportion to my strength, and I have told thee what it behoveth thee to know, and I have taught thee what the Prophets and Apostles preached so that it may be to thee for an admonition, without acting deceitfully about the same and in perfect love. I have drawn thee away from the error of transitory things which are here and from this world which is full of evils, and from the crafty acts of all those who are in subjection thereto. And now it is necessary for me to depart to whence I came, and forthwith I will cast aside my alien disguise and put on my own apparel."

[*How when the prince had examined Baralâm's desert apparel, which was made of bark-cloth, and seen the marks of blisterings and scorchings on his body he determined to receive baptism, and to forsake the world.*]

And Yĕwâsĕf entreated him to show him the apparel which he was in the habit of wearing, and thereupon Baralâm put on again the apparel which he usually wore over his [alien] apparel. And Yĕwâsĕf saw a thing which struck him with amazement, for he saw that the apparel which he put on was [made] of the bark of trees, and he realized that his flesh had

everywhere been worn away thereby, and how his skin had
been blistered off by the heat of the sun, and that he had
become very dark in colour. And he saw that from his loins
downwards to his knees he wore very coarse hair-cloth, and
that he girded his loins with a girdle the like of which the
people there had never imagined. And Yĕwâsĕf marvelled at
the harsh severity of Baralâm's fight, and his mind became
stupefied, and he was quite speechless at the sight of his
patient endurance. And he cried out and wept and said unto
Baralâm, "If thou hadst only come to me [p. 104] to free me
from the bitter slavery of Satan [thou wouldst have done well].
But complete thy benevolence towards me and take my soul
out of bondage, and carry me away with thee, and let us
depart from this place, so that I may deliver myself from the
guile of the world. And I will receive the seal of holy baptism,
and I will become thy companion in this marvellous philosophy, and in this tranquillity which is above the nature of
the children of men."

[*How Baralâm related to prince Yĕwâsĕf the parable of
the rich man and the gazelle.*]

And the honourable Baralâm declared unto him a parable,
saying, "A certain rich man brought up a gazelle in his house,
and since the creature had grown up with him, he was sorry
that it would not become accustomed to him, as a human
being would have done. One day the gazelle strayed away
and found a herd of gazelle and it began to wander about
in the fields near them, but it returned in the evening. And
it escaped again in the morning, through the negligence of
the servants in whose charge it was. And one day it made
friends with the herd of gazelle, and it followed them as it
was wont to do by natural instinct. And the soldiers of the
rich man mounted their horses, and followed its tracks quickly,
and caught it; and they hunted the herd, some of which they
killed and some they hurt badly. I fear that it may happen
to us even as it happened to this herd. If thou followest me,
I may not be able to remain with thee, and I may become

the cause of much injury to my companions; and moreover, I shall be condemned by thy father for ever. But the counsel of God concerning thee at this moment is this: Thou shalt be sealed with the seal of holy and divine Baptism, and thou shalt dwell in thy city accepting everything of the beautiful Faith, and thou shalt be a doer of the commandments of Christ; and when the Giver of good things willeth, He will make an end of this period and hour. And then thou shalt come to us in confidence (or, boldly), and we will dwell each with the other for the rest of our transitory life; and I am confident [p. 105] by God that we shall dwell together in the world which is to come without being separated."

[*How the prince decided to accept Christian baptism.*]

And Yĕwâsĕf let many tears fall from his eyes, and he said unto him, "God's Will be done! And may His Will now assign to me divine, Christian Baptism. Take from me my money and my apparel, and let them be for the food and apparel of you, that is, of thyself and those who are with thee. And depart thou, and take care for thyself in the place of thy tranquillity, and pray on my behalf ceaselessly and continually that I may not turn back ashamed of my hope; and may He make me able to come to thee quickly! Meanwhile I will prepare myself with much labour for that which is profitable."

And Baralâm answered and said unto him, "Have I not already told thee that these poor and wretched folk (i.e. the hermits) have no craving for the things of the world, whilst the rich crave exceedingly for riches unending? The [rich] man is continually heaping up money upon money, and he never resteth from watching and seeking after it, and he craveth for riches without ever being satisfied; now this is the poverty which is absolute. And those who reject transitory things abandon them because of their love for the things that endure for ever. But they esteem this as the finding of riches, and as the gaining of Christ Himself, Who is perfect riches, and they cast aside all anxiety about the food which is transitory, and the apparel which waxeth old. And they set their minds upon God, and put their trust in Him, rejoicing in the renunciation of possessions with a joy that none of those who love the world can obtain. The latter exult in the temporal riches which they lay up and leave to others, whereas the former hope in their minds for the good things that have no end. Verily I say unto thee that the former are far richer than thou and all the kings of the earth. But as for thee, do thou acquire for thyself possessions that resemble this spiritual possession. If thou shalt indeed acquire them perfectly, thou wilt desire [p. 106] to increase them in righteousness, and thou wilt never wish to give any of them away. These are the true acquisitions, whereas the riches which are transitory, having been once acquired, very often go to friends whom they do not benefit. And it is meet for me to call 'perfect poverty' the abnegation of those who long for heavenly riches, and who flee from [transitory riches] with an eager will, even as men flee from before a serpent.

"And if I were to take the enemy whom those who have renounced the world, my brethren and my companions in service, have slain and trodden upon with their feet, and to receive him alive from thee and bring him to them, I myself should become the cause of contention and suffering, and I should moreover be called, without falsehood, a wicked servant. Far be it from me to do this thing! And how could I think of glorious apparel? For how could I put on garments made of skin and rich stuff over my poor apparel before the faces of those who have cast off the cloaks of corruption and the tunics of iniquity, and have rejected them to the utmost of their power? Moreover, as to my friends, I have confidence in them that they desire nothing whatsoever of all these things, for the tranquillity of the desert sufficeth them, knowing well that that is true pleasure.

"And as for thy money and thy apparel which thou dost wish to give away, give them to the destitute, and lay up treasure for thyself in the world which is to come, in the treasury wherefrom things cannot be stolen[1], and make God

[1] Matt. vi. 20.

to be thy helper through their prayers. And do thou likewise make the giving away of riches thy helper, besides the doing of good deeds which shall last for ever. Put on thyself the armour of the Holy Spirit, girding thy loins about with righteousness. Put on the breastplate of righteousness, and set the helmet of salvation upon thy head, and put on thy feet as shoes the devotion of thyself to the work of proclaiming peace, and grasp in thy hand the shield of faith, and the sword of the Spirit, which is the Word of God that cutteth like a knife[1]. And take good heed to thyself in this wise, with strength, [p. 107] and fight the fight against the mind in full confidence until thou dost overcome it and break in pieces on the ground Satan the governor thereof, so that thou mayest adorn thyself with the crowns of victory."

And Baralâm endowed him with strength from the source of life in the right hand of God. And with these Divine laws and words of salvation, and [others that were] like unto them, Saint Baralâm admonished the king's son. And he prepared him to receive Divine Baptism, and he commanded him to fast and to pray, according to the custom which was ordained. And he never separated himself from him, and he kept watch over him continually. And he taught him all the glorious and divine, and different dogmas of the Holy Faith; and he read to him the Holy Gospel, and the Apostolic Admonitions, and he explained to him and made him know the words of the Prophets. For he was a young man instructed by God, and he carried in his mouth every word of admonition of the Old and the New Testaments, and he sent them forth with the word of the Divine Spirit like fire which kindleth into a blaze the knowledge of the True Light.

And on that day whereon he wished to bring him into [the Faith], and to baptize him with Christian Baptism, he began to instruct him, saying, "Behold, O spiritual son, thou art prepared to receive the seal of Christ, and to have impressed on thy face the seal of the light of His face, and thou shalt

---

[1] Ephesians vi. 13-17 ; Hebrews iv. 12.

become a son of God and a habitation of the Holy Spirit, the Vivifier. Believe in the Father, and the Son, and the Holy Spirit, the Head of life, Who is praised, and believe that His Persons are Three, Who is One in His Godhead, Who is holy in His Being, Three recognized Persons, without separation, Who is One in His Substance. Know and be certain that He is One God and One Lord, the Father Who was not begotten, the Son Who was begotten, the Light Who indeed proceeded from the Light, the God Who is in truth of God, Who was begotten before all times. For the Good Father begat the Good Son, and the Light Which was begotten arose from the First Light, and from the self-existing Life broke forth a fountain of life-giving water. And from the Mighty One Who is for ever [p. 108] appeared the power of the Son, Who is the Light of glory, and the Word of God, in One Person, Who was from the beginning with God the Lord, Who was before the world, Who hath no beginning, in Whom everything liveth, both the things that are visible and the things that are invisible. And believe in One Spirit Who sprang from the Father, perfect, the Maker of life, the Lifegiver, and the Giver of holiness, the Compassionate, Blessed in His Person, Mighty in His Person, with One Will. And His Power was with Him before the world in His One Person. Thus shalt thou worship the Father, and the Son, and the Holy Spirit, Three constituted Persons and One God, for Godhead existeth united in Three Persons, and their Nature is One because their Essence (or, Substance) is One, and their Power is One. And there is One Dominion in the unity of the Son and the Holy Spirit, for they proceeded from the Father. And the state of the Father is the state of a Begetter (now He was not begotten); and the state of the Son is the state of one begotten (now He did not beget); and the state of the Holy Spirit is that of what sprang up, for it neither begot nor was begotten. Thus is the matter of the begetting [of the Son] and the springing up [of the Holy Spirit], things that cannot be comprehended, but that are [to be received] with rightness of heart and without doubt: Father, and Son, and Holy Spirit, in every way without [difference], except that of begetting, begottenness, and springing up.

"For the Only Son, the Word of God, came down from heaven to earth for our salvation by the good pleasure of the Father and the Holy Spirit, and was conceived in the holy womb of the Virgin MARY (MÂRÎHÂM), the God-bearer, without seed, by the Holy Spirit, and was brought forth by her without defilement. And He became a perfect man, being Himself perfect God, with One Divine Nature ; manhood with a constituted Person. And thou must accept this, doubting nothing. And thou must by no manner of means seek to find out how the Son of God belittled Himself and became a man with the blood of a virgin, without the seed of man, in incorruptibility. And say not, 'What is this union of two Natures in One Person ?' For we have learned about this dogma, that we should believe it in faith [p. 109] with confidence, for this is a gift concerning which the divine writers have told us. Do thou now believe in the Son of God Who, through his tender compassion, became a man and bore sufferings in His human Nature, which remained uninjured, for He hungered, and thirsted, and toiled, and fought in the Nature of His body, and He tasted death for our sins, and was crucified, and was buried, and He tasted death. His Godhead suffered in no way and remained unchanged, for we are not able to bring suffering upon a nature which is incapable of suffering. But we know that He Who was unchangeable suffered, and was buried, and rose with Divine glory from the dead without [suffering] corruption, and He ascended into heaven, and He shall come again with glory in the Divine Body which He Himself put on, to judge the living and the dead, and to reward each one according to the weighing of his works in righteousness, even as He Himself told us[1].

"The dead shall rise up and those who are in the graves shall awake, even as Isaiah the Prophet saith[2], and those who have kept the commandments of Christ our Lord, and have walked in the path of the True Faith, shall inherit life everlasting.

[1] Matt. xvi. 27.   [2] Isaiah xxvi. 19 ; Ezek. xxxvii. 12.

And those who have acted corruptly and committed sins, and those who have withdrawn themselves from the True Faith, shall be condemned at the Judgement to torture unending. And believe also that evil hath neither shape nor master, and do not think that it hath not a beginning, or that by itself it came from itself, or that there was some one who brought it into being, or that it was from God in the beginning; get thee far from this miserable state, for evil was made by us and by Satan. And it riseth up against us, and it entereth into our interiors side by side with pride in proportion as it hath permission from us, for we have authority over ourselves; by our own free will and good pleasure we can approve, whether we do good or whether we do evil. And in addition to this, believe in one Baptism of water and of spirit for the remission of sins. And receive also the Holy Mysteries of Christ and be sure that they are a certain proof that [p. 110] His Body and Blood are given to the believers, a New Covenant to His disciples and to all those who believe in Him. For He said unto them, Take ye, eat ye, this is My Body, which is broken for you for the forgiveness of sin. And He also took the cup and He gave [it], saying, Drink of it all of you, for this is My Blood, the Blood of the New Covenant which is poured out for you for the forgiveness of sins. Do ye thus for a memorial of Me[1].

"This is the Word of God; behold, He made it known. And the Maker of the Universe performed a work by His might, with His Divine Word, and ordained the statute of the Offering, bread and wine, whereunto there is nothing like. And He placed therein His Body and His Blood, by the help of the Holy Spirit, so that He might sanctify those who received it willingly. And do thou worship truly before the honourable and God-like Image of the Word of God, Who became man for our sakes, being confident that thou art seeing continually the Creator and the Fashioner in the Image. For concerning the honour of the Image one of the saints, whose nature was perfect, saith, 'He Himself is the similitude wherefrom thou

[1] Matt. xxvi. 26–28; Mark xiv. 22–24; Luke xxii. 19, 20.

canst not separate the similitude[1].' For we see the writing which is on the Image, and we look with the eye of our mind at the true similitudes of the Image, and we worship truly and with fear the Image Which became incarnate for our sakes ; and we do not look upon Him renouncing Him, for He is the Image of God Who became incarnate. And we salute with the affection of love, from the depth of our hearts, Him Who shed His Blood for our sakes. And thus do we do also in respect of the image of the pure woman who gave Him birth and the images of all the saints. And we also salute the Sign of the Lifegiving Cross, because Christ God, the Redeemer of the world, was crucified upon it in the flesh to deliver our race from sin. And He Himself gave us the sign so that we might conquer our Enemy thereby, for he is an alien from Him, and he cannot endure the sight of His Power. These are the commandments which we have received. And do thou, O my spiritual son, take them to thyself, and keep them carefully unchanged and unmixed until thou drawest thy last breath. [p. 111] Put away from thee all doubt and all imaginings of the mind, renouncing all [false] teaching, and every word of heresy which would resist this Faith, wherein there is no blemish. And know thou that they are alien to God and remote from Him, for the divine Apostle saith, ' If we, or if an angel from heaven hath taught you anything different from what we have taught you, he shall be cursed and excommunicated[2].' There is no other Gospel, and there is no other Faith besides that to which the Holy Apostles and the Fathers who were arrayed in divinity testified, and they laid down the Law of the General Apostolic Church, each in his own time, and gave it to the General Church."

And when Baralâm had said these things to the king's son, and after he had taught him the commandments of the true Faith which the General Council had drawn up, he baptized him in the Name of the Father, and of the Son, and of the Holy Spirit, in the tank of water which was in the prince's own garden, and the grace of the Holy Spirit dwelt upon him,

---

[1] Compare Heb. i. 3.   [2] Gal. i. 8, 9.

and he shone with the light of the glory of God. And then he took him up into the palace which had been made ready for him, and he completed [his conversion] by the service of the Mystery of the Holy Offering, which is the Body and Blood of Christ. And the young man rejoiced straightway in his soul, and he exalted the glory of Christ Who, in His abundant mercy, had made him worthy of this.

And Baralâm said, "Blessed be God the Father of our Lord Jesus Christ, Who in the abundance of His mercy and compassion hath poured out upon us His Lifegiving Spirit, and hath given us birth again in His hope, and hath made us heirs of the inheritance that neither groweth old, nor decayeth, nor weareth out, and that is preserved in the heavens in Jesus Christ our Lord. Know thou, O my son, that thou this day art set free from sin, [p. 112] and that thou hast become a servant of God, and hast received the pledge of life which endureth for ever, and hast cast aside the apparel of darkness, and hast put on light. And thou hast set thyself in the place of the sons of God, even as it is said, 'To all those who have received Him, and who have believed in His Name through Christ by the Holy Spirit, He giveth power to become the sons of God[1].' Therefore, O my son, do thou take heed that thou art found to be without impurity and without blemish, and that thou doest work of excellence on the foundation of faith, for faith without works is a dead thing, and similarly works without faith are a dead thing[2], even as I have already told thee. Withdraw thou thyself then from every evil thing, and hate thou wholly every work of the old man, for that which is old destroyeth a man like lust. And be thou like the unborn child when his time [of formation] is ended, and he drinketh the milk of his mother, and do thou yearn to drink of the milk of rational excellences, which hath nothing [alien] mingled therein. And do thou fashion thyself therewith and it shall bring thee to the knowledge of the commandments of the Son of God with the capacity of a full-grown man, in the image of Christ. Be not faint-hearted, be not moved and

[1] John i. 12.   [2] James ii. 17 ; Ephesians ii. 8. 9.

made perverse by the strength of the passions when the waves thereof are tumultuous, but be thou a babe in respect of evil, and let thy heart cleave to what is good. And let thy course be consistent with thy calling to which thou hast been called, keeping the commandment of God, and striving with all thy might to hold thyself back from thy former course, which the heathen who were corrupt travelled over in the error of their hearts and in the darkness of their minds. They were remote from the glory of God, and they ministered to their lusts and to their bestial impulses.

"And do thou, if it be that thou shalt become strong as thou approachest the God of righteousness, journey on like the sons of light, for the fruit of the Spirit can only produce goodness, and integrity, and righteousness. [p. 113] The new man that thou hast put on this day shall never become corrupt nor wax old with his former agedness ; but be thou a new man always, in integrity and in righteousness. For this is possible for everyone who wisheth it, even as thou thyself hast heard that ' He giveth those who receive Him the power to become the sons of God, that is to say those who believe in His holy Name.' And for this reason we cannot say that we cannot acquire spiritual excellences. Moreover the path is paved, and it causeth no trouble to the wayfarer. And even if, through the mind of the flesh, it be called narrow and painful, yet it becometh bright, and easy, and straight, because the hope of good things for which we hope will be for those who travel thereon in wisdom ; and these things are understood perfectly in righteousness. And they knew what was the good pleasure of God, and they put on the whole armour of God to do battle against the Enemy who set himself against them, and they themselves showed this plainly in all hope in their entreaties and supplications. And thou, my son, according to what thou hast heard from me and hast learned, add to it the doing of spiritual excellences, perfect, superabundant, and overwhelming, taking to thyself the condition of a soldier of good deeds and excellence. And thou shalt have strong faith and good confidence, thy good deeds being witnesses of the

same, and with perfect patience and pure sincerity shalt take
unto thyself the life that is everlasting to which thou hast
been called. And all the longing and enjoyment, which lead
to the passion that submergeth, thou must put far from thee
not by working only, but thou must put far away from thee
the mind (or, thought) which disturbeth [thee] so that thou
thyself mayest see God. The goodness wherein is no impurity
consisteth not only in our works which can be written down,
but also in our thoughts, which may become to us causes of
rest or causes of punishment.

"And we know of a certainty that in pure hearts Christ
dwelleth, together with the Father and the [p. 114] Holy Spirit.
And behold, we have learned that just as smoke driveth away
the bee, even so doth the grace of the Holy Spirit drive away
evil thoughts from us. In this matter be thou always eager,
and take the greatest pains, and cure thy soul of every worldly
thought, and make it an altar for the Holy Spirit, the Lifegiver. For out of every thought action is perfected. And hath
not everything that is perfected in thought, and that goeth
forth in action, and everything that is done, its beginning in
a small matter? And then growing little by little it attaineth
large proportions which terrify. For this reason permit not
an evil habit to gain dominion over thee, but pluck up the
root thereof from thy heart whilst it is in a tender form, so
that it may not put forth branches and strike roots deep in
the ground; at that period it will neither demand a long time
nor much trouble to uproot it. For by such a thing as this
the weight of sin prevaileth over us continually and over-
cometh our souls. That which is thought to be a little thing,
as for example, an evil thought, or a word of shame, or lewd
or idle talk, cannot be removed from our souls with little
labour. And as an action happeneth through the operation of
the body, and as men make a jest of the lightness of their
wounds, thereby bringing upon their souls a greater and dead-
lier debt, so likewise is it in the case of an action [that taketh
place] through the soul.

"For those who neglect light passions and small sins and

belittle them, themselves make them a means of entrance for great sins, and they are reckoned as great sins when they develop; and their meeting together within them taketh place according to custom, and custom holdeth them to be a light matter, and it belittleth the seriousness thereof. Behold, it is said that if a transgressor cometh to a foul pit, he maketh light of it, and winketh with his eye, so that his soul becometh [like] the pig which rolleth about in the slime of the mud and rejoiceth [p. 115] therein[1]. And thus doth the soul suffer through the habit of evil things, and it acquireth not the desire for the departure of the sins, but it is scourged by them, and it enjoyeth evil as if it were something good. And who can say whether the soul will be able to wake up when the period of its days is drawing to a close, and whether with the sweat of its strenuous labour it will at length be able to free itself from the evil habit to which, of its own free will, it made itself a servant?

"For this reason with all thy might get thee far away from every thought of evil, and withdraw thyself from every destroying thought. Learn to know every habit that appertaineth to the world, and more especially do thou accustom thyself to performing works of spiritual excellence and to rejoice in the performance of the same. When thou hast toiled a little for it thou wilt be able to form a lasting habit, and this shall be to thee, by the help of God, profitable and without fatigue, and thou shalt become conqueror. For if the soul be obedient and it layeth down for itself the habit of doing works of excellence, the habit will become natural to it, and it will enable the soul to obtain the help of God ; and the roughness of the road shall become to thee, as thou wilt then see, something that is necessary for thee. And patience, and purity, and the doing of what is right are difficult for him who moveth about and changeth, for they are habits of the soul, and phases thereof, and characteristics which are impressed on the works thereof. Now, actions are not impressed on our nature, but they come to us from the outside, and if it be that we are in

---

[1] Compare 2 Peter ii. 22.

the habit [of doing them], it is then very difficult to pluck
them up and abolish them. How very much more difficult is
it to do so in the case of performing works of excellence, the
desire to do which was implanted in our nature by the Will
of the Creator! May He be exalted by praise! In the latter
case it is natural [to us], and He Himself helpeth [us].

"And if we labour a little, and we make the root thereof to
go down into our souls with eagerness and ready desire, the
eradication of the same from us then becometh a matter which
is wholly impossible. And behold, a certain man who was
practising this related a story unto me, saying :—'After I had
acquired spiritual visions, that is to say, [p. 116] things that
appeared to the eye of the mind, my soul became strong
through its profitable demonstration thereof. Then I wished
to put the matter to the test, and I covered over my observer,
that is to say, the eye of the mind, and I did not allow it to
rejoice according to its former habit. And I knew straightway
that it was sad and sorrowful, and that its heart was crucified
with longing for vision without any turning back, and it was
unable to constrain its mind which was opposed to itself. And
when I gave the eye of my mind permission [to see again]
straightway it ran with swift steps and returned to its accustomed work, even as David saith, 'As the hart longeth for the
fountains of water, even so doth my soul long for God. My
soul thirsteth for the living God[1].' Behold, then, it is evident
from these words that He purifieth the spiritual excellences
which abide in us. We can make the eye of the mind mistress
if we will, even as we choose, and prefer [the good] to sin.
And those who serve evil are closely attached thereto, and it
is with the greatest difficulty that they can save themselves
from it, even as I have already told thee.

"And now, do thou draw thyself close to Him through the
compassion and mercy of our God, and be thou one who
putteth on Christ as a garment by the divine grace of the
Holy Spirit. Cast thou thyself now on God, and open not a
single door, but adorn thy soul with the perfume of the beauty

[1] Psalm xlii. 1, 2.

of the spiritual excellences of shining splendour. And make thou thyself an altar of the Holy Trinity, and make thou the thoughts of thy heart to be dedicated to the praise of His Name. And sometimes when a man is sent on an embassy to an earthly king he hath the opportunity of talking to him face to face; and all the honour that is paid to the king becometh apparent to him and likewise his glory becometh manifest. And as for the man who is worthy to talk with God, and whose heart inclineth towards Him, blessed is he, for he is held to be worthy of the enjoyment of His word; and he seeth Him as he talketh continually with Him. And as to talking with God, that is to say, praying prayers and making supplication unto Him continually, [p. 117] [I say that] the man who prayeth with a fervent and pure heart, and whose mind is remote from all transitory things, and who standeth openly before God and offereth unto Him supplications in fear and trembling, that man, I say, talketh with God face to face. For our Good Lord and Merciful God filleth full every place, being joined in existence thereto, and He heareth those who pray unto Him in purity, even as David saith, 'The eyes of God are towards His righteous ones[1].'

"And therefore the Fathers say that those who pray are counted as a portion of the mind of God, and they call prayer the 'work of angels,' and the 'beginning of the joy which is to come.' For they have defined prayer as something which is related to God, and as a regent in the kingdom of the heavens, and as an aspect of the Holy Trinity. And they have assigned to it a greatness that is greater than the performance of works of excellence, for the increase of patience at the time of prayer, and the persevering therein, guide the heart to the hall of beautiful confidence; and this is called the similitude of beati-fication. Now not every prayer is like unto this, for there is only one which is meet to be called by this name, namely, that which the Lord taught. He gave His prayer to him that prayed, and that prayer was made public to every one upon the earth, and it was proclaimed by the Lord without any succeeding

[1] Psalm xxxiv. 15.

prayer. Purge thou thyself then anxiously and that prayer shall suffice thee, and it shall lift thee up from earth to heaven, provided that thou hast cleansed thyself from all sin, and from every evil thought. And set it in the perfection of purity, like a clean mirror, the case whereof is new, and withdraw thyself from all stubbornness and from the remembrance of evil, which will prevent the ascent of prayer, and especially from all sinners who will hold it back and keep it from rising to God. And all those who have sinned against thee forgive thou them with thy whole heart, and give alms to the poor and show compassion upon them.

"Increase thy prayer, and offer it unto God with scalding tears. [p. 118] And if thou wilt pray in this manner thou wilt be able to say like David, the Prophet who was king, who protected himself from thousands of adversaries, and kept himself pure among sinners of all kinds, and he said to God, 'I have hated and held in abomination iniquity, and Thy Law have I loved. Seven [times] in my day I praise Thee because of Thy righteous judgement. My soul keepeth Thy testimony and loveth it exceedingly. Let my petition come to Thee, O Lord, according as Thy word is true[1].' If thou criest out like this God will hear thee, and when thou shalt call Him, 'Here am I' will He say unto thee. If thou dost make thyself master of prayer of this kind, behold, thou shalt be a blessed man, for it is impossible for any one to pray with such eager desire as this except with the help of God. And it is impossible for a man to complete his prayer continually, and to fly over the nets of the Enemy, and soar upwards, unless his mind be on fire, even as one of the saints said, 'Rouse up thy soul, and make it to ascend to heaven, and take refuge with thy God.' Remember thy sins and ask forgiveness from Him. And if thou wilt make thy petition with scalding tears He shall forgive thee; for He loveth man, and He is merciful and compassionate of heart. And with these words and thoughts thou shalt drive away all worldly longings, and thou shalt become exalted above the work of the passions of the flesh, and be

---

[1] Psalm cxix. 163 ff.

meet to converse with God, 'What is more beautiful and what is more honourable than this existence?' O my son, may God make thee worthy to attain to this sublime beatitude!

"But now I have shown thee the path of the commandment of God, and I have laboured to tell thee everything that will please God; and behold, I have completed my severe service. Thou art now in thy mind as one who is meet for the Holy God Who hath called thee to Him. And behold, thou must be holy in thy course of life and in thy manner of living, for God saith, 'Be ye holy, for I Myself am holy[1].' And the Chief of the Apostles wrote, saying, 'And even if thou callest Him, Father, it is He Who shall judge, without respect of person, and He will reward every one of you according to his work. [p. 119] Go ye on your way then being in fear all the days of your lives, and know ye that your lives were not bought for nothing, neither with that which your fathers bequeathed to you, nor with the gold nor with the silver which perisheth, but with precious Blood, the Blood of Christ, the Pure Lamb, without blemish and without impurity[2].' Set all this in thine heart, and remember it always, and let the fear of God be before thine eyes, and that which surroundeth the Awful Judge, and the joy of the righteous which they alone shall then enjoy, and the misery of the sinners, and their weeping in the depth of darkness. And know well that all flesh is like the grass, and that all the children of men are like unto the flower thereof; the grass withereth and the flower thereof is stripped off it, but the word of God abideth for ever[3]. Read these words, and those which are like unto them continually, O my son, and the peace of God shall be with thee, and shall make thee to shine, and shall give thee understanding, and shall guide thee to the path of salvation, and shall drive out of thy mind every crafty desire, and shall seal thy soul with the Sign of the Lifegiving Cross, so that none of the evil of the Evil One shall draw nigh unto thee, and it shall make thee ready to perform the work of spiritual excellences. And now,

[1] Levit. xi. 44; 1 Peter i. 15, 16.　　[2] 1 Peter i. 17–19.
[3] 1 Peter i. 24, 25.

mayest thou attain to the kingdom which is to come, which
hath no end and which passeth not away; and mayest thou
rejoice in the light of the Holy Trinity, the Head of life and
the Fountain of the King of glory, Father, and Son, and Holy
Spirit. Amen."

[*How Zardân, the Prince's guardian, having heard the long
conversations between Baralâm and Yĕwâsĕf, becomes afraid,
and tells the Prince that he must report them to the king.*]

With these good words did the honourable chief Baralâm
exhort the son of the king, and then he returned to his solitary
habitation. And the officers of the king and the tutors of the
young man, seeing the master coming continually to the royal
house, marvelled thereat exceedingly. And one of them whom
we have already mentioned, and who was set over them as the
steward, and was faithful, and who loved the king's son and
was beloved by him, and was over the palace of the king's
son—now his name was Zardân—said unto the son of the
king, "O my lord, [p. 120] it is meet that thou shouldst know
how greatly I am afraid of thy father, and how much he
trusteth me, and because of this I fear that he will command
me to be dismissed as an [un]faithful servant. And behold,
I see this alien man talking with thee continually, and I am
afraid lest he may be one of the people of the Christian Faith,
which thy father hateth exceedingly, and that I shall be
deserving of the punishment of death. Now, thou knowest
well thy father's disposition. And if from this time onward
thou dost not cease discussion with this man, and if thou wilt
not do this thing, send me away from before thy face so that
thy father may not revile me, and ask thy father to give thee
another tutor instead of me."

[*How the Prince causes Zardân to hide in the curtains of
the chamber, so that he may hear the conversation which
takes place between the Prince and Baralâm.*]

And Yĕwâsĕf said unto Zardân, "I wish thee to hide thyself
in my curtains and to listen to the words which he uttereth

when he talketh with me." And when Zardân knew [that
Baralâm was coming] he went to the king's son, who placed
him inside his curtains. And Yĕwâsĕf said unto Baralâm,
"Set before me thy divine teaching so that a strong plant
may strike root in my heart."

And Baralâm began to address to him many words of God.
And he said unto him, "Love God only with all thy heart,
and with all thy soul, and with all thy mind. And keep the
commandment of purity with fear and with earnest desire, for
God created everything, both that which is visible and that
which is invisible. Remember that He created man by the
commandment which He commanded, and that man transgressed His commandment, and that He took vengeance upon
His clay because of the transgression. And remember all the
many good things and the glorious things that He took from
us through our transgressing His command, and the sorrows
that we found after we had gone forth from these good things,
and our abundant wretchedness, and remember how He added
and made to follow after this excuses for [His] love for the
children of men, and how the Creator took pains to save us
[p. 121] and sent to us teachers and prophets to inform us
about the incarnation of the Only One, and about the coming
down of the Only Begotten, and His becoming man, and
about the good and marvellous things, and about the sufferings which He bore for our sakes, and His Crucifixion, and
His Death by His own free will. And remember how He
called us a second time, and brought us to the good things
which we had formerly, and the kingdom of the heavens for
which those who are worthy wait. Remember also the punishment of torture which is prepared for sinners, the fire which
cannot be extinguished, and the darkness, and the worm
which dieth not, and all the tortures which those who have
served sin have heaped up together for themselves."

And after Baralâm had finished strengthening him with
these words, and had finished his beautiful doctrine in the
customary manner, he talked to him much concerning the
purity of his strife and life, and concerning the renunciation

and burden of the things that exist in this world; and he condemned the miserable state of those who are submerged in their lust for the same. And he made an end of his words with a prayer for him, and he blessed him so that there might be with him the Faith which is [based upon] right counsel, and the course of life on which nothing should cast a stain, and he prayed that he might act with the holy wisdom that should endure for ever without change or wavering. And Baralâm set a limit to his prayer at this point and brought it to an end, and departed to the place where he performed his ascetic exercises.

[*How the Prince tried to find out the effect of Baralâm's words on Zardân, and how he, being convinced that the Prince had become a Christian, was more afraid of the king than ever.*]

And Yĕwâsĕf called Zardân his tutor so that he might put his mind to the test, and he said unto him, "Didst thou hear just now the discourse which this sower of words addressed to me, and how he tried to persuade me with the persuasiveness of his idle words, in order to make me to withdraw from the joyful pleasure of this transitory world, and the description of his judgement, and how he worshippeth a strange god?" And Zardân answered and said unto him, "If as thou sayest thou art really asking me, thine own servant [my opinion], I know that the word of this man hath come and hath entered the depths of thy heart, and that if the matter were not thus, thou wouldst not hold converse continually with him. Now it is not that I do not appreciate this honour [which thou payest me], but from the time when thy father began the persecution against the Christians, there hath been no way of escape from him. The Christians were driven away from here and their preaching was silenced because of this persecution from that time onwards. Since it hath happened [p. 122] that their counsel is well pleasing unto thee, and it hath been made manifest unto thee, and thou art able to bear his severity and his punishment, the time of thy pleasure hath been in the direction of excellent and good things. But as for me, what can I do who am unable to look forward to these tribulations? Behold, my soul is filled with sorrow and with fear of the king, and with great pain. And what answer shall I make to him in respect of my treachery and my permitting the introduction of this man to thee?"

[*How the Prince entreated Zardân not to report his conversations with Baralâm to the king.*]

And Yĕwâsĕf said unto him, "I know well the exceedingly great nobility of thy love towards me, which is beyond all reward by me, and if I could find the [necessary] height of knowledge I would like to explain unto thee because of my love for thee this good thing which is beyond the comprehension of human nature, then thou couldst inform thyself about what I have found, and thou mightest know also the Creator, and mightest commit thyself to the protection of the Light which illumineth [everyone]. And my expectation concerning thee was that when thou didst hear the account of the things of the Spirit, thou wouldst follow them eagerly, and that thou wouldst lay hold upon Him, and that apathy and indifference would not cause thee to delay [in seeking] Him. But it seemeth to me that I am deceived in my expectation concerning thee, for I perceive that thy speech concerning Him is cold. However, if thou dost tell my father the king this thing, thou wilt only find trouble for thyself, together with sorrow and grief, and if thou wouldst show genuine love for him, thou wilt never cause him pain in the least degree [by mentioning] this matter [except at] the fitting time."

[*How Baralâm bade the Prince farewell and exhorted him to follow the course for which he had prepared him.*]

And on the following morning Baralâm came back, and went into the presence of Yĕwâsĕf, and spake to him about departure. And he could not endure his [approaching] separation from him, and his soul was sad, and tears filled his eyes, and he admonished him with many exhortations, saying unto him, "Be strong in the working of what is good, and [in following] the path of victory which dismay and blemish cannot touch"; and he strengthened his heart with words of consolation, seeking to make him to bid him farewell [p. 123] with joy. And he also said unto him, "The time is not far distant when we shall meet again never to be separated."

[How Yĕwâsĕf entreated him to take with him food and raiment for himself and the monks.]

And Yĕwâsĕf was filled with sorrow and his tears rained down, and [he feared] lest he should cause trouble for the master by increasing weariness, and lest he should prevent him [from following] the way of spiritual excellence which he longed for. And he was afraid lest this [tutor], who was called Zardân, should reveal his affairs to the king, and lest torture and punishment should come upon him. And he said unto him, "O thou who art indeed [my] spiritual father, thou honourable man, stay here among the teachers since thou hast been to me the cause of all excellence. Behold, thou art now about to leave me imprisoned in this useless world, and to depart thyself to a place of spiritual rest; but I would not dare to fetter thee or to make thee to abandon this course. Depart then, and take good care of thyself in the peace of God, and remember continually my wretched state in thy honourable prayer, so that I may be able to find thee and to look with gladness upon thy face at all times. And accept one request from me, even if thou art unwilling to do so, and receive a small [gift] from me; take with thee for the ascetics and for thyself also a little store of food for the way, if only for to-morrow, and some cloth for apparel."

[How Yĕwâsĕf entreated Baralâm to give him his ragged cloak and girdle and to take those he was wearing in exchange.]

And Baralâm answered and said unto him, "If I were to accept anything from thee for my brethren, they would not wish to receive any of the possessions of this transitory [world], wherefrom they have set themselves afar off, and wherefrom they have made themselves remote of their own free will. And how could I accept for myself what I have prevented others from accepting, seeing that I know that the acquisition of possessions is pernicious? Neither for them nor for myself will I take [anything], and we will not fall into the net that snareth and the possessions that cause sorrow." And when Baralâm would not consent either to this or to any other request, Yĕwâsĕf began to make entreaty to him again, and made a new petition to him beseeching him not to treat with contempt his request, and not to pour out upon him abundant sorrow and fear, but to leave with him his ragged hair cloak [p. 124] and his girdle of good things, so that they might be to him a memento and a protection against every Satanic work, and [he said], "Take with thee others instead of them, so that when thou lookest upon them thou mayest remember my feebleness."

[*How Baralâm gave Yĕwâsĕf his cloak and girdle, and received a ragged cloak in exchange.*]

And Baralâm answered, saying, "If I gave thee my cloak, which is worn out, and took from thee a new cloak this would not be right, for I should be receiving a reward for a very little toil; but that thy hope may not be cut off, undertake to give me a ragged cloak like unto that which I am going to give thee." Then Yĕwâsĕf asked for an old and worn out hair cloak and gave it to the master, and he received from Baralâm his cloak and girdle with rejoicing and gladness, and he regarded them as exceedingly precious treasures, and incomparably superior to the purple raiment and glorious apparel which are worn by kings.

[*Baralâm's farewell speech to Yĕwâsĕf.*]

And when the time for Baralâm's departure drew nigh, he began to address to Yĕwâsĕf his farewell words, and he taught him, saying, "O son beloved indeed, and sweet brother, whom

I have begotten in the teaching of the Holy and Honourable Gospel, it is meet especially that thou shouldst know of which King thou art a soldier, and in Whom thou believest and confessest. It is meet for thee now to take good heed to thyself, and to strengthen thy freedom with a ready will; and thou must fulfil what thou hast promised by the Book, having made confession before all the heavenly hosts. If thou dost keep thy word thou wilt be kept safely, and become a blessed one, and thou wilt not desire any transitory thing, but only God and His good things. For transitory things are like unto a dream, and after this [world] cometh the fire of Jahânam, which is everlasting; in it there is no splendour, and its burning never endeth. There is no cessation to the flames and the tortures thereof, and there is none who can reduce it to silence, and there is no end to its punishment. Moreover, what good thing is there to be found in the world? And the world which is to come after is thus: The joys thereof [p. 125] thou shalt rejoice in perpetually with God, Who shall give unto those whom He loveth the kingdom which shall endure for ever; and the beauty thereof is indescribable, and none can resist His power, and His glory abideth for ever. And the good things which He hath prepared for those who love Him are exceedingly sublime, and to all who behold them there is nothing whereto they may be compared, for eye hath not seen it nor the ear heard, and it cannot be imagined by the thought of the heart of man[1]. And mayest thou thyself be the heir thereof, and mayest thou be protected by the hand of God the Mighty!"

[Yĕwâsĕf's farewell speech to Baralâm.]

And Yĕwâsĕf, the king's son, shed tears from his eyes and was sorrowful, and he tore off the skin of his flesh with his nails, and he was unable to bear the separation from the father whom he loved, and from the teacher whose deeds were full of excellence. And he said unto him, "O father, who shall be with me? And who shall fulfil the charge which

---

[1] Isaiah lxiv. 4; 1 Cor. ii. 9.

thou hast committed to me? And who shall be my shepherd and guide like thyself? And what shall I make to be my consolation for the [loss of the] strength of thy affection for thy servant? I was far from God and thou didst bring me nigh unto Him, and thou didst bring me up like a son [and] heir; I was one who was lost and had erred and strayed away in the mountains, and was ready for the mouths of ravening beasts. And thou didst seek me, and by the grace of God wherein is no error, thou didst make me to mix with His sheep, and didst show me the path of righteousness. And thou didst bring me out from the darkness and shadow of death, and didst turn back my foot from the slippery path which carried with it death and tribulation, and which was very rough and crooked. And thou didst become to me the cause of great and marvellous good things, the greatness of which it is impossible for men to describe. And behold, thou didst on my behalf cause God to make complete the deficiency in the great gifts that are from Him, and the deficiency in my thanksgiving, for He alone is the Conqueror and the Giver of the reward of grace to those who, like thyself, love Him."

[How Baralâm prayed before his departure.]

[p. 126] And Baralâm abandoned lamentation and rose up to pray. And he stood up and stretched out his hands towards heaven, saying, " O God, the Father of our Lord Jesus Christ, Who didst illumine the darknesses in primeval time, Creator of all created things, both those which are visible and those which are invisible, Thou hast not renounced Thy clay and hast not permitted us to go after our folly. We give thanks unto Thee, and we give thanks unto Thy power, and Thy wisdom, and Thy WORD, Jesus Christ our Lord, by Whom Thou hast created the worlds. We had fallen down, and Thou didst raise us up. We had committed sin, and Thou didst forgive us. We had gone astray, and Thou didst bring us back. We had been carried away into captivity, and Thou didst redeem us. We were dead, and Thou didst bring us to life by the precious Blood of Thy Son. O Lord, Thou Lover of man, look upon this rational lamb whom I have brought unto Thee, and see if holiness of his soul by Thy power and by Thy grace is not meet for him. Bless him with Thy complete blessing, and protect this vineyard which hath been planted by Thy Holy and Lifegiving Spirit, and grant that he may bring forth fruit, the fruit of integrity and righteousness. And pluck him away from the crafty devices of the Enemy by the wisdom of Thy good and holy Spirit, and teach him to do Thy Will. Remove not Thy grace from him, but make him worthy to be with me, myself, the least of Thy servants, in Thy good things which are for ever and are endless. And be Thou unto him a comforter, and a watcher, and a guide to Thy lifegiving path; for Thou art blessed and glorious for ever and ever. Amen."

[*How Baralâm gave Yĕwâsĕf a last blessing and departed.*]

And when Baralâm had finished his prayer, he turned and kissed the son of a heavenly Father, and blessed him and prayed that he would find peace and salvation, saying, "May God strengthen thee, O my son, in the perfect way, and make thee to find everlasting peace, even as He revealed [it] and gave [it] to thee, with all His saints in the kingdom that never passeth away. Amen."

And after these words Baralâm went out from the royal palace, and he departed to the desert, his dwelling-place, rejoicing, and exulting, and thanking God Who had smoothed for him the path of good things and profitableness.

[*How Yĕwâsĕf prayed after the departure of Baralâm, and devoted himself to acquiring purity of mind and body.*]

[p. 127] And after the departure of Baralâm Yĕwâsĕf roused himself, and gave himself to prayer and the shedding of scalding tears, saying, "O Lord, look Thou and help me; O Lord, haste Thee to my help. For upon Thee the poor cast themselves, and Thou art the Helper of their weakness. Look upon me and have compassion upon me, O Thou Who dost desire the salvation of all [men] and dost wish them to return to the knowledge of righteousness. Deliver me and have compassion upon me, and strengthen me so that I may walk in the path of Thy lifegiving Commandments. For I am weak and miserable, and am useless to do what is good, but Thou art able to deliver me, O Sustainer of all the world. And do not allow me to walk in and follow after the lust of the flesh ; but teach me to do Thy good pleasure, and make Thou me to be meet for the good things which endure for ever. O Father, and Son, and Holy Spirit, One God, of like substance, indivisible, unto Thee do I commit myself, and Thee do I praise, for thou art praised by all created beings ; all the powers of the spirit who have no bodies praise Thee, and blessed art Thou for ever and ever."

And from that time he took great heed unto himself with all care and diligence, so that he might make himself to acquire purity of heart, and mind, and body, by contemplation and prayer, and by making supplications throughout the nights ; for it would happen sometimes that those who dwelt with him would interrupt his rule of life, or perhaps the king his father would visit him or summon him to his presence. And he used to do during the night, with prayers and tears, what he had omitted to do during the day, and he continued to do so until the day broke ; and in him were fulfilled the words of the Prophet who said, " In the night season I will lift up my hands to the sanctuary, and [I] will bless God[1]."

[How Zardân feigned sickness and was relieved of his duties in connection with Yĕwâsĕf.]

And when Zardân, whom we have already mentioned, knew of Yĕwâsĕf's good course of life, grief and sorrow filled him, and he did not know what to do. And when sorrow gained the mastery over him he went to his house, and he caused a report to be noised abroad concerning himself that he was ill ; and when the king heard this he sent one of his confidential servants to stand ready to minister to his son in his stead. And then the king devoted his whole attention to the healing

[1] Psalm lxiii. 2, 4, 6.

of Zardân, [p. 128] and he sent to one of [his] physicians who was exceedingly wise, and he commanded him to take the greatest pains possible to heal him. And when the physician saw that the king was grieved about Zardân, and that he loved him so much, he watched him with the most careful attention until he understood his case thoroughly. Then he went to the king and said unto him, "I have not been able to find any disease in this man, neither can I see any cause for sickness of the body, but I think that his soul is overwhelmed with sorrow." And when the king heard this from the physician he thought that his son might have been a heavy and a disagreeable burden upon Zardân, and that because of this he was sorrowful, and had pretended to be ill, and had departed. And the king wished to understand his case thoroughly, and he sent a message to him, saying, "To-morrow morning I will come and see thee, and I will inform myself as to what is the cause of this sickness of thine."

[*How Zardân went to the king and confessed that his illness was due to grief and sorrow of mind, and not to any disease of the body.*]

And when the message of the king reached Zardân, and he understood it, he rose up in the morning and put on his apparel, and he went to the king and bowed down to the ground before him. And the king said unto him, "Why didst thou force thyself to visit us seeing that thou art ill? I wished to come to thee and to visit thee. All those who are under my authority know well our affection for thee, and the honour in which thou art held by us." And Zardân answered, saying, "My sickness, O king, is not an ordinary sickness which is common to men, but it is a sickness due to grief and sorrow of the soul, and nothing else. And if I have come unto thee quickly, with boldness, according to thine honour, it was so that a rule of folly might not take place through me ; and I was afraid for thy sake lest there should be in thy kingdom dismay and tumult through the disgrace of myself, thy servant here present." And then he informed the king the cause of his sorrow. And Zardân answered and said unto him, "Behold, I have brought destruction upon myself, and an exceedingly great punishment and many deaths are meet for me because of my laziness, for I have treated thy commandment with negligence, and I have become the cause of much sorrow." And the king said unto him, "What hast thou done? Behold, fear envelopeth thee; tell me quickly." And Zardân answered, saying, "O my lord the king, [p. 129] I have neglected to guard carefully thy son, my lord, for an evil man beguiled me. He came to thy son and he taught him the Christian Religion, and he told him a story which gave him pleasure, and he hath become Christ's wholly, for he hath received Him and hath made himself happy by so doing." And Zardân told the king that the name of that master was Baralâm. Now the king had heard before about Baralâm and about the beauty of his righteousness.

[*How the king became filled with wrath when he heard Zardân's words, and how he summoned 'Arâshîsh the astrologer to his presence.*]

And when the king heard these words, sorrow filled his heart, and straightway fear and dismay descended upon him, and his heart burned, and one expected him to choke himself with the violence of the words which were heard [coming] from his mouth. And he caused to be brought a certain man whose name was 'Arâshîsh, whom the king had appointed to be his viceroy, and he used to send for him in connection with all his edicts and the secret matters connected with his decrees. Now 'Arâshîsh was a man who was skilled in the knowledge of the stars, and when he arrived the king told him about that great grief and sorrow that had come upon him. And when 'Arâshîsh saw his dismay and the perturbation of his soul, he said unto him, "Be not dismayed, O king, neither be thou sorrowful. We must not despair, and we must not be without hope that we can bring back thy son and convert him. And I know and am quite certain that thy son will speedily deny the teaching of this deceiver, and will return to thy counsel

B.   10

and thy will" ; and by these words 'Arâshîsh contrived to turn
the anger of the king into joy. And they made a plan(?) to
show him how to bring about the matter.

[*How 'Arâshîsh the astrologer gave the king counsel, and how
the king acted upon it.*]

And 'Arâshîsh said unto the king, " O king, let us act in this
wise. First of all let us seek for Baralâm the evil one. When
we have found him know thou that we must not be ashamed
at what we have thought out, for when we have found him,
we will conquer him with words of argument, and having
terrified him we will force him to say, 'Every word of mine
which I spake was a lie and was only a jest.' And this shall
be sufficient for thy son, my lord. But if we are not able to
find Baralâm I know an old man, a dweller in the desert,
whose name is Nâkôr, who resembleth Baralâm in all his ways
and dispositions that are visible, [p. 130] and his Faith is like
unto our Faith ; and he used to admonish me myself in his
teaching. I will go to him by night, and I will tell him everything very clearly, and I will make him to understand what
he shall do. And I will explain to him that Baralâm is to
be seized, and that he is to have him brought to him when he
is by himself, and that then he is to act craftily and cunningly
and spread a report that he is a supporter of the Christians,
and he will pretend that he is one who suffered sorely on their
account. And after this he will be frightened like one who
hath been defeated. And when thy son, my lord, seeth that
Baralâm is defeated, [he will say], 'Behold, our Faith is a
thing that is overcome,' and thus he will make himself a companion of the victors, and he will join himself unto them,
without making any opposition. And more than this, he will
also be ashamed before the majesty of thy sovereignty, and
will seek to be friendly ; and thus thou wilt find that which
shall make thee to rejoice. And he who in his person shall be
disguised as Baralâm shall convert him, and thy son will consider that it was Baralâm who seduced him."

And the king perceived that that which had been said to

him, and that which Nâkôr had advised him to do was right. But behold, in accepting this counsel he placed his trust in a hope that was vain, and he did not know that Baralâm had departed only a very little time ago.

[*How Nâkôr instructed by 'Arâshîsh sets out on a journey through the desert in search of Baralâm.*]

And Nâkôr departed and made haste to seize Baralâm, and he set men to lie in wait on many roads to look for him ; and he and his attendants mounted their horses with haste, and they departed by a certain road, and there were many mighty men of war with him. And he thought that Baralâm would travel by that road, and he journeyed as quickly as he could to overtake him ; and for three days he tired his body with ready zeal. And he found in that country royal villages which had been built in the open desert, and he rested there and sent 'Arâshîsh and numerous horsemen to seek diligently for Baralâm in the desert. And when he arrived at that place he made a very great stir among those who dwelt there in seeking for Baralâm, and they made him to know and told him, saying, "We have never seen this man." And he departed again into the deserts, so that he might hunt the monks, who lead the life of anchorites, [p. 131] and he went on a little further into the desert asking for Baralâm, and he travelled about over difficult mountains and rivers, where no one had ever been before.

And when he had arrived at a mountain which was exceedingly difficult to travel over, he and all his soldiers who were with him made a mighty effort, and they climbed up to the top of the mountain, and, in the valley below, they saw a monastery of the monks who were solitaries and [the monks] walking about. And by the command of the officer all the soldiers were gathered together, and, without speaking, they descended the mountain, and they strove among themselves who should come down the fastest and who should arrive there first. And when they found the holy men they leaped upon them like mad dogs, and like venomous serpents, the foe[s] of

10—2

the children of men, and they seized the men of the contemplative life, who were clothed with the desert, and on whose faces was the imprint of the contemplative life, and they pushed them along, and made them run, and set them before the officer. But the holy men were not in any way dismayed, and they did not utter one word of abuse, and they exhibited no act of anger. And their Master, because he was the chief, carried a hair scrip which was filled with the bones of the holy men of olden time. And when 'Arâshis, the officer, had scrutinized them carefully and he did not find among them Baralâm, whom he knew, he was sad and sorry, and he repented. And he said unto these holy men, "Where is he who hath deceived the king's son?" And the chief of the monks, who was carrying the scrip, answered and said unto him, "He is not with us, but with you ; he fled from us and went away, by the grace of Christ." And the captain of the soldiers answered and said unto him, "Dost thou know him?" And the desert monk answered and said unto him, "Yea, I know the crafty one and deceiver, that is to say, Satan, who dwelleth with you, whom ye worship and to whom ye minister." And the captain of the soldiers said unto him, "I questioned thee only about Baralâm, and him I want, and because of this I questioned thee about him so that I might learn where he is." And the desert monk answered, saying, "Why dost thou utter a vain word [p. 132] which is unseemly? And thou hast asked before concerning him that hath dealt craftily with the son of the king. If thou art seeking for Baralâm then it is fitting for thee whilst thou art keeping watch over every road to say, 'Where is the man who hath turned the king's son from error and from the crafty deceiver, and hath delivered him from them?' He is our brother, and our companion, and he is bound to us, and for many days we have not seen him."

[*How the monks of the desert refused to tell the captain of the soldiers where Baralâm was and where he lived.*]

And the captain of the soldiers said unto him, "Show me his dwelling." And the solitary answered and said unto him,

"If he had wished to see you he would have gone out with us to receive you; we are not permitted to make you to know the place where he liveth." And the captain of the soldiers was wroth because of these words, and he looked at them with anger, and said unto them, "I will kill you with a terrible death, and I will cut you up into little pieces, if you do not show me where his dwelling is, and if ye do not bring Baralâm to me instantly." And the desert monks said unto him, "What canst thou do to us? Have we any possessions which thou canst carry off from us, and because of which we are drawn to the act of accepting [from thee] this transitory life? Or are we afraid of the death through thee which thou canst bring upon us? On the contrary, we confess clearly before thee that thou wouldst do a good deed for us if thou wouldst take us out of the life of this fleeting world, and wouldst send us into the life that is for ever. But also we do fear with a fear which is not small—we fear the covering over of the eyes at the time of death, and our not knowing what will happen when death shall come to us. Shall we come under the crafty art of Satan and will it make us to delay in doing our own will to another in Whom wé put our trust, that is, God? Work then your will and give up the hope wherewith ye hope of finding him; and make no long tarrying in working your will, for we will not show you where is our brother, who is beloved of God, and we have no wish to escape from this death, even though it be one of torture. On the contrary, it is better for us that we should die a good death confessing the ancient virtues and offering to [p. 133] God the blood of martyrdom with a good and ready mind."

[*How the captain seized the monks and their leader, and bound them in fetters and took them back with him to the king.*]

And this governor, whose heart was dense, was unable to endure their boldness towards him, but he was unable to inflict upon them many scourgings and severe punishment; and that wicked man marvelled exceedingly at their willing-

ness [to die] and at their temerity. And when they would not
submit to him and they refused to discover to him Baralâm,
he forthwith commanded [the soldiers] to drag them out and
to take them to the king ; and they were beaten and bound
with chains of iron, and their bodies were torn [therewith],
and their Master went with them, carrying the scrip wherein
were the bones of the righteous. And in a few days they
arrived at the place where the king was, and the governor
told him about them, and set them before him. And when
the king saw them he was exceedingly angry, and he commanded the soldiers to beat them most severely and without
mercy. And when the king saw that their flesh was torn into
strips by the·wounds caused by the lashes, his fierce anger
against them abated, and afterwards he spake unto them,
saying, "What are these bones of the dead which ye are carrying with you? Are they the bones of people whom ye love
and to whom ye wish to go? I will at this moment make you
like unto them so that ye may mingle with them, and ye shall
thank me forthwith for my goodness." And the Master and
Teacher of those monks, the companion of divine beings,
treated the words of the king as things of no account. And
he answered with humility, and with a shining face, and with
the grace that dwelt in his soul, and said unto him, "O king,
we carry these pure and holy bones as worthy of divine honour,
for they are the bones of righteous men, whose works were
excellent. And we have brought them with us that we may
remember their ascetic excellence and their good course of
life before God, and their love. We have brought them that
we may awaken our souls through them and may make ourselves to resemble them in their departure. And we keep
them that they may be for us a memorial which [p. 134] will
remind us of their virtues[1] and of their bitter deaths, which
shall be exceedingly profitable unto us. And they shall bear
us willingly to the tranquillity of the ascetic life, and by our
approach to this we shall acquire holiness and blessing."

And the king said unto them, "If the remembrance of death

---

[1] Read ትረፋትዎሙ፡

is a profitable thing, even as ye say, why do ye not take to your bodies as a memorial something which doth not at the last decay, and which would be better than these strange things which rot away?" And the Master of the monks answered and said unto the king, " I would have thee to know that we carry about these bones for five reasons (?) ; answer me and tell me [any] one of them if thou knowest. Thou dost laugh at us and dost show signs of amusement at us, but know thou well that the bones of the righteous men who have been long dead establish a memorial which is far better known everywhere than the memorial of the living. If thou dost understand this thing, the bones which thou seest will describe to thee plainly the appearance of death. Why then dost not thou remember thine own death, which is nigh unto thee? It shall come unto thee after a short period of life, and shall make thee like unto them. But thou dost attach thyself to everything which is in opposition to the Divine Law, and dost wage war against the messengers of God, the Most High, and against those who love the splendid Faith, and who have in no wise acted treasonably against thee, but who do not share with thee a portion in this transitory world."

And the king answered and said unto them, " O ye wicked slaves who deceive men, behold, rightly and fittingly will I punish you, for ye lead every one into error and make them to renounce the pleasure of this world and the joys thereof, and to remove themselves far from them, and ye promise them everlasting life in their stead. Ye make men to hate the pleasure of the palate, and the appetites, and the gratifications of the senses which are beloved by them, and to choose this filthy, and abominable, and hard life ; and ye preach to them a rough and stony [p. 135] road, so that ye may transfer the glory of the gods to Christ. But in order that the people may not follow your persuasion, and the land may not become a desert, and that the people may not go far from the gods of their fathers and may not worship strange gods, I will pass judgement upon you and they shall torture you with many tortures."

And the Father and Master of the monks answered and said unto him, "If thou art wishful that every man should share with thee the good things of this world and the luxury thereof, why dost thou not apply unto every man a law whereby he shall enjoy an equal share of pleasure and of money? But thou hast made the greater number of them to be poor and wretched, and thou seizest their possessions for thyself and dost add them to thy possessions! And thou dost not trouble thyself at all about the salvation of the multitude, but only about the glorification of thine own transitory body, and thou dost feed it with dainty and savoury meats. And in addition to this, thou dost deny God Almighty and dost forget Him, and thou dost give the name of God to beings who are not gods, and who commit every kind of uncleanness and fornication. Behold, clearly thou thyself art the seducer and the deceiver, for thou dost prevent the people from sharing the Faith with us, wishing them to be under thy dominion so that thou mayest make to be heavy upon them the burdens of toil and misery, wherein is no advantage; this thou doest that the profit and increase which accrue from them may be thine. Thou art like unto the man who feedeth dogs for hunting purposes, and birds for falconry, which before they hunt are made to be crafty by flattery and persuasion, and when they catch anything during the hunt, the hunter snatcheth it from their mouths. And similarly thou thyself wishest the manifold taxes and imposts on land and sea to be gathered together before thee. Thou pretendest that thou art taking trouble to save them, and that thou thyself wilt protect them, making everlasting perdition the excuse, and the cause of death is to them and to thyself also. And if thy possessions increase, and thy transitory riches, of which nothing shall remain, [p. 136] become exceedingly great, yet are they only like a couple of bread-cakes. Behold, thou art at this moment like a man who preferreth darkness to light. Wake up now from this slumber of thine for to-morrow thou shalt be under the earth. Open thou thy blind eyes and look at our God Who hath made to rise upon every one the splendour of His light, and turn to God, for the Prophet saith, 'O ye who have knowledge, how long will ye neglect to understand that there is no other God except Me? Now our God is One, and there is no other Saviour beside Him[1].'"

And the king answered and said unto them, "Cease to multiply your words, and bring hither to me at once Baralâm, before I destroy you with overwhelming tortures the like of which ye have never before experienced."

And the spiritual fighter, great of patience, and bold of heart, who longed exceedingly for divine wisdom, did not fear one word of the terrifying threats of the king, but he was strong and without fear, and he said unto the king, "O king, do not imagine that we do the works which will bring us nigh to thee, but we do the works which God commanded, God our Lord and Master, and our holy Father. And we were commanded to withdraw ourselves from every pleasure, and the lusts thereof, and to endure patiently torture, and the suffering and evil of every kind which were to come, and all the punishment and torture which thou canst bring upon us, for the sake of our splendid Faith and the good things which are [to come]. Behold, thou art doing us a very great kindness : do whatsoever thou pleasest, for we do not wish to do anything that is beyond what is seemly, but we will not force ourselves [to commit] sin ; and do not imagine that this sin is a little one : we will not deny our Helper Who suffered for us. And even if thou shouldst bring upon us thousands of deaths we shall not lack the ready understanding of the mind, and we shall not cast away the teachings of our philosophy because we are afraid of thy tortures, and we shall do nothing that is not in accordance with [p. 137] the Divine Law. And we are prepared for every torture that thou canst bring upon us, for we shall live again in Christ ; and if we die for His sake it will be great profit to us."

And when the king heard [these words] he became hot with anger, and he commanded [his soldiers] to cut off their divine tongues, and also to pluck out their eyes, and to cut off the hands and the feet of all of them. And when the command

[1] Isaiah xliii. 10, 11 ; xlv. 21.

had gone forth the soldiers surrounded them, carrying their weapons of war to cut off their members without mercy. And they dragged out the tongues of the monks from their mouths with curved iron tailors' awls, and poured water upon them, and they made holes in their eyes with iron borers, and they cut off their hands and their feet with instruments of torture, which had been made specially for the purpose of lopping off limbs. And those holy and honourable men rejoiced in their hearts and minds as if they had been invited to a feast, and they drew nigh to the torture with willingness, each inciting the other to endure, and they chose gladly death for the sake of the love of Christ, without fear and without dismay; and under each and every kind of torture they committed their patiently-enduring souls to God. Now the number of these solitary monks was seventeen. And it is known and it is certain that he who endureth pain patiently hath a mind that loveth the beauty of piety, even as said another, who was not one of our companions, when he praised the martyrdom of one old man, a priest, and the martyrdom of seven young men with their mother, and when he helped them in the place of judgement, "Fight ye for the Religion of your fathers." And these holy fathers, who were pilgrims to the Jerusalem which is above and heirs thereof, did not fall short of the martyrs, and they failed in no way the determination of their minds, and their souls were great even as were theirs.

[*How 'Arâshîs went by the king's command to find Nâkôr the magician, and how Nâkôr agreed to personate Baralâm.*]

And when these holy fathers died their testimony to the shining Faith was made known openly. And then the king turned to 'Arâshîs, the captain of his host, that [p. 138] he might make a second plan, for of the first plan both were ashamed, and he commanded him to bring the man whose name was Nâkôr. And 'Arâshîs went to Nâkôr in the darkness of the night, and he came to his cell; now he dwelt in desert places and he was always practising magic; and 'Arâshîs told him everything that they had planned concerning him, and they completed their plot with him.

And 'Arâshîs came back in the morning to the king, and asked him to give him strong horsemen so that he might go and seek for Baralâm. And he departed into the desert places, and he saw a man coming out from among the rivers, and he commanded his horsemen to bring him to him; and they made their horses gallop, and they overtook him quickly, and they seized him and took him to him. And 'Arâshîs began to question him, and he said unto him, "Who art thou? What is thy name?" And the man said unto him, "I am a Christian and my name is Baralâm" (even as 'Arâshîs had instructed him and arranged with him already), and 'Arâshîs rejoiced in finding Nâkôr, the man of perdition, who had disguised himself as Baralâm; and he led him away hastily. And he went back to the king forthwith and he set Nâkôr before him.

[*How the king held converse with Nâkôr who lied and declared to him that he was Baralâm.*]

And the king said unto him in the presence of all those who were standing before him, "Art thou that evil-doer Baralâm?" And Nâkôr answered and said unto him, "I am the slave of God, and thou must not call me a messenger of Satan, for it is meet that thou shouldst believe in His abundant grace. It was I who taught thy son the good worship of God, and I delivered him from every crafty thing. And I made the God, Who is God indeed, to deal graciously with him, and I taught him and admonished him to perform every kind of work of spiritual excellence."

And the king said unto him after the manner of one who was in a furious rage, "It would be more seemly for us if, instead of hearing one word from thee and giving thee the opportunity to make answer, we killed thee without asking a question, but I will be patient with thee because of my love for the children of men. And I will give thee a period of time, that is to say, up to an appointed day; meanwhile I will investigate thy work publicly, and if I find that thou hast been

loyal unto me, mercy and compassion from me shall be ready
for thee; but if thou hast acted treasonably towards me
[p. 139] thou shalt be destroyed with a terrible destruction."

And this old and wicked man answered, saying, "I should
deserve it. If thou seest thy son careless in respect of admonition, I will rouse him up, and I will remind him of what he
needeth so that he shall never be apathetic (or, lazy)." And
when he had said this he (the king) delivered him over to
'Arâshîs and commanded him to keep guard over him with
all diligence. And he said unto him privily, "If we go beforehand to my son he will add only the word of the Faith; therefore bring Nâkôr, and let him come disguised as Baralâm."

[*How Yĕwâsĕf heard that Baralâm had arrived in the city,
and how God revealed to him the doings of 'Arâshîs and
Nâkôr, and comforted him.*]

Now the report was rumoured everywhere in the city that
Baralâm had been found, and at length Yĕwâsĕf heard it. And
when he heard it his heart was pained, and his soul was sick,
and he could not control himself, and he wept many tears. And
he prayed to God with groaning and lamentation, and he besought Him to help Baralâm, the righteous old man. And the
Doer of good things did not neglect his grief, for He is the
Good Being, and He is the helper of those who cry to Him in
the time of their trouble. And He told the young man and
made him to know everything concerning them in a vision of
the night, and He gave him power and strength to fight for
the Good Faith. And when he woke up he found in his heart
joy and gladness in abundance, and confidence, and God made
him to feel the beauty of the light in his heart, which had
been sorrowful, and sad, and smitten with pain.

[*How the king went to the palace of Yĕwâsĕf and reviled him.*]

And the king wished in his heart to give unto 'Arâshîs many
gifts and great good things, but he did not understand the
words of the prophet David, who said, "The evil doer deceiveth
himself. What is right shall overcome the sinner, and it shall

break him in pieces utterly, and shall destroy the memorial
of him speedily[1]" (and what followeth this). And after two
days the king came to the palace of his son, and though
Yĕwâsĕf went forth to meet him he did not embrace his father
according to his custom, but he behaved like one who was
wroth; and the king went into the royal palace, and was filled
with anger, and sat down. And he called Yĕwâsĕf [p. 140] and
said unto him, "What is this story which hath been poured
into my ears? My soul melteth utterly through fear. I think
in my mind that among the men who have lived before us
there was never one who rejoiced in the birth of his son more
than I rejoiced in thy birth; but I also think that none hath
ever suffered so much evil and sorrow through his son as thou
hast caused me at this present time. Thou hast rejected my
state, and hast removed the light of mine eyes, and hast cut
off the strength of my limbs, and through thee I am obliged
to hold fast to my calamity. Behold, there hath come to me
that which I feared would happen unto me, and I have become the laughingstock of mine enemies. For thou hast
followed a doctrine which is alien to mine own, and thou hast
bent thy will to a man [whose judgement] is immature, and
to the words of those who deceive cunningly. And thou hast
preferred the worship of those who have no understanding,
and thou hast forsaken our great gods, and hast worshipped
a strange god. Why hast thou done this? I hoped that I had
brought thee up with the greatest care and had guarded thee
well, and I hoped that thou wouldst be the strength and stay
of my old age, and the inheritor of my kingdom after me.
Art thou not ashamed to commit such an act of unfriendliness
and hostility towards me? It would have been far better for
thee to obey me, and to follow my Law, than to hearken unto
the word and falsehood of that old man (that hypocrite and
son of perdition!) whom thou obeyest, and who hath promised
thee a life of bitterness instead of a life of pleasure and freedom, and the journeying on the strait and rugged road whereon
the Son of Mary commanded [His followers] to travel. Art

[1] Compare Psalms ix. 5, 6; xxxiv. 16.

thou not afraid of the wrath of the gods, whose glory is great, lest they bring down lightnings upon thee, or snatch thee away in a mighty storm of wind, or lest the earth split and swallow thee up, because it is they who have favoured thee with all the good things of this world? And they have adorned us with crowns of royalty, and have made very many peoples to be in submission unto us. And through my petition and entreaty to them thou thyself wast born, thy coming being [p. 141] scarcely hoped for, and they made thee a partner in this splendid light, and yet thou hast cast them aside and hast utterly rejected them! And thou dost lean upon Him Who was crucified, and they have persuaded thee, with a foolish persuasion, [to believe in] the resurrection of the dead who lived before our time, and thousands of other foolish things. But, O my beloved son, hearken to thy father, and be subject unto him, and withdraw thyself far from this long and distant path, and come nigh and offer up sacrifice to the benevolent gods, and make thyself to be forgiven by them by means of great offerings that are better than one hundred bulls and vows, so that they may grant forgiveness of transgression and remission of sins; for they have the power both to confer happiness and to punish. And let this path be a thing to be talked about by thee only. And do this for our sake also. Through them we have arrived at the exalted position that we hold, and they bestow gracious gifts in return for the glorification of their divinities and majesties, and on those who bring offerings unto them they bestow twofold glory."

[*How Yĕwâsĕf declared to the king his father the existence of God Almighty, and described the reasons for his belief in the Christian Religion, and showed him the futility of the worship of idols.*]

And with this and similar talk at very great length did the king address his son; in it he showed his hatred for our Law and he made a mock of it, and that which concerned the gods he lauded and magnified. And when the divine young man saw [this], he did not wish to teach him and to illumine him, but he raised himself up on a pedestal, and upon a very high place wherefrom he might be very clearly visible, and then filled with courageous daring he spoke to his father face to face. And he spake unto him thus: "The master whom I have made [my guide] I will not deny, for I have fled from the outer darkness, and have come to the light that illumineth, and I have cast behind me error and acquired righteousness. I have rejected the evil Satans, and have followed the Son of God, the Word, in Whom is the Father Who created everything from a state in which it did not exist. He fashioned man out of the dust and breathed into him the breath of life, and He fed him in the Garden of Joy, but having transgressed the commandment of his God he rightly became subject to the punishment of death [p. 142]. And when the Power of Evil drew him aside, the Merciful One, the Maker of the Universe, did not neglect him, and He did not forsake him, wishing [him] to work towards his former glory. And because of this the Creator of the Universe, and the Fashioner of our race, became a man for our sakes in the flesh of a pure and holy virgin. And He went about among men for the sake of us, who were lost slaves, and the Lord accepted death upon the wood of the Cross, so that He might remove from us the fetters of sin and the oppression thereof. And He wished that every man might be as strong as he was formerly, and that [the angel] might open to us the gates of heaven and take us up thither. And He sweetened our natures and laid them upon the throne of glory; and He gave unto those who loved Him a kingdom which is never-ending, and good things (or, happiness) which are beyond the possibility of hearing about, and beyond [the comprehension] of [human] minds. This Being is the Mighty One and the All-Powerful one ; He alone is the Lord of lords, and the King of kings, Who abideth in His saints. Glory be to Him, and to the Father, and to the Holy Spirit, the Holy Trinity, in Whom I have been baptized and placed my trust. Him do I praise, and Him do I worship, Three Persons who are equal, and One Substance without mixture, uncreate and immortal. The First One, Who is unapproachable, and incomprehensible, and indefinable, and incorporeal, and impassible, and unwearyable, and unchangeable, and indescribable, is the source of goodness and of what is right; and He is the primeval Light Which illumined the world, He is the Creator of all created things, both those that are visible and those that are invisible, He is the Protector of everyone and the Keeper of everyone, He careth for every man and He is his Refuge, He is the Sustainer of every man and He is His Lord. Without Him nothing that is could exist, and without His wisdom it would be impossible for anything to stand. He is the life of everyone and the Strengthener of everyone.

"And why, O my begetter, art thou a stranger to One Who is thus good? And why art thou remote from the God Who is thus powerful? He is the God of the dumb graven images which thou thyself hast made, and which return no answer to those who make petitions to them. And in them are abominableness and stinkingness, and one cannot make them to cease from possessing these attributes. And besides this, truly do I say unto thee [p. 143] that devils speak inside them, and they seduce you by their means; and not one righteous and holy man [believeth in them]. I know this, and I hate them with a perfect hatred. I have gotten for myself a God Who liveth indeed, and Him only do I worship, and I shall minister unto Him until my soul leaveth my body, and I have committed my soul into His hand. I have returned from the captivity which is exceedingly evil, and I am one who is illumined with the light of the Holy Spirit. But my soul is sad and sorrowful because thou hast not found that these good things are thus in truth, and because thou hast fled from the shining Faith, and art a servant of evil, and art denying Christ.

"And now, O father, since thou hast discovered my proceedings, hearken unto all the desire of my heart. I will not deny the covenant which I have covenanted with my Messiah, Who purchased me from slavery with His precious blood and from the error of destruction. And because of this it is meet that I should die for His Name by thousands of deaths multiplied

many times. Weary not thyself for my sake by wishing for
my conversion from a confidence which is happy and bright,
for thy wish is just as useless and unprofitable as if thou didst
wish to hold the heights of heaven in thy hand, or to dry up
the fathomless depths of the sea. Know therefore well that
it is impossible for thee to shake me in this my opinion. And
if thou wilt hearken to my advice, make Christ thy God so
that thou mayest find His delights, which are beyond the
understanding, [both] in word and in sublimity. [If thou doest
this] then we two shall be partners, and as we are partners in
the nature of the flesh even so shall we become partners in
the pure Faith. And if thou wilt not do this then know that
certainly and in truth I will remove myself from under thy
authority as my father, and that I shall worship my God, Who
is indeed God."

[*How the king threatened Yĕwâsĕf with his implacable
hostility.*]

And when the king heard all this from him, he was astounded
and was filled with wrath, and madness rushed upon him, and
he gnashed his teeth like a madman, and he said unto him,
"I myself [p. 144] am the source of the causes that make thee
to treat me thus, for I have treated thee as no father ever
before hath treated his son. Rightly did the astrologers tell
me at the time of thy birth that thou wouldst become an evil
man and wouldst show thyself deceitful, and disobedient, and
rebellious towards thy parents. However, if thou wilt not
hold by my advice from this moment and wilt remove thyself
from my fatherly authority, I shall treat thee with hostility,
and I shall inflict upon thee evil the like of which no man
hath ever inflicted upon his enemies."

[*How Yĕwâsĕf accused his father of envying him his salvation, how he threatened to flee from him as from a serpent,
and how he urged him to repent and to seek God.*]

And Yĕwâsĕf answered and said unto him, "Why dost thou
inflame thyself with wrath on my account because I have

B.   11

become worthy of these good things? Who of the fathers of
olden time ever saw his son laden with riches and envied him?
How can a son call such a man 'father,' and how is it possible
for him not to call him 'enemy'? From this moment I will
not call thee 'father,' but I will make myself remote from
thee, even as the man who fleeth from the face of a serpent.
Since the matter is thus I know of a certainty that thou art
jealous of my salvation, and that thou wouldst in fact overthrow me and cast me into the pit of destruction. And if thou
wishest to snatch me away and to force me as thou sayest,
know thou of a certainty that thou wilt gain nothing except
that thou wilt be called a wicked father and a murderer, and
that in comparison with thee the rapacious eagle which
swoopeth [on its prey] in the air is a small matter.

"I will not turn away from the worship of Christ, in Whom
I believe with a happy faith. But do thou get understanding,
O father, and wake up, and remove blindness and darkness
from the eyes of thine heart, and lift up thine eyes that thou
mayest see the light of God which illumineth every man, and
bask thou in this light which is very pleasant. Behold, the
whole of thee is submerged in the sea of sin and in the lust
of the flesh which is unconverted. Know moreover that every
man is as the grass of the field, and that all the work of a man
is as the flower of the desert; for his leaf drieth up and his
flower is driven away, but the word of my God, Whom I preach,
shall remain strong over every man for ever. Let not wrath
and anger have dominion [over thee] as thou pursuest empty
adulation, which is like unto [p. 145] the summer flower that
is beaten to pieces and decayeth, and the pleasure that is
abominable and loathsome, that is to say, the filling of the
belly with food, and the gratification of the filthy passion of
the lower belly, which giveth pleasure to the minds of fools
for a few days, but afterwards there taketh place a rising up
within us of fumes which are more bitter than wormwood, in
this transitory world with its errors and its lying dreams.
And those who are fettered by the love thereof and the doers
of sin [shall dwell] in everlasting sorrow, and in the fire which

burneth and shall never be extinguished, and which hath neither limit nor end.

"Woe is me if thou shalt find thyself imprisoned therein, and shalt suffer torture in the terrible flame thereof in the repentance which is everlasting, because of the abundant evil of thy mind! And thou shalt make manifold entreaties for them to bring thee back to this life, but thou shalt not attain this, and thou shalt remember my words. Now, repentance shall profit nothing there, for in Sheol neither confession nor repentance shall avail thee. For this fleeting time is the time for action, and the time that passeth not away, and that shall assuredly come, is the time wherein to receive reward and retribution. And if there were no passing away to these delights and joys, and if there were no pain or tribulation in connection with them, they would be preferred to the gifts of Christ and to these delights which are exalted far above the thoughts. And as the sun sendeth forth more light than the night, similarly and in the same degree, the good things that God hath promised unto those who love Him are more splendid, more glorious, and greater than all the glory of an earthly kingdom. And now it is meet for thee to choose that which is greatest among things rather than that which diminisheth and becometh little, since every thing that is in this world is transitory and perishable, and is like unto the shadow and the dream; even also are those who are rich therein.

"And now, why dost thou prefer that which is transitory, and the wake of the ship in the waves of the sea, which profiteth not man? O thou fool who hast not sufficient strength to follow the word of righteousness! O thou man lacking in understanding, [p. 145] choose not transitory things in preference to those that abide for ever and are incorruptible, for the pleasure thereof is only momentary, and thou art not able to hear concerning the delights the existence of which is everlasting. Wilt not thou understand this, O my father? And wilt not thou renounce that which to-morrow shall pass away? And wilt not thou take greater heed and be more wakeful in respect of the things that endure? Wilt not thou prefer the habitation that is everlasting to the habitation that is transitory, and the light to the darkness, and the spirit to the flesh, and the life that is everlasting to death and the things that are transitory? Abandon the worship which is to be rejected and is evil, and of the god of this world, who is Satan, and take refuge in Christ, the Good, the Tender-hearted, the Compassionate to all men. And renounce the worship of those who are falsely called 'gods,' and withdraw from them, and worship the True God. Even if thou hast sinned against Him excessively, and hast slain His servants, I know and believe that my God will accept thee, and will forgive thy sins; for He doth not desire the death of the sinner, but that the sinner may return and live for ever[1]. For in His mercy He came to seek us who had gone astray, and He endured for our sakes scourging, and crucifixion and death, and with His precious blood He bought us from the slavery of sin. Glory and praise be unto Him for ever and ever! Amen."

[*How the king was filled with wrath and despair when he heard Yĕwâsĕf's words, and how he cursed his son's birth, and threatened to kill him because of the insults which Yĕwâsĕf heaped upon the gods.*]

And then the king was filled with despondency and wrath at the wisdom of the young man, and at his words to which he found it impossible for him to make answer, and he was unable to turn him by discussion and promises, and he was afraid lest he should bring up against him many other matters of complaint. And he was inflamed in mind greatly because of his audacity, and his blasphemy against the gods, and his derision of them, and he was afraid of his freedom of speech. And he departed, being filled with fury against him, and he said, "It would have been far better for me if I had never begotten thee at all, and if thou hadst never come forth from the womb and seen the light, than for thee to blaspheme the gods and to rebel against thy father's love. But do not treat the gods, who are invincible, [p. 146] with such utter contempt,

---

[1] Ezek. xviii. 32.

and do not blaspheme their great work, for if thou behavest in this manner thou shalt be chastised with every kind of torture, and I will kill thee with a terrible death, and thou shalt become as mine enemy who standeth up against me, and not as my beloved son." And with words of this kind did his father make answer to him, and he went away from him full of wrath against him.

[*How Yĕwâsĕf went into his palace and prayed to God and was comforted by his prayer.*]

And the young man Yĕwâsĕf went into his palace, and he lifted up his eyes to Him Who strengthened him for the spiritual fight, and he cried out to Him from the depth of his heart, saying, "O Lord, my God, Thou sweet Hope, and Word of righteousness wherein is no lie, Thou strong Refuge of those who flee to Thee, consider the contrition of my heart, and reject me not utterly. Be not far from me, be with me until the Day of Judgement, and fulfil to me in truth according as Thou hast promised me, O Thou Who hast strengthened me in this Good Faith, until the day of my death, so that I may be able to endure. Look upon me and have compassion upon me, even as Thou judgest those who love Thy Name. Look [upon me], O King of kings, for my soul burneth mightily with love for Thee, and it is parched like the thirsty man in the time of summer when there is no water, and it hangeth upon Thee. O Fountain of Life which never runneth dry, deliver not over to the wild beasts the soul that is submissive to Thee, and treat not with neglect for ever the soul that is thy pauper ; but hold me to be a sinner so that I may suffer during the whole remainder of my life for Thy holy Name, and I will put my trust in Thee, and sacrifice unto Thee my whole being, for all created things praise Thee and bless Thee for ever. Amen." And when he had prayed in this wise he found Divine consolation in his heart, and his soul was filled with joy, and he passed the whole night praying.

[*How the king, by the advice of 'Arâshis, visited Yĕwâsĕf once again, and spake fair words to him, and tried to convince him that, although he was wholly in sympathy with the Religion of the Galileans, the only right course of life was to worship the great gods.*]

And the king told 'Arâshis, the captain of his host, everything that Yĕwâsĕf had said unto him, and described to him his bold behaviour, which could not be changed. Then straightway the captain of the host advised the king to speak to him with cunningly devised words, and to pretend to love him, and to apply to him words of persuasion. And his father went to Yĕwâsĕf on the following day, and sat down, and called his son, and made him to come near him; and he embraced him and kissed him tenderly and caressingly, [p. 148] saying, "O my beloved son, pay honour to thy father's grey hairs, and hearken unto what I ask of thee. Offer up offerings to the gods and sacrifice unto them, so that they may forgive thee, and may give thee length of days, and glory of every kind, and a reign untouched by tribulation and full of happiness of every kind. In this way thou shalt become profitable to thy father and a joy all the days of thy life. And thou wilt be honoured and praised by all men, for he who obeyeth his father shall be a great man, and every one will praise him; and over and above all this [he shall enjoy] the grace and favour of the gods. Why didst thou think some time ago, O my son, that of my own free will I had withdrawn from the good path, and had chosen the way of the transgressor through ignorance, and lack of understanding and good counsel, and had cast my soul into perdition? And if thou imaginest that I prefer death and evil to life [and what is good], then know thou well, O my son, that thou hast withdrawn thyself from right judgement and from wisdom. Hast thou not observed the abundance of [my] wealth, and how I have prepared an army to fight the enemy? And again, in another way, I have worked at the works at which every man worketh until fatigue, and hunger, and thirst overtook me, and I have wandered about and walked over rough roads, and I have not in any way spared myself. And so much have I regarded my money as a thing of no account, and as a contemptible thing, that I have spent recklessly the treasure of my kingdom in restoring the temples of the great gods, and I have decorated each of them with the decorations that befit it, and I have distributed among the soldiers very much money and treasure. And similarly the desire for pleasure hath been rejected by me, and I have even resisted temptations [successfully]. And when I knew that the Law (i.e. Religion) of the Galileans was honourable I made myself ready to turn to it, and I forsook everything, and I took great pains [to secure] my own salvation. And if one would curse me because I am negligent and deficient in my knowledge in doing what is excellent, understand thou and enquire how many nights I have spent sleeplessly [p. 149] in seeking to learn and in asking questions. And sometimes it hath happened, against my will, that I could not find rest at all for my soul until I obtained the clear explanation of the matter about which I enquired. And there is no one under the sun who is more ready than myself to testify to wisdom and profound knowledge, and to the comprehension of hidden things apparent in any man.

" Behold, I have disputed with many of the wise and learned men, and with those who are called Christians, of my own free will and with attention, seeking knowledge for myself, and at length I found out the works of righteousness from the wise men who were honourable witnesses, and who were men of understanding, in the truth of their words. There is no other way to-day except this—to worship the glorious gods. And there is no place of rest which is more pleasant for a man to meet with than their temple. And we ourselves are among those who delight in and take their pleasure in joy and gladness (which the Galileans cast away in their pride), even the sweet light, and all the joys that the gods have given us. But the Galileans have cast away the hearing thereof, and they await the other hidden life to which they go, though they neither know what they say nor what are the things which [they declare] they know. As for thee, O my beloved son, be thou a comfort to thy father, for by means of a true searching I have found the truth. Behold, moreover, and know that I do not love error, and that I am not one who maketh a mock at good things, on the contrary, I have found them, and have gained possession of them; and as for thee, I prefer to have thee, which is better than to long for thee. Follow thou me, and thou shalt find happiness of every kind, and thou shalt be the inheritor of my kingdom."

[How Yĕwâsĕf showed his father that a man must not imperil his soul through filial obedience, and how he admonished him to cast aside idolatry and follow Christ, and how he described to him the second coming of our Lord, and the day of Judgement.]

And when the young man, who was full of true divine wisdom, heard these words from the mouth of his father, he recognized the craftiness of the cunning serpent, and he knew that a secret net had been prepared for his feet with guile. And he made strong his shining (or, illumined) heart, and he set before his eyes the divine commandment which saith, " I did not come to set peace but the sword and fire, and have come to separate the son from his father, and the daughter from her mother[1]," (and what followeth these words). And [he remembered that it saith], [p. 150] " He who loveth father or mother more than Me is not worthy of Me, and he who denieth Me before the face of man him will I also deny before the face of My Father Who is in heaven[2]." And with all this he pondered at that moment in his heart with divine fear, and he strengthened his heart with strong love, recalling to his mind the words of Solomon, the wise man, who saith, "[There is] a time for showing love and a time for showing hate ; a time for making war and a time for making peace[3]." And he prayed in his heart, saying, " Have compassion upon me, O Lord, have compassion upon me, for my soul confideth itself to Thee, and under the shadow of Thy wings do I trust

[1] Matt. x. 34, 35.   [2] Matt. x. 33, 37.   [3] Eccles. iii. 8.

myself. And I wait until sin shall have passed by. I cry out to God, the Most High, Who hath done good things for me[1]," (and the rest of the Psalm).

And Yĕwâsĕf answered his father, saying, "As for the good pleasure of a father our honourable Lord taught us the memorial thereof, and He sowed in us natural affection. But if it be that the love of parents leadeth to the perdition of the soul, and maketh it to be remote from its Creator, behold, he hath commanded that we must cut it off absolutely from us, and that we must not accept that which will separate us from God. But we must hate these things and renounce them absolutely, even though it be a father who hath commanded us to do what is not right, or a mother, or a king, or a lord of this life; and concerning this love He hath commanded us to withdraw ourselves therefrom. This is not a seemly thing for me to do. Bring not therefore trouble upon me and upon thyself, but bow down and submit thyself, so that both of us may worship the Living God, the First One. For the things that thou worshippest are idols, and they are the work of the hand of man, and they never benefit those who worship them, but only bring upon them perdition and everlasting torment. And if thou dost not wish to do so, do unto me whatsoever thou pleasest, for I am a faithful servant of Christ the Lord, and neither by thy promises nor by thy threats wilt thou be able to separate me from the love of my God, even as I have already told thee ; and I have revealed unto thee the truth. And as for that which thou sayest unto me, I have neither done evil nor acted deceitfully [except] in my ignorance in respect of doing what is good.

"I have learned notwithstanding, through excessive searching and fatigue, [p. 151] that the worship of idols and of the sun, and the lust of sin are the things wherefrom men must withdraw themselves ; and in truth these are not good things. I do not say unto thee that thou doest evil willingly, but the abundant flood which is poured out over thee and thy entrance into darkness prevent thee from seeing the light, and

[1] Psalm lvii. 1, 2.

even a little of the vision of splendour, because thou hast forsaken the path of integrity, and hast fallen into the pit, and because of the overwhelming floods. Behold, I myself have learned the knowledge of this thing. Know thyself, desire not this, and long not for the darkness instead of the light, and choose not death which killeth instead of life. Thou imaginest that this thy counsel is good, but on the contrary, it is thus : the idols which thou dost worship are unclean devils outwardly, and inwardly all their works are unclean. And this life which thou imaginest to be pleasant and full of joy and pleasure is, on the contrary, a vile and filthy thing, and it is even as hath in truth been said about it, ' a transitory thing [which lasteth] a few days only, which smootheth the throat [for a moment] and in the end is far more bitter than wormwood.' And my Master [whose word] is sharper than a two-edged sword, saith, 'How often have I told you about the errors thereof !' If thou wishedst to count them thou wouldst find them very much greater in number than the sands [of the sea].

"[This transitory life] is a path of falsehood upon which are laid as paving-stones filthy lusts and fleeting pleasures, and it leadeth those who are seduced into following it to Sheol and to utter perdition. And the happiness which my Lord promised, which thou thyself didst call the hope of the hidden life, is in truth a thing that is unchangeable, and it hath no end, and decay cannot reach it ; and it is impossible for men to describe it, and no man is able to declare the greatness of that glorious state. But it is not true, as thou sayest, that we shall all die, and that there is none among men who shall live [again]. It is not thus, but thou shalt be raised up when the Lord Jesus Christ, the Son of God, shall come in indescribable glory [p. 152] and in awful power, for He only is the King of kings, and Lord of lords, to Whom boweth every knee which is in heaven, and upon earth, and under the earth, in fear and trembling. At that time the powers of the heavens shall be shaken, and thousands of tens of thousands of angels and archangels shall stand before Him, and divine fear shall seize them all. And the heavens shall roll up like a paper, and the earth shall open her mouth, and the bodies of men who have died, from Adam until that moment, shall be raised up, in the twinkling of an eye, and shall stand as living beings before the throne of God, Who shall discuss with each one concerning what he hath done. Then shall the righteous, who have believed on the Father, and the Son, and the Holy Spirit, and have spent their lives in this world in doing what is good, shine like the sun in the kingdom of the heavens.

"And how can I describe to thee the glory which they shall find? If I compare their splendour and the light of their beauty to the light of the sun, yea, even to the brilliance of the lightning, I cannot make it to compare with that beauty which the eye hath not seen, nor the ear heard, and which hath never been imagined in the heart of man. And this it is that God hath prepared for His beloved ones in the kingdom of the heavens, in the light that cannot be described and in the glory that is boundless. And as for those who have denied the True God, and have forgotten their Creator, and have worshipped Satans and have sacrificed unto devils, and have loved the pleasure of this transitory world, and have wallowed in the deepest depths of sin, like swine in the mire, and have made themselves the habitation of all evil and things of perdition, they shall stand up naked in shame, being filled with sorrow, and they shall be a laughingstock for every creature, and everything that they have said and done shall be depicted in visible form before their eyes. Moreover, after this great disgrace they shall find mocking and shame which they shall not be able to bear, and they shall suffer punishment in Jahânamite fire, in darkness wherein is no light, where are the gnashing of teeth and the worm which dieth not. And these shall be their portion [p. 153] and their retribution for ever, because they have renounced the good things that were promised to them, and have chosen, in return for the pleasure that lasteth but a moment, torture for ever. And because of this [the Christians] withdrew from the enjoyment of this world so that they might find that joy which is indescribable and the pleasure thereof, and the glory which cannot be lauded [sufficiently]. And they shall shine brightly with the angels, and they shall find grace before God, the Bestower of great happiness ; and they shall escape from these bitter tortures which have no ending, and be snatched away from that severe disgrace and agonizing sickness. How very right then is it that we should give our possessions and our bodies, yea, even our souls which we have ! And he who will not learn this hath neither understanding nor knowledge. Will not a man endure the death that lasteth for a moment that he may escape the death [that is everlasting], and inherit imperishable life, and shine with the light of the Holy Trinity, the Source of life and the Creator thereof ? "

[*How the king refused to argue with his son, and spake fair words to him, and invited him to discuss their "idle quarrel" privily with him on another occasion, and how he promised to summon a great Council and to invite both pagans and Galileans to debate the matter before him.*]

And when the king heard how Yĕwâsĕf [spake] these words, and saw the intelligence of the young man, and the vigour of his reply, and that he was not afraid of his father's punishment, and that he would not listen to the words of persuasion, which had been addressed to him, and that the threats of terrifying torture did not frighten him, he marvelled at the eloquence of his mouth, and the beauty of his replies which he was unable to gainsay. And in secret his mind (conscience?) was rebuking him, even as did the words of his son. Now the king was a righteous man, but the evil habits of the life which he lived led him astray, and drew him as with a halter and a bridle, and did not permit him to see the light of righteousness, therefore he scattered (or, sowed) stones like beans, and he strengthened his former resolution to carry out what he had already devised in craftiness. And he said unto the young man Yĕwâsĕf, "It is not seemly for thee, O my son, to give me commands about every matter, and thou shouldst not rebel against me in this manner, and resist me violently, and determine to do thine own will. However, hold firmly to that which thou hast devised and come and let us discuss together concerning this idle quarrel, [p. 154] and let us make peace. Behold, he who hath deceived thee, Baralâm, is bound in fetters in my power. And I will summon a great council and I will gather together to it men of our own religion and customs, and Galileans also, and I will command that a herald shall go round about and shall proclaim with great pomp this matter, so that none of the followers of the Messiah may be afraid, but may accept the invitation safely without fear and with confidence. And we will forthwith seek the occasion for this."

[*How Yĕwâsĕf was warned by God in a dream about his father's duplicity, and how the king assembled his Council.*]

And the truly wise young man Yĕwâsĕf, who was full of intelligence and was bold of heart, learned beforehand in a dream, which was revealed to him by God, concerning the cunning plot of the king his father, and he said unto him, "God's will be done ! Command Thou, O my good Lord God, and may He take us by the right road, which is best. God is Himself the Merciful One, and on Him my soul relieth." And straightway the king commanded to be gathered together the great men of all those who worshipped graven images and of all the Christians, and he sent letters into all the places that were under his sovereignty. And the heralds went round about through all the cities and country places and made the following proclamation : "Forthwith let all the people who are Christians come hither without fear, and no harm whatever shall happen unto them. And by reason of this matter let the people of every race and Faith assemble together with their companions, so that they may enquire into the knowledge of the truth in a manner which shall be without enmity." And the proclamation came to the chiefs and great men of Baralâm, and likewise to those who worshipped idols, the Kaladâwĕyân and the Indians. And all those who were under the king's dominion came without delay, and among them were people of every nation, and men who understood omens, and magicians, and men who made incantations, so that they might conquer the Christians. And a multitude of people that could not be numbered, and that belonged to every kind of Faith were gathered together [p. 155] to the king, but of the Christians there was found only one to help him that was thought to be Baralâm, and his name was Barâkyâs. And as concerning the Christians, some of them had died violent deaths through the anger of the governors of the cities, and some had hidden themselves in the mountains and in caves, being afraid of the deeds of torture which [the governors] would inflict upon them, and some did not dare to show themselves openly in the light of day and worshipped Christ secretly. And this Barâkyâs was the only of them all who was bold and who was victor over his spiritual soul in this matter, and he came to give help to the truth and to fight for it.

[*How the king presided over the Council and ordered Nâkôr, who was disguised as Baralâm, to appear, and how he promised high honours and rewards to those who overthrew the Christians in argument, and threatened them with disgrace and death if they failed.*]

And when the king had taken his seat on the high throne, he commanded his son to take his seat with him, but he did not wish to do this, and he abased himself and sat upon the ground near him. And the learned men, and the men who were wise and understanding, who were rejected by God and whose hearts the lack of knowledge had led astray, came to the exalted places, and of them the Divine Apostle said, "They think in their hearts that they are wise, but they are fools, and they have changed the incorruptible glory of God into the form of a mortal man, and into the form of a four-legged beast[1]." And with these were hypocrites, and those who had come to dispute with the king's son, and their friends, so that the words of the proverb were fulfilled, "The gazelle wisheth to fight with the lion." But Yĕwâsĕf made the Most High a refuge for himself, and he placed himself confidently under

[1] Psalm cvi. 19 ; Acts vii. 41.

the shadow of His wings, whilst those people placed their confidence in mortal judges of this age, and in the sustainer of the world of darkness, unto whom they had made themselves subject in sorrow and misery. And then forthwith they brought forward Nâkôr, who was disguised as Baralâm, according to the counsel of the king and his friends, but they did not know that in addition to the Divine help there was another counsel which would fight against their own counsel. [p. 156] And when the Council of the judges and governors came into the presence of the king he said to the learned men and philosophers, "Behold, the seducers of the people have set before you a fight which is the greatest of all fights, and one of the two contending companies must be [victorious] this day. If ye strengthen and confirm the Faith in which we live, and vilify Baralâm and expose the crafty fraud of that man and of his companions, ye shall find great honour and much favour with me, and with all those who live with me, and ye shall be crowned with crowns of victory. And if ye are conquered ye shall die in the deepest disgrace, and the people shall have permission to plunder all your possessions, and the memorial of you shall perish from the face of the earth for ever. And I will make your dead bodies food for wild beasts, and your children shall perish and be reduced to slavery."

[*How Yĕwâsĕf addressed Nâkôr and threatened him with death and destruction if he were vanquished in argument by the idolaters.*]

And when the king had said these words Yĕwâsĕf answered and said unto him, "Behold, O king, thou hast judged a righteous judgement ; God will make strong thy will. And I also will speak to my teacher." And he turned to Nâkôr and said unto him, "Thou knowest, O Baralâm, in what state of happiness and honour thou didst find me. And thou didst by means of many words make me to forsake it, and to go afar from the Law of my fathers. And I would not perform their customs of error, and I would not worship a strange god, and thou didst make my heart to hope with the hope for happiness

which shall last for ever, which can never be lauded adequately,
and which can never be described in words. And now, take
good heed to thyself, and consider that thou art standing between the two arms of the scales. If thou conquerest and art
the victor, and thy commandment and thy Law also which
thou hast taught me are true, and thou dost heap contempt
upon those who fight against me, thou shalt receive honour
so perfect that no man hath ever attained thereto, and we
will worship Christ, even as thou hast preached to me, until
the departure of my soul from [my body]. But if thou art
conquered thou shalt not live for a single hour, and thou wilt
become to me this day [p. 157] the cause of shame and disgrace. And I will take vengeance upon thee speedily with my
own hand because of my abasement. And as for thy heart
and thy tongue I will seize them and cut them out, and I will
cast them for food to the dogs, and thy whole body also, so
that through thee every man may be warned not to seduce
the sons of kings."

And when Nâkôr heard this he sorrowed with a great sorrow,
and he saw himself fallen into the pit which he himself had
dug, and caught in the net which he himself had hidden, and
he understood the mistake [which he had made]. And he
determined in his heart that he would become one of the followers of Yĕwâsĕf, and would support and strengthen his faith,
so that he might escape the destruction which was appointed
for him; for he knew full well that Yĕwâsĕf had the power
to have him killed. And this took place through the wisdom
of heaven for the strengthening of the faith, so that we might
contend against those who are our opponents.

[*How Nâkôr declared publicly that he was Baralâm, and
denied that he had led the king's son into error, and said
that, on the contrary, he had brought him into the keeping of
the True God.*]

And straightway the king rose up among the servants of
idols, and Nâkôr was like unto Balaam of old, in the days of
Bâlek, who wished to curse Israel and who blessed them with

many blessings of various kinds[1]. And the king sat upon his
royal throne, and his son and his friends, even as we have said,
were there, and all those who had sharpened their tongues
like a cutting sword in order to cut off the truth, and the
learned men who did not know what the prophet said, "he
hath conceived, and suffered and brought forth sin[2]." And
people without number were gathered together so that they
might see their disputing and which party would be victorious.
And one of the learned men who was separated from his companions in the tribunal said unto Nâkôr, "Art thou Baralâm
who with his audacity and boldness hath blasphemed the gods,
and seduced the king's son, and taught him to worship this
[Man] Who was crucified?" And Nâkôr answered, saying,
"I am that Baralâm who hath, as thou sayest, rejected the
gods. As for the king's son, I have not cast him into the midst
of craftiness, but I have saved him from error and stumbling,
[and have brought unto him] the healing of a physician, and
I have set him in the safe keeping of the [p. 158] True God."
And the chief priest answered, saying, "Dost thou blaspheme
the victorious and immortal gods, before whom all the kings
of the earth bow down, and whom all the nobles worship?
How canst thou let thy tongue lie concerning them, and how
dost thou dare to be so bold as to blaspheme them and to say
that they are not gods, and that only the Man Who was crucified is God?"

[*How Nâkôr proclaimed his belief in the God of the Christians
and the futility of the worship of idols.*]

And Nâkôr rose up to make answer to him, and that priest
of idols would in no wise hearken unto him. And with his hand
Nâkôr made a sign to the multitude to hold their peace, and
straightway he opened his mouth, like the ass of Balaam, the
son of Bê'ôr, so that he might say unto the king the words
which he had not beforehand sought to say unto the king
[and he spake, saying], "I came by the wisdom of God into
this world, and I looked at the heavens, and the earth, and

---

[1] Numbers xxiv. 10.   [2] Psalm vii. 14; Isaiah lix. 4.

B.   12

the sea, and the sun, and the moon, and the other created things and I marvelled. And I saw that the world and everything that is therein go on without rest, and I knew that He Who established all created things and He Who sustaineth them is One God. And I knew that everything that He established gaineth strength through their being, and that what He sustaineth gaineth strength through being sustained. Therefore I say, It is the One God Who is the Ordainer of everything, and the Maintainer thereof, the God of olden time, Who is without beginning, Who is exalted above everything, Who is remote from all suffering and disgrace, and is beyond all anger and folly. He hath no desire for sacrifices and offerings, nor for any visible object, but every [creature] that hath need maketh supplication to him. And thus I say concerning God, even as I began by saying.

"And again, let us turn to the race of man, and let us see who of them are there who speak the truth and who ensue it, and who there are among them who do the works of error. It is manifest, O king, and it is well known that the men who are in this world [fall] into three divisions, namely, worshippers of idols, Jews, and Christians. And the first-named division, the worshippers of [p. 159] many gods, may be divided into three divisions, namely, the Kaladăwĕyân (Chaldeans), and the Ṣâbâwĕyân (Sabeans), and Gebṣâwĕyân (Egyptians). And these are they who at an early period taught the rest of the nations to worship gods whose names were many, and to bow down to them. Let us enquire then and consider carefully who among them believed the truth, and who among them spake vanity. The Chaldeans did not know God. They made a mistake and followed after natural objects, and they established the worship of created things instead of the worship of the Creator, and they made for themselves similitudes of things and called them 'gods.' And they made similitudes of these 'gods' in the form of the heaven, and the earth, and the sea, and the sun, and the moon, and the rest of the powers of nature, and the stars ; and they shut them up in temples and bowed down before them and called them 'gods.' These 'gods' they guarded with the strictest guard lest thieves should steal them, and they neither conceived in their minds nor understood that the guardian is more honourable than the thing guarded, and that the creator is greater than the things that have been created. And since it was the fact that their gods could not save themselves, how could they save others? Nay, the Chaldeans were led astray with great craftiness, for their 'gods' could not benefit them but only bring disgrace upon them.

"I am filled with wonder, O king, why those who are called 'philosophers' have wholly failed to understand these natural objects which grow old. First of all, O king, we must know certainly that these things which grow old, and which become changed by the command of the True God, are not gods, and that that God doth not grow old, and doth not become changed, and that He is invisible, that He directeth everyone by His Will, and turneth him and maketh him to be changed; and it is not that I speak concerning natural objects [only]. And those who call them 'gods of heaven' err with manifest error, for we see them changing, and they grow, in fact, and they are created from many substances; moreover, they call [them] 'everlasting,' but it is only the Maker Who endureth for ever, and everything that is made hath a beginning and an end. And His firmament is bright with His stars. Now the stars [p. 160] travel each according to his own ordinance, and each according to his period, and each one maketh his course in his own appointed time, so that they may make complete the summer and the winter. And as they are commanded by God they do not move out of their appointed orbits through an operation of nature, save by the command of the heavenly Master of knowledge. And by this it is known that the heavens are not God, but the work of God, and those who think that the earth is God err with manifest error. For behold, we see that the earth is considered to be a thing of no importance by men, and it is under their dominion. And they treat it in a contemptuous manner, and they make [things] of it, and they consider it to be a substance wherein is no profit, and if they bake it in the fire it becometh a dead thing. For an earthen pot doth not produce any offspring whatsoever, and if it is befouled it is destroyed with its contents, and men trample upon it with their feet, and also all kinds of beasts. And it is sometimes defiled with the blood of the slain, and with the bodies of the dead, and since it is treated in this manner it is not meet for the earth to be called 'God,' but the work of God, which man may fashion.

"And as for those who think that water is God, behold, they go very far astray, for it was only created for the need of men, and it is under their dominion. It is befouled and made dirty, and its substance is changed when men cook with it. Its substance is increased when they add [something] to it, and it is frozen solid by the cold ; and it is contaminated by the blood of many ; and every creature washeth therein. Therefore it is impossible for water to be God ; but it is the work of God.

"And those who think that fire is God make a very great mistake indeed, for fire was only created for the use of men, and in order that they might work at their trades by means thereof, and it is under their dominion, and they carry it about from place to place so that they may cook all the various kinds of meat that are eaten. And moreover, it destroyeth even the flesh of mortal man, especially when the flame thereof is too strong. Therefore it is not meet for fire to be considered to be God, but God is its creator.

[p. 161] "And those who hold the blast of the winds to be God err among mortals, for it was sent for another purpose, and for the sake of men. God ordained the winds to make the ships to sail on the sea, and for the other needs of men, and to make the leaves and branches of trees to mature ; and at the command of God the winds drop and become calm. Therefore the blast of the winds is not God, but the winds are the work of God.

"And those who think that the sun is God err with an error that is manifest. For we can see the sun actually moving, and it turneth and travelleth from Sign to Sign, and it setteth and riseth in order to give heat to the trees and the plants for the benefit of man. And it hath this in common also with the stars; it diminisheth exceedingly in the heavens, and it doth not possess of itself the power which is implanted in it. Therefore it is not right for men to think that the sun is God, but it is a creature of God.

"And those who think that the moon is God err with an error that is manifest. For behold, we see it actually moving, and we see it travelling from Sign to Sign as it goeth to its setting place, and it riseth for the need of man. And it diminisheth more than the sun, for it becometh full and then it diminisheth until it riseth again ; and there are times when it is quite dark. Therefore men must not call it God, but a creature of God.

"And those who think that man is God make a very, very great mistake. For we see him walking about, and he changeth, and he groweth to maturity, and he becometh old. Sometimes he is in a state of joy and sometimes in a state of sorrow, and he needeth to eat and to drink, and to clothe himself withal. And he transgresseth greatly, and he becometh wroth, and feeleth the goadings of envy; he stealeth, he repenteth, and he is corrupt in very many ways by reason of the nature of men and animals, and death hath dominion over him. It is therefore not fitting for men to call man God, but it is God Who is his Creator.

[p. 162] "And now, the Chaldeans are seduced into error with great craftiness, and they err in following their lusts, and they worship objects that grow old (or, are worn out) and die, and graven images, and they do not recognize their error because the things which they lust for are even like unto their error.

"And now let us rise up and enquire into the matter of the Sabeans, and see in what manner they treat God. The Sabeans say, 'We are wise men,' and in this respect they are more foolish than the Chaldeans ; and they acknowledge many gods, one half of them being male and the [other] half female. And in this respect, O king, the Sabeans bring forward a matter which is partly to be laughed at. For they call these [males

and females] 'gods,' and as if reckoning their evil lusts as of
no account [they actually ask them] to help them to commit
wickedness when they go a-whoring, and when they sin and
commit murder, and when they do any disgraceful and abominable act of evil. And if their gods do such works as these
why should not the Sabeans themselves do likewise? And
because of the development of this error much fighting and
slaughter take place among men. But now we would describe
the work of one only of their gods, although we have seen
very much of their contemptible affairs. They say that the
planet which they call 'Zûkhâl[1]' is a god, and they sacrifice
their sons to him, and the men who do thus, O king, become
fornicators, and they have intercourse with males, and they
do other evil deeds, even as do their gods. Now, how can it
possibly be right that he who committeth fornication should
become a god, or one who hath intercourse with males, or is
the murderer of his sons? And after this they bring forward
a lame man[2], and they call him a god, and this man holdeth
a hammer and tongs wherewith to hammer iron so that he
may make gain thereby. And they also say that 'Âṭared[3]
[p. 163] is a god, and he was a merchant, and a magician, and
an interpreter of dreams. And they call Askêlêwôs (Aescu-
lapius) a god; now he was a physician, and he performed
cures and mixed medicines. And they call Apollo a god, who
was jealous, and who carried a bow, a quiver, an arrow (?) and
a lyre. And he distributed gold among men to reward them.
And he married his sister Alânâ (Artemis) the huntress, who
carried a bow and a quiver in her hands, and she used to roam
about in the mountains by herself with dogs hunting the
akarîgêlyôn (or, wild pigs). How can this woman, the huntress,
who roamed about with dogs, be a god? And they say that
the planet Zekhuërâ[4] is a god, although he (sic) committed
fornication with Môlôkh. And they also call a god Adûnî

---

[1] I.e. toħል: or ልተħል:, Arab. الزحل Saturn.
[2] I.e. Hephaestus who, according to Homer, was lame from his birth.
[3] I.e. Mercury. Arab. العطارد
[4] I.e. Azħërâ ኣዝħራ:, Arab. الزهرة Aphrodite?

(Adonis), who was a hunter and who died being chased and wounded by a wild boar. How is it possible for a hunter, or a fornicator, or a mortal, or any other doer of iniquity, to have a care for man? And hereby is it known that men have made their gods their excuse, and have committed every kind of sin, and fornication, and evil, and denial of Christ, and have polluted the earth and the air with their evil deeds.

"And the error and the evil of the Egyptians were greater than the error and evil of every other nation, for they went further astray than all the nations [mentioned above]. They put no faith in the gods of the Chaldeans and the Ṣâbâwĕyân (Sabeans), but they appointed for themselves other gods from among the beasts which speak not, and earthly and mortal creatures from among the trees and the plants. Some of them worshipped a ram, and some of them worshipped a serpent, and some of them worshipped a dove, and a vulture, and an eagle, and some of them worshipped a crocodile, and an ox, and some of them worshipped a flea (?), and a dog and a wolf [p. 164], and some of them worshipped an ape and vipers, and some of them worshipped the leek, the garlic plant, and the onion, and other created things. And they did not understand, the miserable beings, that in all these things there was no power whatsoever, even when they saw men eating their gods, and cooking them over the fire and slaughtering them; but they were blind and did not understand that they were not gods.

"Behold, the Egyptians, and the Chaldeans, and the Ṣâbâwĕyân erred with error which was manifest in considering such creatures as these to be gods. And they made graven images, and they called a graven image which was without flesh and movement 'god.' And I marvel how it was that when they saw the carpenters sawing them, and the masons working on them, and when they saw them old and worn out, and changed in appearance, and melting away, they did not understand that they were not gods, and that they were powerless things, and that they had no strength. How was it possible for such to help man? But the makers of graven images, and the wise men of the Chaldeans, and the Ṣâbâwĕyân (Sabeans), and the Egyptians wished to perpetuate the recital of their traditions and the words of their Books, so that they might obtain honour from their gods; and their disgrace is manifest to every one.

"And behold, a man possesseth many members, but he is unable to cast away one of his limbs, and he dwelleth in oneness with all his limbs complete, being unseparated in his oneness, his word (or, voice) being one. How then in the Nature of God can there be strife and words of different kinds as [there are in] these gods? Now the Nature of God is one. Is anything a god which can be chased and driven away? Is anyone a god whom one can slay? Is anyone a god to whom one can do an injury? Or can anyone be called 'god' who can be chased away by another? Or can anyone be god whom one can slay, or whose skin one can flay off, or who can be stolen and who can wither away? This then is not the manner of a single nature, but [it belongeth] to the many minds of all the workers of evil, and not one of them is to be separated, and the operation of God is not in them at all.

"And now, O king, how could the wise men [p. 165] of the Sabeans do otherwise than fall into error in their words? For they laid down laws, being themselves fettered and kept in restraint by their own laws, for the commandments of the Law become things that are right. But as for their gods, without any untruth, they are wrongdoers, and robbers, and far removed from the Law, and they impute to one the killing of the other, and they commit fornication, and they concoct poison which killeth, and they steal, and they lie with men.

"And they thus consider these works goodness and righteousness, and like unto the works of excellence, and they adopt the works of sin, which are rejected and are antiquated, and the works of their gods, which are themselves hateful to the Law, and are all under the destruction of death. And those who make their gods after the likeness of these are heretics, and the words that are spoken concerning them become mere idle stories, and they are nothing but mere words. And if those who do these things are beings of nature and not gods, then it happeneth to them that they thus become like a story which cometh, and then cometh another story that giveth the first story the lie. Verily they are idle tales and nothing else.

"Behold now, O king, it is well known that the work of those who worship many gods is a work of error and of perdition. And it is not meet to call the things that are visible and the things that are invisible 'gods,' but it is right to worship the God Who is invisible, Who ruleth everything, and Who is the Creator of everything.

"And now, O king, let us describe unto thee the work of the Jews, whose faith is, we see, in God. These are the sons of Abraham, Isaac, and Jacob, and they dwelt in the land of Egypt for a long period of days, and Pharaoh, the king thereof, made them toil for him. And God, the Mighty One, brought them out from Egypt with a strong hand and a stretched-out arm, by the hand of Moses, their Lawgiver, and He drowned the Egyptians by His power, with many signs and great wonders. But these also were wicked men, and gave thanks to Him in an insufficient degree, and they worshipped the gods [p. 166] of foreign nations, and they slew the righteous men and prophets who were sent unto them. And when the Son of God was pleased to come upon the earth they would not know Him, and they behaved foolishly like a drunken man. And then they delivered Him over to Pilate their governor, and they passed on Him sentence of death on the cross. And they did not remember His goodness, and His innumerable wonders which He had wrought among them openly. And now men worship Him as the only God, the Sustainer of the Universe, but the Jews have no knowledge, for they deny that He was the Son of God, and they are even as the [other] nations. Now there are some who consider that they are near the truth. And so much as concerning the Jews.

"And as concerning the matter of the Christians, who are named after our Lord Jesus Christ, the Son of the Most High God, we believe on Him Who came down from heaven for the salvation of men, and became man by the Holy Spirit, and was born of a holy virgin, whose virginity is perpetual, without seed and without corruption. And He took upon Himself from her a perfect body, and He appeared to men that He might call them from the error of death, in His body which He took from us. And He died willingly in His great wisdom, and He rose on the third day by the might of His Godhead, and He ascended into heaven, and His coming was a cause of rejoicing. And the Holy Book which they call 'Gospel' speaketh about Him, and from it thou canst learn these things if thou wilt read it, O king. And He had Twelve Disciples who, after His Ascension into heaven, preached in the countries of the world and the borders thereof, and taught men His greatness. And one of them came to our country and preached unto us the Law of truth, and from that time until the present day those who are called Christians have followed the truth of their preaching. Now these Christians are they who have found out what is the truth more than any [other] people. And they acknowledge God the Creator and Maker of everything, and His Only Son, and His Holy Spirit, and they do not worship any other god beside Him. [p. 167] And the commandments of the Lord Jesus Christ are impressed on their hearts, and inscribed on their minds.

"And they cherish Him, and hope for the Resurrection of the dead, and the life which is to come. And they sin not, and they fornicate not, and they do not become lying witnesses, and they do not covet that which is not theirs. They honour their father and their mother, and they love their neighbour, and they judge rightly and savingly. Whatsoever they wish should not come upon themselves they do not do to others among them. They show love to those who ill-treat them, and they make those who hate them friends, and they entreat kindly those who revile them. They are meek and quiet men, and they withdraw themselves from fornication and from every kind of uncleanness. They neglect not the widow, and they do not make the orphan to sorrow, and he who hath authority among them admonisheth with humility him that is little. If they see a pilgrim they bring him in under the roof of their house and they make rejoicings with him as if they were indeed brothers; and they do not call him a brother in the flesh, but a brother in the spirit (or soul). And they do not boast themselves of their devotion to Christ, although they keep His commandments with scrupulous care and vigour. And they live in truth and in integrity, according as the Lord God commanded them, and to Him they give thanks at all times, when they eat, and when they drink, and with every kind of good works. Verily this is the path of truth which leads those who walk therein to the kingdom that is for ever, which Christ promised them, the life that is to come.

"Know, O king, that I have not spoken these things of my own authority. Look thou in the Christian books and thou wilt find that I have not said anything but what is truth. Ascribe blessing to the understanding of thy son, for in truth I know that I shall worship the living God and Redeemer until the end of time which is to come, and I await His second coming in truth. The wise words [p. 168] of the Christians are great and exceedingly wonderful, for the Christians do not speak with the words of men, but with the word of God. And all nations have erred and have made themselves to err, for they have groped about in the darkness and stumbled about, striking and hurting each other like drunken men. And here is the end of my discourse, O king, wherein I have spoken the truth from the depth of my heart; therefore let the mouths of thy wrong-doing wise men who have uttered falsehood against God be shut. For it is necessary for you, and better for you to worship God the Creator, and to incline your ears to His incorruptible words, so that ye may be saved from the Judgement and from torture, and may enter into the life that hath no trial therein, and inherit it."

[*How the king was wroth and the heathen priests were dumbfounded when Nâkôr finished his speech at the close of the first day, and how the king adjourned the discussion.*]

And when Nâkôr had finished this speech in making answer to him, the king's countenance changed and wrath covered him ; and his chief priests and priests were dumb, and they were unable to answer him except with contemptible and miserable words. But the son of the king rejoiced, and his soul was exceedingly glad, and his face shone, and he praised God Who had laid down a path where there had been none for those that put their trust in Him, and Who confirmed the truth by the mouth of His enemies, who fought against it, and by the mouth of the prince of error, and Who made him a helper and a fighter for the word of truth. And the king was exceedingly angry with Nâkôr, but he was unable to do any harm whatsoever to him, because he had formerly made a pact with him, as we have already said, for he had commanded him to hold converse with the Christians without fear. And because of this he frequently made him to remember by nods and signs, that he must finish his answer and be victorious over the arguments of the high priests of the graven images, even as they had arranged before when they were together alone. And Nâkôr debated the matter with greater zeal and force, and he proved all their questions and the imaginations of their hearts to be futile things ; and he scoffed at the deadliness of their error. And the debate lasted until [p. 169] the time of evening drew nigh, and the king commanded that the Council should break up, desiring the matter to be enquired into further on the following day.

[*How Yĕwâsĕf proposed that Nâkôr should spend the night with him, and the friends of the king with the king, and how the king departed to his palace with his priests and wise men.*]

And Yĕwâsĕf said unto the king his father, "According as thou didst command formerly, let there be a right judgement ; the debate shall now be right [and] perfect in its ending, and one matter shall [proceed] from these two matters. If thou wilt command that my teacher shall pass this night with me we will search for another man that we may dispute by means of him with those who will fight against us to-morrow. And do thou take thy friends with thee, and discourse together according as ye wish, and on the subjects which they themselves shall choose ; or, give me thy friends this night and take my friends with thee. For if they all remain with thee, my teacher will be sorrowful, and fear both of them and of thee will take hold of him ; and thy friends will rejoice and they will expect him to be vanquished, which I do not consider to be a right judgement, but [a display of] the royal power and a breach of the covenant of truth." And the king marvelled at the beauty of his words, and he took with him his wise men and his priests. And he commanded Yĕwâsĕf to take Nâkôr, expecting him also to keep the promise which he had made to them concerning him.

[*How Yĕwâsĕf took Nâkôr with him and informed him that he had penetrated his disguise ; and how, having offered him a reward for his service to the Christians that day, he urged him to become a true Christian.*]

And the son of the king departed after the manner of a conqueror who had overcome his enemies, and had gripped them fast, and Nâkôr was with him. And he called Nâkôr to him privily, and he said unto him, "Thou must not imagine that thy action is hidden from me, for I know of a certainty that thou art not Baralâm, but Nâkôr the diviner ; and I marvel how thou wast able to carry out such a matter as this so successfully. Thou didst imagine that at noon-day thou couldst deceive me so thoroughly that I should take a wolf for a lamb ! Well doth the Psalmist say, 'The heart is evil, it thinketh vanity[1]'; and behold, your counsel and your thoughts are as vanity. And everything goeth forth from the heart, and the thing that thou hast done is full of [p. 170] every kind of wisdom ; therefore rejoice and be glad, O Nâkôr. I trust in thee with great gladness, for thou hast been this day a helper of the truth, and thou hast not defiled thy lips with the foul words and pleasing phrases of perdition. Thou hast purified thyself thoroughly from great uncleanness in thy reviling of those beings who are falsely called 'gods,' and thou didst confirm the truth of the Law of the Christians. And because

[1] Compare Psalm xii. 2 ; Jer. xvii. 9.

of this I was anxious to take thee with me for two reasons. First, that the king might not send thee away, and might not torture thee in secret because thou didst not perform his will; and secondly, that I might reward thee for the act of grace which thou hast performed towards me this day. Enquire of thyself what the reward shall be, and accept it. I will make thee willing and strong to withdraw from the rough path whereupon thou hast walked until this day, and henceforward thou shalt walk on the right path which thou knowest. But, first of all, of thine own free will thou must flee from it, and from the performance of shameful deeds of evil, and from casting thyself down into the pit and abysses of sin. Understand now, O Nâkôr, that there is knowledge in thee; and seek thou to gain Christ only, and the life that is written down for those who have renounced the transitory and corruptible things of this world. For thou shalt not live for ever, on the contrary, thou shalt die after a little [time], and thou shalt depart even as have departed those who were before thee. Woe be unto thee if thou shalt depart thence laden with a heavy load of sin, to the place where there is just punishment and retribution for the deeds which weigh thee down and which cannot there be repudiated, although it is easy for thee to repudiate them in these days."

[*How Nâkôr heard Yĕwâsĕf's words with gladness, and declared his intention to repent of his manifold sins and to seek God.*]

And the soul of Nâkôr welcomed these words with the greatest good will, and he said, "Well hast thou spoken, O king, and I have knowledge of Him Who is indeed the God of truth, through Whom is the certain knowledge of the judgement for which we wait. Behold, we have heard very much [of Him] in the words of the Scriptures, but evil habit and the continued deceit of former days have blinded the eyes of my mind, and have poured out dense darkness over my understanding. [p. 171] And now, by thy words thou hast unrolled the shroud of darkness and stripped it off me, and, committing myself to God, I am going to knock at His gates; peradventure He will have compassion upon me, and will open up for me the path of repentance for having done what is evil. But I think and I say this : It is impossible for me to obtain remission for my sins, which are more in number than the sand of the sea, and which I have committed wilfully and in stupidity, from my youth up to this day."

[*How Yĕwâsĕf preached to Nâkôr Christ's forgiveness and His love for penitent sinners.*]

And when Yĕwâsĕf, the king's son, heard this, he rose up straightway with great warmth of heart, for his heart inclined to Nâkôr in his despair, and he began to encourage him and to hearten him in [his desire] for the Faith of Christ, saying, "Let not thy heart have any doubt about this matter, O Nâkôr, for it is written that 'God is able of these stones to raise up sons to Abraham[1].' And there is nothing [to be done] except this, even as Abba Father Baralâm saith, It is possible for those who do not believe and who are unclean, to be saved from all their transgressions, and to become servants of Christ, Whose sublime love for the children of men is so absolute that He hath opened for us the gates of heaven, which belong to Him, and for all those who come to Him. And He never shutteth the gates of salvation in the face of any man, nay, He welcometh joyfully those who repent. And for this reason He giveth equal rewards unto those who come to His vineyard in the first hour of the day, and at the third hour, and at the sixth hour, and at the ninth hour, and at the eleventh hour, even as saith the Holy Gospel[2]. And although thou hast waited until now, and hast attained to old age in committing sin, thou art meet [to receive] these glorious things as if thou hadst come to the Faith with a fervent and pure belief, and thou shalt rank as the equal of those who have fought the fight from their youth up." And with many remarkable words dealing with repentance the divine young man taught Nâkôr who had worked out his days in committing evil, and he

[1] Matt. iii. 9.   [2] Matt. xx. 1-9.

expounded before him the forgiveness of sins and the blotting out of them, and he made him to hope that Christ would forgive him his sins [p. 172] which were past. And he made his heart to believe that Christ is ready always to receive the erring who turn unto Him with all their hearts; and he made his suffering soul happy by means of his healing words, and he bestowed upon it gracious [words] of salvation and knowledge.

[*How Nâkôr with Yĕwâsĕf's consent left the palace that night and departed to the desert, and confessed his sins with tears to a holy monk, who baptized him.*]

And Nâkôr answered and said unto him forthwith, " O most glorious soul and body, teacher of the mysteries and of the desire for goodness, do thou live in this pleasing confession of the goodness which leadeth unto salvation, and make it to be impressed upon thy heart for ever. And behold, I will depart from here, so that I may seek for the salvation of my soul, and I will make supplication for forgiveness from God, and will make repentance in truth because I have provoked Him to wrath. If God pleaseth from this time forward I will not look upon the face of the king, provided that thou ap- provest of this thing." And Yĕwâsĕf rejoiced and accepted his words with a radiant heart, and he embraced him and kissed him, and he prayed on his behalf to God for a long time, and [then] sent him away from his palace. And Nâkôr went out from his presence with a bold spirit, and he departed like a stag, into a desert which was remote, and he discovered there a monk who had the authority to confer upon him the office of the priesthood, in a place where he had hidden him- self through fear. And Nâkôr bowed down before him in meekness of heart, and he washed his feet with his tears, like the harlot of old[1], and he asked him for Divine Christian Baptism. And that priest, who was filled with celestial grace, rejoiced in him greatly, and having admonished him in the customary manner, made him perfect by bestowing upon him the garment of holy Baptism in the Name of the Father, and

[1] Luke vii. 37.

of the Son and of the Holy Ghost. And Nâkôr lived for a very
long time with the monk in a state of repentance and repented
of what he had done. Blessed be God, Who desireth not the
destruction of any man, but waiteth for the repentance of
everyone, and receiveth those who repent because of His
love for the children of men.

[*How the king fell into a state of doubt and despair, for
although he saw that his gods were vain things he was afraid
to embrace the Gospel.*]

And when the king knew of the matter of Nâkôr he despaired absolutely, for he had placed his confidence in him.
And seeing that his wicked wise men and priests [p. 173] were
wholly vanquished, he was dismayed, and he found no excuse
[for them]. And he poured on these men great abuse, and
cast them away with severity, and covered their faces with
thick darkness. And some of those to whom he had given
commands he scourged very cruelly with whips made of the
tendons of bulls, and he drove them forth from his presence.
And then he began to understand the glory of those beings
who were falsely called "gods." Now he did not wish to see
completely the light of Christ, for thick blackness and darkness covered the eyes of his heart, but he did not pay honour
to the priests of the gods any longer, and he neither celebrated
festivals in their honour, nor offered up sacrifices to graven
images. His mind, however, was distracted by two matters ;
first, he had learned the feebleness of the "gods," and secondly,
he was afraid of the course [laid down by] the Gospel. And
it was exceedingly difficult for him, being drawn by his evil
habits, for he served the desires of the flesh devotedly, and
his whole person was urged on to [the gratification] of evil
passions like a drunken man, even as saith Isaiah the Prophet,
"Without the drinking of wine he is drawn by evil habits as
with a strong bridle[1]." Even so was the king when contending
with the two states of his mind.

---

[1] Compare Isaiah v. 18; xxix. 9.

[How Yĕwâsĕf lived a life of great piety, and converted many by his example, and how he fasted and prayed that he might see Baralâm once again.]

And the understanding of the divine Yĕwâsĕf was filled with royal righteousness of soul and he dwelt quietly in his royal palace, and everyone knew of his victory and the beauty of the nature and disposition that dwelt in him. And his toil and devotion in the performance of the commandments of God were seen and known by all, and the crucifixion of his mind, and the wounding thereof in divine love. And he wished exceedingly to meet with his spiritual teacher Baralâm, and with great longing he strove to see him, and he remembered his shining words in his heart, never forgetting that he was a tree planted by a fountain of water. And he brought forth fruit to be desired to God, and he delivered many souls from the snare of Satan, and presented them as offerings to Christ. And many people used to come to him to hear from his mouth the word of salvation, and then many men, now these were not a few, [p. 174] fled and followed the voice of our Redeemer, and there were others who renounced the world entirely and became remote from it, and entered into the circle of those who led a life of contemplation.

And Yĕwâsĕf was continually fasting and praying, and he cried out openly and spake the following words: "O my King and my God, O Thou in Whom I have put my trust and in Whom I have taken refuge, [whereby] I have been saved from error, grant Thou unto Baralâm, Thy messenger, the reward which he deserveth for having guided me and brought me out of error, for he showed me the life and the true path. O let there not be lacking to me another sight of that angel clothed with flesh, who is beyond all price in this world, and let me fulfil in his company all the days of my life so that I may travel on the divine road, and perform Thy good pleasure, O my Lord and my God, for Thou art blessed for ever! Amen."

[How the heathen priests were dismayed when they saw how the king's interest in their festivals had diminished, and how they appealed to Tawĕdâs (Theudas) to work magic upon him and to restore his love for the worship of the gods.]

And in those days there was to be celebrated a festival in that city in honour of those beings who are falsely called "gods," and the king wished to come to the festival, and [to bring] with him nine bulls for sacrifices. The priests, however, were dismayed when they saw how lukewarm he was about their religion, and how greatly his zeal in following them had cooled, and they were afraid that if he became too lukewarm to come to the temple, they would lose the royal gifts which were ordained for them, and all the [other] gifts. And they rose up and departed and came to a rocky ledge in the outer desert, where dwelt a certain man who fasted and practised magic, and who was ready and willing to be a helper of idolatrous error, and his name was Tawĕdâs. And the king used to pay the honour which was fitting to this man, and he called him "Teacher," and said, "By his magic my kingdom flourisheth and increaseth in extent." And when the priests had come to him they put their trust in him to help them, and they made him to know clearly what had happened to the king in respect of their gods, and they told him about the matter of the king's son, and that through him Nâkôr had declared against them, and how he had blasphemed against the gods, and how he had made them laughing-stocks [p. 175] before the people. [And they said unto him] "If thou dost not help us all our hope will perish, and all our religion will perish, and all our regular offerings whereon we live will come to an end, for thou alone art left unto us as a comforter in tribulations. And behold, upon thee we cast all our hope."

[How Theudas went to the king and entreated him to make a great festival and to sacrifice young men and maidens, and bulls and sheep, in honour of the gods.]

And straightway Tawĕdâs became strong with the Satanic strength which resided in him, and he armed himself, not with

13—2

righteousness, but with the armour of war which is vain, and he summoned certain wicked monks whom he knew to help him, and he roused them up to perform the evil deeds of shame which they had formerly committed with strength and power, and he departed with them to the king. And when the king knew of his arrival he had him brought into his presence, and he came in before the king holding in his hand a palm rod, and he was girded about with a garment. And the king rose up from his throne to welcome him, and he embraced him and kissed him, and led him to the throne, and seated him thereon close to himself, and then Tawĕdâs said unto the king, "O king, live for ever, being under the protection of the great gods! Behold, I have heard that thou hast been fighting a fight with the Galileans, and that thou hast crowned thyself with the shining crown of victory. Behold, I have come so that thou mayest make a great festival of thanksgiving, and that thou mayest offer up goodly young men and beautiful young women to the immortal gods ; and one hundred bulls and many sheep shalt thou sacrifice to them so that they may be an invincible help to us in the future and may make us all glad with the good news of length of days in safety."

[*How the king asked Theudas to explain the victory of the Christians in the debate, and how he at length agreed to make a great festival to the gods in their temple.*]

And the king said unto him, "It is not true that we have conquered, but we have been conquered. For those who were with us rose up suddenly against us, and he (i.e. our enemy) found our soldiers feeble, and drunk, and foolish, and he dashed them to pieces utterly. And now, do whatsoever thou art able to do, and put forth and use every gift of power which thou hast to help our men who have fallen down, and to raise them up again. And explain this thing unto me, for in thee there is wisdom."

And Tawĕdâs answered and said unto the king, "Be not afraid, O king, of the opposition of the Galileans and of their

vain words, for he who speaketh before men who are learned
is not able to speak [p. 176] the things that are [only] known
by judgement and understanding. And if thou wishest I will
conquer them quickly, and will make them like the leaves
that are blown about by the wind, and they shall not be able
to stand before my face. And how can they be able to dispute
with me, and to ask me questions, and to stand up in opposition to me? But let us do this at the festival, in the presence
of all those who are gathered together thereat, so that every
thing which we wish may be simple and easy for us, and our
works may prosper. And do thou thyself be our president in
this matter, and put on armour, and demand the mercy of
the gods; and how great shall be the abundant strength that
thou shalt have!" And thus did the magician boast in his
wickedness, as if he himself were a mighty man of war, and
he sinned every day, even as saith David the prophet, "They
have drunk turbid wine[1]." He boasted in the help of the
depraved spirits which were round about them, and he made
the king to urge forward speedily the service of the gods.

And after this the king wrote many royal letters command-
ing all those who were under his dominion to be gathered
together to their unclean festival. And many people gathered
themselves together, and brought bulls, and sheep, and goats,
and beasts of all kinds, and each tried to outvie the other.
And when they had all arrived the king rose up with Tawĕdôs
and went to their unclean temple, and he had with him one
hundred and twenty bulls, and large numbers of [other] beasts,
and he celebrated the accursed festival and performed the
ceremonies which it was meet [for him] to perform, and the
whole city was moved with the noise of the cries of the beasts,
and [darkened] with the smoke of their stinking offerings.
And the depraved spirits boasted themselves greatly in the
victory of Tawĕdâs, and the priests of the idols confessed that
be had done well.

[1] Psalm lxxv. 8.

[How the king called upon Theudas to make Yĕwâsĕf abandon the Christian religion, and return to the worship of idols.]

And the king went back to his palace and he said unto Tawĕdâs, "Behold, we have done as thou hast commanded, and we have omitted nothing which it was right [to do] in respect of the festival, and we have multiplied offerings. And behold, the time hath arrived when thou must fulfil our expectation, and save my son who is remote from me, and redeem him from the Christian error, and cause him to be forgiven by the glorious gods. [p. 177] For I have carried out every kind of cunning device, and I have moved every hand (power ?), and have acted wisely, but I have not found any relief from the malady, on the contrary, I can see that his mind is more determined than ever. If I talk to him quietly and meekly I do not find that he hearkeneth to me with the ear of his heart, and if I speak to him with authority and sternness I observe that he exalteth his heart exceedingly, and maketh it strong with the purity of his body. And now I cast upon thy wisdom the tribulation which hath found me. And if I am saved therefrom through thee, and I see my son worshipping the gods with me again, and also enjoying himself with the desirable things of this sweet life, and with the glory of royalty, I will make for thee a graven image of gold, so that every man shall pay thee honour equal unto that which is paid to the gods, as long as time unending shall last."

[How Theudas answered the king, and persuaded him that he was able to overthrow by his astuteness any argument which Yĕwâsĕf could bring forward.]

And Tawĕdâs the wicked man inclined his hearing to the king, and he gave him such evil and destructive counsel that his eyes ought to have been dug out and his tongue torn out by its roots. And he said unto him, "O king, if thou wishest to deal wisely with thy son, thou wilt arrange for him a new discussion, for I possess such a measure of astuteness that he will not be able to stand up against it. On the contrary, his

mind, which hath up to now remained unshaken, will make
him to be disturbed, and he will turn and will incline his ear,
and he will become as pliable as the wax which melteth as
soon as it approacheth the fire." And when the king looked
at his vain boasting joy seized upon him straightway, and the
words of Tawĕdâs had savour to him, and he imagined that
the corrupt and unclean tongue of Tawĕdâs could conquer
that soul which had been instructed by God, and was full of
all wisdom and divine philosophy. And the king questioned
him, saying, "What manner of astuteness is thine? Consider
now his astuteness, and how great is its malice, and how difficult it is to escape from it. And examine very carefully the
statements of this depraved man, and what it is possible to
say in reply thereto."

[*How Theudas advised the king to surround Yĕwâsĕf in his
house with a number of beautifully dressed seductive maidens,
so that they might entice him to love them, and to reject the
Christian religion and return to the worship of the gods.*]

And Tawĕdâs said, "O king, dismiss all those who stand
before thy son, and command [thy servants] to procure a
number of the most beautiful women [p. 178] whom it is
possible to find, women who know how to behave cunningly,
and who have sweet and seductive voices. And adorn them
with all kinds of delightful adornments, and dress them in
glorious apparel, and give them orders to minister to the
wants of thy son and to dwell with him continually, and to
eat and drink with him, and to play and enjoy themselves
together, and to entice him to share their beds with them.
And I will send to him one of the spirits who have dominion
in matters of this kind, and I will send upon him the fire of
sexual lust and the power of wrath. And if it be that having
made one of them his wife he doth not do all that thou desirest, it will be meet for me to be cast aside and hated by
thee and I shall deserve every kind of punishment; if, on the
contrary, he doeth thy wish I shall merit honour. For there
is nothing that attracteth the heart of the male so much as

the sight of the naked bodies of women. Hearken now unto me, and I will tell thee a story the hearing of which will cause thee to understand these words of mine."

[*How Theudas told the king the Parable of the youth who had never seen a woman.*]

"There was once a king who was not blessed with any son at all, and his soul was exceedingly sad, and his mind was very sorrowful, for this sorrow was no light one. And whilst he was in this state of sorrow a son was born unto him, and joy ·filled the heart of the king. And the wise and learned men said unto him, 'If this boy looketh upon the sun or fire before he attaineth the age of twelve years, the light of his eyes will be destroyed, for his eyelashes are a sign that this will happen.' And when the king heard this, because of what had been said of the boy, he took great care of him, and thought it right for him to live in a rock-like cave, and he established him there with his teacher and servants, and he did not permit them to let him see the light at all until he had completed his twelfth year. After these years were ended the king had him brought out from the habitation, the boy having seen absolutely nothing in this world. And the king commanded his servants to bring to the boy things of every form and shape and kind. And they showed him men and women, and [took him to places] where there were gold, and silver, and pearls, and mother-of-pearl, and gems of great price, and various kinds of apparel massed together, and shields, and splendid armour, and royal horses [p. 179] which were decorated with royal trappings, and whereon were mounted noblemen wearing armour. And they also showed him herds of cattle, and they showed the youth freely every-thing which was to be seen, and he asked them the names of all of them, and the nobles of the king made him to know each object by its name. And when he wanted them to tell him the name of women, a friend of the king, who smiled as he spoke, said unto him, 'The name of these creatures is Satans, and they seduce men'; and the heart of the youth desired them more than all other possessions. And when they had instructed him about everything they brought him back to the king, and the king asked him, saying, 'Of all the things which thou hast seen which of them appeareth to give thee most pleasure?' And the youth said unto him, 'There is nothing that gave me any pleasure at all except these Satans which lead men into error. Of all the things that I have seen nothing has made me long for them except the love of these. Behold, my soul is on fire.' And the king marvelled greatly at the words of the youth, and he applauded him. There is nothing that is deeper than the love of women, and as for thee, O king, think not that thou canst make the heart of thy son to yield by means of any other thing than this."

[*How the king sent beautiful maidens to the palace of Yĕwâsĕf, and how they ate and drank with him and, following the king's instructions, endeavoured to lead the prince from the path of virtue.*]

And the king accepted the words of Tawĕdâs with joy. And he commanded [his servants] to bring to him maidens with merry eyes and of pleasing beauty, and he arrayed them in beautiful apparel, so that they might seduce and lead astray his son. And he sent messengers and his chosen friends from his palace, and he appointed them to positions over the place where these women were that they might live with his son. And the women began to throw their arms about him, and to kiss his mouth, and they made him to wake up to the beauty of their persons and the sweetness of their voices, and they besought him to gratify the passion of lust with them and to have unclean carnal intercourse with them. And of all the men there was not one who looked at him, or talked with him, or ate with him, for these women used to minister unto him in every matter; thus did the king behave. And after he had given them their orders he went to them and made them know what pretexts [p. 180] would bring them to his son.

[*How Theudas read his books of magic, and sent evil spirits to supplement the endeavours of the women in the palace to seduce Yĕwâsĕf; and how he resisted the attacks both of the women and the devils.*]

And Tawĕdâs departed to his habitation, and he read his books of power so that they might give him help in this matter. And he summoned one of his malignant spirits and sent him to fight against the soldier of Christ Who was slain, but this miserable man did not know that they (i.e. the spirits) were making a mock of him, and that they were laughing at him, and enveloping him and all the Satanic soldiers in disgrace. And that evil spirit took with him spirits which were more wicked than himself, and they came to the palace of the young man who was the conqueror, and they made to descend upon him the flame of fire. And they heated his body with the flame of fornication, and the wicked spirit was burning inside him. And the women also, those who were young, whose bodies were beautiful and whose souls were foul, made him to burn externally with fire of earthly lust. But his pure and holy spirit recognized in his mind the war of the Enemy, and that it was his fighting against him that made him to think evil thoughts, and that made them to course through his mind one after the other. And the saint was frightened and disturbed, and he prayed that he might find rest from these evil things, and that he might preserve pure for Christ, and unspotted with the mire of deadly sin his soul, which had put on the holy purple by the grace of Baptism. And straightway he rose up in the spiritual love which destroyeth the love of the fornicator with divine love, and it made his heart to recall the memory of the joy and the beauty of the glory of Christ, the Bridegroom of pure souls, Whose beauty is indescribable. And it also made him to remember the glory of His palace, and the pleasure of His marriage which is everlasting, and that they (the angels?) would cast out in disgrace the accursed ones, who had defiled their wedding garments, with their hands and their feet bound, and hurl them into outer darkness. And he shed floods of agonizing tears, smiting his breast as he did so, and he expelled from his mind the evil thought which was drawing him into sin.

[How Yĕwâsĕf prayed for strength to preserve the purity of his mind and body.]

And then he rose up and stretched out his hands to heaven, and shed scalding tears, and groaned loudly, and asked God to help him and to give him strength. And he said, "O God, [p. 181] the Sustainer of the Universe, Who alone art Almighty, the Compassionate, Thou Hope of those who are in despair, O Reward (?) of the patient, O Help of the helpless, remember me, Thy servant, in this hour of strife, and look upon me with the eye of Thy mercy, and deliver my soul from the slaughter of Satan and from the power of the dogs[1], and neglect me not, neither forsake me, and let me not fall into the hand of mine enemy, and let him not rejoice over me. Be not far from me, O God, so that I may not become corrupt through the commission of sin, and so that I may not defile my body which I have covenanted to keep pure and undefiled for Thee. Thee only do I love, and Thee [only] do I worship, O Father, and Son, and Holy Spirit, now and for ever." And he finished his prayer by saying "Amen." And straightway there came a Divine Comforter from heaven and rested upon him, and the evil thoughts took to flight being put to shame; and he passed the whole night in prayer until the dawn came. And he knew the crafty devices of the Destroyer, and he began to afflict his flesh with much hunger and thirst, and with tribulations of every kind. And he stood up the whole night reminding himself of the promises of God and His covenants, and he condemned his thoughts, and made himself to remember the joy of the righteous in that other world, and the radiance of their beauty. And he drew in his mind a vivid picture of the fire of Jahânnam, wherein the wicked shall be punished for ever, and of the tortures thereof, and the prolonged duration of the heat of its flames. This he did that the Enemy might not find

---

[1] Psalm xxii. 20.

his soul inert, and stripped of memory and speech, and might not esteem it lightly and sow therein evil thoughts, and that the purity of his mind might not be sullied and the serenity thereof destroyed.

[*How the Devil continued to tempt Yĕwâsĕf, and how he made him to form a friendship with a certain maiden of very great beauty and intelligence with the view of converting her to Christianity.*]

And the Enemy was wholly terrified, and despaired absolutely of gaining power over the nature of Yĕwâsĕf. And the Enemy adopted another method of working evil against him, after the manner of this Evil One who never neglecteth an opportunity of acting craftily towards man and bringing him into disgrace, and he gathered together thousands of evil beings, so that the commandment of [p. 182] Tawĕdâs might be carried into effect, and he renewed his warfare against Yĕwâsĕf. And he entered into one of the young women in the palace—now she had the most lovely face of them all—and she was the daughter of a king, and had been carried off as a captive. And she was a stranger in her father's inheritance, and he had brought her to King Abênêr as a valuable gift because of her beautiful person, which was exceedingly pleasing; and the king sent her to cast her net about his son and to ensnare him. And a certain crafty and plausible man brought her, and he taught her to speak as if she were a learned woman and to use cunning words, for she possessed a trained and understanding mind, and she was intelligent. Now it is a very easy thing for the Destroyer to make anyone able to work with evil craftiness. And this wicked one attacked the son of the king from the right hand, and he infused into his heart love for the maiden because of her understanding and great wisdom, and because of her honourable family which had sprung from a royal race; now she had abandoned her inheritance together with her royal rank and state. And together with this love the Destroyer sowed in the heart of Yĕwâsĕf the thoughts that he might save her from the faith of those who lead men into error, and make her a Christian; and all these ideas were the offspring of the craftinesses of the Serpent, the father of perdition. And when this idea had grown strong in the soul of the king's son, and he did not find in his mind any impure thought or any sinful desire which moved him towards the maiden, with the exception of the feeling of compassion for her which had sprung up in him, he became sorry for her afflicted state and the destruction of her soul. And he did not know that this feeling was due to the craft of Satan, who maketh darkness to appear to be light.

And when the king's son began to converse with the maiden and to talk to her concerning matters of God, he said unto her, "O woman of understanding, learn to know Him Who is God indeed and Who endureth for ever. Destroy not thyself, neither corrupt thou thyself with the error of idols, but learn to know thy Creator, Who created all creatures, and thou shalt become blessed and shalt be the bride of the Immortal Bridegroom." And he taught her these things and many others like unto them. Then forthwith the evil spirit taught her that [p. 183] she must ensnare him by means of seductive words, and draw towards the pit of passion the soul that loved God, even as he had made the race of Adam to be ensnared of old. It was this evil spirit who had driven him forth from the face of God, and from the Garden of Pleasure, to woe and to misery, and he brought him under the power of death, death instead of the life which is blessed and enduring and immortal. And when the maiden heard the words of Yĕwâsĕf, which were full of philosophy, she became stripped of her understanding and she did not comprehend what he said unto her. And she made answer to him, the evil spirit acting as tongue and mouth for her, and she said unto him, "My lord, if thou dost trouble thyself about the salvation of my soul, and dost wish to bring me nigh unto thy God, and to save my feeble soul, fulfil for me one request. Then forthwith I will abandon all the gods of my fathers, and I will worship thy God, and I will serve Him until my soul leaveth [my body], and thou wilt receive thy reward for my salvation and my conversion to God."

[*How the beautiful maiden quoted the Christian Scriptures in support of her request to Yĕwâsĕf, and how the prince answered her.*]

And Yĕwâsĕf said unto her, "What is thy request, O woman?" And the woman, with her face, and her speech, and her looks, and her whole body impelling her to the working of lust, said unto him, "I wish thee to mingle with me in the partnership of marriage intercourse, and [then] I will follow thy commandment with joy." And Yĕwâsĕf said unto her, "O woman, thou hast made an abominable request, a request which it is difficult [to grant], and too unreasonable to perform. As for thy salvation, I will take exceedingly great trouble about it, for I wish to bring thee out from the pit of destruction. For me to defile my body I find very difficult, and I cannot possibly do so." And the young woman was amused at the attitude of the king's son, and she said unto him, "O thou who art filled with all wisdom, why dost thou speak in this manner? Dost thou call intercourse with a woman 'defilement'? Do not I know the books of the Christians? They have spoken to me and I have heard their words. Is it not written in your Books, saying, 'Marriage is honourable, and carnal intercourse undefiled[1]?' And again it saith, 'It is better to marry than to burn[2],' and, 'The man whom God hath joined in marriage shall not be separated[3].' Have not the Scriptures taught us that all the righteous men of olden time [p. 184] and the patriarchs, and the Prophets married wives? And is it not written moreover that Peter, whom ye call the 'Chief of the Apostles,' had a wife[4]? Show me now where thou didst find that one called the wife an unclean thing. It seemeth to me that certain folk have led thee astray and made thee to be remote from the truth of thy Faith."

[1] Hebrews xiii. 4.   [2] 1 Cor. vii. 9.
[3] Matt. xix. 6.   [4] Matt. viii. 14 ; 1 Cor. ix. 5.

And the king's son said unto her, "O woman, it is even as thou hast remembered, and this thing is permitted for those who crave for the carnal intercourse of marriage; but for those who have the hope of becoming one with Christ it is not permitted. And as for myself, when I was purified by the washing away through Divine Baptism of the transgressions of my youth and my folly, I made a covenant with Christ that I would keep myself pure to Him. How then can I dare to break the covenant which I covenanted with God, and put Him to open shame?"

[*How the beautiful maiden entreated Yĕwâsĕf to grant her request in order to secure her salvation, and how she promised to become a Christian if he did so.*]

And the maiden said unto him, "Let this be according to thy good pleasure, even as thou hast counselled thyself, but the little desire which thou canst fulfil for me, if thou wilt, would save my soul; lie with me for this one night only, and allow me to share thy beauty, and thou thyself shalt enjoy the pleasure of my delight, and I will give thee a solemn pledge that in the morning I will become a Christian, and that I will flee from the worship of all my gods and their faith. And thou shalt find forgiveness for this act, and thou shalt be rewarded by thy God, and He will show thee favour because thou hast saved me. For behold, the Book saith, 'There shall be great joy in heaven because of one sinner who repenteth[1].' And if there be great joy in heaven over one sinner who repenteth, how very great shall be the reward of him that is the cause of that sinner's repentance and conversion! Yea, let it be even so; do not set thyself in opposition to me. Have not the masters of your Law often acted with great wisdom, and have not even they transgressed one commandment in order to fulfil another which is greater? Do not ye yourselves say that Paul circumcised Timothy[2] and acted wisely and for the best in so doing, [p. 185] even though Christians made circum-

---

[1] Luke xv. 7. [2] Acts xvi. 3.

cision a thing outside the Law? But this consideration did not prevent Paul from performing this [rite]. And we find in your Books many cases like unto this. And, if thou art in very truth wishing to save my soul, fulfil for me this my desire, which is easy. As for me, I wish for intercourse with thee so that thou mayest be a husband to me; I do not wish to force thee in this matter, but only to do thy good pleasure. Do not put me to utter shame, but hearken unto me for this time only, so that thou mayest deliver me from error, and from the worship of devils, and thou mayest do [with me] what thou desirest all the days of thy life."

And in this wise did she speak unto him with strong affection. And it was her teacher who had given her two ears for evil, and he knew the books of evil, and in truth he taught her effectively according to these errors which she declared unto the king's son. And without shame she made her words tender and affectionate, and set up her nets on the right hand and on the left, so that she might make the fortress of his pure soul to totter and overthrow the steadfastness of his mind. And when the Sower of evil and the Enemy of the righteous saw the tottering state of the soul of the king's son, he rejoiced exceedingly, and he summoned the evil spirits who came with him at that time, and he said unto them, "Do ye not see how very closely that maiden hath come to fulfilling that thing which we were not able to perform? Come now and let us attack him in force, for we shall not in future find the means whereby we may fulfil the good pleasure of him who sent us." And with such words as these did the Father of perdition address his companions, and they came to make war upon the soldier of Christ, and they set in a ferment the whole nature of his soul. And they poured into his heart intense love for the maiden, and they made the fire of lust to burn up fiercely within him. And while he saw that his soul was much urged and inclined towards the commission of sin, his heart yearned to save the maiden and for her conversion to God; and this was due to the setting of the nets by Satan, who made the matter easy for him by the words of

the maiden, "It cannot be a sin to have intercourse with a
woman once only [p. 186] to save [her] soul."

[*How Yĕwâsĕf resisted the maiden, and how he wept and
prayed and then fell into a deep slumber wherein he saw a
wonderful vision.*]

And the saint groaned from the depths of his heart, being
afraid of the hyenas, and he prayed for a long time, and tears
poured down from his eyes like water, and he cried out to the
Holy and Mighty One, Who saveth those who put their trust
in Him, saying, " O God, I have put my trust in Thee, and I
shall never be put to shame, and my enemies who fight
against me shall not triumph over me. Incline Thine ear unto
me at this moment, and make good my path, so that Thy
Name may be praised through me Thine abandoned servant;
blessed be Thou for ever ! Amen."

And when he had prayed a long time, and shed tears, and
made many prostrations to the earth, he lay down upon the
ground and he slept a little. And he saw a vision wherein
certain men, whose faces were most terrifying, snatched him
up and carried him into places which he had never seen. And
they brought him into a vast country wherein were many
rivers, and the landscape thereof was very beautiful, and the
perfumes of its flowers were exceedingly sweet. And he saw
there trees of divers kinds growing all together, and they
bore strange and marvellous fruits which were pleasant to
look upon, and most delicious to the taste. And the leaves of
these trees sang sweet songs, and when they were set in
motion there went forth from them delicious breezes of the
sweetness of which the people could never have enough. And
he saw thrones ornamented with gold, and they were inlaid
with precious stones and mother-of-pearl, and their splendour
shone like the lightning, and the beauties thereof were of
divers kinds. And there were there with the thrones couches
which were furnished with cushions and carpets the splendour
of the appearance of which overcame the splendour of the
thrones; and the gladness [inspired by] their magnificence

was beyond praise. And waters clear as crystal flowed forth, and they caused the beholder to rejoice with great joy.

And having taken the king's son round about through the country the beauty whereof was so marvellous and the spaciousness whereof was so great, and of the things which were therein the appearance was so wonderful, the men brought him into a city the praise whereof cannot be uttered. The fabric thereof was of fine gold, and the walls thereof were of stones the like of which no man hath ever seen. And who is able to describe the beauty of the city? Above it there flashed like lightning a light of two-fold strength, which filled [p. 187] all spaces of the city. And there were soldiers there who were appointed each to his special duty, and to every rank of them there was given a light which flashed like lightning, and by it they marched singing a sweet melody, which hath never been heard upon the tongue of man. And the king's son heard a voice which said, "This is the place of the perpetual rest of the righteous, and this is the joy of the gladness of those who have pleased God."

And these terrifying men wished to put him outside this city, but his whole being was filled with joy and gladness and with the happiness of delight. And he said unto them, "I entreat you not to separate me from this joy which cannot be uttered, but give me one corner in this city wherein I can dwell." And those terrifying men answered and said unto him, "At the present time it is impossible for thee to live here. Thou canst not come here except through much weariness and profuse sweat of the face, and thou must rule thy soul and make thyself to labour."

And when they had said this unto him, they took him away from that city and brought him to places of darkness, which were filled with worms and the smell of which was exceedingly foul; and instead of joy, which did not exist therein, there was sorrow. And he saw a region of darkness wherein was no light, and it was a place of oppression, and a place of sorrow and sadness. In it were a fire that consumed, and the worm of torture which moved about therein. There also were the

Powers which tortured, and there also were those to whom
the care of the fire was entrusted, and they were burning in
the fire many men who lamented loudly, and suffered anguish.
And he heard a voice which said unto him, "This is the abode
of sinners, and in this way do [the Powers] torture those who
defile themselves by working impurity."

And while these things were thus the men with the terrifying faces took him from that place with tears running down
his face like water, and brought him back to the place where
he had been; and by his side were the beauteous forms of
the maiden and of her companions, which stank more than
filth and every kind of offal. And he began to think within
himself and to remember everything which he had seen, and
his heart was suspended [p. 188] on the love of those beautiful
things; and he was afraid and trembled at the idea of those
tortures, which terrified him as he lay upon the bed, wholly
unable to make an answer.

[*How the king heard of Yĕwâsĕf's mental anguish and came
to him and talked with him, and how Yĕwâsĕf described his
vision to him, and appealed to him to desist from troubling
him.*]

And the king learned concerning the suffering of his son,
and he came to him and questioned him about what had come
upon him, and his son began to tell him what he had seen.
And he said unto the king, "Why hast thou prepared nets
for my feet, and brought low my soul? Had it not been that
it was God Who helped me, a very little more and my soul
had been dwelling in Sheol. But God is very loving unto
Israel[1] and unto those who are right in heart, and it is He
Who hath delivered my soul from the nets. I lay down to
sleep, being dismayed, but my God and my Redeemer hath
set me above the heights. And He hath shown me the good
things which He hath set apart for those who have been
careful for their souls, and how great tortures He hath prepared for those who provoke Him to wrath and who act

[1] Psalm lxxiii. 1.

wickedly. And now, O father, behold, incline thine ear and
hearken unto my voice, which shall lead thee to the good
things that the righteous enjoy. Prevent thou me not from
travelling on the path of righteousness, for this is my delight
and my joy, so that I may be saved from all [evil] and may
arrive at the places wherein dwelleth the envoy of God, Baralâm, my teacher, and may live out the rest of my life with
him. And if thou forcest me in [this] matter I shall die in
sorrow and sadness whilst thou art looking on, and thou shalt
not be called by me 'father,' and I shall not be called by thee
' son.'"

[*How the king returned to his palace in despair, and how
the devils, whom Theudas had sent to effect the downfall of
Yĕwâsĕf, confessed to him that they were powerless to resist
the might of the Sign of the Cross when the prince made it
against them.*]

And the king became sorrowful, and his face clouded over
and he fell into despair, and he returned to his palace meditating evil in his mind; and the evil spirits which had been
sent against the divine young man by Tawĕdâs returned to
him, having been put to shame, and they confessed that they
had been vanquished. And that liar Tawĕdâs looked at the
lovers of lies and saw that they bore in their faces the signs
of their defeat, and he said unto them, "Are ye so feeble and
so utterly broken that ye were not able to overcome one
young man?" [p. 189] Thereupon those evil spirits spake
unto him concerning the power of the God of truth, and they
said unto him, "We were unable to approach the mighty one
of Christ, and His Sign, the name of which is 'Maskal' (i.e.
Cross); and when [we attempted to draw nigh] unto it we
were vanquished quickly, and forced to take to flight. Now
all the powers of the air, and all those who sustain the world
of darkness, flee away smitten with great weakness even before the Sign of the Cross is made against them. And when
we attacked this young man with power and made him to
quake, he took refuge with Christ, depending on Him to help

him, and he fortified himself with the Sign of the Cross, and
he drove us off and made us to depart afar off in shame, and
he made for himself a mighty power. And we were neither
apathetic nor careless, and we renewed our attack, but as
soon as we came to him he summoned Christ to help him, and
the fire of wrath descended from the heights above, and it set
us on fire and we took to flight forthwith. And behold, we
are quite certain that we cannot approach him." And thus
did the evil spirits make Tawĕdâs to understand, and they
described to him fully and clearly what had happened.

[*How the king demanded further assistance from Theudas,
and how Theudas went with him to visit Yĕwâsĕf in his
palace, and with gentle and cunning words sought to make
the prince abandon the Christian religion.*]

And the king was wholly disturbed in his mind, and he
caused Tawĕdâs to come into his presence, and he said unto
him, "Behold, we have done everything which thou hast commanded, O master, and we have not gained any advantage
whatsoever. If there be left unto thee any other plan tell me
what it is, so that we may try it, that peradventure we may
find a means of attacking the evil, and a way whereby we may
smite it utterly."

And Tawĕdâs demanded that he might hold converse with
the son of the king, and on the following day he took the king
with him, and departed to visit his son. And when they were
seated together Tawĕdâs took up his parable and began to
admonish him for his resistance in support of an alien Faith,
and for his disobedience. And the young man was bold, and
he cried out, saying, "I shall never esteem anything of more
value than the love of Christ." And Tawĕdâs went into the
interior of the palace, and he said, " O Yĕwâsĕf, dost thou
know what mean remoteness from the worship of our gods,
and abandonment of their Faith, and the provoking of the
king [p. 190] thy father? Thou hast become a thing at which
to blaspheme, and thou art an enemy among all the people,
for it is from them (i.e. the gods) that thou hast thy life. Was

it not the gods who heard thy father's prayer and gave thee
to him? And was it not they who released him from the
bondage of childlessness?" And with many idle and unprofitable words the magician, who would lead the young man
into evil, debated with him, and he began to make his words
pleasant in order to make him to be remote from the Gospel-
preaching, and to encourage him to do the works of error.

[*How Yĕwâsĕf made answer to Theudas, and how he showed
forth the weakness and helplessness of idols, and declared the
power and glory of Christ.*]

And the son of the celestial King who walked in the city
which God, and not the children of men had built, held his
peace, and then he said unto Tawĕdâs, " Hearken, O thou who
art deep in guile, O thou who art blacker than the blackness
of night, thou seed of the Babylonian, thou son of the Chaldeans who built the Tower [of Babel] through whom the
world became mixed [in speech]. O thou declarer of vain
judgement, O thou miserable old man, O thou whose sins are
heavier than those of the Five Cities which were burnt with
the fire of brimstone, how dost thou dare to blaspheme the
Story of Salvation whereby the blackest darknesses have been
illumined, and the erring have found the path of truth, and
those who were lost and those who were captives were saved?
I pray thee tell me what is better than the worship of God,
the Sustainer of the Universe, Who with His Son, the Only-
begotten, and with the Holy Spirit, is One God, uncreate and
immortal, the Creator of what is good, the Fountain of
spiritual excellence, Whose power is invincible, and Whose
glory is incomprehensible? Before Him stand thousands of
thousands, and tens of thousands of tens of thousands of the
angels of the armies of the heavenly beings, and the heavens
and the earth are filled with His glory. By Him all things
were brought into being from a state of not-being; through
Him the Universe is strong and everything is maintained by
His wisdom. Which is it better for men to do? To worship this
God, or to worship the devils of perdition, and the idols which

are without soul, whom men laud and magnify [p. 191] for committing fornication, and for having carnal intercourse with men, and for all the works of the nations which have been written about the gods in the books that treat of their Faith? Will ye not be ashamed to-morrow, O ye who resemble the race of the Chalcedonian, ye miserable men, when ye are rewarded with the fire that never sleepeth? Are ye not ashamed when ye bow down to worship graven images which are the work of the hands of the children of men, who hew stone and cut wood into shape and call these things 'gods?' Moreover, when ye take beasts from the herds and sheep from the flocks, for ye are obliged to provide numerous offerings, and to offer them up as sacrifices to mortal gods, do they make you any happier? O ye foolish and erring men, do ye not know that the sacrifices are more honourable than your idols? For it is a man who maketh the graven image, and it is God Who created the beast.

"Behold, the dumb beast which talketh not hath far better knowledge than thyself, for thou, a being who can talk, hast no knowledge of thy God Who created thee out of a state of non-existence, and in Whom is thy life, and behold thou dost call 'god' a thing which thou didst not know before this. And consider the matter. A man beateth it (i.e. the iron stone) with iron, and melteth it with fire, and hammereth it out, and then dost decorate it with gold and silver, and dost lift it up out of the dust, and dost set it up on high, and then thou dost bow down before a common and worthless stone, a thing which is of less value than thyself. Thou dost not worship God, but dost bow thyself down before the work of thy hands that cannot draw breath. And it is fitting that one should call a graven image 'a dead thing,' for as it was never a living thing it is not meet merely to call it 'a dead thing,' but it is also meet that men should change the name 'dead thing' into some new name which shall be suitable to such a degraded object. For the stone can be split, and a vessel made of potter's earth breaketh, and a man can cut up wood, and brass corrodeth away, and men can melt gold and silver. And men make merchandise of thy gods, some of them being of little price and some of them [p. 192] of great price. And the reverence which is due to God doth not befit this object, for it is an object which passeth away, and which a man can obtain possession of at a price. Who can buy God? Or who can sell Him?

"And as for this motionless object, how can [any] one call it God? Canst thou not see that when any of them are standing up they can never sit down, and that the 'god' which is sitting down cannot stand up? Be ashamed, O thou man in whom there is no understanding, and lay thy hand upon thy mouth, O thou most contemptible of men, who dost praise these objects, for thou art an alien to the truth, and they have seduced thee with the sign of falsehood, and thou makest graven images with thy hands and dost falsely call them 'gods.' Stand up, O miserable man, and get understanding, for thou art an old man, canst thou do thyself any good by making for thyself a 'god,' being a man? How can this thing be? What thou makest is not God, but thou makest the images of men or images of the beasts, which have no tongue, and are unable to make any answer whatsoever. If workers in metal, and carpenters, and masons, did not exist, thou wouldst not be able to find the object that can become to thee God. And if there were none to take care of [the graven images], then thou wouldst make into God a great mountain unto which thou wouldst pray. How great is the folly of the men who whilst worshipping a graven image as God, and whilst praying to it to protect them, appoint a few guardians to protect it, and watch over it so that thieves may not steal it! If the graven image be made of gold or silver they guard it with diligent care, but if it be made of stone or earthenware, or of any ordinary or common substance, they leave it to take care of itself!

"I myself think that in your opinion common earth is stronger than gold. Is it not right and fitting that men should make you laughing-stocks, O ye foolish and blind men, in whom there is no understanding whatsoever, and no sense? For your

works are folly. The man who followeth the profession of
the soldier imagineth that God is a soldier, and he maketh a
graven image for himself and he setteth it up and calleth
Môlôḥ God. And through lust for women he driveth himself
mad because of his passion, and he maketh for himself another
God and calleth it 'Zĕkhuerâ[1].' Another because of his love
of wine maketh a graven image and calleth it 'Yônîsĕs[2].'
[p. 193] And thus is it with the other sins and their images.
Those who lust set up their passions as gods, and they call
sins 'gods,' and therefore in the temples of idols are to be
found [images of] pleasures and delights (which bring in their
train pain), and dancing, and singing and music, and they
decorate them and celebrate foolish festivals in their honour.
Who is able to describe their unclean works? And who could
befoul his mouth by making known their evil deeds? They
are manifest, however, even though we hold our peace.

"This then is thy worship, O Tawĕdâs, O thou who art as
lacking in understanding as thy graven images, and is it
because of it that thou wouldst command me to bow down
before them? Verily thy works are exceedingly evil, and
these and all those who put their trust in them shall be like
unto them. As for me, I will worship my God, and I will
sacrifice myself to Him, the God and Creator, Who directeth
the Universe, our Lord Jesus Christ, our Hope, through
Whom we have found approach to the Father of Lights in
the Holy Spirit, and by Whose Blood we have been bought
from slavery. If He had not abased Himself to become a
servant our race would not have been held worthy of being
called 'sons.' For our sakes He brought Himself down, and
men did not esteem Him as God, but He accepted every
unseemly thing, and He fulfilled all the works of man, sin
alone excepted. And He ascended the Cross in His Body,
and they laid Him in a tomb, and He rose on the third day
after He had descended into Sheol, and brought forth those
who were the slaves of the Evil One, the Lord of the world,
and who were fettered by sin. What is worse than this—thy

---

[1] Aphrodite.   [2] Dionysos.

blaspheming Him by pointing the finger of scorn at Him?
Dost thou not see the sun and consider how very many places
there are which do not benefit [when] he sendeth his splendour into them? How many are the bodies of the dead which
have gone to corruption, which he illumineth! Can one find
in him spot or blemish? Doth he not dry up every unclean
thing and light up the dark places absolutely without suffering contamination himself? And no defilement whatsoever
[p. 194] toucheth him.

"And what hast thou to say also about fire? Doth it not
take into itself the iron which is black and cold, and make
every part of it like unto a blazing fire? Doth the fire take
into itself any of the substance and constitution of the iron?
Dost thou not see that when men beat the iron with hammers
nothing happeneth to the fire and no blemish whatsoever
attacheth itself thereto? Nay, no defect of any evil quality
whatsoever attacheth itself to this substance because of its
intimate association with that which is inferior to it which
cometh to an end. With what words, O man lacking in understanding, O stony-hearted, dost thou deal with me deceitfully
and with mockery! When I say 'Son of the Father' and
'Word of God' absolutely nothing is taken away from the
glory of His Father, but He is God. He came for the salvation
of the sons of men, and He put on the flesh of the children
of men in order that He might make men His partners in
[His] Divine and rational nature, and that He might bring
our race up from the lowest depths of Sheol, and that He
might give it heavenly honour and glory.

"And He put on mortal flesh in order to convince the Angel
of Darkness of this world by His unity in the flesh with the
children of men that He would conquer him and destroy him,
and deliver our race from his oppression. For this reason
He came that He might suffer on the Cross; He Who is
impassible suffered in order to make known the Two Natures.
Because He was a man He was crucified, and because He
was God He made dark the sun, and He made to quake the
earth, and He raised up from the graves the bodies of very

many dead. And again, He died as a man and led Sheol
captive, and as God He rose from the dead. And because of
this the prophet cried out, 'Sheol murmured when He went
down, for it scoffed and it imagined that He was like a man,
and when it saw that He was like God, it was terror-stricken.'
Behold then, He set our nature above everything that was
rejected and lacking understanding, and He set it upon a
throne of glory shining with the glory which is immortal.
What defect came upon the Word of God by this? Art thou
not ashamed when thou blasphemest cunningly [p. 195] against
God and His Word? Which is the better—for men to believe in this God, and to worship the Being Who is so good
and Who loveth man so much, and Who commandeth the
doing of what is right, and the cultivation of the ascetic
life, and the acquisition of purity, Who teacheth mercy, and
bestoweth the gift of faith, and preacheth peace, Who is
righteous, and the Lover of man, and the Doer of good things,
now for such a God as this worship is meet,—or is it meet for
men to worship thy gods whose sins are very many and great,
who are unclean in all their works, even in the giving of
names? Woe be unto you, O ye whose hearts are stones that
are harder than the rock, who are more feeble than the
beasts, ye sons of perdition who are doomed to darkness!
And blessed am I, and blessed are all the Christians, for we
possess a God Who is the Friend of man and is a Being to
be loved. For those who worship Him, if they toil in this
world a little and suffer tribulation, they gather the fruit of
their reward, wherein is no death, in the kingdom of the
heavens which passeth not away, and Divine blessedness which
abideth for ever, the pleasure whereof never cometh to an
end."

[*How Theudas called upon Yĕwâsĕf to prove that the doctrine of the Twelve Apostles was true, and that the Law of
his native land was false, and how Yĕwâsĕf replied to him.*]

And Tawĕdâs answered, saying, "Every generaticn bequeath-
eth [the Law] to those who come after it. This Law of ours

have laid down wise men, and many learned men, and law-givers whose works and proofs of wisdom are marvellous, and all the kings of the country have accepted it as a good and true voice wherein is no error. As for the Law of the Galileans, those who preached it were men who were not priests, and of no account and of lowly position, and they were few in number, that is to say, Twelve. How canst thou take pleasure in the teaching of these few men who were ignorant, being men belonging to the people, of the Law, which many great men who shone like the light drew up? And what is the proof that these were men who were to be believed, and not men who led men into error?"

And Yĕwâsĕf answered, saying, "O Tawĕdâs, I think that thou art an ass in thy speech. Thou hearest the sound of music and dost not understand it, nay, thou art a serpent and dost stop thine ears so that thou mayest not [p. 196] hear the voice of him that reciteth the incantation. Well doth the prophet say concerning thee, 'Can the Ethiopian abandon his skin, and the leopard the spot which is his companion? Canst thou possibly do good deeds, seeing that thou hast learned to do evil[1]?' O thou who art in error and art blind of eye, why art thou unable to learn the power of truth which is praised by many? And thou boastest thyself of thy wisdom which is thy blind and crooked Faith, and thou sayest that many kings [have accepted thy Law], and thou sayest also that it was only a few mean men without learning, who preached the Gospel. Now behold, the strength of our glorious Faith is well known, but your wicked Law is a feeble thing, and although [your] wise men help you by its means, and the powerful men support you, it is a weak and worn out thing. There is no help from the children of men in the Godhead of God. Behold, it shineth with a splendour which is far brighter than the splendour of the sun, and behold, it flourisheth in all the quarters of the world. And if the priests of idols and learned philosophers had established it and mighty kings had given their help to it, thou, O wicked man, wouldst have had

---

[1] Jeremiah xiii. 23.

an excuse and wouldst have been able to say that all this took place through the children of men. But behold now, thou seest that men who were of no account, and men who were fishermen, preached the Holy Gospel, and also men who were driven into exile by all the magistrates and governors who expelled them. And in spite of all this it hath filled the whole world, for their words have gone forth into all the earth, and their doctrine hath reached unto the ends of the world[1].

"And what wilt thou say about the Faith of the gods? Dost thou not fight for the power thereof, so that thou mayest strengthen its works and its counsel in the saving of men, or for a proof which is fitting? O thou man, who art more lacking in knowledge than every other man, thy people are liars, but our people are men who are to be believed, and by this [fact] especially is the word known. And if all their works were not false, and like unto a phantom, this strength which they derive from men [p. 197] would not diminish, and would not become feeble. For behold, the Prophet saith, 'I have seen the sinner great, and exalted like a cedar of Libanus, but when I returned I missed him, I sought and I could not find his place[2].' And the Prophet saith this word concerning you, O ye who are helped by the faith of idols for a moment, 'After a little [time], ye cannot be found, but quickly like the smoke ye disappear[3].' And concerning the knowledge of the Divine Gospel, behold, the Lord saith, 'Heaven and earth shall pass away, but My word shall not pass away[4].' And the Psalmist saith, 'Thou, O God, in olden time didst lay the foundations of the earth, and the heavens are the work of Thy hands. They shall perish, but Thou shalt exist; they all shall wax old like a garment, but Thou shalt tie them up like a bundle; they shall change, but as for Thee Thy years shall not come to an end[5].'

"The fishermen who have drawn into their nets every one from the abyss of perdition are those who have renounced

---

[1] Romans x. 18.   [2] Psalm xxxvii. 35, 36.   [3] Psalm xxxvii. 20.
[4] Matt. xxiv. 35.   [5] Psalm cii. 25–27.

the preaching which belongeth to the wise men of this world, and ye who are indeed debased men, and slaves of sin, are those who have vilified them. For they have made to rise wonders, and signs, and mighty deeds of every kind, even as the sun riseth upon the world. And they gave light to the blind, and learning to the deaf, and the power to walk to the lame, and they bestowed resurrection and life on the dead, for their shadows alone used to heal every sickness that cometh upon man. And they drove out from men the devils which ye made to take possession of them as gods, not only from the bodies of men, but even from this city did they drive them all out by the Sign of the glorious Cross. And they destroyed every magician, and as for their deadly poison, they made it to become like a thing wherein is no strength. These men, I say, healed every creature by the might of Christ. Therefore it is meet that they should be praised by all men who are filled with knowledge, because they were preachers of the truth. What answer now [p. 198] is left unto thee wherewith thou canst answer on behalf of the wise men, and the priests of thy idols, who in the error of their wisdom give their help to Satan, the Liar?

"Tell me, I beseech thee, what have I forsaken in the world which is worthy of mention? And in what things canst thou make one wise except bestial nature, and impurity, and stinkingness, and false wisdom, and every kind of impure conversation, and leading into error, and foolishness [which is derived] from the slime of their law? But these learned men who are able to raise their eyes from their folly for a little speak the truth and their proof is true, for they say, 'These beings who are called gods, are they not men?' And some of them were set as rulers over provinces and countries, and others committed abominable deeds in the world, and yet men call them gods. And they lead men into error by seductive persuasiveness, and they establish ordinances, and each speaketh according to what he knoweth. What is the beginning of the appearances of graven images[1]? This god

---

[1] I.e. how did idolatry start in the world?

existed in days of old, in one period or another, either because he was necessary (?), or because he was thought to be
wise, or because of his association with [some] work, and
another performed some good deed, some deed that remained
in the memory [of men]. And in order to pay such gods
honour men set up graven images to them on pillars. And
those who came after them did not know the wishes of their
fathers, and that they had only made them as objects of remembrance, and that as a mark of their approbation they
set them up on pillars, and so little by little they were persuaded to serve Satan, the Governor of Evil, and were drawn
to the men of old who were exactly like themselves in their
passions. And they served them as gods, and they called
them 'those who die not,' and they offered up to them sacrifices and offerings. And because devils dwelt in the idols,
they committed themselves to their care, and they paid them
honours and sacrificed unto them.

"These men were they who never trained themselves to
obtain knowledge of God, and they wished to set over them
gods for two things ; one of which was that they might honour
idols by this name. [p. 199] The second thing was that it
was pleasing to them to honour as gods, and many burned to
do so, of their own accord, those who had seduced them to
every kind of apostasy and uncleanness.

"And when men arrived at the extremity of this danger,
having clothed themselves in darkness they planted for each
one of them a tree for the fulfilment of their sin and lust
and they called it a god. And through the excess of their
error they became vile, and what was far worse, in their fall
they worshipped it. At length God came in the tenderness
of His compassion, and redeemed from this error us who believed on Him, and taught us the knowledge of the True God.
For there is no salvation except only through Him, and there
is no other god in heaven or upon earth but He only, the
Maker and Sustainer of the Universe, with the Word of His
all-mighty power. For it is said, ' By the Word of God the
heavens were made to stand fast, and all the power thereof

by the breath of His mouth[1]. Everything came into being through Him, and without Him there would have been nothing that is'."

[*How Theudas was dumbfounded at the arguments of Yĕwâsĕf, and how he repented of his error, and sought refuge in God, and proclaimed before the king and all his councillors the greatness of the God of the Christians.*]

And when Tawĕdâs heard these words he knew that they were of the wisdom which was given unto him by God. And he was filled with terror, even as a man who is terrified by the sound of thunder, and he held his peace for a space. And at the time when the sun was setting he returned to the subject, and he began to consider his miserable agitation, for the word of salvation had drawn nigh to the eyes of his heart which was black. And he began to repent deeply for what was past, and he recognized the deceivingness of idols and their power to lead into error; and he went to the true and good light and took refuge with it. And from that moment he went away from under the evil direction of idols, and he made himself hostile to and fought against the vile gods, and he hated them with a hatred that was as great as the love with which he had formerly regarded them. And he rose up straightway in the midst of the assembly—now the king was sitting upon his throne—and he cried out with a loud voice, saying, "O king, behold, the spirit of God dwelleth in thy son. For in truth he hath vanquished us, and we have nothing left to urge against his arguments, and we are unable to blaspheme against what he saith unto us. [p. 200] Verily, great is the God of the Christians, and great is their Faith, and great are the mysteries thereof."

[1] Psalm xxxiii. 6; Heb. xi. 3; John i. 3.

[How Yĕwâsĕf preached the mercy of God to Theudas, and urged him to repent and be baptized with Christian Baptism.]

And he turned towards Yĕwâsĕf the king's son, and he said unto him, "Tell me now, O light of truth, O thou whose soul is illumined, will Christ receive me if I turn to Him, and if I make myself remote from my evil works, and withdraw from them?" And the teller of the truth and the preacher thereof made answer to him [saying], "Yea, most assuredly He will receive you and all those who turn to Him. He will receive you not in the way in which thou thinkest, but like the son who had come from a far country, and whom [his father] welcomed from the path of his sins, and embraced and kissed. And straightway he stripped off him the foulness and uncleanness of sin, and he arrayed him in the apparel of salvation, and he decorated him with the glorious purple of splendid beauty, and he made a festival of joy to the celestial powers, rejoicing at the feast for the return of the sheep that was lost and because of its return. It is God Himself Who saith, 'There shall be great joy in the heavens because of one sinner who repenteth[1].' And again He saith, 'I have not come to call the righteous but sinners to repentance[2].' And unto the prophet He said, 'As I live, I do not desire the death of the sinner, but rather that he may return from his way and live. Turn ye back from your evil way, O children of Israel, and die not, for sin shall not harm the sinner if he returneth from his sin, and worketh truth, and walketh in the commandment of life. He shall live life and shall not die, and all the sins which he hath committed shall never more be remembered against him. For he hath performed judgement and light, and through them he shall live[3].' And He also saith in another place, 'Wash ye, and be clean and pure, and cast away the wickedness of your souls from before mine eyes, and abandon your wickedness

---

[1] Luke, chap. xv.   [2] Matt. ix. 13.
[3] Ezek. xviii. 27; xxxiii. 11–16.

B.   15

and evil, and learn to do what is good. And if your sins be black I will make them to be as snow[1].'

"And with such a hope hath God given to those who turn towards Him the right to hope. Delay thou not, O man, and be not sluggish, [p. 201] and draw nigh unto Christ our God, the Lover of man, and unto the brightness of His light, and let not thy face be ashamed. When thou art baptized with Divine Baptism, all the uncleanness of the old man shall be drowned in the water, and all the weight of thy manifold sin shall be dissolved and done away as if it had never existed. And thou shalt go up from the water purified from all its blemish, and no impurity whatsoever shall be left upon thee, and none of the corrosion of sin. And afterwards it is meet for thee to keep guard over thy soul in the purity which shall be given unto thee by Baptism through the tenderness of the compassion of our God."

[*How Theudas burned his books of magic, and went to the holy man who had received and baptized Nâkôr, and having repented with tears, was baptized by him.*]

And when Tawĕdâs had been admonished by these words, he went out straightway, and departed to the steep rock [where he lived], and he took his books of magic, saying, "This is the beginning of all evil, and is the storehouse of the wickedness of devils; I will burn them in the fire and will consume them utterly." And he ran to the cave of that honourable man, whose works were excellent, and who was clothed with the priesthood, the man unto whom Nâkôr went (whom we have already mentioned, of glorious fame), and he told him everything. And he scattered ashes over his head, and uttered loud groanings, and he washed his body with the flood of his tears, and he told the old man everything about his unclean works. And that old man [wished] to save his soul, and to drag him out of the mouth of the serpent of perdition, for he was indeed a wise man. And he admonished Tawĕdâs with words of salvation, and he explained unto him

---

[1] Isaiah i. 16, 17.

the Law, and made it plain to him, and the abandonment of
sin, and he gave him reason to hope that the Judge would be
forgiving and merciful; and he admonished him a second
time and commanded him to fast for many days. And he
made him pure with the water of Divine, Christian Baptism,
and he strengthened Tawĕdâs in truth and in repentance all
his days, and urged him to repent of his manifold sins, and to
supplicate for the forgiveness of God with continual groanings
and tears.

[*How the king was stupefied when he saw the defeat of
Theudas, how he summoned his councillors to discuss with
him the next step, how Arâshîs, his chief councillor, advised
him to divide his kingdom with Yĕwâsĕf, and how the king
commanded him to carry out this suggestion.*]

And when the king saw the things that had come upon
this famous man he was greatly disturbed in all his person,
and he became utterly depressed, and he had the appearance
of one who was overwhelmed by great trouble; and as for his
mind it was greatly moved and agitated. And once again he
caused to come into his presence all his intimate friends and
councillors, and he took counsel with them as to what he
should do with his son; [p. 202] and there was great discussion on the matter among them. And the man who was
called Arâshîs, whom we have already mentioned, who held
high office among the rulers of the country, and whose advice
was especially pleasing to the king, said unto him, "O king,
what is the right thing for thee to do to thy son [seeing that]
thou art unable to make him to return to the observance of
our Law, and to worship our gods? Unto me it appeareth
that we are following a useless course, for this making of an
excuse is only in accordance with his mind; for he loveth to
conquer and he will never turn back. If thou wishest thou
canst deliver him over to judgement and to torture; it will
be thy own flesh [that will suffer] and thou wilt never again
be able to call thyself 'father.' And thou wilt destroy him,
for I am convinced that he will die for Christ. The only course

15—2

left to thee is to divide thy kingdom, and to compel him to
reign over that portion of it which is to be his. And if natural
impulses and worldly cares can draw him to our Faith he
will be drawn after us, and he will become towards us as we
wish, and as we hope. For it is very hard to fight against a
habit which is firmly fixed in our soul, and it can only be
eradicated with difficulty; but this can be effected by means
of continuous persuasion. Only with difficulty can [the minds
of men] be changed when force [only] is applied. And if he
is strong in the faith of the Law of Christ this should be a
cause of joy instead of sorrow. Destroy not thy son, and
deprive not thyself of him." And when Arâshîs said this all
those who were gathered together hearkened to him, and
they were pleased with his words and accepted them. And
then the king answered and said unto him, being pleased,
"Arrange this matter thus."

[*How the king went to Yĕwâsĕf and offered him the half of
his kingdom, and how Yĕwâsĕf accepted his offer, although he
understood his father's motive.*]

And the king went to his son Yĕwâsĕf and said unto him,
"This is the end of my discussion with thee, O son, who wilt
neither hearken unto my voice nor obey me. And if thou wilt
rejoice my heart, know now that I will spare thee further
search as to what is the power of [my] word (or, voice); for
though I have laboured much I find thee still unconverted,
and disinclined to hear my words. Come, let us divide the
kingdom. Thou shalt live [p. 203] in thy portion in one part
of it, and the people shall call thee king, and thou shalt have
authority to follow whatsoever path thou pleasest." And that
truly glorious soul knew well that the king only did this to
fulfil his will, but Yĕwâsĕf decided that he would hear these
words from him, and [then] take to flight and escape from his
hand, and depart whithersoever he desired. And he answered
and said unto the king, "As for me, what the desire of my
heart is thou knowest well. I would search for that divine
man who guided me to the path of salvation, and I would

abandon everything for him until the end of my life. But if it be not permitted to me, O father, to do my will, I will hearken unto thee and will be subject unto thee; for it is good that sons should be subject to a father in the matter of things in the way of which there is no perdition, and which manifestly and obviously is not remote from God."

[How the king divided his kingdom and Yĕwâsĕf departed to rule over his portion of it.]

And the king was filled with gladness which exceeded by far any joy he had ever known, and he divided the provinces which were under his dominion into two parts, and he made his son king, and he crowned him, and adorned him with every kind of royal dignity, and sent him to the kingdom that had been ordained for him. And Yĕwâsĕf departed in great pomp to it with the music and singing that befit kings. And the king commanded all the chiefs, and all the captains of the host, and all the governors of his chosen men to go with his son who was king, and to choose for him provinces wherein many men lived, and to instruct him in the assumption of sovereignty and dominion. And the king gave him all the armour that was meet for royal state, and thereupon Yĕwâsĕf received royal power.

[How Yĕwâsĕf destroyed the heathen temples, and built a fine church and ministered therein and taught the people.]

And when Yĕwâsĕf came into the region that was his portion to reign therein, he set up the Sign of the Cross upon every fort which was on the city wall, the Sign of the glorious Cross of Christ and God. And he plundered the temples of idols, and threw down their idols, and dug up their foundations, and [p. 204] there was left no trace [of the buildings] of the heretics. And he built inside the city a great sanctuary, a beautiful place, and he commanded that every one should be gathered together to it; and they began the worship of God with the adoration of the life-giving Cross. And he rose up early in the morning before them all, and he made himself

to serve therein with prayer and with the making of long
supplications. And he began to teach all those who were
under the dominion of his power to turn away from the error
of idols, and he proclaimed unto them the preaching of the
Gospel clearly and openly, and the story of the coming down
of the Word of God into the world, and His signs and His
wonders, and he made them to know about His sufferings
on the Cross wherein were salvation and power, and His
Resurrection and Ascension into the heavens. And he also
proclaimed to them the terrible and fearful day of His awful
and dreadful Second Coming, and he told them about the
good things that are prepared for those who believe, and the
tortures that await sinners. And he taught them these things
in a kindly manner and with gracious words. No chosen one
was like this king's son, who, although awful and terrifying
in respect of the height of his royal power and the majesty
of his sovereignty, lived among the people in humility and
meekness, whereby he drew many to him.

He wished to become admirable (?) in his works, and quiet
and simple in his knowledge, and therefore he received the
power of sovereignty with his humility and with his knowledge.
For great humility was a helper and it made all the people to
hearken unto his words. And in this manner in a few days
he made all the people who were under his authority and
power in the provinces and districts to talk about his Divine
words, and to learn the mysteries [thereof]. And they learned
them, and at length they denied absolutely [the existence of]
many gods, and they separated themselves and withdrew from
[their beliefs in] many gods, and the disgrace thereof. And
they became strong in the Faith of the good things wherein
is no error, and they were fashioned anew by his teachings,
and they served Christ. And all those who [p. 205] had lived
shut up in the mountains and caves through the fear of his
father, priests and monks, came forth from their hiding places,
and the bishops with them, and they went to Yĕwâsĕf rejoicing.
And he received those who had suffered the greatest tribulations for the sake of Christ, and he brought them into his

palace, and he washed the dust from their feet and their heads, and he comforted their hearts, and he provided them with everything that they needed, and he consecrated the church which he had built.

And there was among the bishops a certain man who had toiled exceedingly for the Faith, and who had resigned the throne of his office and had appointed thereto a certain chief priest. Now he was a holy man, and he knew well the Canons of the Church, and his soul was filled with divine zeal, and he made ready the means for Christian Baptism, and he baptized in the water those who had returned to Christ. He baptized first of all the noblemen and all the men who held offices of high honour, and after them he baptized the soldiers, and then all the people. It was not only the sicknesses of their souls that were healed, but all those who were suffering from divers sicknesses in their bodies were healed. And they were saved from every sickness when they went forth from the womb of Baptism, pure in their souls, and healthy in their bodies, for they had found healing of both soul and body at the same time. And because of this very many people came to Yĕwâsĕf the king from every place, wishing to acquire from him the knowledge of goodness. And King Yĕwâsĕf began to overthrow all the temples of idols, and he took all their vessels and their furniture which the people had prepared for the graven images, and he built therewith large altars and churches. And he made all their possessions, which were of great price, the property of the churches, and in this way he made that which was transient, and of which the glory was corruptible, an effective and profitable thing. And the unclean devils who were in the habit [p. 206] of frequenting those temples and altars were driven out, and they were doomed to suffer great tribulation, and they cried out, and many heard them wailing and groaning because of the tribulation which had come upon them. And all those provinces found themselves free from the darkness of their error, and they rejoiced in the light of the Christian Faith, which is spotless. And in this wise King Yĕwâsĕf [was teaching] the way of truth to all men, and he nourished many, and he inflamed their hearts to make them to model themselves according to his will, as was fitting for his authority and his position, for all those who were under his sovereignty made themselves like unto him, and they shaped their lives according to his admonitions. And in this way they desired to gain his affection, and they learned his works whereby they became able [to comprehend] a little of the knowledge of their master, and therefore, with the help of God, they grew up in the True Faith, which abounded and increased in them.

[*How Yĕwâsĕf converted his subjects, and how under his gracious rule his kingdom flourished whilst that of his father decayed.*]

And Yĕwâsĕf the king was crucified in his heart by the commandments of Christ and His love, with the wisdom of the word of grace; and he was the haven of many souls, making direct their journey into port. For he knew that it was meet for a king before everything else to teach men the fear of God and to keep guard over their integrity, even as he himself feared God and watched himself. And he made himself strong, so that he might have dominion over the passions, and over all who were under his authority, like a wise governor, and he made fast his feet in the safety of the beauty of the Law. And this king, who was a king indeed, controlled firmly the wishes which he carried into effect, and he boasted not himself of the glory of his fathers, nor of the royal majesty that appertained to him, for he knew that all his begetters were dust, and that the first father of our race was a creature of dust, and that we belong to his nature, both those who are rich and those who are poor. And he thrust his mind down into the depths of humility and into the wisdom which was of the other world, and he understood his life in this world, and he knew well that he would find the things which are in very truth in the other world after his departure from this world, and he knew what these things were exceedingly well.

[p. 207] And he delivered those who were under his dominion
at the same time from the error of their fathers, and he made
them servants of Him Who had bought us with His precious
Blood from the slavery of evil. Carefully then and publicly
he enquired into the beauty of the work of doing virtuous
and excellent things, and the working of purity and integrity
helped him, and he was crowned with purity as with a crown,
and he was adorned with the purple of rectitude, well knowing
the transitoriness of riches, which resembleth the flowing away
of water of the rivers. And he spared no pains in laying up
treasure for himself there where the moth destroyeth not,
and where the thieves do not dig through the walls and steal.
And then he began to distribute his possessions and money
among the poor and needy unsparingly, until there was nothing
left to him. For he knew that he had great power, and that
it was meet that he should imitate God, and he thought that
there was nothing nobler than doing charity, which is more
precious than gems and pearls of great price. And he gathered
together the riches of fair deeds wherein those who perform
them may rejoice in this world, having the hope of the delight
which is to come, and in the next world they will rejoice in
the freedom of the blessed for which they wait. For this
reason he used to redeem those who were in prison and
undergoing punishment, and of those who were bound for
debt he paid the debts and set them free. And he used to
give gladly to all those who were in need, and he was a father
to the orphans, and to the widows, and to those who were in
misery, and he became like their begetter through his love of
doing good, considering that the doing of good to them was
doing good unto himself.

In truth he was rich in gifts, and his soul was rich in truth,
for it was a royal soul and the abode of riches. And he was
an abundant giver to those who were in want; for he hoped
to receive a never-ending two-fold reward when the season
of reward for good deeds should come after a few days. And
the report of him was heard in all places, and every one
desired him at all times, even as do those who run after

sweet perfume with a delicious odour, casting aside from them the necessary things of mind and body. And the mention of his name was sweet in the mouth of every man, but not [p. 208] through fear and terror. For people came to him of their own free will, and with strong love from the depth of their heart, both for the sake of God and for the sake of the beauty of the course of action which was planted in his heart. And straightway there came unto him those who were under the authority of his father, and who had abandoned all error and were rejoicing in the path of truth. And the city of Yĕwâsĕf increased and flourished, and the city of his father decreased and waxed feeble, even as saith the Book of Kings concerning David and Saul[1]. And when his father saw this he repented with great longing at the end of the days of his period of life, and he remembered his sins, and he perceived the weakness of his gods, and their useless craftiness. And straightway he gathered together his faithful councillors, and he followed the light to which he was guided, and all those who were gathered together declared the words of Yĕwâsĕf, the upright [king], to be true; for our Redeemer summoned them from the east, and He heard the supplication of His messenger Yĕwâsĕf.

[*How the king summoned his councillors, how they admitted the truth of Yĕwâsĕf's religion, and how the king wrote to his son and confessed his error and besought him to help him to embrace Christianity.*]

And the king wished to make his son to know this, and he wrote to him on the following day a letter which ran thus: "From the king Anbeyer to the beloved prince Yĕwâsĕf: peace be upon thee, O beloved son! O beloved son, many thoughts have entered my soul and have stirred me up to evil. Behold, I have observed all our works and see that they disappear like smoke; but the working of thy Faith sendeth forth light which is brighter than the radiance of the sun. Behold, I have turned to a mind that believeth. The words

[1] 2 Sam. iii. 1.

that have gone forth from thy mouth are true for ever. As
the deep darkness of sin and apostasy enshrouded us we were
unable to see the truth, and to understand the Creator of the
Universe. Nay more than this, the brilliance which shone
upon us from thee made us cover our eyes, for we wished
not to see it; and we entreated thee very evilly for a long
time, and this we did often, and we caused thee to sorrow.
[p. 209] Woe be unto us! For we have killed many Christians
who, in the strength of the power that helped them, delivered
themselves over to death before the denseness of our hearts.
Behold, however, we have now removed that heavy darkness
from the pupils of our eyes, and we are able to see a little
of the splendour of the truth, and we have begun to repent
of our evil deeds in the time that is past. There is, however,
a second cloud, which is an evil one, for behold, side by side
with this splendour of the truth, thick darkness and cruel
despair have drawn nigh in such a way that they make dark
this splendour and envelop it in many coverings. For I feel
that I am spurned by Christ and that He will not accept me,
whilst I appear to be one who is resisting Him and fighting
against Him. Explain to me quickly and make me to know what
thou wouldst say unto me, O my fair son. Accept these words
and teach me thy father what I ought to do, and draw thy
begetter to the knowledge of what is right, and what I should
make to come to pass."

[*How Yĕwâsĕf received his father's letter, and how he prayed
to God to open his father's eyes and to release him from the
captivity of sin.*]

And when Yĕwâsĕf read this letter and understood what
was [written] therein, his soul was filled with the delight of
Christ and with great wonder. And he folded up the letter and
gave it to him that had brought it, and he went quickly into
his palace and bowed down before the Divine Image. And his
eyes rained tears down upon the ground, and he gave thanks
to the Lord Christ, and he brought and offered up to Him
fervour of his heart, saying, "I will exalt Thee, O my King

and God, and I will bless Thy Name for ever and ever. Amen.
Great art Thou, O God, and very glorious, and there is no end
to Thy Majesty. And who is there that can describe Thy
power and can declare to the full Thy glories, O Thou Who
didst bring water out from the rock[1]? Behold, when he who
was arrogant of heart, whose stiffneckedness was harder than
the rock, saw thee he became as soft as wax before the fire[2].
For Thou art able to draw out of these stones children unto
Abraham[3]. I give thanks unto Thee, O my Lord, Thou Lover
of the children of men, Thou God of mercies, Who hast been
longsuffering towards [p. 210] our transgressions, and hast
borne patiently with us until this moment, and hast not punished
us, although we deserved of old to be cast down before Thy
face like the enemies of the Law who dwelt in the Five Cities
and were consumed by brimstone and fire[4]. But Thou didst
show longsuffering in Thy Spirit, whereto nothing is equal,
and didst show compassion to us, and I the vile one, who am
wholly unworthy to praise Thy goodness adequately, do praise
Thee. I beseech Thy compassionate mercy, which is beyond
all reckoning, O Son and Word of God the Invisible, the
Creator of everything by Thy Word, Who art the Sustainer
thereof by Thy good pleasure, Who didst of Thine own free will
stretch out Thy hands upon the Cross, and didst bestow power
and didst give life everlasting unto those who were bound
in prison, do Thou now stretch out Thy hand which doeth
everything and is invisible, and set free Thy servant, my
father, for ever, from the captivity in which the evil Crafty
One hath led him captive. And reveal Thou to him openly
and clearly that Thou Thyself alone art He Who liveth for
ever, the True God, the everlasting King, Who can not die.
Look Thou upon the contrition of my heart with the eye of
mercy and pity, even as Thine unfailing hope hath been with
me, O Thou Worker, Who dost take thought for every created
thing, let Thy water, unchanged, spring up within me, and
may it give me speech, and open my mouth, and endow me

---

[1] Exodus xvii. 6.   [2] Psalm lxviii. 2.   [3] Matt. iii. 9
[4] Genesis xiv. 8 ; xix. 25.

with a right heart. And let me be well built upon Thee,
O Thou Rock Which satisfiest thirst, and grant unto me Thy
messenger, the worthless and insignificant, power to declare
unto my father the mystery of Thy wisdom in a fitting manner,
and that I may deliver him by Thy power from the wiles of
Satan the Evil One, and that I may bring him to Thee, O God,
Lord of the Universe, Who dost not desire the destruction of
sinners[1], but dost lead us to hope for Thy mercy through repentance. For Thou art glorious for ever and ever. Amen."

*[How Yĕwâsĕf went in state to visit his father, and how he,
by the help of Christ, succeeded in making him to understand
the doctrine of salvation through Christ, and to become a
Christian.]*

And when Yĕwâsĕf had prayed in this wise, being confident
that he would not be put to shame through [the failure of]
his hope, he departed straightway, confessing the tender pity
of Christ, and he rode from his city in royal state, and he
arrived at the kingdom of his father. And when [the servants]
announced to his father the arrival of his son, he went forth
straightway to meet him, and he embraced him, and made a
great festival [p. 211], and rejoiced at his coming; and after
this they sat down together in a place apart. Who can describe
the words which the son of the king spake in wisdom unto
his father on that occasion? And what can we say concerning
what he spake unto him in the words of the Divine Holy
Spirit, through Whom the fishermen of Christ have caught in
their nets the whole world? Now the wisdom of the wise
purified them by the grace of this Spirit whereby this Yĕwâsĕf
was wise.

And Yĕwâsĕf taught the king, and he illumined his heart
with the light of knowledge, but at first he toiled very hard
in teaching him so that he might lead him away from the
worship of idols. What word did he not speak? And what
did he not do to convince him? But [his words] were like
unto those which men speak in vain in the ears of those who

[1] Ezekiel xxxiii. 11.

will not hear. And when God saw the humility of His servant Yĕwâsĕf He opened the closed doors of his father's heart, even as it is said, "He sendeth light into the hearts of those who fear Him, He doeth their will and heareth their prayer[1]." Then the king understood quickly what was spoken to him, and by the grace of Christ his son found the opportunity to make him to agree with him. And his son obtained victory and power over the evil spirits which had dominion over his father, and he freed him from their wiles with an everlasting freedom, and he made him to know openly concerning the Word of salvation, so that he might make the Living God, Who dwelleth in heaven, his own.

And first of all he spake concerning the ordinances of the shining Faith, and he made him to know about them, but in the discourse which he pronounced there was no mention of the great and marvellous things which he had seen and heard. And he taught him many things about God, and explained to him the beauty of His Godhead, and he taught him that there is no other God, either in the heavens above or in the earth beneath, except One God, Who is Father, and Son, and Holy Spirit; and he made him to know the mystery of the Divine Words. And he told him also about created things, both those which are visible and those which are invisible, and how He brought them into existence out from a state of non-existence; and how He created man in His own form [p. 212] and similitude, and how He honoured him by letting him have power to do his own will; and how He gave him power to cultivate all the beautiful [trees] which were in the Garden of Delight; and how He commanded him to keep away from one tree, which was the Tree of Knowledge; and how having transgressed His command God cast him out of the Garden of Delight, because he had slipped aside from his [first] state; and how he fell from the [state of the] race of the children of men into these great errors and vileness; and how [men] fell into the hand of death through the work of the cunning of the Crafty Deceiver, who seized men and brought them under his

---

[1] Compare Psalm iv. 7 ; John ix. 31.

authority in a moment; and how the Deceiver made them to forget God, and seduced them so that they bowed down to unclean gods; and how God then had compassion upon our clay, at the good pleasure of the Father and the Holy Spirit, and was pleased to be born in our image of the Holy Virgin; and how He, the Impassible, endured sufferings, and rose from the dead on the third day, and redeemed us from [our] first rebellion, and made us meet for honour that was greater than that which we possessed before; and how He gathered us together at the time of His ascension into heaven, both those who had come and those who were there; and how we also believe that He will come to raise up our clay and to reward every one of us according to his work.

And he also explained unto him the mystery of the Kingdom of Heaven, and the indescribable good things for which those who are meet for them wait; and he described unto him the tortures which are prepared for sinners, and the fire which is never quenched, and the outer darkness, and the worm which never sleepeth, and the punishment of torture which is laid up for all the slaves of sin. And Yĕwâsĕf spake all these things unto him in gentle words, and he made his father to hearken unto him by the grace of the Holy Spirit which dwelt in him. Moreover, he described to him the depth of the love of God for man, whereof the foundation cannot be found, and how He receiveth the repentance of those who go to Him, and how there is no sin that will vanquish His love, provided that we are strong therein. And he adduced from the Scriptures many testimonies, and [so] made an end of his discourse.

[*How the king abandoned his idols, bowed down to the Cross of Christ, and how all the nobles and people became Christians.*]

And the heart of the king became bold through these [p. 213] words of wisdom, and through the teaching which was from God, and he cried out with a loud voice and with fervour of heart that he believed in Christ our Redeemer. And he

forsook the worship of idols completely, and before all the
people he bowed down to the Cross, the Giver of Life. And he
proclaimed, and all the people heard him, that the Lord Jesus
Christ was God in truth. And he confessed his former denial
[of Christ], and he reviled the hardness of his heart against
the Christians, and his slaughter of them, and he came to the
beauty of worship and to the great sharing therein. And thus
were fulfilled the words of the Apostle who saith, "Where
there was the greatest doubt there especially doth grace
abound[1]." And Yĕwâsĕf, who was the wisest of men, taught
the captains of the army, and the nobles who came, and all
the people, much concerning the Law of God, and the beauty
of His worship; he was like a man of fire, making himself to
resemble the gods, singing a sweet song, and to the assembly
he sang a song of their songs (?). And the grace of the Holy
Spirit rested upon him, and he stirred all the people to praise
God. And all the people cried out with one voice, saying,
"Great is the God of the Christians, and there is no other
God beside our Lord Jesus Christ, Who is praised with the
Father and the Holy Spirit."

[*How the king and his son destroyed the idols and their
temples, and built churches.*]

And then Anbîyar the king departed, being filled with divine
zeal, and he fell with great wrath upon the idols in his Court,
which were made of gold and silver, and he cast them all
down upon the ground and broke them in pieces. And after
this he cut them up into little pieces, and divided them among
the poor, and thus he made to be profitable things which had
had no profit in them. And in like manner he rose up, together
with his son, against all temples and the altars of idols and
overthrew them, even to their very foundations; and he built
in their stead great churches to God, not in the district only,
but in all the countries [round about], and he finished them
with very great care. And the evil spirits which used to dwell
in the temples were driven out from them, [p. 214] and they

---

[1] Romans v. 20; 1 Tim. i. 13, 14.

cried out and trembled at the might of our God, Whom they were not able to resist. And all the people of the city and many of the neighbouring peoples were drawn to the worship of the True Faith.

[*How the king was baptized by a bishop, and how churches were built, and how bishops and priests came forth from their hiding places, and ruled over the new congregations.*]

And at that time a certain holy bishop came and exhorted Anbîyar the king, and he baptized him with holy and divine Christian Baptism, in the Name of the Father, and of the Son, and of the Holy Spirit; and Yĕwâsĕf was his sponsor in glorious Christian Baptism. This was a marvellous thing, for he became the father of his parent who begot him in the flesh. And he became the cause of his second birth in the spirit, for he was the son of the Son of the Heavenly Father, and the fruit indeed of the glorious Root which sprang from the Root which cried out, saying, "I am the Vine of Truth, and ye are the branches thereof[1]"; and thus he brought forth the king a second time with water and with spirit. And Yĕwâsĕf rejoiced with a great joy and he held worthy of divine Christian Baptism all the men of the city and of the [neighbouring] districts. And those who in times past had been black became children of light, and every sickness and every accident that were caused by Satan were driven far away from those who believed, and they all became healthy and perfect in soul and in body. And other marvels took place at the resurrection of the faith, and churches were built, and the bishops, who had hidden themselves through dismay and fear, appeared and took charge of the churches, and priests and monks multiplied, and were appointed to rule the flock of Christ.

[*How the king abdicated in favour of his son, and how Yĕwâsĕf, by his comforting words of grace, brought him out of the slough of despond into which he had fallen.*]

And the king Anbîyar made himself to be remote from his former course of life, and repented of his past deeds; and he

[1] John xv. 5.

B.   16

handed over the rule of the kingdom to his son Yĕwâsĕf.
And finally he departed, and he cast dust upon his head, and
he groaned in his heart, and he bathed his body with his tears,
and he petitioned God the Redeemer in every place, and he
made supplication [p. 215] to Him for the forgiveness of his
sins. And he awakened his soul, which was in a state so lowly
and humble that he restrained himself and was ashamed to
utter the Name of God, nevertheless by forcing himself, and
by fighting the fight, and by exhortation from the mouth of
his son, he at length made bold to utter His Name. Thus was
he changed, and the change in him was good, and he followed
the path which leadeth to the performance of virtues. And
he lived in this state for four years, and he repented honestly,
and lamented [his sins] with scalding tears, and he worked
the works of excellence in all purity and holiness; and thus
he brought his appointed span of life to an end. And then
the illness through which he died seized him, and when the
time of his death drew nigh, fear and dismay laid hold upon
him, for he remembered the evil deeds that he had committed.
And Yĕwâsĕf comforted him with words of consolation, and
he lightened for him the burden of sorrow which was upon
him, and he said unto him, "O father, why dost thou sorrow
and why dost thou disturb thyself? Put thy trust in the Lord
thy God, Who is the Hope of all the ends of the earth and of
those also who are in the sea afar off[1], Who saith in Isaiah,
'Wash ye and be ye clean, and put away evil and wickedness
from your souls before Mine eyes. Learn ye to do what is
good. And though your sins be like scarlet, I will make them
to be white like the snow, and though they be like crimson,
I will make them to be white like wool[2].' Be not afraid,
O father, and doubt not in thy heart that the sins of the
penitent can vanquish the illimitable goodness of God, for
these sins have number, and the will that effected them [had
a limit], whilst the mercy of God and His goodness have
neither number nor limit. Moreover it is not meet that that
which was the dominion of the will and number should van-

[1] Psalm lxv. 5.   [2] Isaiah i. 16–18.

quish Him Who is without limit or number." And with these words and others like unto them, which carried away his father's heart, Yĕwâsĕf exhorted him until he brought him into a state of radiant hope.

[*How the king blessed his son and, committing his soul to God, died in peace.*]

And straightway his father stretched out his hands, and giving thanks to God he blessed Yĕwâsĕf his son, and said, "Blessed be the day [p. 216] whereon thou wast born, O my very dear son, O son who art not mine, but art the son of the heavenly Father. With what reward can I reward thee, O my son? And with what blessing shall I bless thee? And what thanks can I give unto God for thee? I was lost, and I was found through thee. I was dead in sin, and I am alive through thee. I was an enemy and far from God, and He had exceedingly great compassion upon me because of thee. With what can I reward thee for all these things? God Who hath made thee worthy of abundant reward [shall reward thee] in proportion to the abundance of thy merit." And whilst he was saying these words and many others, he kissed his beloved son ceaselessly. And after this he prayed, saying, "Into Thy hand, O Lover of the children of men, I commit my spirit "; and having said this he delivered up his soul into the hand of God, with beautiful penitence.

[*How Yĕwâsĕf buried his father with great pomp and cere-mony, and how he prayed and mourned for him for seven days, and how on the eighth day he distributed all his posses-sions in providing a funeral feast for all the people.*]

And the young man Yĕwâsĕf paid honour to his father with many tears, and he caused all the funerary ceremonies to be performed with great pomp and splendour, and he buried him in a grave among men who were believers. And he did not array himself in royal apparel but in the beautiful garb of repentance. And after this he stood up by his grave, and lifted up his hands to heaven, and poured out tears from his eyes

like the waters of a river, and he cried out to God, saying,
" I give thanks unto Thee, O God, the King of glory, Who alone
art the Almighty, Who diest not, because Thou hast not dis-
regarded my petition, and hast not rejected my tears, but hast
been pleased to turn this Thy servant, my father, from the way
of transgression, and hast drawn him to Thyself, O Saviour of
all men, and hast made him to be remote from the error of
idols, and hast held him to be worthy to know Thee, O God
indeed, Thou Lover of the children of men. And now, O my
Lord and God, the depth of Whose goodness cannot be found
out, nor the foundation thereof, make my father to dwell in a
green place, in a place of rest, where the light of Thy face
shineth. And let his former transgressions be no more remembered, but, according to the abundance of Thy mercy, blot out
his sins and make Thou to be gracious [p. 217] towards him the
hearts of Thy saints whom he killed by the sword and by fire,
and command them not to be wroth with him, for Thou art
all-mighty, and Thou dost teach those who turn themselves to
Thee that Thy compassion is poured out upon all men. And it
is Thou Who dost save those who take refuge with Thee, O my
Lord and God Jesus Christ, unto Whom are meet praise and
thanksgiving until the ages have passed away. Amen."

And for seven days Yĕwâsĕf prayed and made supplication
and treaty to God, and he did not remove himself from his
father's tomb for a moment for seven whole days. And he
never for a moment remembered food, or drink, or sleep, or
rest, but he bathed the ground with his tears, and prayed with
groanings, and never held his peace. And on the eighth day
he departed to his house, and he distributed money and goods
among the poor, and not one man was left among those who
were in misery who lacked anything ; all this work he finished
in a few days and in this way he spent all his treasure, so that
when he wished to enter in at the strait gate he would not
find himself made to lag behind through the weight of [his]
money.

*[How Yĕwâsĕf, at a funerary commemoration held forty
days after the death of his father, summoned the nobles and
people to his presence, and how, having informed them that
he was going to abdicate, he called upon them to elect a king
for themselves.]*

And forty days after the death of his father, he made ready
to celebrate his commemoration, and he invited all the men
of high rank, and all those who were serving as soldiers, and
the assembly of the people of the great city, and he addressed
them all, saying, "Hear, O all ye people ! Behold, ye see that
my father king Anbîyar hath died even like any poor man,
and that there is nothing that can redeem him, neither money,
nor riches, nor royal rank, nor myself, my father's beloved
son, nor any of his friends whom he hath left behind, and that
none of his kinsfolk hath the power to help him, either by
money or riches, at the judgement, wherein no mercy is shown.
But he hath departed to the next world, where there is right
judgement, in order to give an account of his journeying
during the days of his life in this world ; and there is no one
with him of [p. 218] all his friends to help him except his own
deeds, whether they be good or whether they be evil. And this
thing must of necessity come upon all men who are of the nature
of the flesh, and they cannot escape it. And now, hearken ye
unto me, O my friends, and brethren, and people of God, whom
Christ hath purchased with His precious Blood, for He hath
redeemed you from the error of olden time and from the
slavery of the Enemy. Ye know my manner of life among you,
and how since I became a Christian it was meet for me to
become a servant of Christ. I have hated every [god] and
have loved Him alone, and I have forsaken all my lusts. And
the fulfilment of my desire would be to go out from the turmoil of this world, and from the vain pleasure thereof, and be
with Him alone, and to lead a life of spiritual contemplation
wherein there is no turmoil, and to serve my Lord and God.
And as concerning my taking thought for my father, this was
due to the commandment wherewith I had been commanded ;

and by the grace and help of God I have not toiled in vain, and my labour in these [last] days hath not been wasted. For I have cast everything upon Christ, and I have gathered together all of you, and I have taught you to worship Him alone, for he is God indeed and the Lord of all truth. And it is not of myself that I have done this, but through the grace that was with me. And I have set you free from the slavery of evil captivity, and from the deceit of the worship of idols and from the service of graven images. And behold, my time hath now arrived when I must finish that which I vowed to God to do, and I must go to the place whither He Himself will guide me, and I must pay the vow which I vowed unto Him. And now, take ye counsel together, so that there may be appointed one whom ye will choose to reign over you, for from this time forth ye must be strong in the doing of the good pleasure of the Father ; and there is no commandment of His whatsoever which is hidden from you. Walk ye therein, and withdraw not yourselves, either to the right hand or to the left ; and may the God of peace be with you ! Amen."

[p. 219] And when those peoples and the soldiers heard this, straightway there broke out uproar and tumult, and loud cries, and they wept and lamented sorely over their orphaned state. And with many tears and cries of grief the people swore loud oaths, and they shouted loudly declaring that they would never let him go, and that they would rather bind him in fetters than listen to one word of his about departure ; thus did all the people cry out, and all the chiefs and governors with them.

[*How Yĕwâsĕf offered his kingdom to Barâsĕyâs, who had supported him mightily during his disputation with Nâkôr, who pretended to be Baralâm, and how Barâsĕyâs refused to reign.*]

And Yĕwâsĕf made signs to the people with his eyes and with his hands to hold their peace, and he said unto them, "I am not able to stand up against you" ; and then he dismissed them to their homes bearing on their faces the signs of sorrow and suffering. And one of the nobles was with Yĕwâsĕf, whose rank was higher than all the rest, by reason of the beauty of his piety and his marvellously pure course of life; his name was Barâsĕyâs, whom we have already mentioned, and who, when Nâkôr disguised himself as Baralâm, disputed with the philosophers, and became a helper of Yĕwâsĕf, and contended with Nâkôr, for his heart burned with divine zeal. This man did the king take aside privily, and he began to converse with him with humility, and he made earnest entreaties to him to accept his kingdom, and to rule his people in the fear of God, and to follow the course of life which was well-pleasing to himself. And when Barâsĕyâs saw that Yĕwâsĕf absolutely hated the idea of reigning and that he refused to do so, he said unto him, "O king, wouldst thou thus become like a tyrant in thy judgement and in thy word? Is it not the law, which behold, thou thyself hast taught, that thou shouldst love thy neighbour as thyself? For what cause dost thou wish to cast upon me the burden which thou art ready to cast from thyself? And if the kingdom be a good thing take it thyself with happiness, but if, on the contrary, it is a thing of cursing and disgrace in thy sight why shouldst thou cast it on me and desire to trip me up?"

[*How Yĕwâsĕf wrote a letter to his subjects ordering them to accept Barâsĕyâs as their king, and then fled from his palace secretly by night; how the people followed him and found him and how he returned to his palace with them, and swore an oath that he would never reign over them.*]

And when Yĕwâsĕf saw that he spake unto him in this wise, he ceased to hold converse with him. [p. 220] And during the night he wrote a letter to the people which was full of wisdom and knowledge of every kind. In it he described all the beauty of the worship which he openly declared, and how it was meet for them to confess God, and what manner of glorious offerings they ought to offer unto Him, and what manner of praise was due to Him, and what kind of thanksgiving. And over and above this he commanded them to accept as king no one except Barâsĕyâs. And he left this letter in his palace, and he went out from his royal abode in secret and unseen by any. But it was impossible for this matter to be concealed from them, and in the morning when all the people heard this, they forthwith broke out into cries and lamentations, and all the men of the city went forth to seek him, and they scattered themselves on every road so that they might discover whither he had fled. Now their anxiety [to find him] was not in vain, for having occupied all the roads, and searched all the hills, and gone round about the rivers no man could have escaped them, and they found him in a valley with his hands stretched out towards heaven, where he prayed for seven hours. And when they saw him they shed tears, and they made entreaties to him, and they chid him because he had forsaken them and departed, and he said unto them, "Trouble not yourselves in vain, and do not imagine that I shall ever be your king," but when they urged him exceedingly he relented and went back to his palace. And he gathered together all the people, and explained to them his decision, and he took an oath by his own word that he would not live again with them even for a day. And he said unto them, "Behold, I have finished my service to you, and there remaineth to me nothing [to do]. I have not hidden from you anything that it was incumbent upon me to tell you and to teach you, and at the same time I strove to guide every man to the faith in our Lord Jesus Christ, and to show him the path of repentance. Behold, I am going to enter upon the path which I desired formerly, and ye will nevermore see my face. I am innocent of your blood [p. 221] and of yourselves this day, even as the divine Apostle saith, "I am innocent of the blood of you all, for I have not hidden from you anything which I have not told you of all God's good pleasure[1]."

---

[1] Acts xx. 26, 27.

[How the people set Barâsĕyâs upon the throne, and how Yĕwâsĕf crowned him and prayed that God would keep him in the right way.]

And when the people heard this and knew the strength of his will, and that they were unable to make him draw back from his firm determination, they began to lament their orphaned state, and to weep because they could not find a way to prevent [his departure]. Then the king laid hold upon Barâsĕyâs, and said unto the people, "O brethren, appoint ye this man to be king over you"; and Barâsĕyâs opposed this thing very strongly. But though he hated it, against his will they appointed him to the rule of the kingdom, and set him upon the throne, and Yĕwâsĕf put the crown upon his head, and placed the royal signet ring upon his finger. And Yĕwâsĕf stood up towards the east and prayed to the King Who bestoweth sovereignty, that He would keep Barâsĕyâs in the Faith of God, without turning aside, and that he might find the path without withdrawal from the commandments of Christ. And then he made a petition on behalf of the priesthood and all their flocks, and he asked from God for them safety and victory; and every petition which he made was granted.

[How Yĕwâsĕf admonished king Barâsĕyâs, and counselled him as to the ruling of his kingdom and himself.]

And when he had prayed in this wise he turned to Barâsĕyâs, and said unto him, "Behold, O beloved brother, I command thee with the commandment of the Apostle, to protect thyself and all the flock over which the Holy Spirit hath appointed thee king, and to rule the people of God Who hath vivified us by his Blood. And as thou didst know God before me, and thy worship was in the pure Faith, so now do thou show much zeal in pleasing Him, for according to thy deserts is this great appointment from God, and in return therefor it is meet for thee to pay Him back in what is greater. And from him to whom He hath given much are fitting continuous thanksgiving and the observance of His holy commandments, and withdrawal from the way that leadeth to destruction. [p. 222] And it is even as with those who sail on the sea ; if one of the sailors maketh a mistake but little harm befalleth the ship, but if the captain of the ship maketh a mistake the whole ship perisheth. And it is thus in the matter of kings : if one of a king's subjects committeth a fault the evil that cometh upon him because of it doth not come upon all the soldiers of the army ; but if the king committeth a fault evil cometh upon the whole country. And as for thee, if thou shalt be careless about anything whatsoever, then it will be meet for abundant punishment to come upon thee. Do thou take the greatest care to guard thyself in the doing of good, and do thou hate every desire that would draw thee into sin. For the Apostle saith, 'Make ye peace with all men and keep purity, for without it no man shall see God[1].' Consider carefully the circling of the celestial sphere and the revolutions thereof, and how it passeth over the affairs of men, and how it beareth away empty hours, and it maketh them to pass away. And their changing and transient passage shall be to thee a similitude of that which changeth ; for at the time when the heart is changed as a sign of the matter that is therein there cometh a thought (or, mind) that is not true. Be thou strong in doing what is good, and [be] constant in thy words, and magnify not thou the glory that passeth away, and the greatness of the praise that is vain. But with a heart that is pure ponder thou upon the wretchedness and feebleness of thy nature, and upon the swift approach of death in this life—for death clingeth to the flesh—and if thou wilt meditate upon these things thou shalt not fall into the pit of sin. And fear thou thy God Who is in truth the King of Heaven, and thou shalt become the blessed man who liveth in righteousness. For behold, it is said, 'Blessed are all those who fear God, and those who walk in His way. Blessed is the man who feareth God, and who rejoiceth in his commandment exceedingly[2].' And, 'Blessed are the merciful for unto them shall He shew mercy ; and be

[1] Hebrews xii. 14. [2] Psalms cxxviii. 1; cxii. 1.

ye merciful like your Heavenly Father[1].' This is the commandment which those who occupy exceedingly [p. 223] exalted positions should seek to follow above all others. And
it is especially fitting that the man who is appointed to an
exalted position should be like unto Him, Who is the Giver of
power, in all the fair deeds which enable him to show compassion and mercy. And especially in respect of the Law of
His commandment—there is nothing like unto this to draw a
man to love him (i.e. the king). It is like a gift which is given
to the needy with gracious benevolence. He who ministereth
through fear is a worthless creature. Hearken then [to what
I say] concerning fear. Fear is bound up with going astray—
a saying noble and to be praised—[the man who feareth]
leadeth astray those whom men make to come to him. He
who feareth a matter is like unto one who hath found a path,
and who riseth up to contend against it. On the other hand,
he who is bound with the bond of love is strong in the beauty
of His commandment which cannot be set aside. Therefore be
thou a giver to the needy, and open thine ear to hearken unto
the poor, so that the ears of God may become hearkeners unto
thee. For if we become helpers to them in ministering to them
we shall find our God through this matter. And as we hearken
unto them so will He hearken unto us, and as we look upon
them even so will He look upon us with the Eye of His Divine
Kingdom which seeth everything. Let us flee then from
suffering to the desire of mercy, and we shall be rewarded
according as we have worked.

"And moreover, hearken unto another commandment which
is like unto it : Pardon ye, and He shall pardon you ; and if
ye do not forgive men their trespasses your Father will not
forgive you your trespasses[2]. And therefore do not oppose
believers with indignation, but if thou wishest for forgiveness
of thy sins, pardon those who have sinned against thee. He
who forgiveth shall be rewarded with the forgiveness of his
sin, and in return for our compassion upon those who have
treated us evilly, we shall be able to turn aside the wrath of

[1] Matt. v. 7; Luke vi. 36.　　　　[2] Matt. vi. 14, 15.

the Being of Darkness. Moreover we shall find in return for
our non-forgiving of the trespasses of others the non-forgiving
of our own trespasses, even as thou hast heard concerning the
man who owed thousands of talents[1], and who because of the
want of compassion in him reviled with harshness the man who
owed him a debt, and persecuted him relentlessly.

"Therefore it is meet that we should take good heed to ourselves, so that that which came upon him may not come upon
us ; let us forgive everyone, even as it is meet to do, every
feeling of enmity [p. 224] which cometh forth from the heart,
so that He may forgive us the great debt which hangeth over
us. And before everything we must take good heed to preserve
beautiful simplicity, and teach the beauty of worship and the
Faith which thou hast learned, and thou shalt teach it, and no
tares of doubt[2] whatsoever shall sprout therein. Only guard
the divine seed unharmed and pure, so that the Lord may see
the abundance of the fruit thereof, and may reward us according to our works, when the righteous shall shine like the
sun[3], and God shall reward sinners with darkness and sorrow
for ever. And now, O brethren, I commit you to the care of
God and of His grace, which is able to make you strong, and
to give you an inheritance in all holy things."

[How the people wept and bewailed the departure of Yĕwâsĕf.]

And when he had said these words he bowed his knees, and
prayed, and shed scalding tears, and he turned toward Barâsĕyâs, whom he had appointed king, and to all the governors
and men of noble rank and position. Now a great thing happened at that time which is worthy to be wept over, and they
all spoke unto him clearly, uttering cries of lamentation as
they did so, and told him that if he remained with them he
would be their life, and that his departure from them would
be the departure of their very souls. What kind of lamentation is there which was not uttered at that moment ? And what
wail of grief was there which was not ejaculated as they
adjured him not to depart, and kissed him and embraced him ?

[1] Matt. xviii. 24–35.   [2] Matt. xiii. 26.   [3] Matt. xiii. 43.

For the suffering of their hearts made them to be like unto madmen, and they cried out, saying, " Woe be unto us ! Woe be unto us ! O thou who art our deliverer from all evil impurity, O our lord, and father, and redeemer, and creator, through whom we have learned to know God, and through whom we are delivered from error ! Through thee we have found rest, and joy, and gladness, but what will come upon us now ? And what shall we become after our separation from thee ? How many are the evils that shall find us after thy departure ! "

[*How Yĕwâsĕf forsook his palace and kingdom and departed, how the people followed him until the night fell, how he gave his royal apparel to a beggar, and set out on his way in rags and without provisions.*]

And with these words and others which were like unto them did the people make lamentation, and they beat their breasts, and they wept and bewailed the tribulations which would come upon them. And he (i.e. the king's son) spake unto them with words of consolation, and he made many hear, and he promised them that he would be with them in the spirit, though it was impossible for him to dwell with them in the flesh ; [p. 225] and when he had said this he went forth from his royal palace. And they all followed after him, without turning back, and they began to flee from the city, for they were wishing never to see it again with their eyes. And when they had gone forth from the city, after a long time he exhorted them, and rebuked them, and told them to return, and he admonished them, and chid them severely, and they at length left him, and they returned with their eyes full of tears, but their gaze was directed steadfastly towards him, and they were unable to depart. And some among them whose hearts were hot with love for him, repented of leaving him and followed him until the night fell.

And this Yĕwâsĕf, whose heart was bold and willing, fled from among them, and he forsook his kingdom with joy and gladness, even like a man who returneth from exile in a far country, and entereth into his own native city with gladness. He wore as apparel outwardly the garments which he was in the habit of wearing, but underneath them he wore those coarse garments of hair (sackcloth ?) which his teacher Baralâm had given unto him. And that same night he came to the habitation of a certain beggar, and he stripped off the ornamental attire which he had on and gave it to the beggar, so that he might receive a good price for it which would make him glad. And thus by the prayer of this poor man, and [the prayers] of many poor and needy folk, he made God the Most High his Helper, and put on His grace, which is the garb of salvation and the purple of joy. And he took with him neither bread, nor water, nor anything that was needed either for food or apparel, in fact nothing except these rags which we have mentioned, and he increased in the love which is exalted above the love which is natural and in the divine affection for Christ the King which never dieth. He wounded himself, and his whole person became crucified in respect of God, as he burned with love for Him, even as it is said, "Love burneth like fire[1]," and he was drunk with divine love, and athirst for the flame of His love, even as it is said, " As the hart panteth for the brooks of water, even so doth my soul pant for God. My soul thirsteth for my God, the Mighty one, the Living One[2]." [p. 226] For the soul which loveth with a love like unto this crieth out in the words of a song and saith, " I am wounded by love for Him ; shew me Thy face and make me to hear Thy voice, for Thy voice is pleasant and Thy face is beautiful[3]."

O this love unspeakable, this love for Christ which burneth in the heart like fire ! The Company of the Apostles and the Company of the Martyrs forsook everything that is visible, and they preferred Christ to this transitory life, and they suffered and endured tortures of every kind in their love for the divine beauty (or happiness), and they pondered upon the love of the Word of God our Father, in their minds. This fire did Yĕwâsĕf receive in his heart, and he renounced earthly things, and he treated riches, and honour, and the applause of

[1] Compare Song of Solomon viii. 7.
[2] Psalm xlii. 1, 2.   [3] Song of Solomon ii. 5, 14.

men as worthless. He forsook repose and purple apparel, and he held them to be [as transient] as the spider's web, and he brought back his soul with willingness to every kind of suffering and sorrow, and to the life of contemplation and self-denial. And he cried out, saying, " My soul followeth after Thee, and my being awaiteth Thy right hand[1]."

[How Yĕwâsĕf came to the desert, and how he prayed that he might find Baralâm.]

And thus he journeyed onwards with his face set forwards, and without turning back until [he arrived at] the edge of the desert, and he cast aside his association with things transitory, even as a prisoner casteth away [his] heavy fetters. And he rejoiced in [the] spirit, and he looked towards Christ Whom he desired, and he drew towards Him, saying, " Let not mine eyes look upon the good things of this world, and let not my heart rejoice in the transitory things of this world. But fill Thou mine eyes, O Lord, with the shedding of spiritual tears, and strengthen Thou the soles of my feet, and show me the face of Baralâm, Thy messenger, who became unto me the cause of salvation, so that I may learn from him the Rule whereby a man can protect himself in this ascetic life of contemplation, and so that I may not become changed through the failure of my attempt to wage war against the Enemy. Grant Thou unto me, O Lord, that I may find the path that will bring me unto Thee. For my soul is wounded, and it thirsteth for Thee, O Thou Fountain of Life ! "

[How Yĕwâsĕf lived in a great and waterless desert, how he fasted and prayed and overcame the Enemy.]

And with these words did he speak within his heart continually. And he held converse with God by means of prayer, which was united with sublime visions, and in this wise he continued to follow his course of life without weakness. And he suffered [p. 227] very severe tribulations, but by the love of his God he conquered the law of nature, and the craving

---

[1] Psalm lxiii. 8.

for water. And he used to live upon the herbs which grew in
the desert, for he took with him nothing whatsoever, even as
we have already said, except his body and the ragged apparel
which he had on him. Moreover, he lived upon a very small
quantity of herbs, now he was not able to find them in abundance ; for that desert was a very dry one and there was no
water therein. And at the time of noon the heat of the sun used
to burn him severely, but God protected him from the flame
of the thirst for water. And the Hater of what is good, the
Father of lies, could not bear to see Yĕwâsĕf [enjoying] this
happy mind and living in this ardent love of God, and he
raised up against him many trials in the desert, and he tempted
him by making him to remember his royal rank and his noble
and exalted station, and his company of nobles who used to be
round about him, and his kinsfolk, and the members of his
household, and how every soul of them used to hover round him,
and the comfort from each of them. And the Enemy also caused
him to remember how difficult it was to do the things that
are excellent, and also to remember the temptations that are
attached thereto and the infirmity of his body ; and he caused
him to remember that he had not been accustomed to live in
such a state of misery. And the Enemy also made him to consider the weariness of the time and the torture of thirst which
are in the desert, and more especially because there was none
to give encouragement, and none to offer comfort, and that
there was no end to this fatigue ; and the Enemy brought into
his mind intense hatred of the ascetic life, even as it is written
concerning the great man Anthony. And when the Enemy
learned his own weakness before the determination of the
Saint (who was meditating at all times upon Christ, and whose
heart burned with the love of Him, now he was exceedingly
strong in the beauty of his hope, and his belief was bold and
ready), he thought that there was no way of fighting against
him. Thus the Adversary was put to shame at the beginning
of his fight, and he fell down, even as it is said[1].

[1] Psalm xxvii. 2.

[p. 228]

[How the Devil assumed the forms of wild beasts and reptiles and tried to terrify Yĕwâsĕf, and how Yĕwâsĕf reviled him.]

And then the Enemy brought forward another kind of temptation, for [p. 228] cunning devices of the Evil One are very many, and he brought from the regions of the damned divers terrors so that he might cast the spell of fear upon him. On one occasion he appeared unto him in the form of a black man, and on another he disguised himself and pretended to hold a sword wherewith he threatened to kill him, so that he might force him quickly backwards. Another time he took upon himself the forms of wild beasts of various kinds, and they roared at the saint, and uttered terrifying cries and [then] fled. Another time the Enemy took the forms of venomous serpents which coiled themselves round the body of the saint, and another time he took the form of a huge snake, and the forms of vipers and cerastes. But the soul of this victorious fighter and soldier remained without fear or dismay, for behold, he made the Most High his refuge, and his mind was awake, and he scoffed at Satan the Evil One, saying, " O Evil and Crafty One, it is not meet for thee to presume so far as to attempt to seduce me. In times of old it was thou who didst raise up evil against the race of man, and for ever thou shalt be a being of perdition, and thou shalt not cease from stirring up revolt in every place. Truly the form and likeness and similitude of wild beasts and jackals which thou hast assumed befit thee, for the savageness of thy will and thy tortuous depravity are manifest to all. O wretched creature, why cravest thou for that to which thou canst not attain ? And since I have learned that these craftinesses and things that strike dismay into men spring from thee, I shall not henceforward have any fear of thee, and not even one anxious thought, for God will help me, and I shall look upon my wicked enemies, and I shall tread upon vipers and mount upon the back of the serpent, in the forms of which creatures thou dost disguise thyself. And I shall tread upon thee, the lion and the serpent, by the might of Christ, who will make me victorious, and I will

B.   17

say, "All mine enemies shall be put to shame and shall suffer disgrace; they shall be put to shame, and shall depart afar speedily[1]." And Yĕwâsĕf was protected wholly with the Sign of the Cross, the armour which is invincible, and he reduced to nothingness all the devilish [p. 229] devices of the Liar, and straightway the wild beasts and jackals disappeared even as smoke disappeareth, and as wax melteth away when it is brought near the fire even so did they vanish from sight.

And the saint was strong in the might of Christ, and he rejoiced and gave thanks unto God. Nevertheless that desert was seen to be full of herds of wild beasts, and vipers of various kinds, and families of serpents of various appearances and sorts, and the roads through it were filled with fear and terror [for the wayfarer]; but the saint flew over beasts and vipers alike on wings. And as for the terror and fear [they departed from him], according to the verse of the Book, "Love driveth out terror, and as for fear affection maketh it to fly away[2]." and in this wise Yĕwâsĕf fought the fight against hosts of tortures and tribulations for many days.

[*How Yĕwâsĕf wandered about in a parched and fiery desert for two years seeking for Baralâm, and how a pious monk guided him to his cell.*]

And then he came to that desert which is in Sînâ'or wherein Baralâm dwelt, and he found water therein and extinguished therewith the flame of his thirst. And Yĕwâsĕf dwelt in this desert for two years, and he wandered about therein, but he did not find Baralâm—now I think that God was putting to the test the strength of his mind, and the courage of his soul. And he dwelt in the open air. In the daytime the heat of the flame of the sun burned him, and in the night season he froze and shrivelled up with the cold; and he used to search for the glorious old man Baralâm with exceedingly great diligence at all times, like a man who was seeking a treasure of great price. And very many trials came upon him, and many evil spirits

---

[1] Psalm xxxv. 4, 5.　　　　[2] 1 John iv. 18.

made war upon him, and he suffered great privation through
the want of the green herbs whereon he used to live, for they
had withered altogether therein, and there was no green plant
there which was like them. Nevertheless this Christian soul,
which was invincible, burned with great desire [for Christ],
and it suffered gladly, and for this reason it was not put to
shame by supernatural visions. And when two years were
ended Saint Yĕwâsĕf still wandered about ceaselessly seeking
for him the sight of whom he desired, and he made supplication to [p. 230] God, and he shed tears, the tears flowing like
the stream of a river, and he cried out, saying, "O my Lord
and my God, show Thou unto me the man who was the cause
of my learning to know Thee, and of my learning to know these
good things. I have lost him by reason of the multitude of my
sins, but, O Lord, do not permit me to lack this gracious thing,
and make Thou me worthy to see him, and to carry on the
fight of the ascetic life in the same way and to the same degree as he hath done."

And under the guidance of God Yĕwâsĕf found a cell wherein
were footprints of those who travelled along that road, and he
found there a certain monk who was wont to go up and down
through the desert, and he fell upon [his neck] with lowliness of heart, and he kissed him, and he asked him, saying,
"Where shall I find Baralâm?" And he told him his business
and explained to him [his desire], and from that monk he
learned where was the habitation of him whom he sought, and
he found it quickly after the manner of the skilful hunter, who
findeth the track of the prey which he is hunting, and he
recognised the description whereby he knew the old man.
And he went on his way rejoicing in his hope, like a strong
young man who is waiting in hope to see his father after [a
separation of] many years, for when the love of God dwelleth
in the soul it addeth greatly to the natural strength, and
magnifieth its power to do things.

[How Yĕwâsĕf found the abode of Baralâm, how the two holy men embraced each other and rejoiced in their re- union.]

And straightway Yĕwâsĕf stood at the door of the cell of Baralâm, and he knocked thereat, saying, " Bless, O father, bless ! " And when Baralâm heard his voice he went forth from the cell, and through the spirit he recognized Yĕwâsĕf, whom he would not otherwise have been able to recognize quickly, because his appearance was greatly changed from what it had been formerly ; for the face of the young man, which had been like that of a flower and had been radiant with beauty, had become black through the heat of the sun and the cold of the night. Hair had grown over all the members of his body ; his cheeks resembled the burnt-out ashes of a fire, his eyes were bloodshot(?)and seemed to be sunk in holes which were hollowed [in his head], his eyelashes had been burnt away through weeping, and he was in a most emaciated condition. And Yĕwâsĕf knew [his] father in the spirit, and he knew that it was he of a certainty because of the condition in which he lived. And straightway the old man rose up, and turned his face towards the east, and he sent forth prayer to God, and offered up thanksgiving unto Him and made supplication unto Him. [p. 231] And after he had made an end of his prayer and had said "Amen," the two men embraced each other, and they kissed each other, and each paid spiritual honour unto the other with the strength of old affection which was inexhaustible ; and when they had embraced each other for a long time they sat down and began to talk together. And the old man Baralâm said unto Yĕwâsĕf, " Indeed how wonderful is thy coming, O beloved son, thou son of God, and heir of the kingdom of the heavens through our Lord Jesus Christ, Whom thou hast loved, and Whom thou hast desired, and for Whom thou hast prepared thyself, very rightly, from times of old ! Thou art like the wise and understanding rich man, for thou hast sold everything which thou hadst, and didst buy the glorious pearl which is priceless ; and thou hast discovered the treasure which cannot be stolen, and which is hidden in the field of the commandments of God[1]. And thou hast given everything which thou didst possess of transitory things, which pass away quickly, so that thou mightest buy this field for thyself; and similarly God giveth unto thee the things that endure in the place of those that pass away, and the things that never grow old in the place of those that do decay, and thy days shall not come to an end. Tell me now, O beloved son, how it is that thou hast come hither, and tell me what hath happened unto thee since my departure, and whether thy father hath learned to know God, or whether he liveth to this day in his former folly and under the captivity and seduction of Satan."

[*How Yĕwâsĕf related to Baralâm all that had happened since he had withdrawn himself to the desert, and how the two holy men dwelt together for many years.*]

And when Baralâm had said this unto him, Yĕwâsĕf the king began to relate unto him everything which had happened after his departure from him, and how God protected him until the moment of their meeting together. And the old man listened with the greatest pleasure, and he marvelled [at the narrative], and said, "Praise be unto Thee, O our God, Who dost at all times support those who love Thee, and dost give them help. Praise be unto Thee, O Christ, King of the Universe, and Lord of all good things, because Thou hast been pleased with my seed which I sowed in the soul of thy servant Yĕwâsĕf, and hast made it to bring forth fruit an hundred-fold, and because Thou hast made him worthy of this, O Husbandman and Lord. Praise be unto Thee, O Good Spirit, Who art perfect in holiness and grace, and dost bestow grace upon Thy servants the saints [p. 232], and Who hast made Thy servant Yĕwâsĕf meet for this [state of life]. And through him Thou hast set free from the error of the worship of idols many men, and Thou hast illumined their hearts with the knowledge of the light of Thy Godhead which is the Godhead indeed."

[1] Matt. xiii. 44, 46.

And in this wise Baralâm and Yĕwâsĕf sat and held converse together, and they rejoiced in the grace of God. And
the evening of the day arrived, and they rose up to prayer,
and they performed the customary acts of worship, and
after this they remembered their food, and Baralâm brought
forward a glorious table which was full of the food [suitable]
for the life of the spirit. And as for that which appeared
upon it there was nothing except some raw herbs, which the
old man shredded and rubbed down together, and a few
clusters of wild figs which he had gathered in that desert,
and some wild herbs of the desert; and they gave many
hearty thanks to God, and then they ate. And when they
had eaten their portion they drank water from the spring
which was nigh unto them, and gave thanks again unto Him
of the Extended Hand, Who satisfieth all the beasts with
food. And they rose up again, and they finished the prayer
for the night, and then they began to converse on spiritual
matters, and after praying they talked with the words of
salvation, which were full of every kind of heavenly wisdom,
all night long, until the day broke; and love made them to
forget the remembrance of their customary prayer.

And Yĕwâsĕf dwelt for many years with Baralâm, who fought
the marvellous fight, which was above the nature of beings of
flesh, and like a father admonished everyone with lowliness
and humility. And Yĕwâsĕf brought forth fruit to him, and
he ran the course and performed the work of spiritual excellences, and he was admonished by the patient endurance
derived from the fightings against invisible evil spirits. And
because of this he conquered lusts and slew them all, and he
brought into subjection the appetite of the body and the
mind of the spirit, [making them] like a servant before his
master, and he forgot entirely pleasure of every kind and
rest; and on the days wherein the body served him like a
wicked servant, he used to call him with his voice to come
[p. 233] [and obey]. And in this way he fought the fight of
the ascetic life [with such success] that at length Baralâm,
who had endured that life for many years, marvelled at him,

and was overcome at the sight of his patiently-enduring resistance. And in this manner he lived on the dry and tasteless
food, which was scarcely able to support life in him and to
keep him from actually dying, so that he might not lose the
reward of the beauty of his works. Moreover he forced his
natural constitution to keep vigil as if he possessed neither
[human] nature nor body; and his mind was occupied ceaselessly with the work of praying and with the operations of
the mental man. And he passed the days of his life in the
seeing of heavenly and spiritual visions, which never ceased,
either for an hour or during the twinkling of an eye, from
the time he took up his abode in that desert. This was the
man who walked in the ordinances of the true monastic life,
and there was no cessation of his spiritual working, which
was without blemish. This man was bold of heart, and he
was a true apostle who travelled to the resting-places on the
heavenly paths, and who preserved fervour of heart unex-
hausted from the beginning even unto the end thereof; and
he was ever constant in purpose, and went on from strength
to strength. And what was more sublime than this, he added
love to love, and he constantly increased his vigilance over
himself until he arrived at the beatitude that he loved and
longed for.

[*How the time for Baralâm's death drew nigh, and how he
bade farewell to Yĕwâsĕf, and counselled him to continue to
practise the ascetic life in that desert.*]

And thus Baralâm and Yĕwâsĕf dwelt together in happiness
unmoved by any worldly feeling, and each strove lovingly to
outvie the other in spiritual excellence, and their hearts were
free from disorder, and confusion, and the association with
excessive weariness because they were happy in their worship.
And one day the old man called his son in the spirit, whom
he had begotten by the preaching of the Gospel, and he held
converse with him on spiritual matters, and he said unto him
as before, "O Yĕwâsĕf, beloved one, it is meet for thee to
dwell in this desert. Whilst I was praying my Lord Jesus

Christ promised me this thing concerning thee, that I should see thee before my death in this life, and behold, I [p. 234] now see that which I have longed [to see]. And I see thee separated from the world, and from everything which is in the world, and thou hast drawn nigh unto Christ, with a heart wherein is no doubt, and thou hast arrived at the limit of the perfect end. And now, since the time of my departure hath arrived, the habit of desire being associated with me and resisting me, behold, I am going to depart so that I may be with Christ for ever. Behold, do thou carry out the burying of my body, and place dust with dust, and do thou live on in this place. And do thou continue the spiritual fight, and set thou the memorial of my humbleness [in thy mind] at the time of thy prayer, for I am afraid of the multitude of the devils of darkness, lest peradventure they be raised up as stumblingblocks for my soul because of the greatness of my folly.

"O my son, be not thou grieved by the sufferings of the ascetic life, and be not dismayed either because of the length of the time [of its duration], or because of the wiles of Satan; but be thou strong in the might of Christ to resist their infirmities, and do thou scoff at them arrogantly. And in the face of the rigour of tribulation be thou like a man who is always awaiting departure from this world, and that day shall be unto thee as the beginning of the working of thy toil and the ending thereof. Thus do thou live always, forgetting that which is behind thee and pressing on to that which is before thee (being a witness publicly) which is the mark of the reception of the high calling of God in Christ Jesus, even as the glorious Apostle saith[1]. Be not dismayed, O brother, if the external man wax old. Behold, that which is within thee shall be renewed from day to day, for a little sorrow that is over and above the limit will produce for us the honour that shall endure for ever. Let not our desire be directed to that which is visible, for that which is visible appertaineth to time, and that which is invisible endureth for ever. And when thou

[1] Phil. iii. 13, 14.

meditatest thus be bold, and be strong, and become a valiant soldier; take good heed that thou becomest fit to be a soldier. And if the devil of deceit hath brought unto thee thought that is disturbed, take good heed to thyself that thou dost not overthrow the strength of thy mind, and consider carefully [p. 235] the commandment of God which saith, 'Fear ye not his crafty devices. For in this world needs must that ye shall suffer sorrow, but be ye strong, for I have overcome the world[1].'

"And for this reason rejoice in God continually, for He hath chosen thee, and He hath honoured thee [by choosing thee] out of the world, and He hath set thee before Him, and because of this He hath called thee with a holy calling for ever. He is nigh unto thee; take thought for nothing, but in every prayer and supplication have confidence, and give thanks unto God at the time when thou makest thy supplication[2], for He Himself saith, 'I will never leave thee nor forsake thee[3].'" And after this manner do thou think when the spiritual fight becometh difficult, and thy ascetic life of contemplation is disturbed, and rejoice thou in remembering the Lord our God, for he saith, 'I remembered God and rejoiced[4].' And again, if the Adversary dealeth craftily with thee by means of another kind of warfare, and bringeth unto thee thoughts of pride, and showeth unto thee the glory of a kingdom of this world, and all kinds of worldly glory which thou hast rejected, make thou to thyself a breastplate the redeeming word, like a shield, of Him Who said, 'If ye do the work which I command you, say ye, we are lazy servants[5].' For that which is meet for us to do we have done, but we are unable to fulfil that which we ought to do of the commandments of our Creator, Who being rich made Himself poor for our sakes, and suffered in order that He might set us free from suffering. What glory hath a servant if he suffereth even as his master suffered? And as for us we fall very far short of Him in His sufferings. In this wise do thou think in respect of every doubt and

---

[1] John xvi. 33.   [2] Phil. iv. 6.   [3] Hebrews xiii. 5.
[4] Psalms ix. 2; xcvii. 12; Isaiah xxv. 9.   [5] Luke xvii. 10.

every [thought] of pride which magnifieth itself above the knowledge of God. And do thou carry captive all [thy] thoughts to Christ, and be subject unto Him, and bring them to God, Who is exalted beyond all conception, Who shall protect thy heart and all thy mind in Christ Jesus. Amen."

[How Yĕwâsĕf wept and entreated Baralâm to pray to God and to obtain His permission to take him out of this world.]

And when the blessed man Baralâm said these things it was impossible to find the bottom of the limitless flood of tears which Yĕwâsĕf shed, nay, he was like unto a fountain of water wherein are many springs, and [p. 236] he watered his whole body with them and the ground whereon he was sitting. And he lamented bitterly and made supplication unto God that he might journey with him (i.e. Baralâm) on the path of the blessed ones, and that he might not be left in the world after him. And he said unto Baralâm, "O my father, why dost thou seek rest for thyself only and not for thy companion? How will perfect love be made perfect by this? For it is said, 'Love thy neighbour as thyself[1],' and yet thou art departing into rest and art leaving me here in sorrow and misery! I was not trained in my early days to fight the spiritual fight of the ascetic life, and I did not learn betimes concerning the spiritual fights [with devils], nor about their excessive fatigues, and behold, thou wouldst leave me to wage war against them. There is nothing at all left to happen unto me except to fall down beneath their evil craftiness and to die the death of the soul for ever. Woe be unto me, wretched man that I am! for behold, there shall come upon me that which came upon the monks who were called and who were not tempted. But I beseech thee to entreat God to take me with thee, and that I may depart from this world, yea, beseech Him Who rewardeth [every man] in proportion to his work. I beseech thee that I may not dwell in the world even for one day after my separation from thee, and I wish not to wander about in this desert."

[1] Matt. xix. 19.

[How Baralâm showed Yĕwâsĕf that he had not followed the ascetic life long enough to be allowed to die with him, and that it was God's Will that he should remain in the world until he was nearly one hundred years old.]

And when Yĕwâsĕf said this, now he was weeping as he spake, the old man said unto him quietly and with sedateness, "O my son, it is undesirable for thee to resist the judgement of God which cannot be searched out. I have made many supplications to God about this matter, and I have learned from His goodness that it would not benefit thee to cast aside at this moment the burden of the flesh; and thou must endure patiently and quietly [a while] so that He may weave for thee crowns of light. For up to the present thou hast not fought the spiritual fight sufficiently to deserve the great reward which is prepared for thee, and it is meet for thee to toil a little [longer], and then thou shalt come rejoicing into the joy of thy Lord. Behold, at this moment my days are nearly one hundred years, and I have lived in this desert for fully five and seventy years. As for thee, although the allotted space of thy days shall not be as long as that, [p. 237] still it shall approach it, even as God hath commanded, so that thou mayest be the equal of those men and in no wise separated from them who have borne the burden of the day and the heat thereof. Accept thou then with gladness, O my beloved, that [duty] which is well pleasing to God, for there is no man who can control His Will. Endure patiently, and take good heed to thyself by His grace, and watch thou constantly against the thoughts that war against the purity of thy mind, even as thou wouldst watch a treasure of great price; guard thou it from being stolen away, and make thy soul to take refuge in the seeing of spiritual visions. And do thou mount upward day by day, so that in thee may be fulfilled that which our Redeemer promised to His holy ones, saying, 'If there be anyone who shall love and shall keep My word, We will come to him and make a place of rest with him[1].' "

[1] John xiv. 23.

[*How Baralâm administered the Eucharist to Yĕwâsĕf, and addressed further words of consolation to him.*]

And when the old man had said these things and very many others like unto them to Yĕwâsĕf, with holy sorrow of mind, and with a tongue that declared holy things, the sorrowful soul of Yĕwâsĕf was comforted. And the old man sent him also to the brethren whose abode was far away, to bring the things that were necessary for celebrating the Office of the Eucharist, and Yĕwâsĕf went with diligence, and he made haste and fulfilled the mission on which he had been sent, for he was afraid lest Baralâm should die [during his absence]. He was not like any other man, and he could not commit his spirit to God, so that it might not be destroyed, until he had heard Baralâm's voice, and had been received into his charge, and had been prayed over by him and had received his blessing. And thus he departed willingly on that far journey, and he brought back that which was necessary for the celebration of the Eucharist. And the glorious old man Baralâm celebrated the service of God, and he himself partook of the Holy Mysteries of Christ, and gave them to Yĕwâsĕf, and he rejoiced in the Holy Spirit. And they continued to live according to their wont, and Baralâm nourished Yĕwâsĕf also on the words of the teaching which was beneficial for the soul, and he said unto him, "O beloved son, henceforth we must not collect anything whatsoever in this world, and we must feed at one table, for behold, [p. 238] I am about to depart by the road of my fathers. It is meet for thee to make manifest thy love for me by keeping the commandments of God, and by thy patient endurance unto the end in this place, according to the ordinances which thou dost know and which thou hast learned, remembering always my feeble and wretched soul. And now, rejoice with gladness, and be glad in the joy of Christ. For thou hast preferred the things that abide for ever and that do not pass away in the place of the earthly things that perish. Behold, come, receive the wages of thy labour, and take thy reward; behold, He hath appeared and hath now come that He may see the vineyard in which thou hast worked. And His word is true, and His promise is sure, even as Paul saith, 'If we die with Him we shall live with Him, and if we endure patiently we shall reign with Him[1]' in the kingdom which is everlasting and which shall not come to an end. And we shall shine with a light that one cannot look at, and that is impalpable, and we shall be worthy of the illumination of the Trinity, the beginning of everything, the beginning of praise in truth."

[How Baralâm prayed his last prayer.]

And with these and such like words did Baralâm converse throughout the night with Yĕwâsĕf, who uttered cries of lamentation and shed floods of tears, and could not bear the separation from him. And when the day became bright Baralâm made an end of discoursing with him, and he stretched out his hands towards the heavens, and lifted up his eyes, and he magnified God and gave thanks unto Him, saying, "O Lord, my God, Who art in every place, and Whom everyone feareth, I give thanks unto Thee because Thou hast looked upon my feebleness, and Thou hast held me to be worthy to finish my course in this world in Thy True Faith, in the way of Thy commandments. And now, O Thou Lover of what is good, Thou God Whose loving kindness is perfect, receive Thou me into Thine everlasting tabernacle. Remember not all the transgressions which I have committed against Thee, wittingly and [p. 239] unwittingly. And do Thou protect this Thy faithful servant, whom Thou hast held myself, Thy servant, to be worthy to bring unto Thee as an offering, and deliver him from all the wiles of Satan, and make him victorious over the many snares that the Evil One will spread out in order to trip up those who wish to be saved. Give unto him power, O Mighty One, over every being of guile, and drive him away from before the face of Thy servant. And give unto him dominion so that he may trample upon the head of the Enemy, the begetter of destruction and the destroyer of

---

[1] 2 Tim. ii. 11, 12.

souls. And send Thou down upon him from above the grace of the Holy Spirit, and give him power to wage war [victoriously] against the beings who are invisible, so that he may be worthy of and may receive from Thee the crowns of victory. And may Thy Name be glorious upon him, O Father, and Son, and Holy Spirit, One God, for unto Thee are meet praise and glory for ever and ever! Amen."

[*How Yĕwâsĕf prepared the body of Baralâm for burial, and how he dug a grave for it near his own cell and buried him in it.*]

And when Baralâm had said this, he kissed Yĕwâsĕf as a father kisseth his son and gave him the salutation of peace with a holy embrace. And he sealed himself with the Sign or the Cross, and he departed with joy and gladness as one who goeth to a company of men who are making merry, happily and with satisfaction. He who was indeed an old man, and had brought to an end his days in spiritual excellence, departed to receive the wages of the glory everlasting. And Yĕwâsĕt fell upon his father weeping, and he bade him farewell with groaning and tears. And he washed his dead body and wrapped it up for burial in the ragged hair-cloth garment which he had given him when he was in his royal palace, and he rolled him up in it. And he recited over it all day long and all night long the Psalms which are duly appointed, and as he sang he watered the honourable body of the blessed man with his tears. And on the following day he dug a grave near his cell with a willing heart, and he carried thither the pure body of the spiritual priest, and buried it with great honour. And his soul burned like fire, and he devoted himself unto prayer with great vigour, and he said, " O Lord, I beseech Thee with my whole heart, and my soul entreateth Thee, not to turn [p. 240] Thy face from me, and be not wroth with Thy servant; be Thou my Helper, put me not far from Thee, and go not Thou far from me, O my Lord and my Redeemer, for my father and my mother cast me away, and Thou, O Lord, didst receive me. Teach Thou me the way of Thy commandments, and teach

Thou me the path of Thy truth because of mine enemies. Deliver not my soul over unto those who would torture me, for upon Thee have I cast myself, and with Thee have I taken refuge. From my mother's womb Thou hast been my God. Be not Thou far from me, for I have no helper except Thee, and in the multitude of Thy mercies hath my soul put her confidence, O Thou Director of all creation, Thou Who in Thine ineffable watching and wisdom art the storehouse of my life. Make Thou me to know how to walk therein, and deliver Thou me, for Thou art the Good God and art the Lover of men, through the prayer and entreaty of Baralâm, who pleased Thee. For Thou art my God, and Thee do I praise, O Father, and Son, and Holy Spirit."

[*How Yĕwâsĕf saw in a vision the heavenly city, and how the angels showed him the crowns of himself and his father, and how the spirit of Baralâm rebuked him for his thoughts concerning his father's crown.*]

And when Yĕwâsĕf had finished his prayer, he sat down near the grave weeping. And whilst he was sitting [there] he fell asleep, and he saw in his sleep the same august beings whom he had seen when they came to him on a former occasion. And they showed him that great and marvellous city, and they brought him into a great and splendid palace, whereof the beauty was different from that of every other building. And when he went in through the doors other beings, who were shining very brightly with light, received him, and they had in their hands crowns which sparkled with light of indescribable brightness, the like of which the eye of man hath never seen. And Yĕwâsĕf asked them, saying, "For whom are these splendid crowns which appear to me to surpass in beauty every other thing?" And they answered and said unto him, "One hath been prepared for thee because of the multitude of souls whom thou hast saved. And behold, thou shalt see [one] which is more [splendid] than this, because of the life of devotion to God which thou hast led, provided that thou dost finish [thy course]. And this other crown is prepared for thee so that thou mayest prepare it for thy father who, through thee, turned from the evil path and repented with heartfelt repentance to God." [p. 241] And this matter was hard to Yĕwâsĕf, and he said, "How can my father receive a reward like myself, who have toiled with such severe toil? And how can his repentance be considered equal to my toil?" And when he said this Baralâm appeared unto him, and he rebuked him, saying, "O Yĕwâsĕf, did not I say unto thee some time ago, 'If thou hast found great riches do not be greedy?' and thou didst marvel at my words on that occasion. And now, why should it be grievous unto thee if thy father's honour is equal to thine own? Shouldst not thou rejoice in spirit at the news that thy numerous supplications concerning it have been heard?" And Yĕwâsĕf, as was his wont, said unto him, "Forgive me, O my father, forgive me, and make thou me to know in what place thou art dwelling." And Baralâm answered and said unto him, "Behold, I am permitted to dwell in this city of surpassing beauty, inside of which is a magnificent splendour which cannot be defined." And Yĕwâsĕf entreated Baralâm to take him to his abode, and to receive him into happiness. And Baralâm said unto him, "Hitherto the time hath not arrived for thee to come to these habitations, for the burden of the flesh is still upon thee. If thou wilt endure patiently and perform thy service in fear, even as I have commanded thee, thou shalt come [hither] after a little space, and thou shalt be worthy of this abode. And thou shalt find this glory and joy, and they shall be with thee continually for ever."

[How Yĕwâsĕf continued to lead a life of stern self-denial, and how, by fasting and prayer, he acquired superhuman power to resist temptations and to fight the devils.]

And Yĕwâsĕf awoke from his sleep, and his soul was filled with that light and glory, and he marvelled exceedingly, and he ascribed exaltation and glory to God and gave thanks unto Him; and he was wholly strong and was perfect in following the course of life which was indeed Divine. And after the departure of the honourable old man Baralâm he multiplied exceedingly his labours in the life of asceticism and contemplation. In the thirty-fifth year of the days of his life he forsook [his] earthly kingdom, and entered into the spiritual fight of the ascetic life. For five and thirty years he lived the ascetic life in a remote desert, like a man who had no body, and he fought the spiritual fight and led a life of self-denial and renunciation which was beyond the nature of the children of men. And, above everything in importance, [p. 242] he delivered many souls from the mouth of the Serpent, the destroyer of souls, and he brought them as an offering to God, Who saveth those who ask Him [to do so]. And he confessed Christ before kings and governors without shame, and he rose up and became a great apostle and preacher, and he was loud of voice in proclaiming the greatness of God. And after this, that is to say, the renunciation of the kingdom, he departed into the desert, and he fought the fight with many spirits whose wickednesses were of divers kinds, and by the might of Christ he conquered them all. And he obtained favour, and the report of him was noised abroad, and he acquired the sublime gift of Divine Grace, and because of this the eye of his soul became averted from all earthly darknesses, and he saw the things that were to come after as if they had actually happened. And Christ took the place of everything to him, and he was crucified in the love of Christ, and he saw Him existing before his face, and he rejoiced continually in the beauty of Christ, even as saith the Prophet, "I see God continually, He is before me at all times ; He is at my right hand so that I shall not be moved[1]." And again he saith, "My soul followeth after Thee, Thy right hand receiveth me[2]." Verily his soul followed after the Lord Christ, and it clung to Him with a hold that could not be shaken off. And he never changed in this marvellous work, and he never changed in the rule of his ascetic and contemplative life, from the beginning even unto the end thereof ; and he took heed to the body from the days of his youth to the period of his old age. Each day he increased his gain and his exaltation through performing works of excel-

[1] Psalm xvi. 8.　　　[2] Psalm lxiii. 8.

B.　　　　　　　　　　　　　　　　　　　　　　　18

lence, and each day he saw far more of the things that are
hidden than he had seen before.

[*How Yĕwâsĕf died and how a holy man, being warned in a
vision, went and found his body and buried it in Baralâm's
grave.*]

And he journeyed on this road, and he gave to Him Who
called him work which resembled that of Him Who called him.
He crucified the world because of himself, and he crucified
himself because of the world ; thus he journeyed in peace to
the God of peace. He departed to God for Whom he longed
continually. He stood before the face of God in purity, in the
innermost part of the canopy, without restraint. And Christ
adorned him with a crown in the Other World, and He made
him worthy to see the Lord Christ, and to be with Him, and
he rejoiceth continually in the [p. 243] beauty of the Lord
Christ, in the place where is the abode of His messenger
Baralâm, unto whom Yĕwâsĕf committed the charge of his
soul when he was in this world. He departed to the country
of the living where live the lords (?), and where abide all those
who rejoice.

As for his honourable body, a certain man who used to live
near him, a holy man who previously had lodged him when
he was searching for Baralâm, saw a Divine vision, and knew
of the death of the blessed Yĕwâsĕf at that moment. And he
went there and praised him with great praise, and shed very
many tears as a mark of his love ; and he pronounced over
his body all the Christian sentences of burial, and placed him
in the grave of his father Baralâm. Now they had wished that
their bodies should dwell together. Then there appeared unto
that anchorite in a dream a being of majestic form, and he
commanded him with commands that frightened and terrified
him ; and the anchorite awoke in trepidation, and undertook
to do what he had told him.

[How the holy man went to India and reported the death of Yĕwâsĕf to King Barâsĕyâs, and described his spiritual fight; and how the king went to the grave of Baralâm and Yĕwâsĕf and transported their bodies to his capital, and how miracles were wrought at their tomb.]

And he departed to the kingdom of Hend (India), and he went into the presence of King Barâsĕyâs, and told him everything that had happened in the matter of Yĕwâsĕf, the blessed man, and informed him concerning his whole story. And King Barâsĕyâs delayed not, but departed straightway with many horsemen, and came to the cave, and saw the grave, and he wept over it with a burning heart. And he drew back the covering and he saw the dead bodies of Baralâm and Yĕwâsĕf, and he found the limbs in the same state as they were in the days long ago ; and their forms and appearance were not changed in the least degree, and their bodies were in a perfect and sound state, together with their apparel. And having found their bodies in a perfect and sound state, he discovered also that a sweet odour sprang from them and from their apparel, and that neither decay nor corruption had appeared in them. And the king straightway commanded his soldiers to put them into splendid cases, and he took them to his city. And when the people heard the report of them they came from every city and district so that they might worship God, [p. 244] and they saw those holy bodies and they praised [God] before them with many praises. And they lighted many oil lamps and candles in honour, and with joy, and with great sorrow ; and they laid those cases in the church, which Yĕwâsĕf had built there some time before, with much sweet incense and perfumes, according to what was meet for their burial ; for the death of the children of light maketh the children of light and their heirs to rejoice. And as to the healings that appeared—in some cases He healed the demoniacs, and in others He illumined the eyes of the blind, and cured the paralytics, and drove off unclean spirits from men—who is able to count them?—and they all found that they were whole.

And when these people and all the nations saw that God worked signs and wonders, which were beyond the powers of the understanding of the human mind, by His saints, and His messengers, and His righteous men, and that they were made manifest at their tombs, their faith was very greatly increased and they praised God exceedingly. And when besides they heard the story of the spiritual fight of the righteous man Yĕwâsĕf, who desired that it should be like unto that of the sage Baralâm, they glorified God Who had been with him from his youth up. And they were greatly astonished, and they gave thanks unto God, Who at all times enricheth those who love Him, and Who giveth unto them a very great and special reward, and double gifts—to Whom be glory, and honour, and worship, throughout all ages. Amen and Amen.

Here endeth [the history of] the spiritual fight of Saints Baralâm and Yĕwâsĕf. In the peace of God. Amen.

COLOPHON

The completion [of this copy] took place on the day of the blessed eve of the Sabbath, on the fourth day of the month of Khĕdâr in the twelve hundred and thirty-third year of the Era of the Holy Martyrs. May their blessing protect our King Galâwĕdêwôs, and all of us who are his servants! Amen.

I make supplication in spiritual love to him who shall read it (i.e. this book) to remember [in his prayers] me the lacking, poor, and rejected slave, who by reason of his sins and iniquities is unworthy to be called a man, Barsôm, the son of Abu l' Faraj, so that God may have mercy upon him, and may forgive the multitude of his sins, and transgressions, and errors, and stumblings, and may give rest to [his soul and to] the souls of his progenitors, and children, and kinsfolk, and may forgive him his omissions, and his incapacity, and the feebleness of his style and of his writing, for there is no scribe who doth not make omissions. And pray a little for the translator, because of his ignorance of the tongue, that God may reward him also, even as it saith in the Holy Gospel, "With the measure wherewith ye measure they shall measure to you[1]." We beseech Thee, O our Lord Jesus Christ, that Thou wilt help us to do what we have learned, and that which hath been laid upon us by command. And strengthen our old men, and keep our young men, and protect our women, that they may bring up our children in purity and goodness. And grant unto us confidence, and peace, and safety in our cities, and make our judges to give right judgement (?), and may God make long the days of the kingdom of our lord, and ruler, and governor, the sovereign Ruler, honourable and good, Galâwĕdêwôs, and may He bestow victory upon him, and his nobles and his army, whether they be on the march or in camp, and bring him back in peace to his flock. And may He likewise

---

[1] Matt. vii. 2.

preserve us, and lengthen over us the rule of our father, and chief, and shepherd, the father [in] God, great one among the Archbishops, Abbâ John, and may He make us obedient children of his and save us by his prayer. And may He make us worthy of a great share through the intercession of the Lady of Intercession, the Treasury of purity and blessing, the Virgin Mary, Mârîhâm, the pure and holy one, and of Mâr Mark, the preacher to the towns and villages of Egypt, and of all the Martyrs and the Saints, and the Angels who are near, and of all those who have pleased Him, and of those whom He hath made to please Him by their good works. Amen and Amen.

THE PREACHING OF SAINT THOMAS
IN INDIA

[B 231*b* 2] In the Name of the Father, and of the Son, and of the Holy Spirit. [One God.]

Here beginneth the Book of the Preaching of Saint Thomas the Apostle of our Lord Jesus Christ, which he preached in the Country of India. In the peace of our Lord! Amen.

A = Brit. Mus. MS. Oriental No. 678 ; B = Brit. Mus. MS. Oriental No. 683.

And it came to pass that, after the Resurrection of our Lord Jesus Christ from the dead, He appeared unto His holy disciples, and said unto them, "The peace of My Father [A 119 b 1] be with you. What He gave Me I have not hidden from you. Gather yourselves together, and divide ye the world into twelve portions, and let each one of you go unto his portion. And fear ye not, for I will be with you. I know everything which shall come upon you, both the suffering and the tribulation which ye shall endure from men in this world. But bear ye patiently with them, for at length ye shall bring them back from error unto faith in My Name. And remember ye the sufferings which came upon [B 232a 1] Me, and everything which was done unto Me for the sake of the children of men."

Now the lot went forth to Thomas to go unto the country of India. And he bowed down before the Lord, and said unto Him, "Why hath the lot gone forth that I should go unto the country of India? The people thereof are as strong as wild beasts, and their hearts are too hard to hear the Word of the Gospel ; but be Thou [A 119 b 2] with me, O my Lord, in that country." And our Lord said unto him, "Behold, Peter shall guide thee, and he shall go forth with thee into that country." Then all the Apostles made ready to go forth, each one of them unto the country which had fallen to him by lot, and Peter was going forth unto the city of Rome and the regions round about it, and Matthias unto the country of Persia. And Thomas said unto Peter, "O my father, rise up and go with me and my brother Matthias until [B 232a 2] thou hast brought us unto our countries." And Peter said unto him, "I will"; and he went forth with them. And our Lord went up from them into heaven with great glory.

And when they had journeyed for forty days, they came unto a city which was half way to the regions wherein Thomas and Matthias had been decreed by lot to preach the Gospel. And as they were about to enter the city they sat down [A 120a 1] on the high road to the city like travellers. And our Lord Jesus Christ appeared unto them in the garb of an ascetic(?), and He said unto them, "Peace be unto you, O brethren"; and they said unto Him, "And upon Thee also be peace"; and He sat down near unto them on their right side. Then Thomas said unto Peter, "O my father, let us enter into this city and preach therein in the Name of God, for it is the first city to which we have come; peradventure we shall be able to save the people and to bring them back unto the rule of [B 232b 1] God. For God said: Whosoever shall preach in a great city and shall save many men shall have great reward in the kingdom of heaven."

Now whilst they were sitting down there came unto them a certain officer[1] [A 120a 2] of Ḳanṭûkôrôs[2] ቀንጡቆርስ፡, King of India. And he looked at the Apostles as they were seated like travellers, and he said unto them, "Whence are ye, O brethren?" And they said unto him, "Ask what ye desire," and he said unto them, "It is not evil but good. I see that ye are men of goodly stature, and I want to buy a slave who shall be like you." Peter said unto him, "We are three

---

[1] According to the Greek he was called Ἀββάνης, Arab. حَبَّان, Syr. ܢܒܢ.

[2] Gr. Γουνδαφόρος, or Ὑνδοφέρης; old Persian Viñdafra. Gundaforus is, undoubtedly, the king of Parthian descent who reigned over Areia, Drangiana, and Arachosia in the 1st century of our Era; see Lipsius, *Apostelgeschichten*, vol. I. p. 279.

servants of One God, Whose Name is Jesus Christ. He is coming to this country and when He hath come He will sell to you whichever of us thou desirest. Our country is healthy, and all those who dwell in the regions thereof are of goodly stature." Now our Lord Himself was listening to what they were [B 232b 2] saying to each other, and straightway He appeared before them, and speaking unto them in the language which [A 120b 1] they understood, said unto them, "Peace be unto you, ye believers, O noble Peter, and Thomas, and Matthias the meek. Behold, I know you, for I am never absent from you, but am with you always. Behold, I have come, even as I promised you, and I will go before you unto every place whithersoever ye shall go." Now although the officer of the King of India was close to them he could not understand the words which our Lord spake to them.

And after this our Lord appeared unto the Apostles in the garb of a rich man, and He sat down inside the city. And the Apostles said unto the king's officer, "Behold our Master about Whose coming we informed thee ; decide which one of us thou wantest, and He will sell him to thee." And the king's officer said unto our Lord, "Peace be unto Thee, O nobleman. Thy fame and Thy [A 120b 2] garb [B 233a 1] proclaim Thy nobility. Wilt Thou sell me one of these men ? " And our Lord said unto him, "Which shall I sell thee ? This, the eldest, is a native of a great country, and him I cannot sell thee." And the king's officer looked at Thomas, and approved of him, for his body was strong and powerful, and he said unto our Lord, "Sell me this slave of Thine." Our Lord said unto him, " His price is three *arṭâl*[1] ኣርጣሊ of gold"; and the officer said unto Him, "I have bought him from Thee." And he paid Him His price, and said unto our Lord. "Write me a deed of sale, according to the custom of the country." And our Lord said unto him, "Seek not for a scribe to write the deed for thee, for I Myself will write it, and I will declare [A 121a 1] therein

---

[1] Arab. أَرْطَال. The *roṭl* = 144 dirhams = ·99 lb. The Syriac Version (ed. Wright, p. 173) has "twenty pieces of silver."

that I have sold unto thee 'Arbâsôs ኦረበሰሰ, an officer of Gundaforus, King of India, this My slave." And He finished writing the deed of sale as the officer desired, and then went up from them in great [B 232a 2] glory.

After this our Lord appeared unto Thomas, and said unto him, "Take the price of thy sale and divide it among the poor and the needy, and the widows and the orphans in the place whither thou art going. I sold thee for three *arṭâl* of gold because thou art the servant of the Holy Trinity of the Father, and the Son and the Holy Ghost." And Thomas answered and said, "Let Thy grace be with me"; and when our Lord had said these words unto Thomas He departed from him. Then Thomas girded up his loins after the manner of a slave, and he came to Peter and Matthias and said unto them, "Remember me in your prayers." And they embraced each other in [A 121a 2] a spiritual embrace, for this was the last of their meetings in this world, and each and all of them gave thanks together, and with a spiritual embrace they departed in peace. And Thomas went with his master, and Peter and Matthias went on their way.

Then the officer of the king enquired of Thomas concerning his handicraft, and Thomas said unto him, "I am a stone-mason, and a carpenter, and a physician [B 233b 1]. As a carpenter I am skilled in making measures, and scales, and mattocks, and hoes, and spades for digging up thorns from the earth, and whatever else men may want to dig up therefrom. As a stone-mason I am skilled in building temples, and strong palaces, and lofty towers which are useful for kings; and as a physician I can heal the wounds which work decay in the flesh." And when the officer heard these words from Thomas he rejoiced and said, "Right and good. The king is seeking for a man of this kind" [A 121b 2].

And after many days they came unto the country of India[1]. Then the officer went into the presence of the king and told him about Thomas, and he showed him the deed which [his

---

[1] Gr. εἰς ᾿Ανδράπολιν.

Master] had written for him with His own hand ; and when the king saw Thomas he marvelled. Then the officer told the king about the handicrafts wherein Thomas was skilled, and he rejoiced thereat exceedingly, and said unto him, "Take this man and bring him to Lûkîyânôs[1] ሱኪያኖስ, the governor, and let him give him the materials which he requireth, so that he may build a great palace for me" [B 233b 2]. And the officer went to the governor and told him everything which the king had commanded him, and Lûkîyânôs gave Thomas everything he wanted.

And after these things Lûkîyôs (sic) departed to the city of the king, and he commanded his wife 'Arsônwâ አረሶንዋ (Arsenia?), saying, "Let not this man who hath come unto us in these last days do the work of the slave, but let him toil at his handiwork until I come back from the presence of the king." And after he had departed [A 121 b 2] Thomas came to 'Arsônwâ, the wife of the governor, and read to her the Gospel of our Lord Jesus Christ and the prophecies of the Prophets. And he said unto her, "I see that thou art in great darkness, and art serving these gods of gold and silver ; thou sayest that they are gods, but they are not gods. What thou doest for them profiteth thee nothing whatsoever, for they cannot speak, nor hear, nor see, and if there were an earth-quake they would not be able to save themselves, but would fall down and break in pieces. I beseech thee to bring me into the temple wherein ye bow down before them that I may see their power." And the woman [went and] showed Thomas her gods. And when Thomas saw them he lifted up his eyes to heaven, and prayed, saying, "O God, the Sustainer of the universe, the Father of our Lord Jesus Christ [A 122a 1], Thy Son, Thy Beloved One, and the Holy Ghost, Whom when they hear the devils tremble ; Thou art the Good Shepherd, the Good Lamb, the True Light which shineth in our hearts, Thou art He Whose Name all creation feareth, Who didst send me into this city to bring back unto Thee those who dwell therein.

---

[1] Lipsius has Vecius.

Thou art the Creator of all the races of the children of men, and all created things are subject unto Thee. When Thou lookest upon the earth it trembleth, [B 234a 2] and the sea, and all that therein is, and all the creatures thereof and all the waves thereof are silent when they hear Thy voice ; and vipers and all reptiles bow low before Thee, because Thou art He Who judgeth them. Yea, O my Lord and God Jesus Christ, make manifest through me wonders and marvellous signs in this city, so that [the men] thereof may praise Thee ; for unto Thee belong glory and thanksgiving for ever [A 122a 2]. Amen."

Now as the Apostle was praying thus the house wherein were all the gods trembled, and all the gods who were resting on their stands fell down upon their faces on the earth, and all the devils that dwelt in them cried out, saying, "Woe unto us ! Woe unto us ! For behold, our power is destroyed, and our shame is multiplied, and henceforward there shall be no God except Jesus Christ, the Son of the Living God." And when ·Arsenia saw what had befallen the gods she feared exceedingly, and she fell down upon the earth before the holy man [B 234b 1], and Thomas stretched out his hands and raised her up. Then she took hold of him, and made supplication unto him, and said unto him, " O servant of the Good God who hast come into my house, art thou, O man, a slave or a god? What is the Name of this Jesus on Whom thou didst call ? For when thou didst utter His Name the house [A 122b 1] shook, and all the gods wherein I used to put my trust fell down upon their faces on the ground, and they became like wind. Hide not thou from me the power which is with thee, O servant of the Good God, for from this hour I will put away the dominion of false gods from me, and I will advance in the knowledge of our Lord Jesus Christ, the Son of thy God, and I will believe in thy God."

Then Thomas the blessed Apostle answered and said unto her, " O Arsenia, if thou believest with all thy heart, forsake this fleeting world which passeth quickly away. Know that thy glorying in gold, and silver, and in the beautiful apparel which is perishable and which the moth [B 234 b 2] consumeth, and in the perishable beauty of the flesh, and in everything wherein man glorieth in this world, shall quickly come to an end. And if a man looketh for the beauty of his person, his face will become sad, the eyes becoming blind and the tongue speechless [A 122 b 2]. And where shall a man be then? He goeth unto his everlasting house [i.e. the tomb]. Seek God, O Arsenia, and thou shalt find Him, and hold not thyself aloof from those who seek Him with all their hearts. Referring to God the prophet saith, "I am the Living God, and I cling closely to thee like the garment which thou dost put on." And again he saith, 'Repent, O ye children of Israel, for I am the God Who desireth not the death of a sinner, and I desire that he will turn and save his soul alive[1].' And again He saith, 'Turn ye unto Me, O ye children who have transgressed against Me; return and ye shall find me, for he who seeketh after God shall find [B 235 a 1] Him; and unto him that calleth upon Him He hearkeneth[2].'"

And as Arsenia, the wife of the governor, hearkened unto him, her heart turned to the fear of God, Who opened the eyes of her heart, and all those who were in her house believed [A 123 a 1] on God, as did many of the people of the city. Then she went into her house and cast aside her splendid apparel, and she bowed down and sprinkled ashes about her, and she entreated God and made supplication unto Him, saying, "I believe on Thee, O my Lord Jesus Christ, Thou God of the stranger who hath come into my house, and become my guide into the path of life. I beseech Thee, O my Lord, the Merciful One, Whom I have only learned to know this day—yet behold, Thou dost hold me worthy of the knowledge of Thee, O my Lord Jesus Christ, Son of the Living God—to forgive me all the sins which I have committed in times past, and the error wherein I have [B 235 a 2] dwelt until this day under the dominion of impure gods. Behold now, I turn to Thee, O my Lord Jesus Christ, Thou art my Light,

---

[1] Ezekiel xviii. 32; xxxiii. 11.
[2] Compare Jeremiah iii. 22 ; Matthew vii. 7.

my Deliverer, my [A 123a 2] Hope, my Strength, and my Refuge ; and in Thee I put my trust."

And when she had finished her prayer she went out to the Apostle with her face covered with ashes, and she said unto Thomas, "O servant of the Good God, rise up and baptize me in the Name of the Father, and of the Son, and of the Holy Spirit, whereby thou canst deliver me." And the Apostle rejoiced and saw her faith and said unto her. "O good woman, behold, the grace of God hath descended upon thee." And Arsenia answered and said unto him, "The faith of thy God dwelleth in my heart, and mind, and soul, and I give thanks unto my Lord Jesus Christ Who hath brought back the sheep that was lost." Then Thomas rose up quickly [B 235b 1] and baptized her and her household, in the Name of the Father, and of the Son, and of the Holy Ghost. And he took pure bread, and filled a cup with wine, and he gave thanks, and brake [the bread] and gave unto the people who had [A 123b 1] been baptized the Body and precious Blood of our Lord, and he and all the baptized brethren sang the Psalms of David and prayed all night. And they brought unto him all those who were sick of divers kinds of diseases, and those who were possessed of devils, and the blind, and the lame, and the lepers, and he healed them all. And Thomas went out into the city every day and preached in the Name of our Lord Jesus Christ, and told the people the story of the Holy Gospel. And he said unto them, "Bring forth unto me all the sick folk, and I will heal them for nought, and I wish for no reward from any man." Then all those who believed the words of Thomas assembled in the house of Arsenia, the governor, and all the people of the city [B 235b 2] believed and became Christians. And the Apostle used to read unto them the Gospel, and the Books of the Prophets, and he taught them the Law of Faith [A 123b 2], and afterwards he baptized them in the Name of the Father, and of the Son, and of the Holy Ghost. And he dwelt with them from the time that he entered the city, that is to say, for four years, and their faith waxed strong in our Lord Jesus Christ.

And when Vecius, who had been with the king, entered his city, his wife and all the people went forth to meet him. And when he looked at his wife and saw that she was dressed in humble garb, he was much grieved, for he thought that thieves had stolen everything that he had in his house. And he called one of her servants unto him and said unto him, "What hath taken place in my house?" And the servant said unto him, "No evil, but only good, hath happened therein since thou didst leave it." And Vecius went to the bath and then returned to his house [B 236 a 1]. And he called his wife Arsenia, and when she came to him he, in accordance with the custom of men of this world, spake to her concerning companying with her. And [A 124a 1] with tears she answered and said unto him, "O my lord, God hath removed from my heart the desire for this evil and profitless thing, and to-day is the Sabbath of God." And in great wrath he answered and said unto her, "What are these words which thou sayest unto me? I never before heard such from thee. Thou shalt not leave me until I have known thee. Woe be unto thee! Of a surety this strange slave who hath come unto us recently hath bewitched thee." And Arsenia answered and said unto him, "O my lord, God forbid that thou shouldst say such things about him ; for sorcerers cannot heal dead bodies, and this man healeth not only dead bodies but [dead] souls. Utter no foul word against him, but do thou thyself hearken unto his words."

And when [B 236a 2] he heard these words from his wife Satan's anger filled his heart, and he said [A 124a 2] unto her, "If he be a sorcerer and a magician he shall heal himself of the scourgings which shall be inflicted upon him." And straightway he commanded the soldiers of his guard to bring unto him [Thomas] and all the executioners who were in the city, and they brought them unto him. And he cried out and said unto Thomas, "O thou wicked slave and sorcerer, where are all the works of thy handicraft concerning which thou didst say, 'I can make them'? Where are the temples thou wert to build? Where are the palaces concerning which thou didst say, 'I will build them'? Where are the measures,

and the scales, and the mattocks, and the hoes, and the spades?
Where is thy work? Where are thy healings and the good
which thou hast wrought?" And Thomas answered, saying,
"Behold, I have finished all my handiwork and have made an
end thereof." And Vecius said unto him, "Wouldst thou
mock me? [B 236b 1] O wicked servant, I will beat thee to
death." And Thomas said unto him, "Without delay [A 124b 1]
I will inform thee rightly about the matters which I have not
made known unto thee until this day, and I will tell thee truly.
The temples and palaces which I have built are the souls who
have purified themselves and have believed, and these are the
palaces which I have beautified for the heavenly King Who
liveth in them. And the mattocks and the hoes and the spades
are the Holy Gospels, wherewith all hatred is dug out from
the hearts of those who believe and who seek God with all
their hearts. And the work of the craft of the physician is
the Holy Mysteries which root out every evil thought, and
every pain, and every desire, from the hearts of all those
who seek after purity. This is the noble handicraft which God
hath taught me."

And Vecius said unto him in wrath, "O thou wicked slave,
where are the things which thou didst promise me?" And he
commanded the soldiers to cast Thomas into prison. And they
laid him out there and made a wheel [A 124b 2] in the ground
and bound him upon it, and Vecius commanded [B 236b 2]
the executioners to strip the skin off his body, and said unto
him, "I will put thee to the torture, and thou shalt not die
speedily but only when I please." Then the people of the city
wept bitterly and said, "Woe be unto us! What can we do
for this righteous man who hath healed us of every kind of
sickness? If we lay hands upon him God will be wroth with
us, and will bring down His anger upon us, and will send fire
from heaven to consume us, but if we do not do what this
wicked man Vecius commandeth us, he will kill us. Behold,
we have seen many miracles of this holy man. One day a wild
boar came into the field of a poor old woman, and the young
men could not drive him off. Then the woman came and cast

herself down before that righteous man, and besought him, saying, 'O my lord, help me!' And he had pity on her, and went out into the field [A 125a 1] and said unto the wild beast, 'Get thee out of this poor [B 237a 1] woman's field, and lay not waste her crops.' And when the boar refused to depart straightway fire came down [from heaven] and consumed him. We are greatly afraid of this man's God."

Then Saint Thomas answered and said unto them, "Rise up and fulfil the commands which Vecius hath given you. I know that ye have received your commands, and that ye do not perform them willingly but through your fear of the foolish governor." And Vecius commanded them to flay the holy Apostle. And Thomas lifted up his eyes to heaven, and cried out with a loud voice, saying, "O my Lord Jesus Christ, Thou Son of the Living God, help me in this tribulation." And when Arsenia heard the words of the executioners and the weeping people—now she was looking at them from a hidden opening in her house—and saw the skin being stripped off the body [A 125a 2] of the Apostle, she was greatly moved, and she fell upon her face and died straightway. [B 237a 2] Then Vecius cried out and said, "Behold, O wicked slave, my wife hath died through thee! I will [not] cease from torturing thee until I know the full extent of the evil which thou hast done." And when the parents and kinsfolk [of Arsenia] heard these things they came and wept and wailed over her, and they cried out, saying, "Woe be unto us! But for this stranger thou wouldst not have died. Nevertheless, our hearts rejoice because thou hast died in the faith of our Lord Jesus Christ, and at the command of the blessed Apostle." Then Thomas answered and said unto them, "Weep not; be silent. Since she died through me I will raise her up again." And Vecius said unto him, "Think not that thou shalt end [thus]; I will torture thee as [long as] I wish, and will not let thee escape." And he commanded them to bring him vinegar and salt to rub into the body [A 125b 1] of the Saint. And the Apostle [B 237b 1] cried out, saying, "O my Lord Jesus Christ, help me in this mine hour of tribulation, for behold, my heart and body and spirit are on

B.   19

fire, and are very weak. O my Lord Jesus Christ, Thou merciful and compassionate God, let Thy help draw nigh unto
me, and remember that I am a stranger here, and a man
without kinsfolk. I have here in this city no father, no
mother, no brethren, no kinsfolk, and no friend. O my Lord
Jesus Christ, Son of the Living God, Thou art my Helper,
and in Thee have I put my trust. Thou art my Redeemer ; it
is Thou Who didst send me into this city, and I have not
disobeyed Thy commandments. O my Lord and God, I have
rejected everything in this world for Thy Name's sake, and as
soon as I heard Thy voice I forsook father, mother, kinsfolk,
and everything which I had. Thou didst send me into this city
to save the people, and behold, [A 125b 2] Thou seest what
hath come upon me therein. Since Thou, O God, [B 237b 2]
didst suffer for me, it is meet that I likewise should bear
patiently and joyfully the suffering which hath come upon
me here. Remember Thy word on the day of Thine appearance unto Thy beloved Apostles, when Thou didst rise from
the dead. I was not with them, and when they told me that
they had seen Thee, I remembered Thy words 'Make trial of
the spirits, for many shall come in My Name, and shall lead
astray many[1],' and I said unto my brethren the Apostles,
'Unless I see our Lord, and see His hands in which they drove
the nails, and put my fingers in the places wherein the nails
were driven, and my hand into His side I will not believe.'
And Thou didst appear unto me and show me that which I
asked of thee, and I believed in Thy Resurrection, and was re-
proached for the littleness of my faith. If, O my Lord Jesus
Christ, Thou didst suffer by this thing through me, [A 126a 1]
I beseech Thee to forgive me, O Lord, for Thou art the Good
[B 238a 1] and Merciful God, and dost turn unto those who
turn unto Thee with all their heart."

And when he had spoken these words he wept. And our
Lord had compassion upon him and appeared unto him upon
a shining cloud, and said unto him, "O Thomas, My beloved,
endure joyfully and be strong, for thou shalt overcome thine

---

[1] Matt. xxiv. 5; Mark xiii. 6; Luke xxi. 8.

enemies and all those who fight against thee. Verily, verily I say unto thee, all the scourgings which shall come upon thee for the sake of the sons of men, until I have delivered thee from the hands of the Enemy, are as nought by the side of one hour of the rest which I shall make thee to enjoy, and the grace which I shall give thee, or the place which thou shalt have on My right hand in My kingdom. Thou wast surnamed 'Twin,' and thou art beloved by Me. Endure patiently, for thy reward shall be great, and thine honour at My hands shall be abundant, and through thy skin a great number of wonderful deeds shall be made manifest. Let thy heart be strong [B 126a 2], and make haste to show forth thy true faith [B 238a 2] and My dominion in this city. After these things thou shalt depart unto a city in the East which is called Quantaria, and thou shalt dwell therein and shalt turn the people thereof to the Faith in My Name. Behold, the whole world is filled with the grace of My Father, and through My Blood, which was shed for the salvation of the world, His mercy is upon all created beings." And having said these things unto Thomas, our Lord touched His flesh with His hand, and healed his wounds ; and then He was no longer seen by Thomas.

Then Thomas, being made whole, rose up and came unto the place where the wife of Vecius was, and he laid upon her his skin which had been flayed off him, and said, "In the Name of our Lord Jesus Christ, and of the Father, and of the Spirit, let the word which came to Lazarus raise thee up." And straightway she opened her eyes, and saw the Apostle [A 126b 1] standing by [B 238b 1] her head, and she rose up and bowed down before him. And when Vecius saw this wonder and the great miracle which had been wrought by Thomas the Apostle, he rose up in fear, and bowing down before him, said, "Verily there is no god except thy God, Whom thou servest. I beseech thee, O servant of the Good God, to forgive me the evil thing which I have done unto thee, for I did it in ignorance." And Thomas raised him and said unto him, "Fear not, God taketh not vengeance upon

those who repent and confess their sins." And straightway
Vecius and all the men of his dominion believed, and at once
Thomas baptized him and all the nobles of the city, for they
all likewise believed with him. Then Thomas commanded them
to bring forth bread and a cup, and he prayed and administered unto all of them the Holy Mysteries, and they all became
Christians. [B 238 b 2.] And he set Vecius [A 126 b 2] over
them, and gave them the commandments of the Law of Faith
and the admonitions of the Gospel ; and he dwelt with them
three days teaching them the Holy Scriptures each day. And
he said unto them, "If it be the Will of God I shall return
unto you, but behold, our Lord hath commanded me to go
unto Him in a certain city which lieth to the east of you."
And he departed from them, and they set him on his way with
tears, saying, "Stay not away from us over long, for we are
only young plants." And the Apostle prayed over them, and
blessed them, and gave unto them the salutation of peace, and
departed unto Quantaria to preach therein, even as our Lord
had commanded him.

And when he arrived at the city and had entered in through
the gates thereof, he found an old man there who was weeping
bitterly ; and his apparel was ragged, and his appearance was
wretched. And the Apostle came up and said unto him, "O
aged man, why do I see thee in this sorrowful state and
weeping bitterly ? Behold, thou [B 239 a 1] art making thy
heart sad." And the old man said unto him, [A 127 a 1] "Depart from me, O my brother, for my sorrow is great." And the
Apostle said unto him, "I beseech thee to tell me what hath
happened unto thee ; peradventure my Lord Jesus Christ will
heal thee through me." And the old man said unto him,
"Hearken unto my words. I had three sons, and the eldest I
betrothed to the daughter of an elder of the city so that she
might become his wife. When the time came for him to marry,
he said unto me : Father, be not angry with me because
[I stop] the marriage, for I will not marry [any] woman. Behold, I have renounced the world and all the lust thereof.
When I heard him say this I grieved in my heart, and he

seemed to me to be mad when he spake these words unto me. And I said unto him : Behold, the appointed time hath come, and I want to bring thy wife for thee to marry, and yet thou sayest these words unto me. Then he said unto me : I have sworn by the Majesty of the King, Who is the King of Kings, [A 127a 2] Jesus Christ, since thou dost order [B 239a 2] me concerning this matter, that I will depart to the desert, and after this day thou shalt never again see me. And I said unto him, What vision hast thou seen ? Tell me.

"And he said unto me : I will tell thee what I saw. Last night I was sleeping on my bed, and I saw a young man with a beautiful face. He was dressed in apparel which was brighter than the sun, and the odour of flowers went forth from Him, and the place was filled with the scent thereof. On His head was a royal crown, and in His hand was a gold sceptre, and when I looked upon Him I feared exceedingly and I fell down on my face at His feet like a dead man. And He stretched out His hands, and lifted me up, and said unto me : ' Take good heed, and hearken not unto those who would advise thee to marry a wife, but guard thy body and keep it pure, that thou mayest be like unto Myself, and become the head of the Church. Behold, the Apostle Saint Thomas shall come to this [A 127b 1] city, and he shall bring the Faith unto thee [B 239b 1], and shall give thee the seal thereof, and shall be constantly with thee, and shall make thee worthy to receive the Holy Mysteries. Know that I am the God Who became incarnate for your sakes, and it is meet that ye should not be slothful concerning the salvation and life of your souls.' And as He said these words unto me He laid His hands upon my head, and blessed me, and went up out of my sight into heaven with great glory. For this reason, O my father, I will not forsake the gift of grace which God hath given unto me, so that the King may not be wroth with me, and blot me out because of the transgressions of His Word.

"When I heard these words from my son I held my peace, and I sorrowed in my heart, [thinking] that perhaps it was the god of the city who had appeared unto him. Then I went to certain of the nobles of the city, and I told [A 127b 2] them all that my son had told me, and I sent to the father of the maiden, and told him all that the nobles had heard from me. And he was furiously angry and said unto me, 'Dost thou treat my rank and dignity with contempt? Wouldst thou [B 239b 2) put my daughter to shame with such lying words as these?' Then he went to the king, and took us, that is to say, myself and my son, into his presence, and said, 'They have stolen the property of the temple'; and the king sent and killed all my seven children at once. For this reason thou seest me weeping and sorrowful. And besides this, the money which I borrowed—now I gave it to the damsel—they now require of me; since the death of my children I have been smitten with fear, and I have no means whereby I can restore their money. If only one of my sons had been left to me he would have helped me to give them what they demand from me."

And when the Apostle heard these words from him, he answered and said unto him, "Weep [A 128a 1] not, O aged man. Behold, I have heard thy words, and thou must bring me, Thomas, unto the place where thy children are, and my Lord Jesus Christ will graciously grant unto them the gift of life." Then the old man went to the place where his children were buried [B 240a 1], and many people followed them, saying, "If this counsel prove right we ourselves will believe in the God of this man." And when they had come to the grave, the Apostle gave his skin to the old man, and said unto him, "Go into the grave, and lay this skin upon each of thy children, and say, In the Name of the Father, and the Son, and the Holy Ghost, rise up, my children, and become alive as ye were formerly. I Thomas may not do this lest they say of me, He is a sorcerer." And the old man did as Thomas commanded him, and he laid the Apostle's skin upon his children, and they became [alive] as they were formerly. Now there were there in the tomb [A 128a 2] a number of other people's children who had died before his children, and because of what was done they all rose up alive. Now they were fifteen in number. And they went forth to the blessed Apostle, and bowed before him and said unto him, "We beseech thee, O Apostle of our God, to give us baptism, which is the fulfilment of life." And when the multitude saw [B 240a 2] these things they cried out with a loud voice, saying, "Truly there is no God but Jesus Christ, the Son of the One Living God, the God of Thomas."

Then certain of these men went to the temple of Apollo, and told the priest of the temple everything that had happened. And when the priest heard the Name of Jesus he rent his garments and said, "Woe unto me! This man is one of the disciples of Jesus who came forth from the land of Judaea, and who go round about the whole world leading into error [A 128b 1] all those who hearken unto them. They are the disciples of the man called Jesus, Who was a sorcerer, Whom as we have heard, Pilate crucified. And these men stole his body, and they go about in the world, and say that He hath risen from the dead." Then the priest said unto them, "Rise up, O people, and let us go to him, and curse him and revile him, and tell him that his words are lies, and that all that he doeth is by means of sorcery." So the priest and all the people [B 240b 1] with him rose up and went to the place where Thomas was—now they found him in the highway of the city with all the people gathered together about him there, for he was casting out from a man the Satan who possessed him. And the priest said unto Thomas, "O sorcerer and deceiver, what doest thou in this? Were not the land of Judaea and the dwellers therein sufficient for thee, that thou must come into this city? Who is this Jesus? If He [A 128b 2] was God, why did He not deliver Himself from the Cross? Ye stole His body and now ye testify unto all creation that He rose from the dead. But know thou that the people of this city are men of understanding, and that they are not to be led astray like the other peoples whom thou hast made to err." Then turning his face to the people he said unto them, "Let each of you take a stone in his hands and cast it at this sorcerer, so that henceforth he shall not find another opportunity to lead the people astray." And the people did as the priest commanded them, and stooped down [B 240b 2] to pick up stones to throw at St. Thomas, but straightway their hands withered on the stones and they could not stand up. And they all cried out with a loud voice, saying, " We entreat thee, O servant of the Good God, to beseech thy Lord God to have mercy upon us, and to heal us so that we may rise up and stand upon our feet. Then will we believe in thy God, and behold, we shall know that [A 129a 1] there is no God but thine either in heaven or upon earth ; reward not us according to our folly."

Then the Apostle prayed and said, " I give thee thanks, O my Lord Jesus Christ, for behold, Thou hast not withheld that which I asked for from Thee, and I have revealed Thy story to these multitudes that are assembled before Thee. I beseech Thee to send down Thy divine power from heaven, and let the priest hang in the air head downwards, for he hath blasphemed Thy holy Name." And straightway the priest was hung up in the air [B 241a 1] head downwards among the people ; and they saw the might of God Most High Who had done this thing to him. Then he who hung in mid-air cried out, saying, " I believe in the Name of our Lord Jesus Christ, and I do not believe in the gods. Indeed Thou art my God, Whom in my folly, I blasphemed. Thou art the God of the gods [A 129a 2] which are made by man, the which it is not right to call gods. Nay, Thou wast God before the world existed, and Thou, O God of heaven, and earth, and of what is under the earth, Thou, O Jesus Christ, art He in Whom I have placed my trust. Thou art my King and my hope." And the priest having made this confession as he hung in mid-air came down to earth whilst the people were looking at him. And the people who had seen him believed and were saved, and they asked the Apostle to baptize them in the Name of the Father, and the Son, and the Holy Ghost.

And when they were confirmed in the faith he took them to the [B 241a 2] temple, and they overthrew the stands of the gods and made the temple into a church. And Thomas appointed the priest to be bishop over them, and the seven brothers, the sons of the old man whom he had raised from the dead, he made to be [A 129b 1] priests and deacons, and he set them in the church that they might minister to the sanctuary. And he dwelt in the city many days, teaching the people all the mysteries of the faith, and many wonders took place through him. And he used to carry his skin on his neck, and to take it with him whithersoever he went. And after these things he departed from the city thanking and praising God. And our Lord appeared unto him, and took his skin and set it about his body, and Thomas became as he was formerly. And He embraced Thomas, and he did away his sorrow, and said unto him, " Seat thyself on this cloud, and it shall bring thee unto the place where are thy brethren the Apostles [B 241b 1] in peace. And I will be with you in every place where ye are, for ye are those whom my Father hath chosen to preach in the world." And our Lord went up into heaven [A 129b 2] with great glory. Then Thomas mounted upon the cloud as our Lord had commanded him, and it bore him along and brought him to Mount Nîya'anâdîn-'Ênsîs ነየአናዲን፡ኤንሲስ. And he found the Apostles gathered together there, and Paul, and MARY, the God-bearer, were among them. And he embraced them with a spiritual embrace, and they made mention of the wonderful things which God had wrought through them, and they remained assembled there for eighty days, and they glorified God together. To God be glory, and honour, and thanksgiving, for ever and ever! Amen. Amen. And Amen.

THE ACTS OF SAINT THOMAS IN INDIA

THE FIRST ACT

[To be Read on the Eighteenth Day of the Month Maskarram (Sept. 15)] [A 152a 1; B 139a 2.]

And it came to pass in those days that all the Apostles were in Jerusalem, that is to say, Simon who is called Peter, and Andrew his brother, and James the son of Zebedee, and John his brother, and Philip and Bartholomew, and Thomas and Matthew, and Thaddeus and James, the son of Alphaeus, and Simon Zelotes, and Judas the son of James. And we counted up the countries of the world together, and divided them among us, and we departed unto that which had come to each of us by lot when our Lord sent us forth among the nations. Now the country of India had fallen to the share of Judas Thomas, that is Didymus, and he was unwilling to go there, and said, "I cannot go there because of the fatigue of the body [on the journey], for I am a Hebrew. How is it possible for me to go to India and preach the Gospel there?" And whilst he was thinking and speaking thus our Redeemer appeared to him by night, and said unto him, "Fear not, O Thomas. [B 130b 1.] Get thee to India, and preach My word there, for I Myself will be with thee." [A 152a 2.] Then Thomas said unto Him, "I do not wish to go. I would that Thou wouldst send me unto another country, for unto the country of India I cannot go."

And whilst Thomas was speaking in this wise, a certain merchant who was from the country of India came nigh unto them; and his name was Abbanês ('Αββάνης), and he had come from the king of Gônâ[1] who had sent him to bring workmen and tools. And as our Lord was standing by the side of Thomas, He saw Abbanês in the market going to his workshop.

---

[1] Read "from king Gundaforus" (Γουνδάφορος).

And He said unto Abbanês, "Dost thou wish to find a work-man?" And Abbanês said unto Him, "Yea, my Lord, I wish to buy a workman (or, slave)." And when he had said these words unto Him our Lord showed him Thomas in the distance, and He made a covenant with Abbanês to sell him for one pound of silver. And He wrote for him a bill, saying, "I [Jesus], the son of Joseph, sell and deliver unto thee My servant Thomas to go to Gônâ." And when the bill was executed according to the law, the Saviour took Judas, and gave him to Abbanês and said [B 139 b 2] unto him, "Behold thy master." Then the Apostle [A 152 b 1] answered and said unto Him, "Yes, he is my master." And Abbanês said unto Thomas, "I have taken thee"; and the Apostle held his peace.

And at dawn the following morning the Apostle prayed unto the Lord and said, "I will go whithersoever Thou wishest, O Jesus, and Thy will be done." And he departed with Abbanês the merchant who took with him nothing except what he had bought; and our Lord saluted him and said unto him, "Behold, thou hast thy merchandise with thee, and My peace shall be with thee whithersoever thou goest." And the Apostle found Abbanês loading up his goods into a ship, and he was his slave. And when they had gone up into the ship and were seated there, Abbanês asked the Apostle and said unto him, "In what handicraft art thou skilled?" And the Apostle said unto him, "In wood I can make the implements which are used in ploughing, such as yokes, and the bent ends of ploughs, and oars and steering poles for ships, and wheels (or, wheeled carts?). And as for stone I can make picks (?), and spades (?), and columns, and ornaments for pillars and tombs and sepul-chral monuments for kings." And Abbanês the merchant [A 152 b 2] said unto him, "Thy knowledge of thy craft is sufficient for my needs." So they put to sea and journeyed on with fair winds, and they sailed on happily [B 140 a 1] until they arrived in the country of India, and came to the city of the king[1]. And when they had come down from the

[1] I.e. Andrapolis or Sandarûk; see Lipsius, *op. cit.* vol. I. p. 249; Wright, *Apocryphal Acts*, vol. II. p. 148.

ship, and had entered the city, they heard the sounds of flutes and organs which rent the heavens, and with them were mingled the blasts of horns, and the blare of trumpets, and the sounds of the harp, and voices singing sweet songs of divers kinds. Then the Apostle asked, saying, "What is the festival in this city to-day?" And the men said unto him, "The angels have brought thee hither to take part with [the people of] this city. The king hath a daughter [called Pelagra], and he hath given her in marriage to the bridegroom [Diony-sius], and so there is great rejoicing this day. This is the reason for the festival about which thou hast enquired. The king hath sent forth a herald to proclaim this and to invite to the marriage feast everyone, rich and poor, bond and free, stranger and citizen; and if there be any one who will not come [A 153a 1] to the feast he will be condemned to suffer according to the king's pleasure." And when Abbanês the merchant heard this, he said unto [B 140a 2] the Apostle, "Come, let us also go, lest we be punished by the king, even though we be new-comers." And the Apostle said unto him, "Yes, let us go"; and having gone into the public guest house they rested a little while and then went to the feast.

And when those who were seated looked at the Apostle as he sat down, they saw that he had the look of a poor stranger, and of one who was from a foreign country. Now Abbanês, who was dressed like a nobleman, took his seat in another part of the building; and the people ate food and drank their wine, but the Apostle took no food whatsoever. And those who were sitting near him said unto him, "Why hast thou come hither? Thou neither eatest nor drinkest." And the Apostle answered and said, "I did not come here for meat and drink, but because it was the king's wish that I should do so. For the herald cried out, saying, [A 153a 2] 'If there be any man who doth not come to the feast, he shall suffer the king's punishment.'" And when the people had eaten and drunk, the servants brought them sweet perfumes, and scented unguents, and garlands, and wreaths of flowers [B 140b 1], and every man took something from them; and some anointed their faces, and some their beards, and others their bodies. And the Apostle anointed his skull and head, and he placed a little of the unguent in each nostril and each ear. And the garland which came to the Apostle was made of lentil flowers, and other sweet-smelling herbs, and he took the garland and put it on his head, and he took a reed and held it in his hand. And a certain singing woman, who was of the people of the Hebrews, took her tambourine in her hand, and went about among the company singing, and when she came to the place where the Apostle was, she stood still near him and sang a song before him. And the Apostle was looking fixedly on the ground, and one of those who had eaten with him lifted up his hand and smote him. And lifting up his eyes [A 153b 1] the Apostle looked at the man who had struck him, and said unto him, "My God may preserve for thee in the world which is to come the hand wherewith [B 140b 2] thou hast smitten me; may He forgive thee this injury! But He will show thee His wonders in this world, and I shall see the dogs carrying off the hand wherewith thou didst smite me." And when the Apostle had said these words unto him, he began to sing this song[1] concerning the Church.

"The Church is she in whom is the splendour of royalty. She is pleasant of aspect and lovely, Beautiful is she to him that looketh upon her. Her garments are like unto flowers of every kind, And the odour thereof cometh forth and anointeth the head. The king giveth food gladly to those who are with him the mighty ones. Truth is upon her head, and joy with her feet. It appeareth in her mouth, Which openeth in a manner which is seemly. The praises of her by this tongue are twofold. Whosoever forgetteth [to praise her] shall straightway become....... And he who rejoiceth according to the mind....... [A 153b 2]. Her neck, which towereth upwards and is made of brass hath the God thereof made. Her two hands make

---

[1] This song or hymn is poorly rendered in the Ethiopic text, and almost impossible to translate in its present form. For the Syriac text see Wright, *op. cit.* vol. I. p. ܐܠܡ and Burkitt, *Studia Sinaitica*, IX. pp. 25–44; for the Greek text see Tischendorff, *Apocalypses Apocryphae.* (*Acta Thomae*, ed. Bonnet, Leipzig, 1883.)

manifest and reveal the places of beauty which He hath made, and proclaim where they are; her ten fingers point out the ante-chamber thereof. Her bridal chamber is made of light, the sweet odour thereof is on the tongue, together with beautiful odours of every kind, and incense, and sweet spice, and every sweet thing whatsoever, the savour of which ariseth from its essence. [B 141a 1] And the Bridegroom shall be adorned, and he shall hold the reed of the Seven whom he hath chosen, and the guardians of the Bride are seven also. Those who are before her and those who are behind her are twelve; they await the Bridegroom and baptism, and expect to live with Him for ever. They will go out and wait for Him in the great Assembly with righteousness. It is meet that they array themselves in royal apparel, they shall put on shining raiment with joy and gladness, and shall belong to Him to Whom great splendour belongeth. They shall be welcomed in heaven, and shall shine in the Divinity of God [A 154a 1]. They shall receive the food which is without spot or blemish of any kind, and shall drink of the wine which will not permit them to thirst again. And the King shall give them their souls' desire, and they shall sing praises to Him and glorify Him with the hearing ones, and with the souls of the Fathers who have gone to their rest in the confidence which is begotten of wisdom, and henceforth they shall praise Him with perfect praises."

And when he had said these words all who were there looked at him, and they saw that his visage was changed [B 141a 2] and his whole form different; but they did not understand what he had said, for he was a Hebrew and his speech was Hebrew. The singing woman alone heard and understood what he said, for she was a Hebrew. Then she left the Apostle and continued to sing and to beat her tambourine, but she was thinking about him, and looking at him and watching him frequently. And she loved him because she knew that he was a man of her people, and he was, moreover, of more goodly [A 154a 2] form than any man there. And when she had finished her song, everyone praised her, and she went and sat down in front of Thomas, and continued to look at him and to watch him with great care. But the Apostle never took his eyes off the ground even for a moment, and he was waiting for an opportunity to escape from the place.

And the man who had sat at meat with Thomas and had struck him, went down to the well to draw water, and a lion sprang upon him suddenly and slew him and tore his body and left him. And the dogs carried away the members of his body, and one of them, a black dog [B 141 b 1], seized his right hand with his mouth, and brought it to the men who were seated in the great chamber. And when they saw this they were all horrified, and they asked, saying, "Who is the man that is dead?" And they recognized the hand of the man who had served them and had smitten the Apostle. Then the singing woman took her tambourine and cast it away from her, and she went and sat down at the feet [A 154 b 1] of the Apostle, saying, "This man is either God or an Apostle of God. For I heard what he said in Hebrew to the serving man, and now I see the dog carrying the hand which smote him. Behold, ye all can see that it hath come to pass even as he spake." And some believed and some did not.

And when the king heard of this he drew nigh unto the Apostle and said unto him, "Rise up, and come with me and pray for my daughter, for she is my only child and I have this day given her in marriage." And the Apostle refused to go with him, because our Lord had not as yet [B 141 b 2] revealed Himself unto him in that place. But the king, in spite of his refusal, compelled him and took him into the chamber of the bride that he might pray on their behalf. And the Apostle stood up and he began to pray thus: "O my Lord and God, [A 154 b 2] Who dost guide Thy servants and lead them, and dost toil for those who believe on Thee, Thou art the Refuge and Asylum of the afflicted, the Hope of the poor, the Deliverer of the captives, the Healer of sick souls, the Saviour of created beings, the Lifegiver of the world, the Strengthener and Fortifier of souls. Thou, O God, knowest what will come to pass, and what is to be fulfilled by us. Thou,

O our Lord, art a hidden Mystery, and dost teach those who know Thee not. Thou, O my Lord, dost plant good trees, and through Thee they bring good works to perfection. Thou, O my Lord, art in our every aspiration, and Thou livest in Thy work, and in all Thy works Thou art hidden [B 142a 1], Thou Jesus Christ, the God of mercy, the perfect Saviour, Christ, Son of the Living God, God Almighty, Thou Mighty One unconquered by the Enemy. [A 155a 1] Thou art the Word which the Principalities heard, and which made the Powers and the Dominions to tremble. Thou wast sent from heaven and didst go down to Sheol and open the gates thereof, and didst bring up those who had been held captive there from of old and had dwelt in the mansions of darkness, and Thou didst show to those who would be guided the way whereby to return. O my Lord Jesus Christ, I entreat Thee on behalf of these young folk ; be pleased to help them and to grant unto them the things which are good and excellent, and lay Thy hand upon them." Then the Apostle said, "My Lord be with you," and he left them in their place.

And the king having gone forth he besought the friends of the bridegroom to depart from their chamber. And when they all had gone forth, and the doors were shut, [B 142a 2] the bridegroom drew the curtains of the doors so that he might take the bride to himself. And he saw our Lord Jesus Christ [A 155a 2] in the form of Judas Thomas, talking to the bride even as when he blessed the bridegroom and bride, and it seemed that Thomas had not left [the chamber]. [And the bridegroom said unto him, " Lord, Thou didst go out first ; how then hast Thou come back?"]¹ Then our Lord said unto him, "I am not Judas Thomas, but I am his brother"; and He sat down there and told them to sit on the couch, and He said unto them, "Remember, O My children, what My brother hath said unto you, and unto Whom he committed you. Know ye that if ye renounce carnal union which is impure, ye shall become holy and perfect in purity. Then shall ye escape labour and sufferings, both the seen and the unseen, and ye

¹ Supplied from the Syriac Version.

shall be free from worldly cares, and the children who would form your posterity will not come into being. If ye beget many children ye will, for their sakes, become avaricious oppressors, [B 142b 1] and ye will afflict the orphan and the widow, and ye will become unjust persecutors. And if ye do all these things [A 155b 1] ye will suffer sore chastisement. And the greater number of children become wicked and fall into error, for devils attack them either secretly or openly, or they become mad, or foolish, or deaf, or left-handed, or lame, or paralysed. If they escape these things they become unprofitable evildoers, or workers of abominations, or they become the companions of avaricious men and thieves, and in any case ye suffer labour and sorrow. But if ye be steadfast and keep yourselves pure to God, there shall be born unto you [spiritual] children which shall be free from all these defects which I have described to you, through your own strength. Ye shall rest and not be separated in the place of beauty, ye shall be free from sorrow and pain, and shall await [B 142b 2] the marriage that never endeth. [A 155b 2] And ye shall be the friends of the Bridegroom, by Whom ye shall be recognized when ye come to the never-ending marriage, and into the perfect light."

And when the young man and the young woman heard these words they believed on the Lord and dedicated themselves to Him ; and they forsook their impure lust, and remained as they were in that place the whole night. And our Lord passed from them, saying, "The grace of God be with you."

Now when the morning dawned the king came and prepared a table, and he went to the bridegroom and bride and found them sitting and talking together ; the face of the bride was uncovered, and the bridegroom was exceedingly happy. Then the mother of the bride came to her and said unto her, "O my daughter, why art thou sitting unashamed in this manner? Ye sit and behave like people who [A 156a 1] have been married for many days." And her father said unto her, "Is it for the sake of [B 143a 1] thy husband that thou dost not cover thy face?" And the bride answered and said unto him, "O my father, verily I am in love with God Almighty, and I pray that I may abide in this love which I learned to know during the past night, and may possess this man concerning whom I have understanding this day. For this cause I am not ashamed. The shame which is made known by the mirror hath passed away from me, and henceforth I shall never be ashamed. I shall never veil myself, for the works of shame have departed from me, and are hidden away far from me. Henceforth I shall not feel that I am a stranger, and none shall make a stranger of me; and I shall live in light and gladness, and in the day of my joy I shall not be moved. I have put aside this man and have not hitherto been united to him; but I shall be united [A 156a 2] to the true Husband Who shall come at last, Whose soul is full of mercy, and then evermore shall I have greater enjoyment."

And whilst the bride was saying these words the Bridegroom [B 143a 2] answered and said, "I give thanks unto Thee, O God, because through this stranger Thou hast glorified Thyself before us, and hast revealed Thyself unto us. Thou hast removed me from vanity and hast sown life in me, and hast taken from me the sickness which is incurable and everlasting; and Thou hast graciously bestowed upon me the life of abstinence. Thou hast shown me Thyself, and depicted to me all the [evil] works wherein I lived, and hast saved me from stumbling and hast guided me into [the path] which is good. Thou hast led me away from destruction and hast brought me to the place where I shall neither die nor be overcome. Thou hast abased Thyself and descended to my humble estate in order to give me joy and gladness, and hast not withheld Thy mercy from me, the sinner. Thou hast taught me to seek myself, for I did not know where I was, [A 156b 1] and the works which were alien unto me Thou hast now put away from me. Moreover, I am now as one who knoweth Thee, for Thou didst seek me when I knew Thee not. And Thou wilt receive me into the place where [A 143b 1] Thou now art. I cannot forget this, for love moveth me, but I am unable to speak to Thee. I would speak great things concerning Thee, and my trust in Thee is as great as my praise of Thee. Boldness is unseemly for me, but even if I knew Him not my love for Him would make me say what I want to say."

And when the king heard these words from the bridegroom and bride he rent his garments, and said unto those who stood near him, "Get ye out quickly and go round about the city and seize and bring hither that man, that sorcerer who came to this city with evil intent, and whom I myself [A 156b 2] brought into my house and told him to pray over my wretched daughter. Whosoever shall find him and bring him to me to him will I give whatsoever he asketh." And they all departed, and went round about through the city seeking for the Apostle, who had gone to another city. And they went to the house where he had lodged in that city, and found [B 143b 2] there the dancing woman who was weeping and lamenting because the Apostle had refused to take her with him ; and they told her about everything which the Apostle had done to the young man. And when she heard these things she rejoiced greatly, and she ceased to be sorrowful and said, "Now shall I find rest here." And she rose up and went to the bridegroom and bride, and tarried with them whilst the Apostle returned to the king. And many of the people who had been with him believed, and when they heard where the Apostle was, and that he was living in the [A 157a 1] country of India and teaching the people thereof, they departed and joined themselves unto him.

Here endeth the First Act of St. Thomas.

THE SECOND ACT OF SAINT THOMAS IN INDIA.

[To be read on the ninth day of the month Ṭeḳemt (Oct. 6).]

[B 144a 1] And when the Apostle had entered the country of India[1] with Abbanês the merchant, Abbanês went to greet Gondapôr (Gondaforus) the king, and to tell him about the workman whom he had brought with him. And the king rejoiced and told Abbanês to bring him into his presence. And when the Apostle came before him the king said, "What is thy handicraft?" And the Apostle said unto him, "I am a carpenter and a stonemason." And the king said unto him, "What canst thou make in wood and what in stone?" And the Apostle said, "In wood, ploughs, yokes, measures, wheels, ships, oars and steering poles; in stone, statues and houses and royal palaces." Then the king said unto him, "Canst thou build me [A 157a 2] a palace?" And the Apostle said unto him, "Yea, I can build [one] and finish it, for I have come hither for the purpose of working at my trade of stonemason and carpenter." And the king took them [B 144a 2] and they went out through the gates of the city. And the king began to hold converse with the Apostle concerning the building of the palace, and where he would dig out and lay the foundations for it, and at length they came to the place where the king thought he would build [his palace]. And the king said, "Here is the place where I wish to build"; and the Apostle said, "Yea, this place is excellent and suitable for the purpose." Now the place was marshy and swampy, and there was much water there. Then the king said unto him, "Begin to build here [now]," but the Apostle answered and said unto him, "I cannot begin to build now, but only at the [proper] season." And the king said unto him, "When wilt thou be able [to begin]?" And the Apostle said, "After two months. I will

---

[1] See Lipsius, *Apostelgeschichten*, I. p. 252; Wright, *Apocryphal Acts*, II. p. 159.

begin to build at the new moon of the month of Ḥadar
(November), and I will finish it in the month of Mîyâzyâ
(April)." And the king held his peace and marvelled at him.
Then he said unto him, "All buildings are built in the summer.
Art thou able to build [A 157 b 1] the palace in the winter ?"
And the Apostle said unto him, "It must be [done] thus, for
there is no other way." And the king said [B 144b 1], "If
thou thinkest it must be built then, mark out on the ground
for me the place where the palace will stand, and later I will
return hither." Then the Apostle took a reed and measured
the ground, and marked out the dimensions of the palace, and
the position of the foundations, and the site of the large hall.
He made the site of the building to face the east whence
cometh the light of the sun, and its windows (or, openings)
to face the west whence cometh the wind ; the doors of the
bakehouse (or, kitchen) [faced] the south, and by the side
flowed a stream of good water. When the king saw the plan
he said unto the Apostle, "Verily thou art a cunning handi-
craftsman, and it is fitting that thou art in the king's service";
and he gave him much money and departed. And the Apostle
began to build, and the king sent to him money, and everything which the men who were working with him needed.
[A 157 b 2] And he took the money, and went about teaching
and giving alms to the poor, and the sick, and the needy, and
the destitute, and thus he gave them relief. And he said,
"What belongeth unto the king shall be given unto the king,
[B144 b 2] and many shall enjoy relief." Such was his desire.

And after these things the king sent a messenger unto the
Apostle with a letter, saying, "Write unto me an account of
all the work. Tell me what I am to say concerning thee, and
send me word about whatsoever thou art in need and I will
despatch it to thee." And the Apostle wrote unto him, saying,
"The palace is finished, but there is no roof on." And when
the king heard this, he sent unto him much gold and silver,
and he wrote to the Apostle, saying, "I have built the palace,
and I must make it complete with a roof." And the Apostle
prayed to God and said, "I thank [A 158a 1] Thee, O God,

for all things, and [especially] because through Thy death I shall live for ever, and because Thou didst sell me as a slave so that I might bestow freedom from bondage upon many." And the Apostle ceased not to teach and to comfort those who were in sorrow, saying, "O God, bestow upon them the gifts of grace, for it is Thou Who dost feed [B 145a 1] and protect the orphans, and Thou dost support the widows and the castaways, and dost give them rest and peace."

And when the king came into the city and enquired of his friends concerning the building which Judas Thomas had built for him, they said unto him, "He has built neither a palace nor anything else," and, they added, "he hath done nothing except go about the city, and through the region round about it, and what thou didst give him and all that he himself had he hath given to the poor and needy. He hath taught the people a new God, and healed the sick, and cast out devils [A 158a 2], and performed many wonderful things. We thought that he was a sorcerer, but the things which come from his hands are mercy, grace, and healing; and the humility and wisdom which he showeth through his Faith make us believe that he is indeed an Apostle of the God Whom he preacheth. And he fasteth and prayeth always. [B 145a 2] His food is bread alone, his drink is water, his apparel, both in summer and winter, is a single garment, he taketh nothing from any man, and whatsoever he hath he giveth unto others."

Now when the king heard these words, he rubbed his face with his hands, and he smote his head [with them] being filled with wrath. And in that same hour he sent and caused the Apostle to be brought unto him ; and also the merchant who had presented him to the king. And the king said unto him, "Hast thou built the palace for me?" And the Apostle answered and said unto him, "Yea, I have built [it]." And the king said unto him, [A 158b 1] "When can we go and see it?" And the Apostle made answer, saying, "Thou canst not go to see it now, but only when thou hast departed from this world wilt thou be able to see it." Then was the king exceedingly wroth, and he commanded them to cast the merchant and Judas Thomas into prison. And they took Judas Thomas to the prison-house to torture him so that they might find out unto whom he had given the king's money; [B 145b 1] and when they had tortured him they were to kill him and the merchant who had brought him to the city. And Judas Thomas went into the prison-house with rejoicing, and he said unto the merchant, "Fear thou nothing whatsoever. Only believe in the God Whom I preach, and thou shalt be saved in this world, and receive life in that which is to come."

Meanwhile the king was meditating upon the manner in which he would punish them, and he determined to do so by means of fire, after they had been flayed. And it came to pass on that same night that Gâdôn (Gad)[1], the brother of the king, fell sick by reason of his sorrow for the fraud committed upon the king, and for the king's grief. Then the king's brother sent for [A 158 b 2) the king, and said unto him, "I commit my house and my children to thee for safe keeping, because I am stricken down with sorrow by reason of the fraud which hath been perpetrated upon thee, and because of it I shall die; and thou wilt not give my soul any rest after death unless thou shalt seize that worker of sorcery and slay him." And the king said unto his brother, "This very night have I been thinking out the means whereby I shall punish him, and I have decided to burn him in a fierce fire after he and the merchant who brought him here have been flayed." [B 145b 2] Now whilst the king was speaking in this wise, the soul of Gâdôn, the king's brother, departed. And the king mourned for his brother, for he loved him dearly, and he commanded that he should be buried with royal pomp and honours.

And whilst all these things were being performed, the angels took the soul of Gâdôn, the brother of the king, and carried it to heaven. And they showed it the region where it would dwell, and they asked it, saying, "In which part wouldst thou dwell?" And having come to the building which Thomas had built for the king there, the soul of Gâdôn looked upon it, [A 159a 1] and said unto the angels, "I beseech you, O my

---

[1] See Wright, *op. cit.* p. 162.

lords, to allow me to dwell in this mansion." And the angels said unto him, "Thou canst not dwell in this building," and the soul of Gâdôn said unto them, "Why not?" Then the angels said unto him, "Because this is the palace which the Christian hath built for thy brother." And the soul of Gâdôn said unto the angels, "I beseech you, O my lords, to allow me to go to my brother, and to buy this [B 146a 1] palace from him, for as he knoweth nothing whatsoever about it, he will sell it to me."

And when the angels released the soul of Gâdôn, it returned to his body when they were swathing it for burial, and it spake unto those who were standing by it, saying, "Call ye to me my brother, so that I may ask him a certain question." And straightway the men went, and told the king what had happened, saying, "Thy brother hath returned whence he had departed and hath come back to life." And the king and many people ran thither, and when he arrived at the place where his brother was, he went in and stood by the bier, and he was unable to speak with him. [A 159a 2] Then his brother answered and said unto him, "Know, O my brother, and be certain that if thou wilt grant unto me the petition which I shall make unto thee on my own behalf that I will give unto thee even to the half of my kingdom; therefore grant me my only request for a price." And the king answered and said unto him, "What is the petition which thou wouldst have me grant unto thee?" And his brother said unto him, "Swear thou unto me by thy Faith that thou wilt grant it unto me"; and the king sware [B 146a 2] an oath unto him, saying, "Whatsoever thou askest of me, if I possess it, I will give it unto thee." Then he said unto him, "Sell to me this palace which thou hast in the heavens." And the king said unto him, "Where have I a palace in the heavens?" Then his brother said unto him, "I mean the palace which the Christian hath built. The Christian is the man who is now in prison, and he is the same man who was brought unto thee by the merchant, who bought him from a MAN Whose Name was Jesus. This Christian is the Hebrew slave whom thou wishest to suffer death because he defrauded thee, and because of whom, through sorrow for thee, I died. But, behold, now I am alive." And straightway the king perceived and understood, and knew of a certainty that good deeds would endure for ever, [A 159 b 1] and that they would benefit him. And he said unto Gâdôn, "I pray and beseech that I may enter in and dwell there, and that God will grant unto me a portion like unto that which He hath given unto those who are therein. And as for thyself, if thou art thinking of building a similar palace, behold, he who built my palace is [still] alive, and he can build a better one for thee."

Then straightway the king sent and brought the Apostle [B 146 b 1] and the merchant who was with him in prison, and he said unto him, "I entreat thee, even as one entreateth a priest of God, to pray for me, and to beseech Him Whose messenger thou art, to remit unto me, and to forgive me for everything which I have done unto thee, and everything which I meditated upon doing unto thee, and to let me dwell in that palace, at [the building] of which I have in no way toiled; for thou alone hast laboured thereat, the grace of God being thy helper. And let me evermore [A 159 b 2] become the minister of this God Whom thou preachest, and let me serve Him." Then the king's brother bowed low before the Apostle, and said unto him, "I beseech and entreat thee by the presence of thy God that I also may become the minister of Him Whose angels have made Him known unto me." And the Apostle rejoiced and said, "I give thanks unto Thee, O Lord, because Thou hast revealed Thy righteousness, and because Thou, the God of righteousness, art God alone, and there is no other God besides Thee. Thou knowest every hidden thing, and Thou showest mercy unto all, and Thou art pitiful unto men; [B 146 b 2] forgive Thou the wicked and the ignorant and the men who have no understanding. And now, I pray and beseech Thee to accept the king and his brother. Lead Thou them among Thy flock, and in Thy compassion cleanse them, bring over them that which is right, guard them against the Satans, and bring them unto Thy haven, and give them Thy

[A 160a 1] gracious gifts, and let them drink of Thy fountain which never faileth. May they beseech, and entreat, and ask Thee in mercy to grant them escape from the Enemy who hath in times past hated them, and would have slain them, even as for our sakes all these things did come upon Thee. And forgive us, O Thou Who art indeed the Shepherd, and grant unto them that they may come to their right minds with Thee, and that they may obtain help from Thee. Let them await the hope of their salvation from Thee, and let them abide in Thy mystery, and receive Thy gracious gifts, and perform what Thou wouldst have them do, and let them rejoice in Thy service, and finally [B 147a 1] let them array themselves in the apparel which is from Thy Father, because they have believed in Thine Apostle."

And when the Apostle had thus spoken Gandâpôr (Gonda-forus) the king and his brother Gâdôn departed, and they withdrew themselves from him and waited for him to ask them for whatsoever he wished ; and they became an asylum for everyone, and asked that they might receive the seal of his words [A 160a 2]. And the Apostle said unto them, "Prepare yourselves, and entreat God earnestly, and then I will bestow upon you the seal itself." And they said unto him : "We have heard thee say that the God Whom thou preachest knoweth His own sheep by His seal." And the Apostle answered and said unto them, "I rejoice, I beseech you to receive this seal, and to associate yourselves with me in fasting, and giving of thanks for the blessing of God, and to become perfect wholly in God, Jesus Christ, in Whose Name I preach, and to believe in the Name of the Father of righteousness, concerning Whom [B 147a 2] I have taught you." And he commanded them to bring oil, and to receive the seal, and they brought oil and lighted many lamps, for it was night. Then the Apostle rose up, and prayed over them with his voice, saying, "Peace be unto you, O my brethren." Now they heard the voice only [A 160b 1], but they did not see [his] form ; for as yet they had not received baptism. And the Apostle took the oil and poured it over their heads,

and recited prayers over them, and he answered and said,
"Let the Name of Christ, which is over all things, come ! Let
the Name which is holy, and exalted, and perfect in mercy,
come ! Let Thy mercy come ! Let Thine excellent union with
us come ! Let that which is a hidden mystery come ! Let the
mother of the seven mansions come, and let thy rest be in
the eighth habitation ! Let the intercession of wisdom, and
counsel, and understanding come and unite itself unto
[B 147b 1] these young men ! Let the Holy Spirit come and
cleanse their hearts and reins ! " And he prayed over them in
the Name of the Father, and of the Son, and of the Holy
Ghost. And when the exorcisms had been said a young Man
appeared unto them, and He held a lighted lamp in His hand,
and straightway all the [other] lamps died down, and flickered,
and became extinguished. [A 160b 2] Then the Apostle said
unto the Lord, "O Thou Who art almighty, we cannot bear
the light which Thou hast revealed unto us, for Thy Grace is
more mighty than ours." And when the dawn came and it
was morning, the Apostle gave them the Bread of Union, and
they stood up in thanksgiving to Christ, and rejoiced and
were glad.

And many other people believed and were added unto
them, and came to Christ as a refuge. And the Apostle ceased
not to teach and to preach, and he said unto them, "O men
and women, young men and maidens, old and young, bond or
free, flee from greed (or avarice) and from fornication and the
service [B 147b 2] of the belly, for under these three sins are
[found] wickednesses of every kind. For fornication burneth
up the mind, and darkeneth the eyes of the soul, and it
maketh the body to cease from the doing of good works ; and
ye know that a woman turneth away a man's mind from them,
[A 161a 1] and leadeth him into suffering. And avarice
bringeth the soul into fear and shame, and when it dwelleth
in the body, it plundereth the possessions of others, and it
preventeth a man from giving to his neighbour what is his
due, and restoring to others what is theirs. And the service
of the belly cloudeth the mind, and casteth sorrow into the

soul, and it meditateth whether it will have need of this or of that, and it seeketh the things which are alien to it, and how it can escape from the things which must come upon it, and how it can obtain ease. Dwell ye without fear and anxiety, and this Saviour Whom I proclaim shall dwell with you. And ye shall take no thought for the morrow, for the morrow shall take thought for the things of itself. And remember ye [B 148a 1] these words which were spoken in olden time concerning the ravens : "Consider the birds of the heavens, for they neither sow, nor reap, nor gather into barns, and God feedeth them ; how little is the faith which [A 161a 2] ye have[1] !" But ye must accept Him Who shall come, that is to say, our Lord, in Whom your hope shall be. And believe in His Name, for He shall be the Judge of the living and of the dead, and He shall reward every man according to his work. At His coming, and when He appeareth at the last day, there shall be no word which a man can utter that will excuse him, for He shall judge according to the Law, [and it will avail men naught to say that] they did not hear. The word of His preaching is in the four quarters of the world. Understand ye then that which is preached and believe ye these words at this present time, and take upon you the yoke which is easy and the burden which is light, so that ye may live and not die. Keep ye these things, and confirm yourselves in these commandments, and go forth from the darkness, so that ye may be received into the light. Come ye unto the Good One so that ye may receive of His gracious gift, [B 148a 2] and may fill yourselves with the doctrine which is His."

And when the Apostle had said these things, some of those who stood there said unto him, "It is time [A 161b 1] for those to whom a debt is due to be paid." And he answered and said unto them, "Always doth God take from some so that He may remit the debt to him that asketh it ; but let us give that which is meet unto Him." And he blessed them, and he took bread, and oil, and sheep's flesh, and salt, and gave unto them, but he himself continued to fast until the

---

[1] Matt. vi. 26; Luke xii. 24, 28.

dawn of the Christian Sabbath came. And in the night our
Lord came and stood by the Apostle, near his pillow, and said
unto him, "Rise up straightway, O Thomas, and at dawn, at
the time of prayer, go forth by the road that leadeth to the
east for a distance of two stages, and there I will show thee
My glory. And because of thy going many shall come and
take refuge in Me, and the strength and the will of the
Enemy shall be rebuked." And when the Apostle rose from
his slumber, he said unto the brethren who were with him,
"My children, [B 148b 1] and brethren, [A 161b 2] God hath
the desire to work miracles and do wonders through me. Let
us pray and entreat Him that there may be no cessation of
them through us, but on the contrary, that they may never
cease; and now let it happen unto us according to His
Counsel and His Will." Then, having said these words, he
laid his hand upon them, and blessed them, and said unto
them, "Let thanksgiving be with you, and mercy, and compassion, and may it not be for judgement!" And they said,
"Amen."

Here endeth the Second Act of Saint Thomas.

THE THIRD ACT [B 205a 2]

[TO BE READ ON THE SECOND DAY OF THE MONTH OF
YAKÂTÎT (JANUARY 27).]

The Miracle of the Snake.

And the Apostle departed to go forth unto the place whither
our Lord had commanded him[1]. And when he had drawn nigh
thereto, being about one stage from it, he withdrew a little
from the highway, and by chance he saw a young and handsome man lying dead. And the Apostle said unto our Lord,
"Was it because of this, O Lord, that Thou didst make me to
go forth and come hither, in order to make me undergo this
trial? Nevertheless, since thou hast sent me, Thy Will be done

---

[1] See Lipsius, *op. cit.* vol. I. p. 255; Wright, *op. cit.* vol. II. p. 169.

in this matter." And he began to pray, [A 162a 1] saying,
"O God, Thou Judge of the quick and the dead, the quick
being those who are standing upright, and the dead being
those who are lying down, Thou God of all, Father of those
who are in the body, and of those who have departed from
the body, and are in the spirit, O Lord, Thou art the Judge in
this hour, and therefore I cry unto Thee, let me make manifest
Thy glory through this dead man who is here." Then the
Apostle turned unto those who were following him, and said,
"This is no light matter. The Enemy himself hath performed
it so that he might have possession [of his soul]; but behold
ye, [B 205b 1] he hath not power to do it to any other man,
and he shall do this only to him that is obedient unto him."
Now when he had said these words a large snake, which was
by the side of a stone, put forth his head and shook it, and his
tail was in the earth. And he cried out with a loud voice,
saying, "I will declare before thee in the following words the
story of the quarrel which I had with this [young man], for,"
he continued, "I know that thou hast come hither in order to
rebuke my deeds." And the Apostle said unto the serpent,
"Yea, speak." Then the serpent said, "There was a certain
beautiful [A 162a 2] woman who lived in the village opposite,
and since she lived there I saw her, and I loved her, and I
followed her, and I watched over her. And I found that this
young man was wont to kiss her, and to lie with her, and to
work other things with her, which it would be easy for me to
declare, but it is not meet for me to reveal them before thee,
for I know that thou art the twin of Christ, Who doth continually destroy our souls. I did not slay him when he was
with her, but I watched over her until the evening had come,
and then I struck at him, [B 205b 2] and killed him because
he was wont to do this thing on the Sabbath of the Christians."
And the Apostle answered and said unto the serpent, "Of
what kith and kin art thou?" Then the serpent said, "I am
he who moveth and is moved. I am an oppressor and have
the power to oppress. I am the son of him that sitteth upon
the throne in the heavens, and who gathereth together those

belonging unto him who have been avenged. I am the son of him that fettereth the drunken man. I am the kinsman of him who is on the outside of the [A 162b 1] Ocean, and whose tail is in his mouth. I am he who was born in the Garden (i.e. Paradise), and I dwelt therein, and I came in with Eve, and I held converse with her, and I spake [unto her] the things which my father commanded me to speak. I am he who stirred up Cain and made him burn to slay his brother, and through me the thorn and the thistle sprouted, and flourished on the earth. I am he who made the angels to come down from on high, and I snared them with the lust for women, so that the children of earth might spring [B 206a 1] from them, and I worked my will [in them]. I am he who hardened the heart of Pharaoh, and who made him to slay the children of Israel and them to serve under a cruel yoke. I am he who led astray the people in the desert when they made the graven image. I am he who moved Herod to wrath, and I incited Caiaphas when [the Jews] made false accusations before Pilate against Him Whom it is meet that I should worship. I am he who made Judas to betray Christ and to deliver [A 162b 2] Him over unto death. I am he who layeth hold upon the depth of the......although the Son of God desireth it not. I am he who hath led the way, and whatsoever He hath chosen from me He hath chosen. I am the kinsman of him who shall come from the east, and to whom hath been given the power to do whatsoever he pleaseth on the earth." These are the things which the serpent spake whilst all the multitude was listening.

And the Apostle answered and said unto him, "Hold thy peace, and [hearken unto] what I shall say unto thee, O abominable one, and thou shalt be put to shame. For the time for thy destruction hath arrived, and thou shalt never [B 206a 2] again speak these words wherein thou didst proclaim what thou didst do for those who hearkened unto thy speech. In the Name of Jesus, Who hath lived up to this present, and Who shall live for ever, because of these elect who are here, I command thee to suck out and to withdraw from this [young man] the poison which thou didst cast into him." And the snake spake again, saying, "The time hath not yet come for my destruction, as thou sayest, and why wilt thou make me to withdraw that which I have cast into this young man? Why should I die before my time? [A 163a 1] It was [my] father himself who made the poison, and who took it and cast it into the world, and destruction thereby took place." Then the Apostle said, "Show me now what thy father made." And the serpent having drawn nigh, put his mouth into the wound, and in the presence of all the multitude sucked out his poison, and, little by little, the colour of the young man, which was purple, changed and became white even as it had been formerly. And the serpent became puffed out as he drew the poison into himself from [B 206b 1] the young man, who leaped up and embraced the feet of the Apostle, and straightway the serpent became swollen to his full extent, and he burst asunder and all his venom and poison were poured out. And the earth was rent asunder to a great depth and also the place where the venom was poured out, and the serpent was swallowed up in the abyss. And the Apostle commanded the king and his brother, and they brought slaves, and filled up the chasm, and laid foundations and built upon it houses wherein the poor might dwell.

Then the young man spake unto the Apostle, saying, "In what have I sinned against thee, O thou man whose grace is twofold? [A 163a 2] What thou thinkest upon that thou obtainest, and unto thee there is nothing impossible, even as I see from this man who is standing by thee. And moreover, he telleth me that I shall see many miracles through thee, and that through thee I shall perform many mighty works, and that I shall fulfil them in such wise that there shall be a reward [unto me], and that many shall be saved by them, and shall attain unto the rest and the light which is for ever, and shall become children of God. Now thou hast given life unto me, a young man who was held fast by the Enemy, [B 206b 2] and thou hast placed me under thine own protection; thy coming among us was for good, and unto good things thou wilt guide us. I have become free from sorrow and trouble, and I have returned from darkness into the light. I have ceased to serve the world, and I have been saved from him that would urge me to perform the deeds of error. And I have forsaken him who was born in darkness, and who would have forced me to commit sin by my acts. But now I have found Him Who will give me light, and Who will be a kinsman and a Redeemer unto me. And He will [uncover] our eyes, and will draw onwards [A 163 b 1] those who hearken unto Him, that they may have knowledge, and may work, and may feel shame, and showing themselves penitent may be saved (?). I have seen this deed, which is of the light, and is one which, indeed, cannot be put to shame. I am delivered from the work of darkness and error, and I shall not be put to shame. I have found him who will do good unto me, and who will drive away evil from me. I have come unto him that is indeed the son and kinsman of the WONDER, Who will scatter the clouds, and illumine the world, and heal our wounds, and overthrow [B 207 a 1] hatred of Him. O servant of God, I beseech thee to show Him again unto me so that I may know Him, and may hear His marvellous voice, which cannot be described, for the music of [His] Person is beyond that of Nature."

And the Apostle answered and said unto him, "If thou art saved, and hast placed thy trust as thou hast known how to do, even as thou sayest, Who is He Who hath done this for thee, and hath given thee knowledge and proof? Because thy love [for Him] is certain unto thee, thou desirest to [A 163 b 2] see Him, and to be with Him for ever, and to abide among His own creatures, and to have thy rest in His joy. If it be not true that thou hast fled unto Him for refuge, and if thou hast returned unto the works which thou didst aforetime, then thou must forsake the beauty of the work of His goodness, which hath now appeared unto thee, and the light of His baptism, which thou now desirest. And if thou forsakest Him thou shalt lose not only this life which perisheth, but also that which is to come, and thou shalt return to thy former state, which is behind thee, of which thou speakest."

And when the Apostle had thus spoken, he came into the city holding the young man [B 207a 2] by the hand, and he spake unto him all these words : "[The things seen] are only a few out of many of the things which are with God ; He doth not inform you concerning the things which are seen, but He showeth you things which are greater. As long as we are in the body we cannot declare and proclaim openly the things which He hath prepared for those who believe on Him ; and even if I would declare unto you the light [A 164a 1] it would be a hard thing for me to do. And if we tell you that He is rich, since His riches do not appear in this world, we can only make mention [thereof] and cannot seek them. For He said, 'It belongeth unto what is difficult for a rich man to enter into the kingdom of heaven[1].' And it hath been heard and said, 'Those who wear fine linen are found in the palace[2].' And because of those who are pure the banquets of which we have been wont to partake have been proclaimed and condemned, that we might know within ourselves that we must not overload our bodies with strong drink or with worldly care. 'Take not thought for yourselves what ye shall eat, and what ye shall drink, nor for your bodies [B 207b 1] what ye shall put on ; for the soul is of more account than the food, and your bodies are of more account than the raiment[3].' If we speak of the enjoyment of a little food, a judgement is waiting thereon. But we may speak concerning Him that is above the world, and concerning God and His Angels, and concerning the Saints and the Watchers, and concerning the way [A 164a 2] of joy, and concerning the drinking of the wine of the true Vine, and concerning the putting on of apparel which abideth and groweth not old, which the eye hath not seen, nor the ear heard of, and which it hath not entered into the heart of sinful man to imagine, and which God hath made ready for those who love Him[4]. Of these things do we speak, and of such things do we preach. Believe

---

[1] Matt. xix. 23, 24; Mark x. 25; Luke xviii. 25.
[2] Luke vii. 25.   [3] Matt. vi. 25.
[4] Isaiah lxiv. 4; 1 Corinthians ii. 9.

thou then in Him that thou mayest live, that thy hope may
be upon Him, and thou mayest not die. He desireth not a
gift, and even if thou wouldst give Him one He cannot be
appeased thereby ; and He asketh not thee to offer up sacrifices to Him. Put thou thy trust in Him, and He will not
reject thee ; turn thou unto Him, and He will not forsake
thee. [B 207b 2] For His goodness will make thee to love
Him, and when thou hast turned unto Him He will never forsake thee."

And when the Apostle had said these things unto the young
man many people flocked to him. And the Apostle looked at
them, and saw that they were thrusting up their heads that
they might see him, and that they were going up on to higher
ground so that they might look at him. Then he said unto
them, "O ye men who [A 164b 1] have come that ye may believe in the works of Christ, know ye and understand henceforth that unless ye raise yourselves a little above the ground
ye cannot see me who am a man like unto yourselves. How
then will ye be able to see Him Who dwelleth in the height
and in the depths unless, first of all, ye withdraw yourselves
from your former habits, and from the works wherein there is
no benefit ? I desire that ye keep yourselves from that wherein
there is no profit, and from the riches which perish, and from
the possessions which grow old and decay in the earth, and
from [rich] apparel, and from the meat which cometh to an
end and perisheth [B 208a 1]. And moreover, all your bodies
also wax old, and they are buried in the ground, and turn into
dust, and return to their former state and become ashes.
This is [the fate of] the body which worketh. But believe ye,
and be baptized in Christ Jesus, Whom we preach, so that He
may become your hope, and your life shall be everlasting. He
shall be your guide in this [A 164b 2] land of violence, and
He shall become a haven for you among the billows of the
sea. He shall be a fountain of pure water for you in this land
of thirst, and He shall be your food in every place, and an
asylum for your souls, and a healing for your bodies."

And when the multitudes of people who had gathered

together to him heard these words they wept, and they said unto him, "O man of the God Whom thou preachest, O man of the God Who is God, it is not meet for us to say that we are His, for the works which we have been wont to do are [B 208a 2] alien unto Him, and remote from Him, and they are not well-pleasing unto Him. But if He will have compassion upon us, and will show mercy unto us, and redeem us, and will deliver us from our former works, and from all the evil and from the error wherein we have erred and gone astray, and will neither keep in mind, nor remember against us our transgressions of former times, we will conform unto His Will, and we will keep His commandments wholly."

Then the Apostle answered and said unto them, "He will neither keep in mind, nor remember against you your transgressions, nor the error wherein ye have lived, [A 165a 1] and He will not keep beneath His eye the sins which ye have committed."

THE FOURTH ACT

To be Read on the Second Day of Yakâtît (January 27).

How an ass spake to the Apostle.

Now whilst the Apostle was standing in that place and talking with the multitude, the colt of an ass came and stood before him. And the colt opened his mouth and said unto the Apostle, "O kinsman of Christ, and Apostle of the Most High! Thou art full of the word of Christ, thou art he who knoweth hidden things. Thou who wast a free man, like the Son of God, didst become a [B 208b 1] slave, even as did He, that thou mightest redeem many. Thou who art of noble race didst bind thyself unto an enemy, and didst deliver his chosen one, and didst become the means of life unto many in the country of India. And thou didst come unto sinful men, who at the appearance of thee, and through the voice of God, have turned unto the things which God sent thee to teach them. If thou wilt mount me and ride me thou canst have rest until thou enterest the city."

And the Apostle answered and said, "O Jesus, by Whose desire Thy mercy is given for the perfecting of patience, Who speakest by means of animals which speak not, [A 165a 2] Who art the hidden rest, Who art only revealed by divers means, our Redeemer, our Nourisher, and our Guardian, Who givest rest to the body and salvation to our souls, Thou art the Sweet Spring and the Pure Fountain which never fail and never become polluted. Thou art the Merciful One, Thou art the Helper of those who are Thy servants and who fight for Thee. Thou turnest back the Enemy, and dost make him to withdraw from us, Thou wagest war on our behalf in many combats, and we prevail by Thee, Who art [B 208b 2] indeed the Athlete and Angel who cannot be overcome, Thou holy, victorious and glorious God! Thou givest unto Thine elect the joy which never endeth, and the rest which is without labour. Thou didst give Thyself on behalf of Thy sheep, and didst vanquish the wolf, and didst deliver us who are the sheep of Thy pasture, and Thou didst lead them in the Commandments which are good. Thee we glorify, Thee we praise, together with Thy Father, Who is invisible, and the Holy Ghost, for Thou art the One righteous God in all the world."

And whilst the Apostle was saying these things to the colt of an ass, the multitude were looking at the Apostle, and were waiting for the answer [A 165b 1] that he would make unto the animal. And the colt having stood there astonished for a long time, with his gaze fixed upon heaven, the Apostle said unto him, "Who art thou? Unto whom dost thou belong? For that which hath gone forth from thy mouth is astonishing and glorious, for thereby many marvellous and secret things [are revealed]." And the colt of the ass answered and said unto him, "I am of the offspring of the ass which served Balaam, and upon my father, [B 209a 1] from whose seed I have come, did thy Lord and Teacher sit. And now, I have been sent unto thee that I might give thee rest, and that thou mightest sit upon me." Then the Apostle believed and said in his heart, "This is my portion which hath come to me through thy labour; I will go. Rise up." And the Apostle said unto the ass, "He Who hath given unto thee this gracious gift is able to make it perfect for thee from generation to generation; this thing is too honourable for me, and I am not meet for it." And he refused to ride upon the colt of the ass. Then the colt of the ass asked and entreated the Apostle to allow him to receive a blessing from him ; and he stood still, and the Apostle mounted him and bade him [A 165b 2] [to proceed]. And all the people followed him, some running in front of him and some behind him that they might see the conclusion of the matter, and how he would leave the colt of the ass. And when the Apostle came to the gates of the city, he cast himself from the colt of the ass and said unto him, "Go, and take heed where thou goest." And straightway the colt of the ass fell down before him and died. [B 209a 2] And all those who were there were terrified, and said unto the Apostle, "Bring him to life and raise him up again." Then the Apostle answered and said unto them, "I have the power to raise him up through the might of Jesus Christ, but he is better thus. He Who gave him a voice to speak with is able to make him not to die and to raise him up again, but He wisheth it not. This state is best for the colt." And the Apostle commanded those who were standing there to dig a hole and bury the body of the colt of the ass.

THE FIFTH ACT

To be Read on the Fourteenth Day of the Month Magâbît [B 221a 1; A 166a 1] (March 10).

How a Devil seized and took possession of a woman, and tarried with her, and dwelt in her for five years.

And the Apostle came into the city[1], and all the multitude followed after him. And he decided to go unto the kinsfolk of the young man who had been killed by the serpent, whom he had made to live, for they besought him earnestly to go to

---

[1] See Lipsius, *op. cit.* vol. I. p. 257; Wright, *op. cit.* vol. II. p. 182.

them. Now when the Apostle had come into the house there was a certain woman there who was beautiful, and she cried out with a loud voice, and said, " O thou new Apostle of the new God, who hast come unto the country of India, through whose coming the salvation of our souls hath arrived, through whom, if they believe in Him, the bodies of such as are sick by reason of the sickness of the Enemy are made whole, thou art the means of life unto all those who turn to Him. Give thou to me the command to approach thee, so that I may declare everything that hath happened unto me. Then shall I, through thee, have hope, and those who are standing by thee also shall have hope in the God Whom thou preachest. Behold, for five years not a little torment [B 221a 2] have I suffered through the Enemy, and during that time I have been like [A 166a 2] unto a woman who was in suffering and sorrow, although formerly I was at peace with everyone, and I had no care or anxiety whatsoever. Now, one day, as I was coming out of the bath, there met me a certain man who appeared to be in haste, and he was troubled, and his voice was weak and trembling within him. And he said unto me, 'Stand still in front of me, for thou and I are one, and our love shall be one, and we will have union together after the manner of a man with a woman.' Then I answered and said unto him, 'I had nought to say to my betrothed, for I wished not to have union with him; how then canst thou desire union with me, except as a harlot?' And having thus spoken I passed on my way. Then I said unto a woman who was with me, 'Didst thou see this man who was not ashamed to speak openly with me of fornication?' And she said, 'I saw an old man talking to thee.' And when I had entered my house, and had eaten my supper, I fell to thinking much about the young man whom I and my friend [B 221b 1] had seen, [A 166b 1] and whilst I was engaged in thinking I fell asleep. And in the night the man himself came in person and had union with me ; when the day came I fled from him, but at nightfall he returned and stayed with me. This he hath been in the habit of doing during the last five years, and behold, though he weareth me out he will not leave me. I know of a surety that devils, and unclean spirits, and Satans are subject unto thee, and that they tremble [before thee] and at thy prayer. Pray then thou for me, and drive away from me my tormentor, so that I may be free from him, and may return to my former condition, and may again receive from my kinsfolk the gracious treatment which they have withdrawn from me."

And the Apostle said, "What evil can the Enemy work that cannot be put down? There is no opposition which cannot be overcome, and no evil for which there is not a remedy." [And the Apostle said unto the man who tormented the woman,] "Thou, O Evil One, hast many aspects, and thou appearest in any form thou pleasest, and thy nature changeth with each; thou art without faith, and thou destroyest him whose works are good. [B 221 b 2] Thy nature is bitter, and thy fruit is from Diabolos. Thou art shameless Error, and thy errors [A 166 b 2] burn like the venom of the serpent." And when the Apostle had said these words the devil came forth into his presence, though none saw him except the woman, and he cried out with a loud voice before the people who were listening, "What have I to do with thee, O Apostle of the Highest? What have I to do with thee, O thou servant of Jesus Christ? What have I to do with thee, O friend of the Holy Son of God? Why dost thou wish to destroy us before our time? Why dost thou wish to take away the power which is ours? For we had hope and opportunity, like thyself, and we had dominion, and in thee and in me is the same dominion (or, equal power?). And what is the power whereby thou hast come to have dominion over us? Now we also have in us the knowledge of another through which thou shalt not gain the mastery over us. [B 222 a 1] And why dost thou covet for thyself, like an unjust man, that which belongeth unto another, and dost make thyself like unto the Son of God, Who hath [A 167 a 1] guided us, and having come hither, dost pretend thou doest things by the strength which is thine own? Now we imagined that we could hold Him with our hand, like a man, but we understand [Him] not, for He hath turned us and brought us back with His hand. We knew Him not, for He came in the similitude of a man, and He hid Himself and abased Himself. And we looked at Him, and imagined that He was a man Who had put on flesh, and we knew not that it was He Who could give life unto man. He gave us power over our enemies, and we had dominion over them for many days, and we led them into error, being lords over them, and we made them to go round about. Now thou desirest, without opposition, to exceed the power which was given unto thee, and to cast us away."

And when he had said these words the devil wept and said, "Must I leave this my kind and [B 222a 2] beautiful wife with whom I have dwelt for [many] days, and in whom I have found my place of rest? Must I leave thee now, O my most beloved sister, my most dear one, in whose body I have been well pleased? [A 167a 2] I know not upon whom I am to call, or who will hear me and give me rest. But I know what I will do. I will go into places where I have never been, where the authority of the Apostle ruleth not, and I will find another [woman to take] thy place." And lifting up his voice the devil said, "Dwell thou in rest and peace, for thou hast received one who is greater than I. I will go and seek for some one who is like unto thee, and if I find her not I will return unto thee. For I know that since thou art near this man thou wilt take refuge with him; but when he hath departed thou wilt be unto me as thou wast aforetime when thou hadst not seen him and chosen him. And when the time hath come I shall appear openly, but I fear Him Whom this man preacheth." And having said these words [B 222b 1] the devil went forth amid fire and smoke and was no more seen, and all who were there marvelled. And when the Apostle [A 167b 1] saw this he said unto them, "There is nothing marvellous about what this devil hath done, except his nature, by which he hath been brought to nought; for it is his own fire which hath consumed him, and the smoke of his burning is scattered."

And the Apostle answered and said, " O JESUS, Thou hidden

Mystery which hath been revealed unto us, Who art not hidden, it is Thou Who hast created me, and [made] me greater than my fellows. Thou hast spoken unto me three words whereby my mind shall be revealed unto others, but I am unable to declare them. Jesus, Thou Man Who wast slain and buried, Jesus, our God and Redeemer, Who gavest life to the dead, Who didst heal the sick, there is no man whom, if he ask Thee, Thou wilt not save in Thy mercy. Thou didst catch fish for the evening and morning meals [of the multitude], and with very little bread didst satisfy them. Jesus, Who didst rest Thyself after a journey even like a man, but Who didst walk upon the waves of the [B 222b 2] sea like God, Thou art the Word of the Most High Who dost manifest Thyself in the hearts of the perfect. [A 167b 2] Thou art the perfect (or, absolute) Saviour, and the Right Hand of the Light. Thou didst destroy Satan by Thy power, and didst blot out all his works, and every similitude of him, O Thou Only-begotten, Who art above all the firstborn of many brethren, Thou God Who art from God, Thou Exalted One Whom men have rejected and despised until this present. O Jesus Christ Who didst not make Thy grace to be remote from us, we cry out unto Thee, O Thou Who hast become the source of life to all the race of men. For our sakes Thou didst endure condemnation, and didst suffer pain, and wast shut up in prison. And Thou didst set free all those who were therein, and those who had been cast aside, and those who had gone astray, and Thou didst redeem from the path of error those who believed in Thee. I beseech Thee, O my Lord, on behalf of those who are standing [here] and believing on Thee, who await Thy grace, and Thy place of refuge, and who hearken with their ears to Thy word [B 223a 1] which is spoken unto them by Thee, let Thy peace come, and let Thy joy and Thy faith [A 168a 1] dwell upon them, and make new their works in the time which is past, and let them put away their old works and put on the new [man] which is preached unto them by me."

Then the Apostle laid his hand upon them and blessed

them, saying, "The grace of our Lord Jesus Christ be with
you for ever and ever. Amen." And the woman made entreaty
to him, saying, "O Apostle of the Most High, give me the seal
so that this evil enemy may not come back upon me." And
the Apostle set her before him, and he laid his hand upon her,
and he made the sign of the Cross over her in the Name of
the Father, and the Son, and the Holy Ghost. And many
other people were sealed with her with the sign of the Cross.
Then the Apostle commanded them to bring a table, and they
placed a bench which was there in position, and the Apostle
spread a linen cover over it, and set thereon the Bread of
Blessing. And [B 223a 2] standing up, he said, "O Jesus,
Who hast caused me to appear that we may give thanks unto
Thee, and may partake of Thy holy Body and Thy precious
Blood, because of Thy grace towards us we offer [A 168a 2]
thanksgiving unto Thee, and we proclaim Thy Name to be
holy. Come now and accept us, and let the grace of the Most
High come, and let Thy mercy come, and let the human
nature whereto Thou hast united thyself come, and let Thy
doctrine which hath knowledge of hidden mysteries come, and
let the mighty companion come, and let the mighty warrior
come, and let the storehouse of life come, and let the grace
of the elect come, and let the grace which is of old come, and
let it reveal great and marvellous works. And let that which
is hidden be manifest openly, and let grace and rest be given
unto those who think with me, and let it come and mingle
itself with this thanksgiving which we make in Thy Name,
and in Thy love, and let us be blessed unto Thee." And having
said these words the Apostle made the sign of the Cross over
the bread, and he brake it and offered it unto the [B 223b 1]
woman over whom he had made the sign of the Cross, and
said, "This shall be unto thee for the remission of sin and
transgression, and it shall be unto thee for everlasting life."
And [A 168b 1] after this he gave it unto those who were
with her, and they were sealed with the sign of the Cross and
were blessed.

THE SIXTH ACT

To be read on the Twentieth Day of the Month Sanê (June 14).

How a woman was slain in a shop.

Now[1] [B 245b 1] there was a certain young man who had committed a very wicked act, and he was rebuked. For he drew nigh and partook of the Blessing, and gave thanks, and he was about to put the Bread in his mouth when both his hands dried up, and he was unable to do so. And those who were standing there saw what had happened, and they told the Apostle. The Apostle called the young man and said unto him, "Tell me, O my son, and fear not, what didst thou do before thou didst come here ? For the grace of God hath rebuked thee. Now the grace of God is a healing unto many, and especially unto those who receive it in faith and love, but thee hath it caused to wither, because of the sin and transgression which thou hast committed." And when the young man saw that the grace [A 168b 2] of God had rebuked him, he drew nigh and bowed down at the feet of the Apostle, and he made supplication unto him, saying, " I have committed an abominable act [B 245b 2], although I intended to do what was good. Behold, there was a certain woman who lived outside the city, and she trafficked in merchandise, and she loved [me exceedingly]. And when I heard how thou didst preach Christ, the living [God], I came and I received from thee the sign of the Cross together with everyone. And thou thyself didst say, 'If any man joineth himself unto foul impurity, and especially if he hath union with a woman who hath a husband, he shall not receive forgiveness of sins from God.' And because of these words, and because I loved her, I should have been well-pleased for her to live with me in purity of heart, even as thou didst teach me, but the woman importuned me greatly, and when she refused to desist, I took a sword and killed her, for I could not bear the sight of her." And when

---

[1] See Lipsius, *op. cit.* p. 258; Wright, *op. cit.* vol. II. p. 190.

the Apostle had heard these words, he said, "O evil [A 169a 1]
lust, which couldst not be constrained, thou hast caused this
man to commit a foul act in wrath. Thou hast made him to
commit in a shameful way an act of the [B 246a 1] Evil One."

And the Apostle commanded them to bring unto him water
in a washing bowl, and they did so. And the Apostle said, "O
water which hath come unto us from the Water of Life! O
grace which hath been given and sent unto us from Grace!
O rest which hath been sent unto us from Rest! O Might of
the redemption of Christ which vanquisheth all things and
which doeth all things! Yea, O Lord, let Thy command come
and abide upon this water, so that the grace of the Holy
Spirit may be upon this water." Then the Apostle said unto
the young man, "Go, and wash thy hands in this water"; and
the young man washed, and was healed, and became as he
was aforetime. Now before the young man had washed, the
Apostle said unto him, "Dost thou believe that Jesus Christ
is able to do all things?" And the young man said, "Let not
this my punishment be too severe for me because I did this
evil thing, for I committed the deed [A 169a 2] in faith,
[B 246a 2] imagining that I was doing a good deed, and I did
it because of my belief. I made supplication unto her, as I
have already told thee, and she refused to keep herself in
purity, and I did this thing unto her."

And the Apostle said unto him, "Come now, and lead me
into the house of the woman to whom thou hast done this
evil, and let me see her." And the young man went with the
Apostle, and when they arrived at the place, they found the
woman ready for burial. Now when the Apostle had seen
her he was sorrowful, for she was fair to look upon, and of
graceful stature, and he commanded them to bring her out
into the garden. And they brought her out and laid her upon
a bed outside [the house]. And they did even as he commanded them. Then the Apostle laid his hand upon her, and
said, "O Jesus Christ, Who withdrawest not Thine hand, and
Who makest not Thy face to be remote from those who call
upon Thee, Thou Jesus Who appearest at all times, whenever
we wish and whenever we call upon Thee, Thou hast given

this power [B 246b 1] that we may receive it. [A 169b 1]
And not this only hast Thou commanded us, but Thou hast
taught us to pray: and Thou dost not only instruct man, but
Thou appearest to him and he seeth Thee. Iniquity is not
hidden from Thee, and Thou hast shown Thy works openly
unto men. Thy works, as far as we are able to comprehend
Thee, are unmeasurable. O Thou Who hast given unto us
this gracious gift, Thou hast said unto us: Ask, and it shall
be given unto you; seek, and ye shall find; knock, and it
shall be opened unto you[1]. We make supplication unto Thee,
knowing our sin. We beseech Thee neither for riches nor
possessions, nor for gold and silver, nor for anything desirable
whatsoever which returneth unto the earth. But we beseech
and entreat Thee, for Thy holy Name's sake, to raise up by
Thy might and glory her who hath fallen down, so that those
who are here present may believe." Then the Apostle said
unto the young man, "Go, take hold of her and say unto her,
I slew thee by an iron weapon with my own hand, but Christ,
by my own hand, [B 246b 2] through faith, shall raise thee
up." And having drawn nigh unto her the young man said,
[A 169b 2] "I believe in Thee. O Jesus Christ, grant Thou
unto this woman the gift of life. As for me, draw nigh unto
me, and [increase] my faith." Then he drew the hand of the
woman towards him, and she arose, and turned round and sat
up, and all those who were there saw her. And [when] she
saw the Apostle standing in front of her, she left her couch,
and rose up and bowed low in homage at the feet of the
Apostle. And she took hold of the hem of his garment, and
said unto him, "I beseech thee, O my lord, [to tell me] where
is the other being, who was with me and who would not let
me remain in the place of abomination, but handed me over
into thy care [and said], "Let this woman return unto her
place, and let her dwell as she hath dwelt in the time which
is past." And the Apostle said unto her, "Tell me, whence
hast thou come?" And she answered and said unto him,
[B 247a 1] "Dost thou, who wast with me, wish to hear into
what place I came?" Then she began to speak unto the

[1] Matt. vii. 7; Luke xi. 9.

Apostle, and she said unto him, " A man who was altogether black, and whose apparel was altogether filthy, carried me away [A 170 a 1] and set me in a place where there were many pits that reeked with a foul smell. Then he led me out from that place and set me in another where I saw before me a pit of blazing fire. Here there were wheels which went round, and to these wheels were bound souls which shrieked and cried out, but there was none to deliver them. And the black man said, 'These are the souls of people like thyself, who when their days [upon earth] have come to an end, are delivered over to this punishment, for being men they made themselves to be as women.' And I also saw little children, one above the other [B 247 a 2]. And the black man answered and said unto me, 'These are the children of those souls, and God hath placed them here to disgrace them.' And the black man took me to another pit, and I looked and saw an abyss filled with worms, and the souls therein were writhing, and they were gnashing their teeth and uttering piercing cries. And the black man [A 170 a 2] said unto me, 'These are the souls of the women who have left their husbands, and have committed fornication with other men, and of the men who have left their wives and committed fornication with other women; behold, they have entered upon their punishment.' Then he showed me another pit, and I looked and saw therein souls that were hanging, some by their tongues, and some by the hair of their heads, and some by their hands, [B 247 b 1] and some by their feet, and some with their heads downwards; and the smoke of pitch was fuming below them. And the black man said unto me, 'The souls that are hanging by their tongues are the souls of those who were guilty of falsehood, and who spake lies without being ashamed. The souls that are hanging by their hair are the souls of those who were perverse, and who never had reverence for man or woman. The souls that are hanging by their hands are the souls of those who robbed and plundered the poor, who never gave [alms] to those who were in affliction, who stole the possessions of others, and who neither remembered nor observed the Law of God. The souls that are hanging by their [A 170 b 1] feet are the souls of those who followed after evil desire, and who never regarded those who were in misery, or those who died and remained unburied. Each soul shall be rewarded according to its deeds.'

"Then he set me in another place of darkness wherefrom there proceeded a filthy smell, and multitudes of souls were gazing from that place that they might see the [B 247b 2] light, and those who had charge over them were preventing the souls from looking towards the light. And the [black] man who was with me said unto me, 'Such are the punishments of the souls whom thou seest. When a company of souls have received the punishment which is assigned to them, according to their work, another company take their place. Some souls are destroyed after they have received their punishment, but others are condemned to endure further punishments.' And the guardians of the souls which were in darkness said unto the [black] man who was leading me, 'Give us this soul to place with its friends until the time for its judgment shall arrive.' And he said unto them, 'I will not give it up unto you, but unto Him that [A 170b 2] sent me, for He commanded me not to leave it here but to take it with me until a decree concerning it should come forth.' Then the [black] man took me and set me in another place wherein were men walking about, and one who was like unto thee [B 248a 1] took me, and gave me unto thee, saying, 'Take her, and keep her, for she belongeth unto the sheep who have gone astray in times past.' And now, behold, I am here before thee; and I beseech and entreat thee not to let me depart to that place where the punishments which I have seen are inflicted."

Then the Apostle said unto those who were there with him, "Hear what this woman saith. But there are punishments which are more cruel than those which she hath described, and these ye shall receive if at your death ye do not turn unto the Lord Whom I preach unto you, and forsake the evil works which ye did, through ignorance, in the times that are past. Believe in our Lord Jesus Christ that He may remit to you the sins which ye have committed, and may cleanse you from all your sins, and from all your evil mind, and [B 248a 2]

may be with you [A 171a 1] continually. And now, having
heard these things, put off from you the old and array yourselves in the new apparel. Put away your former works and
lusts. Let those who have stolen steal no more, but let them
love work and gain possessions for themselves. Let those who
have committed fornication do so no more, lest having enjoyed
the pleasure of a moment they find the pain which is eternal.
Now for a man to go with a man as with a woman is the
worst sin of all before God. Flee fraud, and oppression, and
plunder, and strong drink, and blood-guilt, and reward not
with evil him that doeth evil unto you, for all these things
against which I preach are abominations unto God. Dwell ye
in faith, and believe ye meekly, holily and hopefully, and walk
ye in the path wherein God is well-pleased. Be ye followers
of Him, and ye shall receive the gift of grace which [B 248b 1]
many shall receive at this present."

Then all the people believed and gave themselves unto God,
and they marvelled at Thomas's exalted works and at his
[A 171a 2] holy service. And they collected much money to
give to the widows, for the Apostle was wont to give unto them
with his own hands on certain days each month whatsoever
they needed, whether raiment [or food]. And he never failed
to preach and proclaim that it was written that Christ should
come, and be crucified, and raised up again on the third day.
And again and again he showed them from [the Books of] the
Prophets, from the beginning to the time when Christ Himself
appeared, that whatsoever they had said concerning Him was
fulfilled by Christ when He came.

Now the report of the Apostle came into every country and
city, and from the places wherever there were sick and diseased
folk among them, and people possessed of devils, and lunatics,
and cripples, and [B 248b 2] men sorely afflicted, they came
unto him. And those who were bedridden were carried to
him by those who could walk, and they carried them and laid
them by the roadside where the Apostle would pass and he,
by the might of God, healed them [A 171b 1] all. Those who
were sick were healed, and those who were infirm and crippled
stood up, and they all said with one voice, "Glory be to thee,

O Jesus Christ, Who hast bestowed healing alike upon all of us by the hands of Thy servant Thomas! We praise Thee, and beseech Thee to be allowed to enter Thy fold, and to be [counted] among the number of Thy sheep. Receive us, and remember not the sins which, in our ignorance, we committed in times past."

And the Apostle said, "Glory be unto Thee, O One, Only-begotten of the Father, Glory be unto Thee, O Thou Firstborn, Who givest life unto many, Glory be unto Thee, Thou Who rebukest and receivest those who turn unto Thee. Thou Who slumberest not dost raise up those who [B 249a 1] slumber, and givest life unto the dead. O our Lord Jesus Christ, the Son of the Living God, the Saviour, and Helper, and Refuge, and Rest of all those who labour [to do] Thy Will, Thou givest healing unto those who walk in Thy Name, and who bear the burden and heat of the day. We give thanks unto Thee for Thy gracious gift which hath been given unto us, and for Thy help [A 171b 2] which hath been with us, and for Thy grace which hath come forth from Thee upon us, O Lord, for Thou hast loved us and truly hast shown Thyself unto us. And look upon us, O Lord, for on Thee we have set our mind, and for Thy sake we have become alien unto our desires. And look upon us, O Lord, for for Thy sake we have left our possessions so that we might find Thee, the Great Treasure. And look upon us, O Lord, for for Thy sake we have forsaken our kinsfolk so that we may mingle with Thy kinsfolk. And look upon us, O Lord, for for Thy sake we have forsaken [B 249a 2] our fathers, and our mothers, that we might see Thy Father, and obtain from Him the food of blessing. And look upon us, O Lord, for for Thy sake we have left our wives and families, that we might enter into the companionship with Thee which, in truth, endureth and never perisheth. And let us find the fair offspring which shall be given unto us by Thee, and let us not be separated from this our present state of purity, and let us be pure, and may we all unite with Him for ever and ever. Amen."

Here end the Acts of Saint Thomas the Apostle in India.

LIST OF BIBLE PASSAGES QUOTED
OR REFERRED TO

PLATE X

1. King Abenner seated on his throne (by the side of which is an idol on a pillar), pronouncing a decree ordering the persecutions of the Christian ascetics and their expulsion from his country.
2. The ascetics and monks departing into the desert.

PLATE XI

The Christian official in Abenner's service having entreated the king to embrace Christianity, is ordered to depart forthwith. Near the king sit and stand personifications of anger, etc.

PLATE XII

1. The Queen in childbed. The child Ìòasaph being bathed by his nurse. At the foot of the bed are men presenting doves and lambs for offerings. The king standing and asking the idol on the pillar what his son's future will be.
2. The wise men, magicians, and astrologers consulting the stars.

PLATE XIII

1. The king and one of his nobles, who was a Christian, hunting in the forest, where they find a man who has been mauled by an animal.
2. Abenner consulting with Hosinaise.
3. Abenner giving commands to two of his servants.

PLATE XIV

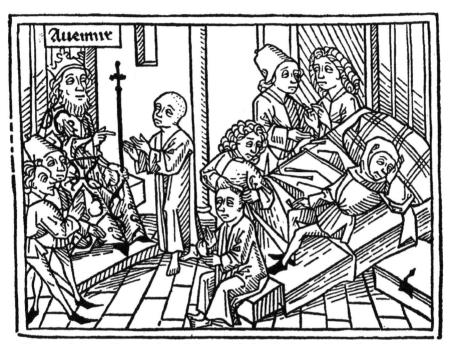

1. The wounded man from the forest lying on a bed in the house of the Christian noble.
2. The nobleman, having shaved his head and dressed himself in mean attire, appeasing the wrath of King Abenner.

PLATE XV

King Abenner riding through the forest with his men and dogs meets two monks, whom he forthwith condemns to be burnt in the fire.

PLATE XVI

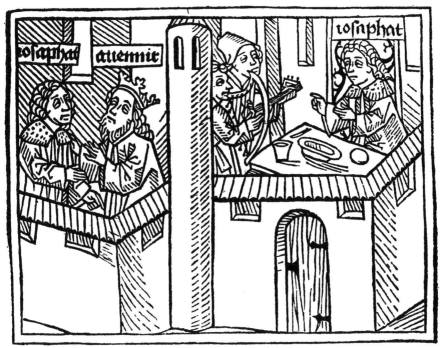

1. Iôasaph seated at table in his palace with musicians playing the harp and an instrument like a banjo to him.
2. Iôasaph entreating his father to let him ride outside the palace grounds.

PLATE XVII

Iôasaph rides outside the palace grounds with Zardan and sees, for the first time in his life, a blind man, a cripple going on sticks, and a decrepit old man on the point of death. The trumpeters had made a proclamation for the streets to be cleared, but failed to remove these men. Abenner seeing from his palace what is taking place.

PLATE XVIII

1. Barlaam comes to the prince's palace disguised as a merchant carrying a casket.
2. He changes his attire and is introduced into the presence of the prince, to whom he presents the casket. Our Lord is looking on.

PLATE XIX

1. Illustrates the Parable of the King who alighted from his chariot to greet Two Ascetics and was rebuked by his nobles for lack of dignity.
2. The herald blowing the Trumpet of Death before the house of the king's brother.
3. The king and the boxes of jewels and decaying bones.

PLATE XX

1. Barlaam expounding the doctrine of the Trinity to Ïóasaph.
2. The Three Persons in the clouds of heaven.
3. The Expulsion of Angels who had rebelled.
4. The Serpent coiled round the Tree of Good and Evil; on the right is Eve, and on the left is Adam.
5. Noah in the Ark.
6. The wicked being drowned in the waters of the Flood.

PLATE XXI

Barlaam pointing to the figure of an idol and explaining to Iôasaph the helplessness of idols and the absurdity of worshipping blocks of wood and stones. He also relates to him the Parable of the Hunter and the Nightingale.

PLATE **XXII**

1. Barlaam exhorting Iôasaph to repulse the lusts of the flesh, which are caused by the devils seen at his feet and their leader, from whose mouth a devil is emerging.
2. The Prodigal Son, starving in a strange land, sees men eating and drinking, and determines to go home.
3. The Prodigal Son on hands and knees wishing to eat the husks in the trough from which the swine eat.

PLATE XXIII

1. Barlaam instructing Iôasaph in the Christian Religion.
2. Christ(?) casting out a devil from a sick man; the devil is issuing from the sick man's mouth.
3. A saint being tortured(?).
4. Monks entering a church.

PLATE XXIV

1. Barlaam relating the Parable of the Man in the Well and the Rhinoceros (Unicorn).
2. The Man in the Well.
3. A man and a woman standing in the mouth of a Crocodile.

PLATE XXV

1. Iôasaph asking Barlaam questions about his life and habits.
2. Barlaam, naked, plucking herbs to eat.
3. Barlaam, naked, being fed by an angel.
4. Barlaam in prayer.

PLATE XXVI

Barlaam relating to Iôasaph the Parable of the man elected King for one year only.

PLATE XXVII

1. Barlaam preaching the beauty of almsgiving to Iôasaph, who is giving money to the poor from a bag.
2. Christ admonishing a money-changer, who is seated at his table with piles of coins heaped up on it.

PLATE **XXVIII**

Barlaam relating to Iòasaph the Parable of the rich young nobleman who refused to marry the daughter of a rich man, and married a poor but exceedingly pious maiden.

Plate XXIX

1. Barlaam sailing to India.
2. Our Lord in heaven.
3. Barlaam proclaiming to Ioasaph that God is the Creator of everything.

PLATE XXX

Barlaam relates to Iôasaph the Parable of the Man and his Three Friends—how the two of them for whom he had done most forsook him in the day of adversity, whilst the third, whom he had lightly esteemed, saved him from ruin.

PLATE XXXI

1. Barlaam exhorting Iôasaph to be baptized.
2. Barlaam baptizes Iôasaph.
3. Illustrates the Parable of the Tame Gazelle.

PLATE XXXII

1. Zardan, seated between Barlaam and Iôasaph, noting their conversation.
2. An angel taking a soul to heaven, and an angel appearing to a suppliant and giving him succour.

PLATE XXXIII

1. Iôasaph stripping off his royal robes to put on the garb of Barlaam.
2. Barlaam and Iôasaph bidding each other farewell.
3. Barlaam setting out on his road to the desert.

PLATE **XXXIV**

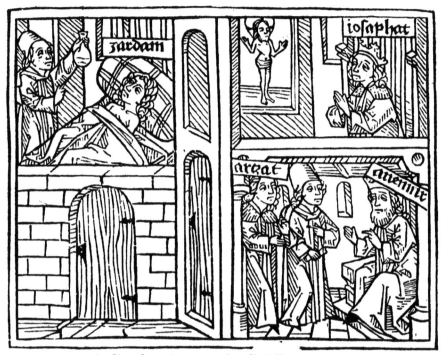

1. Iôasaph praying to an eikon (?) of Christ.
2. Zardan takes to his bed and feigns sickness.
3. King Abenner doubts the reality of his sickness.

PLATE **XXXV**

1. Arachis giving the King evil counsel.
2. Arachis riding out to seek for Nachor.
3. Arachis and Nachor meet in the forest.

PLATE **XXXVI**

1. Arachis, riding in search of Barlaam, meets some holy monks carrying relics in their hands.
2. He seizes them and causes them to be executed.

PLATE XXXVII

1. Arachis brings into the presence of King Abenner the wicked magician Nachor, who has disguised himself and pretends to be Barlaam.
2. Iôasaph praying.

PLATE **XXXVIII**

1. King Abenner riding to visit his son in his palace.
2. King Abenner reviling Iôasaph for allowing himself to be led into error by Barlaam, and for neglecting the worship of his father's gods.

PLATE **XXXIX**

1. Ióasaph trying to turn away his father's wrath.
2. Magicians consulting the stars.
3. People in a crocodile's mouth, symbolic of hell (?).

PLATE XL

1. Iôasaph praying. He discovers through a vision the plot which his father and Arachis are hatching against him.
2. Abenner and Arachis plotting together.
3. Abenner riding out secretly by night.

PLATE XLI

Nachor (*not* Arachis) is caught in his own net and is brought into Iôasaph's council as if he were Barlaam.

PLATE XLII

Nachor, in the presence of Abenner and Barachias, preaches in favour of the Christian Religion and against the errors of the Chaldeans.

PLATE XLIII

Abenner, Arachis, and the Greeks and Egyptians worshipping the Moon, Mercury, Venus, the Sun, Mars, Jupiter and Saturn.

PLATE XLIV

1. Abenner holding his sceptre.
2. The Jews nailing Christ to the Cross.

PLATE XLV

Nachor (*not* Arachis) pretending to be Barlaam and proving the truth of the Christian Religion to Abenner.

PLATE XLVI

1. King Abenner with his counsellors after the defeat of the priests.
2. Nachor and Arachis going to Ioasaph by night.

PLATE XLVII

1. Iôasaph instructing Nachor in the Christian Religion.
2. Nachor being pardoned by Christ.
3. A priest baptizing Nachor.

PLATE XLVIII

Abenner the king, whilst witnessing the overthrow of some of his idols, is visited by
Theudas the magician.

PLATE XLIX

Abenner the king, persuaded by Theudas, offers sacrifice to an idol. On the left his subjects are seen bringing animals for sacrifice.

PLATE L

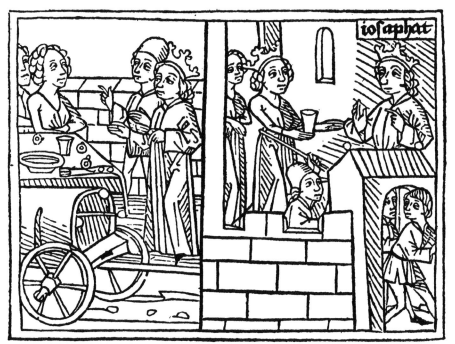

1. Theudas, the magician, advising King Abenner to employ beautiful maidens to tempt Iôasaph to commit fornication, and to make him abandon the Christian Religion.
2. A princess, with her maidens, bringing wine to Iôasaph.

PLATE LI

1. Iôasaph sitting at meat with a princess and her beautiful maidens, behind whom are devils urging them to seduce him.
2. As a result of Iôasaph's prayers, the Devil, in the form of a black goat, is expelled from the dining hall.

PLATE LII

1. Iôasaph driving away from him the devil of lust.
2. The devil re-entering by her mouth the princess who had tempted Iôasaph.

PLATE LIII

1. Iôasaph holding conversation with a woman, and the devils of lust and fornication tempting him.
2. An angel showing Iôasaph in a vision a righteous man receiving his crown from God in heaven, and a wicked man suffering torture in the flames of hell.

PLATE LIV

1. Iôasaph falls sick through grief, worry and anxiety and is visited in bed by his father Abenner the king. In the window is one of the devils who has been tormenting him.
2. Theudas the magician and his devils in council.

PLATE LV

Iôasaph and Theudas disputing in the presence of King Abenner. Near Iôasaph is a figure of Christ on the Cross, and near the king is an idol on a pedestal.

PLATE LVI

Theudas and Iôasaph disputing in the presence of King Abenner. 1. Iôasaph vanquishing Theudas in argument. 2. Theudas being baptized. 3. Theudas burning his books of magic.

PLATE LVII

The debate between the Christians and the idolaters. On the one side is Iôasaph declaring Christ's Gospel to Theudas the magician, and on the other, Abenner and his people worshipping an idol on a pillar. Theudas defeated confesses his sin to Nachor.

PLATE LVIII

1. Abenner entreating Iôasaph.
2. Abenner, on the advice of his councillors, announcing to his son that he will divide his kingdom and give him half of it.

PLATE LIX

Iosaphat iosaphat

1. Iôasaph preaching in a pulpit.
2. A bishop baptizing the people.
3. Iôasaph handling portions of a human body.

PLATE LX

1. Iôasaph praying to a figure of Christ on the Cross.
2. Abenner taking counsel with his officers.
3. Abenner seeing God in a vision.

PLATE LXI

1. Iôasaph converting his father Abenner to Christianity.
2. The baptism of King Abenner, who stands in a font.
3. Iôasaph and Abenner embracing each other.

PLATE LXII

1. King Abenner in mental distress in his chamber.
2. Iôasaph ministering to his dying father.
3. Iôasaph prostrate on the tomb of his father.

Plate LXIII

Iôasaph, having abdicated, sets out from his palace to go to Barachias, whom he intends
to make king in his stead.

PLATE LXIV

The subjects of Iôasaph searching for him in the desert. They find him, but having brought him back to the palace he crowns Barachias king.

PLATE LXV

1. Iôasaph bidding his friend Barachias farewell.
2. Iôasaph, having forsaken his kingdom, sets out on his journey through the desert to seek for Barlaam.

PLATE LXVI

Iôasaph passing through the desert jungle in his search for Barlaam. Fiends and devils and savage animals endeavour to bar his progress.

Plate LXVII

Iôasaph, wandering about in the desert enquiring for Barlaam, being attacked by devils in the form of winged animals, and is directed to his abode. Barlaam and Iôasaph meeting and embracing each other.

PLATE LXVIII

Barlaam and Iôasaph praying together to God in heaven. Barlaam and Iôasaph eating together in the desert, with the hills behind them. Barlaam instructing Iôasaph and pointing to a figure of Christ on the Cross.

PLATE LXIX

Barlaam pointing to the heavens where God and the angels abide, announces to Ióasaph
his departure from this world, and comforts him.

PLATE LXX

Barlaam holding converse with Iôasaph. He administers the Sacrament to Iôasaph, and dies, and is buried by him.

Plate LXXI

Ióasaph weeping on the grave of Barlaam. He is being carried in the spirit by angels to heaven, where he sees Barlaam who has been carried into the presence of the Trinity by an angel.

PLATE LXXII

Iôasaph in the desert. He dies and an angel receives his soul. A fellow monk buries him in the same grave as Barlaam. Above, seated in glory among the clouds, are the Father, Son and Holy Ghost.

PLATE LXXIII

The exhumation of the bodies of Iôasaph and Barlaam in the presence of King Barachias, and the departure of the same in coffins for the country of India.

INDEX

For Product Safety Concerns and Information please contact our EU
representative GPSR@taylorandfrancis.com Taylor & Francis Verlag GmbH,
Kaufingerstraße 24, 80331 München, Germany

Batch number: 08153782

Printed by Printforce, the Netherlands